God's Knowledge of the World

God's Knowledge of the World

*Medieval Theories of Divine Ideas
from Bonaventure to Ockham*

Carl A. Vater

The Catholic University of America Press
Washington, D.C.

Copyright © 2022
The Catholic University of America Press
All rights reserved

Library of Congress Cataloging-in-Publication Data

Names: Vater, Carl A., author.
Title: God's knowledge of the world : medieval theories of divine ideas from Bonaventure to Ockham / Carl A. Vater.
Description: Washington, D.C. : The Catholic University of America Press, [2022] | Includes bibliographical references and index.
Identifiers: LCCN 2022033773 | ISBN 9780813235547 (hardcover) | ISBN 9780813235554 (ebook)| ISBN 9780813241272
Subjects: LCSH: God (Christianity)—Omniscience—History of doctrines—Middle Ages, 600–1500. | Scholasticism.
Classification: LCC BT131 .V38 2022 | DDC 231/.4—dc23/eng/20220906
LC record available at https://lccn.loc.gov/2022033773

To My Wife and Children

Table of Contents

Abbreviations ix

Introduction 1

Part I: The Imitability Theory of Divine Ideas 11
    Chapter I: St. Bonaventure (ca. 1217–1274) 13
    Chapter II: St. Thomas Aquinas (ca. 1224/1225–1274) 43
    Chapter III: Henry of Ghent (before 1240–1293) 87

Part II: The Infinite Intellect Theory of Divine Ideas 121
    Chapter IV: Peter John Olivi (ca. 1248–1298)
    and Petrus de Trabibus (fl. 1290s) 123

Part III: The *Obiectum Cognitum* Theory of Divine Ideas 135
    Chapter V: James of Viterbo (ca. 1255–1308) 137

Part IV: The *Creatura Intellecta* Theory of Divine Ideas 147
    Chapter VI: Richard of Mediavilla (ca. 1249–1302) 149
    Chapter VII: Bl. John Duns Scotus (ca. 1265–1308) 157
    Chapter VIII: Early Thomists and Scotists 195

Part V: The Nominalist Theory of Divine Ideas 207
    Chapter IX: Peter Auriol (ca. 1280–1322) 209
    Chapter X: William of Ockham (ca. 1285–1347) 229

Conclusion 257

Bibliography 275

Index 291

Abbreviations

General Abbreviations
- a./aa. — *articulus/articuli*
- arg. — *argumentum*
- CUP — *Chartularium Universitatis Parisiensis*, ed. Henricus Denifle. Paris, 1889–97.
- fm/fa — *fundamentum/fundamenta*
- d./dd. — *distinctio/distinctiones*
- *In Sent.* — An author's *Commentary on the Sentences*
- p. — *pars*
- PG — *Patralogia cursus completus*, series graeca, accurante J.P. Migne. Paris, 1857–.
- PL — *Patralogia cursus completus*, series latina, accurante J.P. Migne. Paris 1844–.
- q./qq. — *quaestio/quaestiones*
- *Quodlibet* — An author's *Quaestiones quodlibetales* or *Quaestiones de quodlibet*
- s.c. — *sed contra*

Algazel
- Met. — *Metaphysica*

Aristotle
- AL — *Aristoteles latinus*. Corpus philosophorum medii aevii, Academiarum consciatarum auspiciis et consilio editum. 1939–.
- Anal. post. — *Posterior Analytics*
- EN — *Nichomacean Ethics*
- Met. — *Metaphysics*

Augustine
- *Conf.* — *Confessionum libri tredecim*
- *De civ. Dei* — *De civitate Dei*
- *De div. qq. 83* — *De diversis quaestionibus octoginta tribus liber unus*
- *De vera rel.* — *De vera religione*

Averroes
- *In De anima* — *Commentarium Magnum in libros De anima*
- *In Met.* — *Commentarium Mangum in libros Metaphysicorum*

Avicenna
- Met. — *Liber de philosophia prima sive scientia divina*

Bonaventure
    De reductione   *De reductione artium theologiae*
    De scientia Christi   *Quaestiones disputatae de scientia Christi*
    De mys. Trin.   *Quaestiones disputatae de mysterio Trinitatis*
    In Hex.   *Collationes in Hexaemeron*

Godfrey of Fontaines
    PB   *Les Philosophes Belges*, edited by De Wulf and Pelzer. Louvain, 1904–37.

Henry of Ghent
    Summa   *Summa Quaestiones Ordinariae*

John Duns Scotus
    Lect.   *Lectura*
    Ord.   *Ordinatio*
    OPh   B. Ioannis Duns Scoti, *Opera philosophica*, 5 vols. (St. Bonaventure, NY: Franciscan Institute Publications)
    Rep.   *Reportatio Parisiensis*

Peter Auriol
    Scriptum   *Scriptum super primum Sententiarum*

Pseudo-Dionysius
    De div. nom.   *De divinis nominibus*

Thomas Aquinas
    De ente   *De ente et essentia*
    De malo   *Quaestiones disputatae de malo*
    De potentia   *Quaestiones disputatae de potentia*
    De prin. nat.   *De principiis naturae*
    De sub. sep.   *De substantiis separatis*
    De veritate   *Quaestiones disputatae de veritate*
    In De Trinitate   *Super Boetium De Trinitate*
    In De anima   *Sentencia libri De anima*
    In De div. nom.   *In librum Beati Dionysii De Divinis nominibus expositio*
    In Ioan.   *Super Evangelium S. Ioannis lectura*
    In Liber de causis   *Super librum De Causis expositio*
    In Met.   *In duodecim libros Metaphysicorum Aristotelis expositio*
    In Phys.   *Commentaria in octo libros Physicorum Aristotelis*
    SCG   *Summa Contra Gentiles*
    ST   *Summa theologiae*

William of Ockham
    Ord.   *Ordinatio*
    In Porph.   *Expositio in librum Porphyrii de praedicabilibus*

All critical editions of texts will be cited on the following model:
    Author, *Text*, internal textual divisions (Edition, volume.page:line–line).
    Bonaventure, *In I Sent.*, d. 35, q. un., a. 1 (Quaracchi, I.600).
    Aquinas, *ST* I, q. 15, a. 3 (Leonine, 4.204).

Full citation information for the editions cited can be found in the bibliography.

Introduction

Sources for Theories of Divine Ideas

A theory of divine ideas was the standard Scholastic solution to the question, "How does God know and produce creatures?" A theory was deemed to be successful only if it simultaneously upheld that God has perfect knowledge and that he is supremely simple and one. Scholastic discussion of divine ideas relies on three primary sources: Sacred Scripture, the Fathers of the Church, especially St. Augustine and Pseudo-Dionysius, and the philosophers. Sacred Scripture is the preeminent cause for discussion of divine ideas. From the very first verse of the Bible, it is declared that God created the heavens and the earth.[1] Creatures were not merely formed out of preexisting matter, nor did they emanate from God out of necessity or chance. God created them. Creation is the result of an intellectual and voluntary act. Moreover, Sacred Scripture affirms that God did not gain knowledge from some external source.[2] He did not learn about creatures from something other than himself. Knowledge of creatures is somehow part and parcel of what it means to be God.

Again, according to Sacred Scripture, God does not know creatures vaguely; he knows the minutest details of each aspect of creation. He knows our sitting and our standing.[3] He knows every sound we utter.[4] He foreknows our thoughts.[5] He knit us together in our mothers' wombs.[6] He has counted the hairs on our heads.[7] A sparrow does not fall to the ground without him knowing.[8] He thoroughly penetrates every division in creation such that "no creature is invisible in his sight; everything is nude and has been laid bare to his eyes."[9] All of creation is God's art, and the divine artist has crafted all of creation.[10] Finally, Sacred Scripture insists that God does not merely know of creatures. God remains intimately connected to creation by providence. His providence works toward the good of all creation. He feeds the birds of the air that neither sow, nor reap, nor gather grain into barns,

---

1. Gn 1:1.
2. Is 40:12–14.
3. Ps 139:1–2.
4. Wis 1:7.
5. Ps 139:3.
6. Jer 1:5.
7. Mt 10:30.
8. Mt 10:29.
9. Heb 4:12–13.
10. Eph 2:10; Rom 11:36.

and he makes the lilies grow.[11] God knows and guides all the workings of creation. Sacred Scripture declares *that* God knows creation intimately, but it is silent as to *how* he can have such knowledge. As such, Sacred Scripture provided Scholastic thinkers with certain conclusions that their arguments should achieve, but it did not offer the premises of those arguments. As a result, the Scholastics turned to the Fathers of the Church and philosophers.

Scholastic authors turned first and foremost to St. Augustine and Pseudo-Dionysius for insight on divine ideas. St. Augustine spoke of divine ideas most explicitly in q. 46 of his *On Eighty-Three Diverse Questions*. In this short question, St. Augustine explains that ideas have their origin in the thought of Plato, how to translate the Greek term *eidos* into Latin, and how he thinks an idea ought to be understood. The term *eidos* is best translated into Latin as either *form* or *species* (*forma vel species*). The term reason (*ratio*) will suffice, but it is not as good a translation since *ratio* usually translates the Greek term *logos*. Ideas, St. Augustine says, are certain principle, stable, and unchangeable forms or notions of things. These forms are not made, and so are eternal, that is, they never come to be or pass away. Moreover, they are contained in the divine intelligence. Since they are in the divine mind, only the rational part of the soul has any access to them, but only if it is holy and pure. Nevertheless, even those who cannot intuit them should not dare to deny them because everything that exists, that is, each thing that is contained in a proper genus and nature, has its origin in them. They are the reason according to which all things have been made. Additionally, St. Augustine says, man and horse are not made according to the same reason because it would be absurd to think that this happens. Each one is created in its proper reason.[12]

Scholastic authors also made frequent reference to Pseudo-Dionysius, who offers penetrating insight into divine exemplarity. In book V of his *On Divine Names*, Pseudo-Dionysius refers to 'predefinitions' as exemplar reasons preexisting in God. These reasons are the substances of things that define and cause things. They are found in God because God, who is above the category of substance, predefines and produces all things.[13]

Authors also developed theories of divine ideas to respond to certain philosophical errors coming from Aristotle, Avicenna, and Averroes. These philosophers were the source of many of the metaphysical, epistemological, and logical tools that the Scholastics used to articulate theories of divine knowledge of all possible creatures and divine production of creatures, but their theories of divine knowledge were highly deficient. Aristotle argues that God (the Unmoved Mover) knows only himself. God does not know finite beings, nor is he their efficient cause. He is only

---

11. Mt 6:26, 28.
12. Augustine, *De div. qq. 83*, q. 46 (PL 40:29–31). For an in-depth analysis of St. Augustine's theory of divine ideas, see Lawrence F. Jansen, "The Divine Ideas in the Writings of St. Augustine," *Modern Schoolman* 22, no. 3 (1945): 117–31; Theodore J. Kondoleon, "Divine Exemplarism in Augustine," *Augustinian Studies* 1 (1970): 181–95; Vivian Boland, *Ideas in God According to Saint Thomas Aquinas: Sources and Synthesis* (New York: Brill, 1996), 33–88.
13. Ps.-Dionysius, *De div. nom.*, V, c. 8 (PG 3:823C). See Boland, *Ideas in God*, 94–146.

their final cause, explaining their motions.[14] Avicenna argues that God, whom he frequently calls the Necessary Being, is the efficient cause of all beings other than himself, but he knows creatures in a universal way only. He does not know particular beings or their actions.[15] Averroes argues that God's knowledge is beyond the categories of universal and particular. As a result, God has indeterminate knowledge of particular beings.[16]

Averroes's theory of divine knowledge is worth dwelling upon because it was the proximate cause of the explosion of literature on divine ideas. Many viewed Aristotle's theory of divine knowledge with suspicion, but some authors were willing to give a charitable reading of the texts.[17] The texts of Aristotle by themselves would have been concerning for the Scholastic authors, but they might have been reconcilable with fundamental Scholastic tenets. The real trouble was the fact that Averroes's reading of Aristotle's theory of divine knowledge is contrary to the Scriptural understanding of divine knowledge. In his *Long Commentary on Aristotle's Metaphysics*, Book XII, comment 51 (*In XII Met.*), Averroes argues that God cannot have determinate knowledge of singular beings, and he argues that this position is the proper interpretation of Aristotle. Scholastic authors took these arguments as serious challenges to the Biblical account of God, and they responded with theories of divine ideas. William of Ockham even went so far as to respond to each of Averroes's arguments individually.[18]

Before moving to the responses, it is worth looking at the arguments that Averroes presents. Averroes offers eight objections to divine knowledge in *In XII Met.*,

---

14. Aristotle, *Met.* XII, c. 9 (AL 25/3.2.264–265). See R. A. Gauthier and J. Y. Jolif, *L'Ethique à Nicomaque*, vol. 2 (Louvain: Publications Universitaires de Louvain, 1970); Leo Elders, *Aristotle's Theology: A Commentary on Book Λ of the Metaphysics* (Assen, The Netherlands: Koninklijk Van Gorcum & Co., 1972); Joseph Owens, *The Doctrine of Being in the Aristotelian Metaphysics: A Study in the Greek Background of Mediaeval Thought*, 3rd. ed., rev. (Toronto: Pontifical Institute of Mediaeval Studies, 1978); Joseph Owens, "The Relation of God to World in the Metaphysics," in *Études Sur La Métaphysique d'Aristote: Actes Du VIe Symposium Aristotelicum*, ed. Pierre Aubenque, 207–28 (Paris: Vrin, 1979).

For a different interpretation of the Unmoved Mover's knowledge, see Richard Norman, "Aristotle's Philosopher-God," *Phronesis* 14, no. 1 (1969): 63–74; Thomas De Konick, "Aristotle on God as Thought Thinking Itself," *Review of Metaphysics* 47, no. 3 (1994): 471–515. There was concern among Scholastic authors that the proper interpretation coheres with the sources cited in the previous paragraph.

15. Avicenna, *Met.* VIII, cc. 5–6 (van Reit, 405–19). See Peter Adamson, "On Knowledge of Particulars," *Proceedings of the Aristotelian Society* 105, no. 1 (2005): 257–78; Michael E. Marmura, *Probing in Islamic Philosophy: Studies in the Philosophies of Ibn Sīnā, al-Ghazālī, and Other Major Muslim Thinkers* (Binghamton: Global Academic Pub., 2005), 71–95. Deborah Black argues that Avicenna's discussion of individual intentions contains the necessary premises to articulate a theory of divine knowledge of individual human souls, but he failed to draw those premises together. See "Avicenna on Individuation, Self-Awareness, and God's Knowledge of Particulars," in *The Judeo-Christian-Islamic Heritage: Philosophical and Theological Perspectives*, ed. Richard C. Taylor and Irfan A. Omar, 255–81 (Milwaukee: Marquette University Press, 2012).

16. Averroes, *In XII Met.*, c. 51 (Iunctina, VIII.157va1–20).

17. Already by ca. 1235, Robert Grosseteste had declared that Aristotle's philosophy contains grave errors and that it cannot be taken wholesale without emendation (*Hexaemeron* [Dales and Gieben, 60:30-61:11]). St. Thomas Aquinas, writing ca. 1272, is one of the authors that interprets Aristotle charitably (*In XII Met.*, lect. 11, n. 2614 [Spiazzi, 608]).

18. Ockham, *Ord.*, I, d. 35, q. 2 (OTh IV.436:7–8).

comment 51, four of which are pertinent. As a prelude to these arguments, Averroes says that God must have understanding since he is the noblest of all beings. One can have understanding in two ways, in act or in potency. Something is in act when it is using or exercising a certain ability that it has. The being is in potency when it is not doing so now. The distinction between act and potency looms large because potency is related to act as the imperfect to the perfect. A sleeping man is imperfect because he is thinking in potency, not in act. Since God must be the noblest and most perfect being, his knowledge cannot be in potency; it must always be in act. But what does he understand?[19]

This question leads to Averroes's first argument. God is so noble that he will be nobler than any other being concerning understanding. Intellection—the act of understanding—is the perfection of the one understanding. This claim follows from the relationship between act and perfection. A being in act is more perfect than a being in potency to act. The act by which someone understands is called intellection. Thus, intellection is the act that perfects the knower. Since that which perfects is more perfect than what it perfects, the object of knowledge, that is, the thing known in the act of understanding, is in a sense more perfect than the knower. Thus, whatever knows something other than itself is not the most perfect and noblest being. But God cannot be perfected by anything else; he must be perfect of himself or else he is not the noblest being. Therefore, he does not understand anything other than himself.[20]

This conclusion could be read in two ways. Averroes could mean (1) that God has no other principle or source of understanding or (2) that which God understands—the object that he knows—is only himself. If Averroes means (1) the principle of God's understanding, then Averroes's claim is that God has no other source of knowledge than himself. God does not look to separately existing forms to know possible creatures like Plato's Demiurge. This reading would not necessarily prohibit God from knowing things other than himself. All it would entail is that God knows everything that he knows by knowing himself. This point would not be controversial. In fact, all Scholastic authors agree that the divine essence is the only means by which God knows.[21] However, as will become clear from the other arguments, Averroes means (2) the objects that God knows. Averroes's remaining arguments show that God cannot have distinct knowledge of anything other than himself because God's perfection does not depend upon a creature.

In the second argument, Averroes argues that the noblest principle does not acquire nobility except through its act of understanding. God's nobility and perfection come from what he is, what his substance is. Averroes has already determined that God's substance is his understanding. Thus, God's act of understanding is his nobility and perfection. Therefore, if God, the First Principle, understands

---

19. Averroes, *In XII Met.*, c. 51 (Iunctina, VIII.157va1–20).
20. Averroes, *In XII Met.*, c. 51 (Iunctina, VIII.157va21–25).
21. See, e.g., pp. 67, 88–89, 160, 214–15. For an explanation of the Platonic position, see Thomas M. Ward, *Divine Ideas* (New York: Cambridge University Press, 2020), 9.

INTRODUCTION

base things (*vilia*), then his nobility would come from understanding lower, less noble things. As a result, the noblest principle's act of understanding will be the basest of actions. Therefore, if noble beings must flee low acts, then God must not understand lower things. Averroes takes it to be obvious that noble beings must flee low acts because there are some things that we are better off not knowing because of their baseness. Therefore, God only understands himself, and not things other than himself.[22]

Third, Averroes asks whether what God understands from himself is one simply or many composed. Everything that does not have matter is not divided, as we find with human understanding. For Averroes, matter is the principle of potency in material things that distinguishes two individuals of the same species from each other. Absent some matter, two things are only divided if there is some formal or specific difference between them. In the case of our understanding, what is understood is the same as the understanding itself with the result that they cannot be divided. Yet, in our understanding, we can find some cause of division because that which is understood is in some way other than the intellect. Our intellect and the thing understood are not in every way one in us. This otherness is the cause of multitude. Our intellect is free from matter in itself, but it is not freed from matter absolutely because that which we understand must be abstracted from matter. If there is a being free from matter absolutely, then understanding and understood are identical in it. God, the First Principle, is absolutely one without any multiplicity. Understanding and that which is understood are one in every way. Therefore, God's simplicity excludes a multitude of things known.[23]

This argument brings to the fore a central principle for Averroes: divine cognition is unlike ours. Thinking that God's knowledge is like ours is "the principal source of error" because we must recognize that "the mode of divine cognition is not analogous to the human mode."[24] By 'mode' (*modus*) is understood the way or manner that cognition is carried out. Averroes's point is that the way God knows is not analogous to the way that we know. We cannot gain any insight about how God knows by examining how we know. Averroes makes this point definitively in the *Decisive Treatise*, a text to which the Scholastic authors had no access. In that text, Averroes says that the term 'knowledge' is used equivocally for human knowledge and for divine knowledge.[25]

Fourth and finally, Averroes argues against God's knowledge of things other than himself by means of an argument about universals and particulars. Averroes does not mention any names, but this argument is intended to be a qualified defense of Avicenna's theory of divine knowledge, and an attack on Themistius's interpretation

---

22. Averroes, *In XII Met.*, c. 51 (Iunctina, VIII.157vb7–26).
23. Averroes, *In XII Met.*, c. 51 (Iunctina, VIII.158ra3–68).
24. Miguel Cruz Hernandez, *Abu-L-Walid Ibn Rusd (Averroes): Vida, Obra, Pensamiento, Influencia* (Cordoba: Monte de Piedad y Caja de Ahorros de Cordoba, 1986), 155. Unless otherwise mentioned, all translations in this text are mine.
25. Averroes, *Decisive Treatise*, n. 17 (Butterworth, 13–14).

of Aristotle.[26] Themistius argued that God knows all things from the fact that he understands himself to be the principle of them all. Averroes agrees that God knows all things insofar as he causes their *esse*, but he takes issue with Themistius's understanding of the term 'all.' If God is to know all things, then he must know them with either universal knowledge or particular knowledge. An example of universal knowledge is knowing Socrates insofar as he is a man but not as this particular man. Universal knowledge is knowledge in potency to the further knowledge of the particulars that fall under the universal.[27] God's knowledge is not in potency. Therefore, he does not know things with universal knowledge. God's knowledge is not particular either because particulars, Averroes says, are infinite. The infinite is incomprehensible and so not able to be comprehended. Since God's knowledge is neither universal nor particular, it is indeterminate for things other than himself. His knowledge breaks our categories, transcending the disjunction between universal and particular. We can say that God knows all things as cause, but we have no access to what it means to say that God knows all things.[28]

Averroes's theory presents three challenges to an account of divine knowledge that ensures that God knows each possible creature thoroughly and distinctly. First, the Scholastic authors must explain why God's supreme nobility is not contrary to his knowledge of things less noble than himself. Second, authors must explain how we can have access to the mode of divine cognition. Third, authors will have to explain how God's knowledge can extend to every possible creature. Answering these difficulties will require authors to make precise metaphysical, epistemological, and logical distinctions. These challenges to divine knowledge make it clear how Averroes could be a source for a theory of divine ideas without speaking of them at all. A robust theory of divine ideas shows how God's perfection requires that he knows every possible creature distinctly.

THE STATUS AND SCOPE OF DIVINE IDEAS

Scholastic authors raised a variety of questions to explain how God knows all possible creatures and produces creatures, which can be divided into two types. The first type of question concerns what I call the *status* of divine ideas. These are questions such as What is an idea? Does God have ideas? Are ideas speculative or practical? How many divine ideas are there? If there are more than one, how are they many? How are divine ideas related to God? What sort of existence, if any, does a divine idea have? What is the status of the ideas according to which God chooses never to create, that is, what is the status of non-existing possibles? The second type of question concerns what I call the *scope* of divine ideas. Of what are there divine ideas? Are there divine ideas of singulars, evil, prime matter, genera, species, and number?

---

26. The core of this argument reappears in Averroes, *Decisive Treatise*, n. 17 (Butterworth, 13–14).

27. For example, knowledge of *animal* is in potency to knowing the species that fall under that genus, *goat, duck, shark*, etc.

28. Averroes, *In XII Met.*, c. 51 (Iunctina, VIII.158rb16–32). Averroes does not defend the claim that particulars are infinite in number in this text.

These questions cause the Scholastic authors to articulate, among other things, their positions on the nature of knowledge, relation, exemplar causality, participation, infinity, and possibility. Many of the changes that we find from one theory to another arise because of a change in one of these positions. In particular, I argue that later authors primarily take issue with the theory of relations articulated by their predecessors. They object that their predecessors' theories of relations are incompatible with the nature of knowing, divine simplicity, or both. The earliest theory of divine ideas in this study, the Imitability Theory, argues that God knows possible creatures by means of the relations of imitability that they could bear to him if created. Later theories object that a relation can only be known after the two related things are known.

OUTLINE OF THE FOLLOWING CHAPTERS

The following chapters trace the way reflection upon divine ideas and connected theories developed between the years ca. AD 1250 and ca. AD 1325, St. Bonaventure to William of Ockham. I choose these dates because the theories of divine ideas articulated during this time show a certain trajectory. Divine ideas occupy a preeminent place in Bonaventure's thought. To deny divine ideas is to abandon the search for truth in its fullness and to deny the Uncreated Word.[29] It is at least tacitly heretical for a Christian to deny divine ideas. In contrast, William of Ockham's theory of divine ideas is practically no theory at all. His theory of divine ideas is superfluous to his theory of divine knowledge. He seems to preserve divine ideas more out of deference to the tradition of St. Augustine than because they are explanatory. In a span of approximately 75 years, divine ideas go from having as prominent a place as possible to having hardly any place at all.[30]

This book is divided into ten chapters corresponding to the ten major authors and groups examined. I have chosen these authors because they are the central figures in various theories of divine ideas. The centrality of earlier authors is confirmed by the fact that later authors engage with their thought. Bl. John Duns Scotus, for example, critiques the thought of St. Thomas Aquinas, Henry of Ghent, Peter John Olivi, and James of Viterbo, and he appropriates some of the views of St. Bonaventure. Thus, the story of the development of theories of divine ideas requires a close look at the thought of each of these authors. I deem later authors central either because they inaugurate a new theory of divine ideas or because they advance the thought of an earlier author.

The first three chapters (Part I) examine St. Bonaventure, St. Thomas Aquinas, and Henry of Ghent, who hold what I call the "Imitability Theory." Their theories

---

29. Bonaventure, *In I Sent.*, d. 6, a. un., q. 3 (Quaracchi, I.130a): "qui negat ideas esse, negat Filium Dei esse." Cf. Augustine, *De div. qq. 83*, q. 46, n. 2 (PL 40.30).

30. Historically, Ockham does not eliminate discussion of divine ideas. Later authors certainly discuss divine ideas. John Wyclif (ca. 1330–1384), for example, articulates a theory of divine ideas, although it is a highly problematic one. See Stephen E. Lahey, *John Wyclif* (New York: Oxford University Press, 2009), 87–93.

of divine ideas are characterized by saying that divine ideas are secondary objects (*obiecta secundaria*) of the divine intellect when it knows the divine essence. The divine essence itself is the primary object of God's knowledge and the divine essence as imitable is the secondary object. When he knows the ways his essence is imitable, God knows all the real relations that possible creatures could bear to him. God knows creatures as a result of knowing this imitability. They also insist that divine ideas play two roles: a cognitive role because God knows possible creatures through them, and a causal role because God creates according to them. This theory of divine ideas was the most popular theory of its kind in the second half of the thirteenth century.

Chapter IV (Part II) examines Peter John Olivi and his student Petrus de Trabibus, who hold what I call the "Infinite Intellect Theory." This group of theorists argues that divine ideas are identical to God's infinite act of understanding (*intelligere*). Olivi and Petrus are the first to raise serious objections to the Imitability Theory. Their objections are appropriated and expanded by Scotus and provide the impetus for him to rethink divine ideas, even though Scotus rejects the Infinite Intellect Theory.

Chapter V (Part III) considers James of Viterbo's theory of divine ideas, which I call the "*Obiectum Cognitum* Theory." This theory bears some similarities to the Imitability Theory, but it argues that the divine ideas are the very object cognized. The divine essence is God's intelligible means of understanding, but he understands divine ideas insofar as he knows his essence as a cause. A cause necessarily entails an effect distinct from the cause, and so divine ideas are the effect as the object cognized. Scotus praises this theory as the best of his predecessors' theories despite its fundamental flaws.

The next three chapters make up Part IV of the book, which considers what I call the "*Creatura Intellecta* Theory." This theory holds that God knows possible creatures directly. Like the Imitability Theory, the complete character of a divine idea includes a relation of imitability, but, unlike the Imitability Theory, the relation of imitability is posterior to God's knowledge of the possible creature, not prior to it. This theory is inchoately held by Richard of Mediavilla (Chapter VI), and it emerges fully in Bl. John Duns Scotus's thought (Chapter VII). The *Creatura Intellecta* Theory is perhaps the most important theory in the study. It presents serious objections to every preceding theory, and it offers a compelling account of how God can know possible creatures, how God and creatures can be related, and how God can produce creatures.

Chapter VIII gives credence to the importance of the *Creatura Intellecta* Theory by examining the positions of the early Thomists, John of Paris and Thomas of Sutton, as well as the positions of one early Scotist, Henry of Harclay. I use the term 'Thomist' loosely because while they adopt many of Aquinas's positions and defend them against the criticisms of their contemporaries, both John and Sutton are willing to criticize and reject certain positions of Aquinas, including divine ideas. Both authors endorse the *Creatura Intellecta* Theory. These Thomists show how devastating Scotus's arguments were and how they quickly brought endorsement of the

Imitability Theory to an end. Henry of Harclay endorses two different versions of the *Creatura Intellecta* Theory, which he arrives at in part because of an ambiguity in Scotus's articulation of his theory. Harclay's earlier theory denies that divine ideas include any sort of relation, and his later theory argues that divine ideas include a rational relation as a *sine qua non*, but that relation is not how God knows possible creatures.

Chapters IX and X (Part V) explain what I call the "Nominalist Theory" endorsed by Peter Auriol and William of Ockham, respectively. This theory eliminates the need for a theory of divine ideas in large part because of a dramatically different account of relation than their predecessors. Earlier theories rely heavily on the distinction between a real relation and a rational relation to explain divine ideas. Nominalists deny that the distinction is relevant when speaking of divine things. Instead, God just knows a variety of objects when he knows his essence. Just as our intellects can know many terms as a single proposition, so too God can know both himself and all possible creatures in the single act of knowledge. Their predecessors' robust and complicated theories of relation thus become superfluous and erroneous.

The book concludes with a recapitulation of the foregoing chapters and offer a systematic overview of the points of agreement and disagreement among the theories. Despite the many differences in the theories, there are several points on which the authors agree. Finally, I offer a suggestion for determining the best theory of divine ideas. This question cannot be determined simply by comparing the theories themselves. A determination of the best theory of divine ideas can ultimately be decided only after it is determined which theory of essence is true, which points to the fact that the question of essence is prior to the question of divine ideas. Even Bonaventure's theory of divine ideas, which occupies a preeminent place in his metaphysics, relies on his theory of creaturely essences.

I have tried to present a systematic account of each author's theory. As a result, I do not offer a detailed examination of each place that the author discusses a certain aspect of divine ideas. Such a close analysis would unnecessarily swell the length of this already lengthy study. I break with this practice only in certain cases where the author, especially Aquinas and Henry of Ghent, changes his mind about divine ideas. In these cases, I present some of the earlier theory, but focus on the mature thought.

Part I.
The Imitability Theory of Divine Ideas

The first theory of divine ideas covered in this study is what I call the Imitability Theory, which has several characteristic marks. First, divine ideas are secondary objects of the divine intellect when it knows the divine essence. The only principle or source of God's knowledge is his essence. When he knows his essence, the primary object that his essence makes him know is himself. Things other than God are known as secondary objects. In particular, they are known because when God knows his essence, he knows all the ways that his essence could be imitated (or, in Bonaventure's terminology, expressed). Thus, divine ideas are a result of God's knowledge of his essence. If, *per impossibile*, God did not know his essence, then there would be no divine ideas.

Second, these divine ideas perform a cognitive role and a causal role. Divine ideas are the means by which God knows possible creatures, and he has no epistemological access to creatures except through divine ideas. Divine ideas are also exemplars to the imitation of which God creates the world. Imitability Theorists insist on these two roles to ensure that their account preserves the fact that God acts reasonably. If divine ideas did not perform these roles, then God would create without knowing what he created, in which case the creatures that are created and the very order of creation would be due more to chance or necessity than forethought. God would learn *de novo* about creatures after he created them. Moreover, if he did not know what actions creatures, in particular men and angels, perform, then he could not justly mete out eternal reward or punishment.

Third, adherents of the Imitability Theory insist that divine ideas are relations. In particular, they are the rational relations or respects (*respectus*) that God knows exist from himself to the creature. They will sometimes also say that a divine idea is God's knowledge of the possible real relation that a creature could bear to him. Both these expressions are ways of reiterating that a divine idea is God's knowledge of the ways his essence can be imitated. Each creature is what it is because of a unique relation of imitation that it bears to the divine essence.

The fourth point flows from the third point. There are many divine ideas because there are many possible imitations of the divine essence. The plurality might seem contrary to divine simplicity, but Imitability Theorists argue that it is not. In reality (*secundum rem*), there is only one divine idea because everything in God is one. According to reason (*secundum rationem*), there are many ideas because God knows many possible imitations of his essence. The plurality of divine ideas is only a plurality of rational respects, and this sort of plurality is not contrary to unity or simplicity at all. That which (*id quod*) God knows is one, but that to which (*id ad quod*) his knowledge extends is many. These authors insist that the plurality of divine ideas is prior to and the cause of the multiplicity of creatures.

Imitability Theorists disagree over a host of details about God's knowledge of things other than himself. Nevertheless, they agree on these points. For them, divine ideas are relations or respects through which God knows a possible creature. Knowledge of one term of the relation, namely, himself, and the relation suffice for knowledge of the other term of the relation, namely, the creature.

Chapter I.
St. Bonaventure (ca. 1217–1274)

THE PLACE OF DIVINE IDEAS IN ST. BONAVENTURE'S THOUGHT

St. Bonaventure of Bagnoregio's theory of divine ideas is, in many ways, indebted to his predecessors.[1] Yet, Bonaventure is an apt figure to begin this study because his thought is extremely influential for later authors, especially other Franciscans, and because divine ideas have a preeminent place in Bonaventure's thought. A theory of divine ideas is paramount to any metaphysical system because it explains the exemplar and pattern of all creatures. This second point is worth expanding before turning to Bonaventure's theory of divine ideas itself.

Metaphysics is the study of essence (*esse*).[2] *Esse* exists in only two ways. In the one way, *esse* is from itself, according to itself, and because of itself. In another way, *esse* is from another, according to another, and because of another. We can call these sorts of *esse* primary *esse* and secondary *esse*, respectively. Secondary *esse* traces back to primary *esse* in three ways. Primary *esse* is the reason for the origination, exemplifying, and end of secondary *esse*. As Bonaventure also puts it, primary *esse* is the principle, medium, and end of all secondary *esse*. The metaphysician begins with secondary *esse* and traces it back to primary *esse*, but his task is not always unique to him. Insofar as he considers the originating principles of all things, his work corresponds with the physicist's work since they consider the first efficient cause. Insofar as he considers the ultimate end of all things, his work coincides with the ethicist's work since they both consider the good. When he considers the reason for the exemplification of all things, he does not share his work with another, and he is a true metaphysician. As Fr. Christopher Cullen writes, "so central is exemplarism to metaphysics that the only real metaphysician is the one who considers being in the light of that principle which is the exemplar of all things."[3] The mark of the metaphysician, then, is the investigation of exemplarity.[4]

---

1. For the influence of Alexander of Hales and John of La Rochelle on Bonaventure, see Riccardo Saccenti, "*Sic Bonum Cognoscitur et Similiter Lux*: Divine Ideas in the First Franciscan Masters (Alexander of Hales and John of La Rochelle)," in *Divine Ideas in Franciscan Thought*, 1–24.

2. For a justification of this translation of *esse*, see George P. Klubertanz, "*Esse* and *Existere* in St. Bonaventure," *Mediaeval Studies* 8, no. 1 (1946): 169–88.

3. Christopher Cullen, *Bonaventure* (New York: Oxford University Press, 2006), 72.

4. *In Hex.*, col. I, nn. 12–13 (Quaracchi, V.331a–b). Cullen puts the matter more technically: "The central concern of metaphysics, then, is the ultimate ground of being under a particular aspect: namely, as the source for reality's having meaning or making sense at all, as the source of things being what they are and not other things, and as the source for being graspable by mind at all" (*Bonaventure*, 73).

Just as exemplarism is the central and preeminent consideration of the metaphysician, so a theory of divine ideas is the central and preeminent aspect of exemplarism. A theory of divine ideas is so pivotal because divine ideas account for God's knowledge and production of creation. For Bonaventure, "reality reflects the divine ideas that are exemplars in the divine mind," so reality cannot be understood without understanding divine ideas.[5] A theory of divine ideas is the bridge that allows the metaphysician to trace back secondary *esse* to primary *esse*.

Exemplarism, and especially a theory of divine ideas, is central for Bonaventure both philosophically and theologically. A philosopher who omits exemplarism is not a metaphysician because he loses sight of the most fundamental aspect of creatures. At its core, every creature is a sign pointing to God, that is, it is an imitative likeness (*similitudo imitativa*). Thus, Bonaventure claims that Aristotle, who denies Plato's conception of Ideas in many places, was not a true metaphysician. Aristotle focused too much on knowledge of things for their own sakes, rather than as signs pointing to God.[6] Bonaventure holds Aristotle in high regard because he safeguarded an important form of knowledge, but things lose their stability without an exemplar. Since he did not investigate the exemplarity of things, he had to consider them as subsisting for their own sakes. When finite beings are considered in this way, "they become for us simple objects of curiosity" and not part of the pursuit of wisdom.[7]

Theologically, investigating exemplarity is the closest that man can, by his natural reason, come to investigating Christ, the Son of God. Christ is the center and mediator between God and man, and he holds a central position in all things.[8] Since all the treasures of God's wisdom and knowledge are hidden in Christ, he is the center of all the sciences.[9] He is the eternal Art in which the world has been described from eternity. He is the Word through whom all things were created.[10] To investigate divine ideas, then, is to investigate Christ, although not *as* Christ. Moreover, since "if you understand the Word, you understand all knowable things," a theory of divine ideas is the closest that reason can come to perfect, comprehensive knowledge.[11]

Divine ideas are so central to Bonaventure that he declares it heretical to deny them: "He who denies that ideas exist, denies that the Son of God exists."[12] They are so central to God's knowledge, the act of creation, the very essences of things, and our knowledge that no one could both deny them and be a Christian. This claim is worth noting because no later author is as insistent upon the point as Bonaventure is.

---

5. Cullen, *Bonaventure*, 76.
6. *Christus unus omnium magister*, n. 18 (Quaracchi, V.572a).
7. Étienne Gilson, *La Philosophie de Saint Bonaventure*, troisième édition (Paris: Vrin, 1953), 143.
8. *In Hex.*, col. I, n. 10 (Quaracchi, V.330b). See Zachary Hayes, *The Hidden Center: Spirituality and Speculative Christology in St. Bonvaenture* (New York: Paulist Press, 1981).
9. *In Hex.*, col. I, n. 11 (Quaracchi, V. 331a).
10. *In Hex.*, col. I, nn. 16–17 (Quaracchi, V.332a).
11. *In Hex.*, col. III, n. 4 (Quaracchi, V.344a): "Si igitur intelligis Verbum, intelligis omnia scibilia."
12. *In I Sent.*, d. 6, a. un., q. 3 (Quaracchi, I.130a): "qui negat ideas esse, negat Filium Dei esse." Cf. Augustine, *De div. qq. 83*, q. 46, n. 2 (PL 40.30).

THE STATUS OF DIVINE IDEAS

Bonaventure's systematic discussion of divine ideas occurs in two places: *In I Sent.*, dd. 35–36 (ca. 1251) and the *De scientia Christi*, qq. 1–3 (1254).[13] Many have noted that Bonaventure's thought remains consistent throughout his career, and divine ideas are an excellent example of this consistency.[14] Although his articulation of the theory is slightly different in *In I Sent.* and *De scientia Christi*, the differences are only a matter of emphasis.

What Is an Idea?

Idea

Before asking whether God has ideas, it is prudent to ask what an idea is. Bonaventure approaches this question from the perspective of what an idea is not. Ideas cannot be the true essence and quiddities of things because ideas are not other than the one who has them. If an idea were the true essence and quiddity of a thing, the artist would have the same essence as the art he produces. The sculptor would have the same essence as a statue, which is absurd. The case is even worse, for, in God's case, to deny that the Creator and creatures have different essences is to endorse pantheism or at least panentheism.[15] If the statue is not the sculptor, far less is any creature the Creator. Thus, Bonaventure says, an idea must be an exemplar form and representative likeness of things. Since they are representative likenesses of things, ideas are thus the intellectual means of knowing (*rationes cognoscendi*) things because cognition, precisely as cognition, entails an assimilation and expression between the knower and the known.[16]

Cognition involves the assimilation of the knower and the known.[17] Since Bonaventure has ruled out that the assimilation can occur by essence, it must occur by likeness; "likenesses are mandated by the very nature of knowing."[18] Even if we were to know by our essence, we would still know through a likeness. In that case,

---

13. For these two texts, I follow the chronology of John Francis Quinn, "The Chronology of St. Bonaventure (1217–1257)," *Franciscan Studies* 32, no. 1 (1972): 168–86.

14. For a brief bibliography of the issue, see Hayes, *The Hidden Center*, 7n7.

15. Pantheism is the theory that God and the world are identical. Panentheism is the theory that the world is in God or part of God, but God is greater than the world. Pantheism reduces God to the world, and panentheism claims that God is not exhausted by the world. For a good introduction to panentheism and a history of its adherents, see John W. Cooper, *Panentheism, the Other God of the Philosophers. From Plato to the Present* (Grand Rapids, MI: Baker Academic Press, 2006).

16. *De scientia Christi*, q. 2 (Quaracchi, V.8b), esp.: "cognoscendi rationes sunt, quia cognitio, hoc ipso quod cognitio, assimilationem dicit et expressionem inter cognoscentem et cognoscibile." See Cullen, *Bonaventure*, 73.

17. *De scientia Christi*, q. 2, fm. 4 (Quaracchi, V.7a). See Aristotle, *De anima* III, c. 8, 431b20–21 (Leonine, 45.1.235a).

18. Christopher M. Cullen, "The Semiotic Metaphysics of Saint Bonaventure" (PhD diss., The Catholic University of America, 2000), 145.

our intellect would not need a likeness taken or received from some external object. It would still use itself as a likeness to know other things.[19]

Three things stand out in this account. An idea is a *ratio cognoscendi*, a representative likeness, and an exemplar form. These three show that an idea can perform two distinct roles: as a cognitive principle and as a causal principle. An idea is the means by which the artist knows what he can produce and the exemplar to whose imitation he produces. To understand what Bonaventure means by 'idea,' we will have to investigate both roles.

There are three things to note about the cognitive role. First, the cognitive role of an idea is prior to its causal role because, as R. P. J.-M. Bissen notes, "an idea is strictly speaking a likeness and does not necessarily entail production."[20] Nothing has to be produced for the character of an idea to be completed. The character of an idea is complete in serving the cognitive role. The causal role of an idea is entirely predicated upon its first being a cognitive principle.

Second, an idea has its cognitive role because it is a representative likeness. Bonaventure distinguishes two types of likeness. In one way, there is a likeness through the agreement of two things in a third, which Bonaventure calls a likeness of univocation or of participation. Peter and Paul are like each other because of humanity. A man and a horse are like each other because of animality. In each case, the two are like each other because of a third thing that, as it were, stands as a higher genus. In another way, there is a likeness when one thing is like another, which Bonaventure calls a likeness of one to another. In this case, there is no third thing common that makes one thing like another. Rather, "the likeness is itself like."[21] Bonaventure further distinguishes the likeness of one to another into an imitative likeness (*similitudo imitativa*) and an exemplative likeness (*similituda exemplativa*) corresponding to the way that the two things that are related. The imitative likeness is expressive, and the exemplative likeness is expressing.[22]

Bonaventure explains expressing and expressive likenesses through a distinction between knowledge that causes a thing and knowledge that is caused by a thing. When knowledge is caused by a thing, the thing known is expressing, and there is an imitative likeness in the knower because the likeness has its source *ab extra*. The likeness in the knower imitates the thing known, and it causes a certain assimilation between the knower and what is known. The likeness in the knower is expressive of what is known. The thing known is expressing because it causes the likeness in the knower. The received and imitative nature of the likeness in the

---

19. *De scientia Christi*, q. 2, ad 7 (Quaracchi, V.9b).

20. R. P. J.-M. Bissen, "Des Idées Exemplaires En Dieu d'après Saint Bonaventure" (PhD diss., The University of Freibourg, 1927), 15; R. P. J.-M. Bissen, *L'exemplarisme Divin selon Saint Bonaventure* (Paris: Vrin, 1929), 22–23. Bonaventure's emphasis on the cognitive role shows the influence of Alexander of Hales, *Glossa*, I, d. 36 (Quaracchi, 357:21–30). See Saccenti, "*Sic Bonum Cognoscitur et Similiter Lux*," 14.

21. *In I Sent.*, d. 35, a. un., q. 1 (Quaracchi, I.601b): "similitudo se ipsa est similis."

22. *De scientia Christi*, q. 2 (Quaracchi, V.8b–9a). Cf. *In I Sent.*, d. 35, a. un., q. 1, corpus and ad 2 (Quaracchi, I.601). The names of the types of likeness are from *In I Sent*.

knower also entails some composition and addition in the knower's intellect. The imitative likeness in the knower involves the addition of new knowledge and bespeaks the imperfection in the knower who must pass from knowing in potency to knowing in act.[23]

When knowledge causes a thing, there is an exemplative likeness in the knower. This likeness neither has its source *ab extra* nor implies any imperfection. Instead, it entails every manner of perfection. In a finite artist, we can imagine that such an exemplative likeness might be of mixed perfection. The architect surely thinks up the building himself, and his idea of the building is perfect in that sense. Nevertheless, the various buildings that he has experienced and studied inspire the architect. His idea, then, is partially the result of an imitative likeness of other buildings, and partially the result of his thinking up a new building. As we will see below, Bonaventure insists that God's ideas do not have this mixed perfection because God does not receive knowledge *ab extra*. Divine ideas are the result of God being the supreme light and fullness of truth, and so they are perfect in every way.

The third thing to note about an idea is that only an exemplative likeness is an idea. Neither a likeness of univocation nor an imitative likeness is an idea. Only the sort of knowledge that causes a thing, or at least can cause a thing, deserves to be called an idea. This restriction means that an idea is fundamentally a principle of practical cognition. Bonaventure does not draw out this point explicitly, but it follows from what he has said. A knower cannot have ideas of things that he cannot cause. The carpenter can know a chair and a cheetah, but he can only have an idea of the chair because he can produce the chair but not the cheetah.

Although Bonaventure emphasizes that ideas are exemplative likenesses, an exemplative likeness is intelligible only in tandem with an imitative likeness. An exemplative likeness does not exemplify if nothing can imitate it. Ideas, then, are the sort of things that can be imitated. In other words, central to the character of an idea is imitability. This is the reason I say that Bonaventure articulates a version of the Imitability Theory. Bonaventure's focus on exemplative likeness can obscure his Imitability Theory because he does not speak in terms of the imitability of the divine essence. However, when Bonaventure speaks of exemplative likenesses, he is speaking of imitability. The terms "exemplative likeness" and "imitative likeness" allow Bonaventure to talk specifically about one term of a relation. However, that term is only part of the relation because of the other term. Bonaventure does not use the terminology of 'imitability' in his theory, but he articulates the substance of the theory just the same.

Exemplar

Turning to the causal or productive role of divine ideas, we find that this role is marked by a shift in terminology. Bonaventure consistently uses the term "idea" to describe the cognitive role of an idea, but when he speaks of the causal role of an

---

23. *De scientia Christi*, q. 2 (Quaracchi, V.9a).

idea, "the word 'exemplar' often replaces the word 'idea.'"[24] Ideas belong primarily to the genus of likeness, which is accomplished through cognition only, but an idea can also serve as an exemplar in production. A complete account of an idea then, requires investigating what Bonaventure means by 'exemplar.'

In the *Breviloquium*, Bonaventure says that an exemplar is "an idea according to the act of foreseeing; a word according to the act of proposing; an art according to the act of accomplishing; a *ratio* according to the act of perfecting because it adds the intention of an end."[25] An exemplar, then, has four aspects: it gives knowledge, proposes for production, carries out the act of production, and adds the intention of an end. The discussion of the cognitive role of an idea above should suffice for a discussion of the first aspect of an exemplar. The rest of this section will be concerned with the other three aspects. Given the contexts in which Bonaventure discusses these three aspects, the existence of divine ideas will be assumed, even though Bonaventure's arguments for their existence will not be examined until the next section.[26]

Word

An exemplar is a word because of its act of proposing. Bonaventure says that words are spoken in two ways: either to oneself (*ad se*), that is with oneself (*apud se*), or to another (*ad alterum*).[27] These two ways of speaking correspond to the two words that God has spoken: the interior word and the exterior word. God's interior word is the Divine Word, and his exterior word is creation. God's interior word corresponds to the Divine Word because speaking to oneself is nothing other than conceiving mentally. This understanding results in the conception of something like yourself. By speaking to himself, God conceives a word that is progeny like himself.

Our minds generate many conceived words, but the Father conceives only a single Word that is simultaneously the imitative likeness of the Father and the exemplative likeness of things and the operative likeness of things.[28] It is through the Divine Word that the Father foreknows and conceives all that he will do. The Word is what allows us to say that the Father acts rationally.[29] The Divine Word is both the perfect image and Word of the Father and the exemplar of creation. To be an exemplar is proper to the whole Trinity insofar as an exemplar is a *ratio cog-*

---

24. Bissen, "Des Idées Exemplaires," 16.
25. *Breviloquium* I, c. 8 (Quaracchi, V.216b), "Ad exemplar autem spectat idea, verbum, ars et ratio: idea, secundum actum praevidendi; verbum, secundum actum proponendi; ars, secundum actum prosequendi; ratio, secundum actum perficiendi, quia superaddit intentionem finis."
26. See p. 36.
27. *In I Sent.*, d. 27, p. 2, a. un., q. 1 (Quaracchi, I.482b).
28. *In I Sent.*, d. 27, p. 2, a. un., q. 2 (Quaracchi, I.485b).
29. *In I Sent.*, d. 27, p. 2, a. un., q. 4 (Quaracchi, I.490a): "Nam sicut homo nihil operetur rationabiliter, quod non praecogitet et mente concipiat, sic Deus Pater omnia in Verbo disposuit." See *Breviloquium* I, c. 3 (Quaracchi, V.212a).

noscendi, but it is also appropriated to the Word insofar as wisdom is proper to the Word.[30]

As the wisdom of the Father, the Word is generated principally by nature and only concomitantly by the divine will. Bonaventure's account of agents that produce by nature will be explained in more detail in the next section. For now, it suffices to say that an agent produces by nature if it produces the same sort of thing that it is. A man generates a man by nature. When Bonaventure says that the Word is generated principally by nature, he is saying that the Father produces the Word by producing the same sort of thing that the Father is. Since an act of the will presupposes an act of the intellect, if the Word proceeded primarily through the divine will, then God would have willed blindly and about things he did not know.[31] Furthermore, since God communicates to creatures through his will, saying that the Word comes by will would entail that the Word is a creature, which is false.[32] Thus, Bonaventure claims that the Word is generated from the Father by nature primarily.

The claim that the Divine Word is generated from the Father by nature primarily impacts Bonaventure's account of divine ideas. Since divine ideas are appropriated to the Divine Word and since that the Divine Word is generated naturally and necessarily, the Divine Word exemplifies all possible creatures naturally and necessarily. As Bonaventure says, "although the actual production of a creature be voluntary, yet the potency of producing [it] and the knowledge is necessary."[33] God necessarily has all the knowledge that he has, including the knowledge of possible creatures. He also necessarily has the ability to create any of the possible creatures that he necessarily knows. This knowledge and creative potency are necessary if Bonaventure is to say that God produces creatures rationally. The Divine Word is the guarantor of divine rationality because it expresses the ability to know and express others. This analysis makes clear why Bonaventure argues that he who knows the Son of God knows all things and why a denial of divine ideas amounts to a denial of the Son of God.[34]

Art

The discussion of 'word' naturally leads to a discussion of art because a discussion of the notion of exemplifying, which makes the production of creatures possible, leads to a discussion of the production itself. The term 'art' specifies the term 'exem-

---

30. *In I Sent.*, d. 6, a. un., q. 3, corpus and ad 2 (Quaracchi, I.130). To say that the term 'exemplar' is appropriated to the Divine Word means that it belongs especially to the Divine Word to be an exemplar, even though it does not belong exclusively to the Divine Word. Appropriations are taken from Sacred Scripture. Given that Sacred Scripture names the Second Person of the Trinity the Word (Jn 1:1), and given Bonaventure's description of what the Word is, it belongs especially to the Second Person of the Trinity to be called an exemplar. See *New Catholic Encyclopedia*, 2nd ed., (2003), s.v. "Appropriation."
31. *In I Sent.*, d. 6, a. un., q. 3, fm. 4 (Quaracchi, I.127a).
32. *In I Sent.*, d. 6, a. un., q. 3, ad 3 (Quaracchi, I.128b).
33. *In I Sent.*, d. 27, p. 2, a. un., q. 2, ad 2 (Quaracchi, I.486a): "quamvis actualis productio creaturae sit voluntaria, tamen potentia producendi et scientia est necessaria."
34. *In Hex.*, col. III, n. 2 (Quaracchi, V.344a); *In I Sent.*, d. 6, a. un., q. 3 (Quaracchi, I.130).

plar' by adding the act of accomplishing. Just as 'word' implies a speaker, the thing spoken, and the relationship between the two, so 'art' implies an artist, the artifact, and the relationship between the two. To understand the artist, we must consider the distinction that Bonaventure makes between a natural agent and an intelligent agent. A natural agent produces through natural forms, as when man generates man. A natural agent is the sort of thing that it produces.

In contrast, "an intelligent agent produces through forms that are not something of the thing, but ideas in the mind."[35] A natural agent's form constrains it to produce only according to that one form, but an intelligent agent can produce a host of artifacts that vary in form. Insofar as he is a natural agent, a man can only generate another man, and never a shark. Insofar as he is an intelligent agent, a man can make any of the artifacts of which he has ideas. Bonaventure uses the example of a carpenter crafting a chest. The carpenter is not a chest, but the chest proceeds from him because of the idea of the chest in his mind. Thus, he assimilates the wood to the form he has in his mind whenever he wills to do so.

Although his actions are infinitely more eminent, God produces things in the same way as the carpenter. God has ideas by which he foreknows all the things he could make. Just as the chest is not produced except by the will of the carpenter, so neither are the things God knows by his ideas produced except by the will of God. This analogy can only take us so far, however. Strictly speaking, God does not *have* ideas because that would imply that they are distinct from him. Instead, the ideas *are* God.[36] God has one art because he is a single knower.[37] Aristotle was right, Bonaventure says, to criticize Plato for saying that ideas were separate substances existing outside of God because this position takes both cognition and operation from God. However, Aristotle was wrong to deny that God has ideas because such a position takes cognition of things other than himself away from God.[38]

The claim that ideas are the divine exemplars according to which God creates tells us something of the artist and something of the artifact, but it does not yield much insight into the relationship between the two. The discussion of idea above supplies that relationship.[39] The artist and his artifact have a relationship of assimilation.[40] There is assimilation because the artist fashions the artifact to be like his idea. Just as the carpenter first conceives the house he will build as an idea and word in his mind, and then he crafts it so that it will express the exemplar in his mind as much as possible, so God preconceives all things as likenesses of divine truth before creating them. Bonaventure stresses that the assimilation between the exemplar and the imitation need not be great to count as an actual assimilation:

---

35. *In II Sent.*, d. 1, p. 1, a. 1, q. 1, ad 3 et 4 (Quaracchi, II.17b): "agens per intellectum producit per formas, quae non sunt aliquid rei, sed ideae in mente."
36. *In II Sent.*, d. 1, p. 1, a. 1, q. 1, ad 3 et 4 (Quaracchi, II.17b).
37. *In I Sent.*, d. 35, a. un., q. 3, ad 2 (Quaracchi, I.608b).
38. *In II Sent.*, d. 1, p. 1, a. 1, q. 1, ad 3 et 4 (Quaracchi, II.17b).
39. See pp. 15–17.
40. See *In I Sent.*, d. 36, a. 3, q. 1 (Quaracchi, I.628a).

"the least assimilation suffices for the notion of an exemplar."[41] So the fact that there is always a greater dissimilarity between a creature and the Creator does not preclude creatures from being the products of divine art.[42] That a creature is fashioned after a divine idea is enough to say that the idea is an exemplar.

This analysis further illuminates the distinction between knowledge that causes a thing and knowledge caused by a thing. Knowledge that causes a thing is exemplary and perfect because the knowledge brings about the thing, meaning the knowledge is the standard of judgment. The thing that is caused by the knowledge is measured against the standard of the knowledge. The more a thing is assimilated to the knowledge, the better an imitation it is. And it is proper to speak of assimilation here because all knowledge involves an assimilation of knower and known. Since art involves an intelligent agent producing something according to the form in his mind, there will always be an assimilation involved.

Ratio

The last aspect of an exemplar to be discussed is *ratio*.[43] An exemplar is "a *ratio* according to the act of perfecting because it adds the intention of an end."[44] The *ratio* perfects the exemplar precisely by adding the intention of an end. Since a divine idea is not caused by the thing in any way, but rather causes it, the divine idea causes the thing in every way. Not only does the idea make a thing be the sort of thing it is, it fully determines its nature. Divine ideas determine both that Peter will be a man and what it means to be man. A divine idea determines everything characteristic of the essence, including its characteristic acts and its end. Unlike the finite artist who might not determine the end of what he makes, God does not borrow his model from anywhere else. He establishes the model after which he makes creatures because he is supremely expressive truth. He perfects the natures of things, which natures he has established himself.

Conclusions

Four conclusions can be drawn from Bonaventure's discussion of idea, word, art, and *ratio*. First, exemplarity belongs to intelligent causes. The character of an

---

41. *In I Sent.*, d. 36, a. 3, q. 2, fm. 4 (Quaracchi, I.629a): "minima assimilatio sufficit ad rationem exemplaris."

42. This point is especially important since the Fourth Lateran Council (1215) stated that "inter creatorem et creaturam non potest tanta similitudo notari, quin inter eos maior sit dissimilitudo notanda" (Henricus Denzinger and Adolfus Schönmetzer, eds., *Enchiridion Symbolorum Definitionum et Declarationum de Rebus Fidei et Morum*, 32nd ed. [Rome: Herder, 1963], n. 806). By claiming that even the least assimilation fulfills the notion of an exemplar, Bonaventure both upholds the council's declaration and art's requirements.

43. The inspiration for this discussion of *ratio* is Gregory Doolan's parallel insight into Aquinas's definition of idea (*Aquinas on the Divine Ideas as Exemplar Causes* [Washington, DC: The Catholic University of America Press, 2008], 28–33).

44. *Breviloquium* I, c. 8 (Quaracchi, V.216b): "ratio, secundum actum perficiendi, quia superaddit intentionem finis."

exemplar includes the character of a *ratio cognoscendi* and a notion of exemplifying. Natural forms can exemplify insofar as what is generated is like what generates, but natural forms are not *rationes cognoscendi*. Natural forms do not require any sort of cognition for generation to occur. Again, the form by which it generates is not a likeness in it. Natural agents really are the sort of thing that they generate, but it is characteristic of an exemplar to exemplify by a likeness. The intelligent agent assimilates his effect to the exemplar in his mind.

Second, assimilation between the exemplar and the imitation can be far from perfect. The immense gap between the perfection of God and the minimal perfection of the lowest creature does not hinder the creature's assimilation. All that is required is that the imitation be assimilated to divine truth in some way. The fact that a creature is always more dissimilar to God than similar does not preclude God's exemplarity or the creature's imitation.

Third, ideas and exemplars are common to both God and men. Man can have ideas and exemplars precisely because he is an intelligent agent. Likenesses received from things cause man's knowledge initially. This receptivity is evidence of the potency and imperfection of man's knowledge, but man's knowledge is not merely receptive. He uses those imitative likenesses to fashion ideas and exemplars of possible artifacts. Insofar as he is an artist, man imitates God's art and has ideas. Despite this similarity, the divine art infinitely surpasses human art because God can create natural things whereas man can only make artifacts. God creates the whole of things; man only fashions out of what has already been created. Nevertheless, man does exercise real exemplarity regarding those artifacts, including establishing the end of the things he makes. To borrow an example from Aquinas, man not only makes a knife, but also establishes the end for which the knife is made, namely, cutting.[45] This example can be taken one step further. Not only does the artist establish the end of knife in general, he also establishes that that the end of the fillet knife is for separating the skin of a fish from the fillet and that the end of the cleaver is for separating big joints. Each knife is crafted precisely because of the end that it can fulfill, which end was established by the knife-maker.

Finally, for Bonaventure, the causal or productive role of the exemplar is posterior to the cognitive role of the idea. All ideas are the likenesses by which the knower knows things that he could produce, and they are also the exemplary forms by which he actually produces them, but the cognitive role takes center stage. In the case of divine ideas, the cognitive role is primary in part because it is necessary. God necessarily has all the ideas that he has. He does not necessarily have any exemplars because it was not necessary that he will to create anything. Preserving this distinction safeguards God's power to know more than he creates and his ability to create freely. God necessarily foresees everything that he could make, but he does not make all of it.

---

45. Aquinas, *De prin. nat.*, n. 4 (Leonine, 43.45:104–8).

Does God Have Ideas?

Having seen that an idea is a principle of practical cognition that serves as the intellectual means of knowing (*ratio cognoscendi*) by which a possible effect is known, we ask whether God has ideas. Bonaventure offers three arguments why we ought to posit divine ideas and an argument how we ought to posit divine ideas in God, two of which are pertinent.[46]

Bonaventure bases each of his arguments that God must have ideas on our inability to account for an aspect of reality without them. If we do not posit divine ideas, then we cannot account for the fact that God acts rationally (*rationabiliter*), that we can know with certainty, and that all finite beings are imitations of God. The first argument is as follows.

> Every agent that acts rationally (*rationabiliter*), and not by chance or out of necessity (*non a casu vel ex necessitate*), foreknows a thing before it exists. Every knower has the thing known either according to truth (*secundum veritatem*) or according to a likeness (*secundum similitudinem*). But things, before they exist, cannot be had by God according to truth. Therefore, they are had according to a likeness. But a thing's likeness, through which a thing is known and produced, is an idea. Therefore, God has ideas.[47]

The first premise of this argument takes for granted that God acts rationally and not by chance or out of necessity. Since God is pure act and truth itself, it follows that he acts rationally. Moreover, if God acted by chance or out of necessity, then finite beings would not be the result of divine love, so Bonaventure can reasonably be granted this premise. Once this point is granted, it follows straightaway that the agent has foreknowledge of what it causes because these three possibilities are exhaustive. Agents either act rationally, by chance, or out of necessity (whether that necessity be a necessity of nature or coercion). Knowledge involves an assimilation of the knower to the thing known, which can only occur according to truth or according to likeness. The thing known is in the knower according to truth only if the knower is the thing known in reality. This possibility can be ruled out on a variety of grounds, but Bonaventure chooses an easy route. If the things known were in God according to truth, then God would really be those things. In that case, the things would be eternal like God, and it would not make sense to speak of "before they existed." The creature would be both eternal and finite, which is impossible. This position would amount to pantheism or at least panentheism because a

---

46. I omit the argument based on divine illumination found at *In I Sent.*, d. 35, a. un., q. 1, fm. 3 (Quaracchi ed., I.600a). For more on divine illumination, see Stephen P. Marrone, *The Light of Thy Countenance: Science and Knowledge of God in the Thirteenth Century*, 2 vols. (Leiden: Brill, 2001).

47. *In I Sent.*, d. 35, a. un., q. 1, fm. 2 (Quaracchi, I.600a): "omne agens rationabiliter, non a casu, vel ex necessitate, praecognoscit rem, antequam sit; sed omnis cognoscens habet rem cognitam vel secundum veritatem, vel secundum similitudinem; sed res, antequam sint, non possunt haberi a Deo secundum veritatem: ergo secundum similitudinem. Sed similitudinem rei, per quam res cognoscitur et producitur, est idea: ergo etc."

creature and God would be identical. Since the thing known cannot be in God according to truth, it must be in God according to a likeness. The likeness by which a thing is known and produced is an idea. Therefore, God has ideas.

Bonaventure takes his second argument from the fact that God creates the world.

> Because things are produced by God, therefore they are in him as in an efficient cause, and God is most truly an efficient cause. Similarly, because they have their end from him, therefore, God is most truly an end. So, by the same reasoning, because they are cognized and expressed by him, God is most truly an exemplar. But an exemplar in itself must have ideas of the things exemplified. Therefore, God has ideas.[48]

This argument relies on the unstated principles that everything makes something like itself and nothing can give what it does not have. If creatures have been brought into existence, then their producer must be an efficient cause, but for an effect to imitate a cause is for the cause to be an exemplar. Creatures could not be imitations of God if their likeness did not preexist in God, and God could not make creatures if creatures did not imitate him in any way.

Bonaventure then turns to the question of how there are divine ideas. A divine idea "signifies the divine essence in comparison to or in respect to a creature."[49] There are several points to note from this statement. First, divine ideas are in the divine intellect. A comparison of the divine essence could only happen through a knowing power. If the divine essence remained unknown, then there would be no ideas. Second, the source of God's ideas is the divine essence. All his knowledge is the result of the divine intellect knowing the divine essence. Third, the comparison of the divine essence to a creature occurs because the divine intellect is the supreme light, full truth, and pure act. Divine light is sufficient to express all things. Since this expression is an intrinsic act, not the extrinsic act of creation, it is an eternal act of God. The divine intellect eternally expresses the exemplar likenesses of all things. God is truth itself and each creature is a likeness of that truth. Since divine truth is supremely expressive, it follows that the expression will be most lucid, most expressive, and most perfect. Therefore, God's knowledge will be most perfect, most distinct, and most integral. There is no possible aspect of creatures that could escape his understanding.[50]

It might seem *ad hoc* that Bonaventure does not explain why truth is expressive in detail. His account relies heavily upon the analogy of knowledge to light. Just as

---

48. *In I Sent.*, d. 35, a. un., q. 1, fm. 4 (Quaracchi, I.600): "quia res a Deo producuntur, ideo sunt in Deo tanquam in efficiente, et Deus verissime est efficiens; similiter, quia ab ipso finiuntur, ideo verissime est finis: ergo pari ratione, quia ab ipso cognoscuntur et exprimuntur, per se ipsum Deus verissime est exemplar. Sed exemplar non est, nisi in quo sunt rerum exemplatarum ideae: ergo etc."

49. *In I Sent.*, d. 35, a. un., q. 3 (Quaracchi, I.608a): "hoc nomen 'idea' significat divinam essentiam in comparatione sive in respectu ad creaturam." Cf. Alexander of Hales, *Summa theologica*, p. 1, inq. 1, tr. 5, sect. 1, q. un., mem. 2, c. 4 (Quaracchi, I.250b).

50. *De scientia Christi*, q. 2 (Quaracchi, V.9a). See *In I Sent.*, d. 35, a. un., q. 1 (Quaracchi, I.601b).

light does not stay confined in its source but shines out as much as it is able, so too God's knowledge does not remain confined to knowledge of the source, namely, the divine essence, but extends to all likenesses of the divine truth. But, if God is pure act and fullness of truth, why should his knowledge extend to anything else? If we consider what he says about the expressiveness of divine truth based on his arguments for the necessity of divine ideas, we see that divine truth must be expressive. If divine truth were not expressive, then God would not know or produce creatures rationally.

Bonaventure's insistence on speaking of divine truth as expressive obscures the fact that he is talking about the imitability of the divine essence. Other versions of the Imitability Theory emphasize the imitability of the divine essence as known.[51] But speaking of divine truth as expressive is speaking of knowing the imitability of the divine essence. Divine truth expresses all the ways that possible creatures could imitate the divine essence. Since a divine idea signifies the divine essence in comparison to or in respect to a creature, and since creatures relate to the divine essence as imitations, divine ideas are the ways the divine essence is known to be imitable.[52] Divine ideas concern the imitability of the divine essence. Once again, Bonaventure's theory is found to be a version of the Imitability Theory. The fact that Bonaventure does not use a term that becomes standard in later accounts does not mean he holds a different theory.

Thus, God must have divine ideas because they are necessary to account for the fact that God knows creatures, produces creatures, and that rational creatures know with certitude. Divine ideas exist because God is truth itself and truth itself is supremely expressive. When God knows his own essence, he does not just know himself; he also knows all the likenesses of himself. By knowing these likenesses, God eternally, most perfectly, most distinctly, and most integrally knows all possible creatures.

The Unity and Multiplicity of Divine Ideas

The question of the unity and multiplicity of divine ideas is particularly thorny because both options seem necessary and impossible. On one hand, there should be only one divine idea because of the unity and simplicity of the divine essence. If divine ideas are just the expression of divine truth knowing the divine essence, then they should be one like divine truth. Yet, if there be only one divine idea, then it seems that God does not know creatures distinctly. The understanding of "animal" is not the same as the understanding of "white," so how could a single idea result in perfect and distinct knowledge of both? It seems, then, that divine ideas must be both one and many, but how is it possible? Bonaventure argues that the seeming contradiction can be overcome by making important distinctions between the source of divine knowledge and the things known. Divine ideas are one in reality

---

51. See pp. 56–61 and 89–91.
52. *In I Sent.*, d. 35, a. un., q. 3 (Quaracchi, I.608a).

(*secundum rem*) and many according to reason (*secundum rationem*). This section will investigate each of these claims in turn, and then it will explain the sort of theory of relations that allows Bonaventure to make this distinction.

The Unity of Divine Ideas

Bonaventure begins his discussion of the unity of divine ideas by noting how tempting it is to say that ideas are many in reality (*secundum rem*). Some have tried to argue for the position as follows. Consider how forms exist in God, in the soul, and in matter. In matter, forms have distinction, composition, and opposition because they exist materially. In the soul, forms have distinction and composition, but not opposition because they are present in the soul spiritually. In God, forms have distinction but not composition or opposition because of God's supreme simplicity. Although the forms are distinct in God, they are still one exemplar just as the many particular forms in a signet-ring make one seal.[53] We might update the example by imagining a picture that is made up of smaller pictures. When we look at the picture from a distance, we see a single image, but when we look closely, we see a host of smaller pictures.

Bonaventure thinks this position seems probable, but it ultimately contains an error. If ideas were posited to be really different or distinct, then there would be a real plurality, but the only real plurality in God is the plurality of the divine persons. Thus, this position requires positing as many divine persons as there are ideas plus three. God would no longer be a Trinity, but an Infinity. If someone tries to avoid this abhorrent conclusion by saying that this position does not posit a plurality that is absolutely other, but only relatively so, then what is the status of that relative otherness? It could only be something or nothing. If it is nothing, then there is no real distinction at all. If it is something, then it cannot be relative to anything except the divine essence. But everything essential is one in God. So divine ideas would really be one.[54]

Having ruled out that divine ideas can be many in reality (*secundum rem*), Bonaventure offers a variety of arguments for the position that divine ideas are one in reality, of which two are worth examining. First, God can know and produce all things through one divine idea because that idea is a likeness entirely outside of every genus. Since it is not in any genus, it is not limited to anything. A likeness that is constrained by a genus cannot be the likeness of things in other genera. The likeness of a living thing cannot be the likeness of a nonliving thing precisely because living and nonliving differ generically. A likeness that is outside of every genus can express all things through the mode of an exemplar likeness. The reason it can be a likeness of one thing is the same reason it can be the likeness of another, and the reason it is a likeness of some part of something is the same reason it is a

---

53. *In I Sent.*, d. 35, a. un., q. 2 (Quaracchi, I.605b).
54. *In I Sent.*, d. 35, a. un., q. 2 (Quaracchi, I.605b), esp.: "Nam si in Deo esset ponere ideas realiter differentes sive distinctas, tunc esset ibi alia pluralitas realis, quam sit pluralitas personalis." See also *De scientia Christi*, q. 3, fm. 13 (Quaracchi, V.13a).

likeness of the whole. Divine truth is this sort of likeness, and so God's divine idea is this sort of likeness as well. God is outside of every genus precisely because he is pure act. Every genus involves the limitation of act to a certain range of potencies. And so, since God has no potencies, he is outside of every genus and can be the likeness of every act of every genus.[55]

I think this argument is sound, and its strength lies in its appeal to God as pure act. Since God is pure act, he has no limitation that would prevent him from being the perfect exemplar of every possible creature. As a result, there is no need to appeal to another principle or idea to make God the perfect exemplar. Bonaventure tacitly seems to be using a principle of parsimony in this argument. Since the one divine truth is the perfect exemplar of every possible creature, there is no need to multiply ideas to cover God's exemplarity of every possible creature. Adding more ideas in reality would be redundant.

Bonaventure's second argument is taken from the unity of divine truth. An idea in God entails a likeness that is a means of knowing (*ratio cognoscendi*). A *ratio cognoscendi* could be understood in two ways. In one way, it can refer to that-which-is (*id quod est*), and in another way, it can refer to that-to-which-it-is (*id ad quod est*). *Id quod est* refers first and foremost to that through which things are cognized, and this is nothing other than divine truth. Divine truth, that is, God's knowledge of his own essence, is the one and only source of divine knowledge. And since divine truth is one in reality, it follows that there is one divine idea in reality.[56] *Id ad quod est* refers to the things known, and will be treated below.

These arguments show why divine ideas must be one in reality (*secundum rem*) and why their unity is not opposed to their being the perfect likeness of many things. The second argument shows the impossibility of many divine ideas in reality, and the first argument shows how that one divine idea is a perfect exemplar of many possible creatures. Divine ideas must be one in reality because God has but one source of knowledge. If divine ideas were many in reality, God would come to know from multiple sources, and there would either be many divine essences, or God's knowledge would be at least partially due to some external source. Both options are impossible, so there is just one source of divine knowledge.[57] Since God has but one source of knowledge, his truth is one and that one truth is the only likeness of all things other than himself. The fact that there is numerically one likeness of all possible creatures is not a problem, however, because that likeness is not limited to any genus. Since it stands above every genus, it exemplifies in them all equally. The one divine idea exemplifies in the category of substance for the same reason that it is able to exemplify in each category of accidents.

---

55. *De scientia Christi*, q. 3 (Quaracchi, V.13b–14a), esp.: "Potens est autem divina veritas, quamvis sit una, omnia exprimere per modum similitudinis exemplaris, quia ipsa est omnino extra genus et ad nihil coarctata." See *In I Sent.*, d. 35, a. un., q. 2, ad 2 (Quaracchi, I.606).

56. *De scientia Christi*, q. 3, fm. 11 and corpus (Quaracchi, V.13a and 14a). See *In I Sent.*, d. 35, a. un., q. 2 (Quaracchi, I.605b–606a).

57. *De scientia Christi*, q. 3, fm. 8 (Quaracchi, V.12b–13a).

The Multiplicity of Divine Ideas

There is one divine idea *secundum rem* because a divine idea "has an ontological identity with the divine essence."[58] The divine essence as it is known and expressed in divine truth is the only source and likeness of all possible creatures. The arguments above show *that* God's one idea could be a likeness of all things, but they do not show *how*. The one divine idea is a likeness of all things because it is many according to reason (*secundum rationem*). Divine ideas must be many according to reason because of the requirements of knowledge. Before God produces things, he knows them actually and distinctly. There is no distinction in God the knower or in the thing known, so the distinction must be in the *ratio cognoscendi*.[59] If there are no distinctions in the *ratio cognoscendi* whatsoever, then it cannot be the source of distinct cognition. God's one idea would be a general likeness of all creatures and not the proper likeness of any particular creature.[60] Thus, any distinctions that are found in beings would be unknown to God except perhaps in some general way. God would not know creatures distinctly. Moreover, the distinctions found in beings would not have God as their source. They would be the result of some secondary cause or chance. Therefore, Bonaventure needs to be able to show how there can be many ideas according to reason in such a way that does not contradict their unity.

He argues for the multiplicity of divine ideas *secundum rationem* in three steps. First, he insists that divine ideas are not merely the divine essence; "the name 'idea' signifies the divine essence in comparison or in respect to a creature."[61] Without this comparison, the objections based on distinct cognition would hold. God would only know in an indistinct way because his knowledge would not entail a distinct assimilation of any particular creature to his essence.

Second, Bonaventure specifies the comparison or respect (*respectus*) of the divine essence to creatures.[62] Ultimately, there are many divine ideas because there are many things connoted in God's understanding.[63] The term 'connotation' signifies that the knowledge of one thing directly includes or entails the knowledge of something else indirectly. When it comes to divine ideas, what is known directly is

---

58. Cullen, "Semiotic Metaphysics," 168.
59. *In I Sent.*, d. 35, a. un., q. 3, fm. 4 (Quaracchi, I.607b).
60. *In I Sent.*, d. 35, a. un., q. 2, arg. 3–4 (Quaracchi, 605a); *De scientia Christi*, q. 3, arg. 14–16 (Quaracchi, V.11b–12a).
61. *In I Sent.*, d. 35, a. un., q. 3 (Quaracchi, I.608a): "hoc nomen 'idea' significat divinam essentiam in comparatione sive in respectu ad creaturam."
62. I will consistently translate *respectus* as 'respect' to distinguish it from 'relation' (*relatio*) because Henry of Ghent will make a distinction between *respectus* and *relatio* that is crucial for his account of divine ideas. See p. 102. Jeffrey Brower translates *respectus* as "outward-looking-ness" because the term "draws on a visual metaphor to suggest that relations are that in virtue of which a substance 'looks out toward something' (*respicit ad aliquid*)" (*The Stanford Encyclopedia of Philosophy* [sect. 2.1, 2018], s.v. "Medieval Theories of Relations").
63. *In I Sent.*, d. 35, a. un., q. 3, ad 1 (Quaracchi, I.608b). See *De scientia Christi*, q. 3, ad 15 (Quaracchi, V.16a).

the divine essence. Possible creatures are known indirectly as a result of knowing the divine essence directly.

Speaking in terms of connotation has several advantages. First, it preserves that God has but one source of knowledge. To say that a divine idea is the divine essence in comparison or relation to a creature does not mean that God is looking away from the divine essence or acquiring knowledge from another source. God knows the comparison to the creature with the knowledge of the essence itself. Second, many things can be connotated from a single source. "The White House" denotes a certain building in Washington, DC, but it connotes both the office of the president of the United States of America and the current president. Bonaventure thus preserves God's knowledge of many creatures by speaking of them as connotated. Third, if we consider the connotated things insofar as they are connotated, we find that they can be connotated both eternally and temporally. Things are connotated eternally when a habitual respect is implied as when a creature is predestined. It does not exist in act, but only habitually. Things are connotated temporally when an actual existence is implied as when the possible creature is actually created. Thus, the connotation extends both to the possible creatures that God will create at some time and to those that God will never create.[64]

In his third and final step, Bonaventure points out that there are many things connotated and known by the one idea. This step takes up Bonaventure's distinction between that-which-is (*id quod est*) and that-to-which-it-is (*id ad quod est*). As noted above, *id quod est* refers to the source of God's knowledge, and so *id quod est* can only be divine truth.[65] *Id quod est* entails examining divine knowledge from the perspective of the knower. God is a single knower with a single source of knowledge. Examining *Id ad quod est*, by contrast, considers divine knowledge from the perspective of the things expressed in that knowledge, and a plurality is found here. Bonaventure explains this plurality using an example adapted from Augustine and Avicenna: "to express a man is not to express a donkey."[66] Again, to predestine Peter is not to predestine Paul, nor is creating a man the same as creating an angel. Therefore, divine ideas are many according to what they signify or connote, that is, according to that to which they are compared.[67] There are divine ideas because there are many possible creatures connotated by knowledge of the divine essence.

Bonaventure is quick to remind the reader that the comparison between God and possible creatures does not entail any real respect in God because God is not really related to anything outside of himself. Instead, these comparisons entail only

---

64. *In I Sent.*, d. 35, a. un., q. 3, ad 3 (Quaracchi, I.608b).

65. See p. 27.

66. *De scientia Christi*, q. 3 (Quaracchi, V.14a). Cf. Augustine, *De div. qq. 83*, q. 46, n. 2 (PL 40.30); Avicenna, *Met.* V, c. 1 (van Reit, II.228:26–29). Both Augustine and Avicenna use the example of "man and horse" instead of "man and donkey."

67. Bonaventure's reasoning here is inspired by Alexander of Hales, *Glossa* I, d. 36, nn. 5 and 7 (Quaracchi, I.358–59), esp.: "nam sapientia nominat plus ex parte Dei cognoscentis, quod est omnino unum; ratio vero medium nominat; idea vero ex parte rei cognitae. Et ideo, sicut res cognitae sunt plures, ita ideae plures." Alexander expresses the same theory again at *Glossa* I, d. 45, n. 13d (Quaracchi, I.454).

a way of understanding (*ratio intelligendi*) to which corresponds a real relation on the part of the things, whether in act or in aptitude.[68] This claim is crucial for Bonaventure's theory of divine ideas because it means that a divine idea is fundamentally a relation. God knows the possible real relation that could exist from a creature to him. When God knows his essence, he knows first and foremost himself, and he simultaneously knows all the possible real relations that creatures could bear to him as connotations.

Bonaventure concludes that divine ideas are one in reality (*secundum rem*) and many according to reason (*secundum rationem*).[69] This distinction arises from whether we consider divine ideas on the part of the expressing knower or on the part of the things known in the expression. On the part of the knower, there is one divine truth from the one divine essence. On the part of the things known, there are many ideal reasons because of the many relations connotated from the one divine likeness.

Before turning to the question of what sort of relation a divine idea is, I want to reemphasize that Bonaventure's theory of divine ideas is a version of the Imitability Theory. A divine idea is "the divine essence in comparison or in respect to a possible creature."[70] A divine idea is God's knowledge of the way a possible creature relates to him. We have already seen that that relation is exemplifying on God's part and imitative on the creature's part. Once again, he emphasizes that the way the divine essence is imitable by creatures characterizes divine ideas, even though he does not use those terms explicitly.

Real Relations vs. Rational Relations

Bonaventure's discussion of the unity and plurality of divine ideas relies heavily on a distinction between real relations and rational relations. However, he does not flesh out that distinction in the places that he treats divine ideas. All we can glean from the texts we have examined so far is that there are two distinct types of plurality in God and that both real relations and rational relations exist in God. There are real relations from the divine persons of the Trinity and there are rational relations from the divine ideas. Both pluralities and their relations must be articulated in such a way that they neither contradict with God's supreme unity and simplicity nor become confused with each other.

Bonaventure gives us just such an articulation in *In I Sent.*, d. 30, a. un., q. 3. There he argues that there are two types of relations: real relations and rational relations, the latter of which he describes as a mode of understanding. Real relations

---

68. *De scientia Christi*, q. 3 (Quarcchi, V.14a): "Et quia ad illud sunt non secundum realem respectum, qui sit in Deo, quia Deus ad nihil extrinsecum realiter refertur, sed solum secundum rationem intelligendi, cui correspondet realis respectus in actu vel aptitudine ex parte rerum." See also, *In I Sent.*, d. 35, a. un., q. 3 (Quaracchi, I.608).

69. *In I Sent.*, d. 35, a. un., q. 3 (Quaracchi, I.608b); *De scientia Christi*, q. 3 (Quaracchi, V.14a).

70. *In I Sent.*, d. 35, a. un., q. 3 (Quaracchi, I.608a): "hoc nomen 'idea' significat divinam essentiam in comparatione sive in respectu ad creaturam."

are threefold. Sometimes a real relation is founded upon an accidental property, as when a likeness is in two white things. Sometimes a real relation is founded upon an essential dependence, as the respect or relation of matter to form. Sometimes a real relation is founded on a natural origin, as an effect to a cause and a son to a father. The first two sorts of real relation cannot exist in God because he has no accidental properties or dependence upon anything. The third sort of real relation, however, is in God with respect to the Divine Persons because it does not entail any composition or inclination of dependence like the first two do.[71] Instead, the third sort of real relation posits only distinction and order.[72] For Bonaventure, diversity from origin is not properly diversity because it does not imply any composition of addition.[73] Thus, such a real relation is compatible with supreme simplicity.

Creatures are really related to God according to all three sorts of real relations, but God is not really related to creatures. God cannot even be really related to creatures according to the third sort of real relation—a relation founded on natural origin—because creatures are distinct from God not merely by natural origin, but also by essence. God's causality with respect to creatures must be beyond a real relation because a real relation from God to creatures would make God dependent upon creatures.[74] Anything that is really related to another that differs in essence can be influenced or acted upon by that other. If God were really related to creatures, then creatures could act upon God. In that case, God would be in potency to being acted upon by creatures. He would not be pure act, which is impossible.

Despite not being really related to creatures, God must be related to creatures in some sense because he knows them. Since all knowledge requires an assimilation, God must have some logical relation to all possible creatures. Bonaventure tries to capture this logical relation by calling it a relation according to a mode, according to a mode of understanding, according to reason, according to a means of understanding, and according to a means of speaking. These expressions emphasize that these relations are founded upon the requirements for distinct knowledge. Since God's knowledge of possible creatures is perfect, he knows the possible real relations that they could have to him perfectly. Since the real relation that one creature has

---

71. For an explication of Bonaventure's account of the relations of the Divine Persons, see, *inter alia*, John Francis Quinn, *The Historical Constitution of St. Bonaventure's Philosophy* (Toronto: Pontifical Institute of Mediaeval Studies, 1973), 575; Zachary Hayes, "Bonaventure: Mystery of the Triune God," in *The History of Franciscan Theology*, ed. Kenan B. Osborne, 39–125 (St. Bonaventure, NY: Franciscan Institute, 1994); Kenan B. Osborne, "The Trinity in Bonaventure," in *The Cambridge Companion to the Trinity*, ed. Peter C. Phan, 108–27 (New York: Cambridge University Press, 2011); Russell L. Friedman, *Intellectual Traditions at the Medieval University: The Use of Philosophical Psychology in Trinitarian Theology among the Franciscans and Dominicans, 1250–1350*, vol. 1 (Leiden: Brill, 2012).

72. *In I Sent.*, d. 30, a. un., q. 3 (Quaracchi, I.525b). Cf. *De mys. Trin.*, q. 3, a. 2 (Quaracchi, V.76a).

73. *In I Sent.*, d. 8, p. 2, a. un., q. 1, ad 2 (Quaracchi, I.166b).

74. *De mys. Trin.*, q. 3, a. 2, ad 4 (Quaracchi, V.77a): " respectivam includit quandam dependentiam, ac per hoc et defectum dicit a simplicitate summa."

to God is not identical to the real relation that another creature has to God, the relations are intelligibly many.[75] The relations that pluralize divine ideas do so by reason of the things understood. Since there are many (possible) real relations to God and none of these relations can be substituted for another (that is, they are not interchangeable), it takes many ideas to know them.

The relationship between creatures and God, then, is 'mixed.' It is real on the part of the creature and rational on the part of God. Bonaventure finds support for this way of articulating the relationship both in Pseudo-Dionysius, who claims that the relationship between a cause and an effect is not reciprocal, and in Aristotle, who argues that knowledge is referred to the knowable but not vice versa.[76] Just as some external object is indifferent to being known by some knower and is not changed when it comes to be known or is forgotten even though it causes a change in the knower, so God, who is pure act, is not changed by some creature being really related to him, even though it is God who causes the creature's relation to him.

The Infinity of Divine Ideas

Since he has determined that there are many divine ideas, Bonaventure naturally turns to the next logical question: how many are there? Is there some limit on the number of divine ideas or are they unlimited? There are good reasons for both sides. Since God is both omniscient and omnipotent, how could there be any limitation on the number of things he could know or produce? However, if his knowledge comprehends an infinite, then it would seem to render what he knows finite, and so there would seem to be only a finite number of divine ideas. Even worse, Bonaventure must contend with Averroes's argument that the infinite is unknowable.[77] If it is unknowable, then God cannot have an infinite number of ideas. Despite these last two difficulties, Bonaventure sides with an infinite number of divine ideas because "the mind of God is infinite."[78]

Bonaventure's first argument is from St. Augustine. God cognizes every species of number. By "species of number," Bonaventure means that each number has its own distinct properties such that knowledge of one number is not sufficient for knowledge of any other number. God cannot be said to know every number simply by knowing the number one. Therefore, they all have distinct ideas in God because each species of number has its own distinct properties. The species of number are infinite. Therefore, God has an infinite number of ideas. It is futile to respond that numbers are only infinite for us and not in reality because all species of number

---

75. See Quinn, *Historical Constitution*, 495.
76. *In I Sent.*, d. 30, a. un., q. 3, fa. 1–2 (Quaracchi, I.525). See Ps.-Dionysius, *De div. nom.*, c. 9, sect. 6 (PG 3.914–15); Aristotle, *Praedicamenta*, c. 7 (AL 1.18–23) and *Met.* V, c. 15 (AL 25.3.2.112–114).
77. See pp. 5–6.
78. Cullen, *Bonaventure*, 73.

exist in reality, so it follows necessarily that an infinite number of things exist in act. If all the species of number are ideas in act in God, then God has an infinite number of ideas.[79]

This argument is beautiful because it does not appeal to any species other than number. Since numbers are beyond counting, they are infinite, but which of these numbers does God not know? If God's knowledge is perfect, and his knowledge of things other than himself is always through ideas, then just from the fact that God knows all numbers, it follows that God has an infinite number of ideas.

Bonaventure's second argument is based on God's omnipotence. The number of creatures that God could create is potentially infinite.[80] What he actually creates is finite, but his possibilities are infinite.[81] God must have cognition and an idea of what he produces, so he has ideas of an infinite number of things. But a plurality of things indicates a plurality of ideas. Therefore, ideas of an infinite number of things yields an infinite number of ideas.[82] Although he does not make all the things he knows, the fact that he could have made things different from the way they are shows that God has ideas of more than just the things that actually exist at some time. He has an idea of anything that he knows he could have made.[83]

In response to the sorts of objections raised at the beginning of this section, Bonaventure admits that God renders an infinite number of things finite by comprehending it. It follows that, from God's perspective, there are a finite number of divine ideas, but this finitude only applies to God because only God can comprehend them, while they are numerically infinite to any other being.[84] Again, the way we think about the intelligibility of the infinite depends upon what we mean by 'infinite.' 'Infinite' can be understood either through defect or through excess. Infinity through defect is in creatures as in matter, and so is imperfect. This sort of

---

79. *In I Sent.*, d. 35, a. un., q. 5, fm. 3 (Quaracchi, I.611a). See *De scientia Christi*, q. 1 (Quaracchi, 4b–5a); Augustine, *De civ. Dei* XII, c. 18 (PL 41.367–68).

80. In *In I Sent.*, d. 35, a. un., q. 5, fm. 4, Bonaventure states "Deus potest infinita producere" (Quaracchi, I.611a). The Quaracchi editors note that Bonaventure means in potency, not in act. (Quaracchi, I.611n5). This caution is well taken because Bonaventure argues in *In II Sent.*, d. 1, p. 1, q. 2, fa. 1–6 (Quaracchi, II.20b–21a) that God cannot make an actual infinite. Bonaventure seems to think that there are certain conditions under which an actual infinite could thought possible, but those conditions cannot be realized. For more discussion on this point, see *inter alia*, Olivier Bonaseo, "The Question of an Eternal World in the Teaching of St. Bonaventure," *Franciscan Studies* 34, no. 1 (1974): 7–33; Antonius Coccia, "De Aeternitate Mundi apud S. Bonaventuram et Recentiores," in *S. Bonaventura 1274–1974* (Rome: Collegio S. Bonavenura, 1974), 279–306; Francis J. Kovach, "The Question of the Eternity of the World in St. Bonaventure and St. Thomas: A Critical Analysis," *Southwestern Journal of Philosophy* 5, no. 2 (1974): 141–72.

81. *De scientia Christi*, q. 1 (Quaracchi, V.5a); *In I Sent.*, d. 43, a. un., q. 4 (Quaracchi, I.74–75). See Cullen, *Bonaventure*, 74–75.

82. *In I Sent.*, d. 35, a. un., q. 5, fm. 4 (Quaracchi, I.611).

83. *De scientia Christi*, q. 1 (Quaracchi, V.5a).

84. *In I Sent.*, d. 35, a. un., q. 5, ad 1 (Quaracchi, I.612a). Note that Bonaventure is playing on the meaning of *infinitum* as "unbounded, without limit." Since God can comprehend an infinite number of divine ideas, he bounds and limits them by his knowledge.

infinite is not in God. Infinity through excess is found in God because he is supremely perfect, not created, composed, or limited.[85]

Summing up, Bonaventure rejects Averroes's argument that God's knowledge cannot be particular. Averroes had argued that for God's knowledge to be particular, he would have to know an infinite number of particulars, which Averroes declares to be impossible.[86] Bonaventure agrees that God would have to know an infinite number of particulars, and he declares that God can do it. An infinite being can know an infinite number of objects because infinity is not necessarily a mark of incompleteness. God's infinity is an infinity through excess and a mark of perfection because it entails the lack of anything that would limit God. God does not have to go through the infinity of divine ideas one-by-one. It is impossible to know an infinite in this way because the infinite cannot be traversed.[87] As an infinite being, God can know an infinite number of divine ideas, and he does so perfectly, knowing them all at once.[88]

The Existence of Things in God and the Possibles

The last aspect of the status of divine ideas to be considered is the sort of existence that a divine idea enjoys. Bonaventure says that a thing has a twofold existence, namely, in itself (in its own genus) or in its cause (in its exemplar).[89] Bonaventure argues that things can be in something in three ways: according to actual presence, which is how things are in the universe, according to the presence of likeness, which is how things are in a knower, or according to causative potency, which is how things are in their cause. The second and third ways apply to God because he knows and produces all things other than himself. Since God has knowledge from eternity, the things he knows also exist from eternity.[90] Divine ideas, then, are eternal. Bonaventure specifies that we should not say that they are eternal because of the divine essence or a divine person, but because things "are in God as in a cause."[91] Divine ideas are eternal because God eternally expresses all the possible ways that truth could exist.

But what sort of eternal existence do they enjoy? Bonaventure argues that divine ideas have life (*vita*) in the divine intellect. Life extends not just to divine idea of things that God elects to create at some time in history, but even to divine ideas of things that will never exist—it extends to divine ideas of possibles. Since life extends to ideas of possibles, then things are life in God according as God is an

---

85. *In I Sent.*, d. 35, a. un., q. 5, ad 4 (Quaracchi, I.612b). Cf. Alexander of Hales, *Summa theologica*, p. 1, inq. 1, tr. 5, sect. 1, q. un., mem. 3, c. 2, ad 2 (Quaracchi, I.252b).
86. See pp. 5–6.
87. *In II Sent.*, d. 1, p. 1, a. 1, q. 2, fm 3 (Quaracchi, 21a): "Impossibile est infinita pertransiri."
88. Scotus argues on similar lines saying that God can know an infinite number of divine ideas since God's own infinity is the cause of the infinity of divine ideas. See pp. 191–92.
89. *In I Sent.*, d. 39, a. 1, q. 1, ad 3 (Quaracchi ed., I.686b). See Cullen, *Bonaventure*, 71 and 202n52.
90. *In I Sent.*, d. 36, a. 1, q. 1 (Quaracchi, I.620b–21a).
91. *In I Sent.*, d. 36, a. 1, q. 2 (Quaracchi, I.622b): "sunt in Deo ut in causa."

expressing exemplar, not as he is a producing principle or conserving end. These latter two extend only to what has existence in time, not to all possibles.[92]

An objection arises here: God represents things as they truly are, so how can all things have life in God if not all things have life in reality? How can a rock have life in God? Bonaventure responds that God does not have to represent a thing in the same way as it would exist in itself. Corporeal things need not be known corporeally.[93] Moreover, divine ideas are the divine intellect's intellectual means of understanding (*rationes intelligendi*). Since understanding is an act of life, divine ideas must be living and even life itself because God's means of understanding is his intelligence (*intelligentia*).[94]

Since divine ideas are life itself, Bonaventure concludes that they are spiritual, invariable, and incorruptible. He draws this conclusion from the statement in the *Liber de causis* that "life is a spiritual and continuous act, flowing from a still and sempiternal being."[95] Bonaventure explains that the author of that text chooses the word 'spiritual' (*spiritualis*) to exclude corporeality, the word 'still' (*quietus*) to exclude variability, and the word 'sempiternal' (*sempiternitas*) to exclude corruptibility. Divine ideas, then, are incorporeal, invariable, and incorruptible.

Things in God have an elevated mode of existence precisely because they are in God. God's excessive nobility is shared with all things in him because everything in God is one. But if things enjoy such an elevated existence in God, then do they exist more truly in God or do they exist more truly in their proper genera? Bonaventure argues that both sides of the dichotomy are correct depending on the meaning of 'exists.' If 'exists' is taken as a comparison of one and the same thing to its diverse modes of existing, then a thing exists more truly in its proper genus because a thing exists simply in its proper genus, according to intrinsic and proper principles, and in its proper being.[96] If 'exists' is taken as a comparison of a thing to its likeness, then a thing exists more truly and more nobly in God because all things in God are God himself. Divine ideas are God himself, and since there is nothing truer or nobler than God, everything exists more truly and more nobly in God than in its proper genus or in a created intellect.[97] Since divine ideas are God himself, and God himself is spiritual, invariable, and incorruptible, divine ideas are spiritual, invariable, and incorruptible.

Bonaventure's position on the existence of things in God, then, is straightforward. All things in God are one and they share in divine life. As likenesses of the supremely expressive divine truth, divine ideas are truth itself, spiritual, invariable, and incorruptible. They exist eternally and necessarily as in a cause because God

---

92. *In I Sent.*, d. 36, a. 2, q. 1 (Quaracchi, I.624a).
93. *In I Sent.*, d. 36, a. 2, q. 1, ad 3 (Quaracchi, I.624b): "non oportet, quod ratio repraesentationis sit talis omnino, quale est representatum."
94. *In I Sent.*, d. 36, a. 2, q. 1, ad 4 (Quaracchi, I.624b).
95. *Liber de causis*, prop. 17(18), n. 145 (Pattin, 173:46–47): "vita est processio procedens ex ente primo quieto, sempiterno." Bonaventure substitutes *actus* for *processio*.
96. *In I Sent.*, d. 36, a. 2, q. 2, s.c. 1–3 (Quaracchi, I.625).
97. *In I Sent.*, d. 36, a. 2, q. 2 (Quaracchi, I.626a).

knows that he could create creatures according to them. Importantly, they enjoy divine cognitive being only. None of them has any sort of existence independent from being known by God. So, going beyond Bonaventure's text itself, we can conclude that if *per impossibile*, God would stop thinking about a certain divine idea, it would immediately cease to exist.

THE SCOPE OF DIVINE IDEAS

The questions of the status of divine ideas aim at determining *what* a divine idea is. The questions concerning the scope of divine ideas aim at determining *of what* God has ideas. A partial answer to the question of the scope of divine ideas is already evident from the foregoing discussion: God has ideas of the infinite number of things he could create. God has ideas of all the things that the supremely expressive divine truth expresses. This response glazes over certain difficulties, such as, does God have a distinct or unique idea for each and every singular thing that he could create, or does he just have an idea of a species or genus? Are there ideas of evil things? If so, how is that compatible with divine perfections? What about imperfect things like matter, and so on? This section will examine Bonaventure's answers to these questions.

Singulars, Species, and Genera

The question of divine ideas for singulars is, at heart, a question about what distinguishes divine ideas. Are divine ideas many because of the individuals, the lowest species, intermediate species, or highest genera that God knows? The analysis of Bonaventure's thought thus far has shown that God has many divine ideas because of the things he knows, and that number is even infinite because God's possibilities are limitless. Nevertheless, it is easy to imagine that that infinity is an infinity of species, not an infinity of individuals. Thus, Bonaventure must determine specifically what makes divine ideas many.

Bonaventure argues that there are good reasons for thinking that divine ideas might be diversified at the level of species only. It seems in keeping with his nobility and his simplicity that divine ideas extend only to species. A created artist can produce many things through one idea, as when the builder builds houses through the same idea. Therefore, since God is nobler than the created artist, he should produce many things that are numerically diverse through one and the same idea.[98] Again, the singular is more proper than the universal, which is more common. So, if God had an idea of a universal *qua* universal (e.g., man) and an idea of a singular *qua* singular (e.g., Peter), then he would have one idea that is more common and one that is more proper. Since the common is prior to and simpler than the proper, God would have a real order and essential composition within him, which is contrary to his simplicity.[99] Thus, divine ideas would seem to be multiplied only to the level of the species.

---

98. *In I Sent.*, d. 35, a. un., q. 4, s.c. 2 (Quaracchi, I.610a).
99. *In I Sent.*, d. 35, a. un., q. 4, s.c. 4 (Quaracchi, I.610a).

Bonaventure contends there are compelling reasons to think that there are divine ideas of singulars too.

> Cognition of a thing is truest when it captures the totality of the thing. Singulars add something beyond the universal. Therefore, since God knows the totality of the thing, he has an idea of the singular in addition to the idea of the universal.[100]

Again, since divine ideas are multiplied because of a respect and relation to the thing ideated, any real distinction among the things ideated is evidence of distinct divine ideas. Since divine ideas are really multiplied according to individuals, divine ideas are also distinguished at the level of the individual.[101]

In his response, Bonaventure argues that there are divine ideas of both universals and singulars. An idea in God is identical to God in reality. However, insofar as it is an intellectual means of understanding (*ratio intelligendi*), an idea is a likeness of the thing known. Thus, this likeness is an expressive means of knowing not only the universal but also the singular. Bonaventure specifies that the idea itself is not universal nor singular, just as God is not universal or singular. Furthermore, since divine ideas are a likeness of both the universal and the singular, they are multiplied both according to the multitude of universals and singulars.[102]

The analogy to the created artist breaks down here. The created artist can produce many houses with one idea of house because he applies that one idea to different matter each time. If he had no recourse to matter, then he could know numerically one house with his one idea. God knows the diversity of singulars in a simple glance, and so his ideas must include the proper differences and properties of all the singulars.[103]

There are two things worth noting about Bonaventure's reply. First, his account of divine ideas is as full as possible. God is the fontal fullness (*fontalis plenitudo*) who has a likeness of all possible creatures and all possible aspects of those creatures.[104] Not only does God have an idea of Peter, but he has an idea of man,

---

100. *In I Sent.*, d. 35, a. un., q. 4, fm. 2 (Quaracchi, I.609): "cognitio rei verissime est secundum rei totalitatem; sed singulare aliquid addit supra universale: ergo cum Deus totum cognoscat, non tantum habet ideam universalis, sed etiam superadditi, scilicet singularis; similiter et alterius singularis." Henry of Ghent uses this argument, but he denies the minor premise. Thus, he concludes that there are no divine ideas of singulars. See Henry, *Quodlibet* II, q. 1, arg. (Leuven 6.3:11–17), and pp. 114–16.
101. *In I Sent.*, d. 35, a. un., q. 4, fm. 4 (Quaracchi, I.609b).
102. *In I Sent.*, d. 35, a. un., q. 4 (Quaracchi, I.610).
103. *In I Sent.*, d. 35, a. un., q. 4, ad 2 (Quaracchi, I.610b): "si habet [artifex creata] solum ideam una, impossibile est intelligere, quod secundum illam simplici aspectu cognoscat diversa; Deus autem simplici aspectu cognoscit singularia ut diversa, ita quod secundum totum et secundum proprias differentias et proprietates; ideo non est simile."
104. Bonaventure uses the term *fontalis plenitudo* to describe God, especially the Father, in many places. See, *inter alia*, *Itinerarium*, c. 3, nn. 7–8 (Quaracchi, V.301b); *De myst. Trin.*, q. 8, ad 7 (Quaracchi, V.115); *Breviloquium* I, c. 3 and IV, c. 5 (Quaracchi, V.212a and 246a); *De reductione artium ad theologiam*, n. 1 (Quaracchi, V.319a).

mammal, animal, and so on. Since God knows all the distinguishing features of singular beings in a single glance, without any reference to matter, we are left somewhat in the dark about what Bonaventure thinks the singular adds to the species. The implication seems to be that there is something formally present in Peter that distinguishes him from Paul. An investigation of Bonaventure's theory of individuation would help to clarify this question, but I think Bonaventure is not especially concerned with that question.[105] All that matters for this discussion is the fact that knowing Peter is not the same as knowing Paul. This phenomenon alone is sufficient to require that there be a distinct divine idea for each singular.

The second thing to note about this response is that it includes a direct response to Averroes. Averroes's third and fourth arguments focused on God's knowledge being so unlike our own that it was ontologically one and elevated beyond the categories of universal and particular.[106] Bonaventure grants Averroes's major premises and denies his minor premises. Ontologically, divine ideas are one and identical to God himself, but this identity does not prevent them from being distinguished by the objects known through them. Moreover, Bonaventure agrees with Averroes that divine ideas are neither universal nor particular. Nevertheless, while they themselves are not universal nor particular, divine ideas are likenesses of things that are universal or particular. God's knowledge includes both the universal and the particular. An infinity of particulars is not concerning for Bonaventure because they do not escape God's power. Rather, the infinity of particulars depends upon God's supremely expressive truth.[107] God's knowledge certainly exceeds our own, and it strains our intellectual abilities to understand it, but "knowledge" is not said equivocally of God and creatures. God does have determinate knowledge of all universals as universal and of all singulars as singular.

Evil

The question of a divine idea of evil is particularly thorny. On one hand, God must have knowledge of evil to mete out punishment justly. Since divine ideas are the intellectual means by which God knows creatures, it seems he must have an idea of evil. On the other hand, divine ideas are the likenesses of things and their creative exemplars. If God has an idea of evil, then he would seem to be the creative cause of evil, which is repugnant. Thus, it seems he must not have an idea of evil.

In his reply to the question, Bonaventure argues that evil things are not in God, nor does he have an idea of them. Still, God still knows evil things through his idea of the good things of which the evils are privations. He justifies this position by appealing to two principles: Aristotle's principle that the straight is the judge of both itself and of the curved, and the principle that a divine idea is a likeness that

---

105. For Bonaventure's theory of individuation, see Peter King, "Bonaventure (b. ca. 1217; d. 1274)," in *Individuation in Scholasticism: The Later Middle Ages and the Counter-Reformation 1150–1650*, ed. Jorge J. E. Gracia, 141–72 (Albany, NY: State University of New York Press, 1994).
106. Averroes, *In XII Met.*, c. 51 (Iunctina, VIII.158ra3–68). See pp. 5–6.
107. See pp. 191–92 for Scotus's argument about one infinity depending upon another.

entails a certain assimilation.[108] Aristotle's principle justifies the claim that God knows evil things. Knowledge of a perfect imitation is sufficient for knowledge of what falls short of perfect imitation. Since God is supreme truth, light, and act, he cognizes both himself and the oblique, dark, and deprived. Nevertheless, evil things are not in God because they are known through privation, that is, through a lack of what ought to be present. If they were in God, then God would cooperate with them in some genus of causality (especially formal and exemplar causality). But no cooperation is even possible precisely because evil things are privations, and this is where the second principle comes into play. Since divine ideas are exemplars, they entail some manner of assimilation, even if only a minimal assimilation. Privation is, by definition, opposed to assimilation. Thus, evil things *qua* evil cannot be in God except through something that will assimilate, that is, through some good thing. There are not divine ideas of evil things, then, but only of good things, and it is through a privation of these good things that the evil things are known.[109]

Imperfect Things: Matter, Passion, Multitude

Bonaventure's response to the question of a divine idea of evil raises a question about whether there are divine ideas of certain other aspects of reality. If there is no divine idea of evil things because evil is a privation, what about other things that also entail some manner of privation? Matter, passion, and multitude are a certain privation of form, act, and unity, respectively. Are there distinct divine ideas of them, or only of what completes them? Bonaventure argues that there are divine ideas of these imperfect things.

He explicitly denies that imperfect things are known through an idea of the perfect because each of the imperfect things entail some being (*dicant aliquam entitas*), and thus they entail some truth. Since they entail some truth, they necessarily have some assimilation to the first truth, and so have a notion of exemplarity. Consequently, imperfect beings satisfy the requirements for having divine ideas in God. To make this claim hold Bonaventure makes a distinction between considering an imperfect thing as a thing or as imperfect. The consideration of a thing as imperfect entails a privation and so is a consideration of the imperfect thing insofar as it is unassimilable. Therefore, there are no divine ideas of imperfect things by reason of their imperfection. The consideration of an imperfect thing as a thing entails some essence, and so entails some degree of assimilation. Therefore, there are divine ideas of imperfect things insofar as they are things.[110] Since imperfect things exist and everything that exists is assimilated to God to some degree, imperfect things are assimilated to God, even if it is only to a minimal degree. Imperfect things bear a likeness to God, which means that there is a divine idea of them in God.

---

108. Aristotle, *De anima* I, c. 5, 411a5–7 (Leonine, 45/1.58b).
109. *In I Sent.*, d. 36, a. 3, q. 1 (Quaracchi, I.627b–28a).
110. *In I Sent.*, d. 36, a. 3, q. 2 (Quaracchi, I.629), esp.: "Cum enim ista omnia dicant aliquam entitatem et ita veritatem, de necessitate aliquam assimilationem habent ad primam veritatem, et ita rationem exemplaritatis; et ideo necessario sunt in Deo."

Lest some reader think that knowing imperfect things render God's knowledge imperfect, Bonaventure insists that God's way of knowing is perfect. Just as there are living ideas of nonliving things in God, so there are perfect ideas of imperfect things in God.[111] Bonaventure seems to be making a veiled critique of Averroes's second argument against God's knowing things other than himself distinctly here.[112] Averroes argues that if God knows base things, then his perfection will come from something less noble and so he would be less noble. Bonaventure is denying that base things must be known in a base way. Instead, the thing known is known in the way proper to the knower. Since God's way of knowing is perfect, everything that he knows is known in a perfect way. Therefore, no possible object of knowledge debases God's act of knowing.

I find the distinction Bonaventure draws between evil things and imperfect things satisfying. Since evil is privation alone, it is impossible for there to be any sort of assimilation to God, and thus, no divine idea of evil. Imperfect things do entail a privation—which is why they are imperfect—but they are not mere privations. Thus, there can be divine ideas of imperfect things insofar as they are something. This answer also presents a beautiful account of created being on a spectrum. Every creature, as Augustine says, has some mixture of being and nonbeing.[113] Having something of nonbeing, each creature is imperfect, but not all creatures have the same level of imperfection. More perfect creatures have a greater share of being than nonbeing, but even the most imperfect beings have some share in being. Thus, every possible creature both has some privation and some being. Therefore, God has a divine idea of every possible creature insofar as it something of being and not insofar as it has some privation. This analysis is true of every creature from the most perfect to the least perfect.

RECAPITULATION AND CONCLUSIONS

Divine ideas are the likenesses of things known that serve as the means of divine knowledge (*rationes cognoscendi*) of things other than God. They are also the exemplary forms for any creatures that God wills to create. Thus, divine ideas play two hierarchically ordered roles in Bonaventure's thought. Their primary role is cognitive and explain how God knows possible creatures. Their secondary role is causal because they are the patterns according to which God creates creatures. Bonaventure employs this hierarchy because God does not have to create. Creatures only exist because God willed that they exist. Yet, God did not will to know them. Divine ideas necessarily flow from divine truth because it is supremely expressive. When he knows his essence, God does not just know himself, but also knows his essence in comparison to creatures. It is only because he knows them that he can create them. Thus, the cognitive role of divine ideas is prior to their causal role.

---

111. *In I Sent.*, d. 36, a. 3, q. 2 (Quaracchi, I.629b).
112. See pp. 4–5.
113. Augustine, *Conf.*, VII, cc. 11–12 (PL 32.742–43).

Divine ideas are a likeness of one thing to another. In this sort of likeness, the imitation is like the exemplar directly, not because of some third thing. The expressive likeness and the imitative likeness are related in such way that the expressive likeness is the total cause of the imitative likeness and knowledge of the expressive likeness is perfect and without composition. God is the perfect expressive likeness because he does not need anything external to have perfect knowledge of himself and of all possible creatures. Since he is pure act, he is sufficient for knowing all things, which he knows by expressing them. The things that God expresses, the imitative likenesses, all have God as their source and point back to him as signs of his truth. They are all assimilated to God because he determined them to be what they are.

Bonaventure consistently speaks of divine ideas in terms of divine truth expressing itself. Such a characterization is not surprising for two reasons. First, since Bonaventure privileges the cognitive role of divine ideas, it is reasonable that he would associate divine cognition and divine truth. Second, although he never says so explicitly, there would be no divine ideas if God did not know himself. The divine essence is necessary for divine ideas, but the divine essence by itself does not yield divine ideas. The divine essence is only a likeness insofar as it is a means of knowing, that is, insofar as there is an intellectual act of comparing it to a creature.[114]

Since divine ideas are expressions of divine truth, they can be considered with reference to their knower, God, or with reference to the things known. Insofar as they are considered in the first way, divine ideas are numerically one because they are identical to divine truth, which is God's one and only means of knowing. Strictly speaking, God has one idea. Insofar as they are considered in the second way, divine ideas are many according to the many things known. They are many because the knowledge of one possible creature is not the knowledge of another possible creature. Therefore, divine ideas are one insofar as they signify the one divine truth, and they are many insofar as they connote the variety of things that God knows by means of them. Since the things that God knows are infinite, divine ideas are numerically infinite. Divine ideas receive cognitive being from God. They have no existence independent of being thought by God.

The multitude of divine ideas extends to each singular being as well as to each universal being. Each singular being has a unique relation to God and so there must be a unique idea that accounts for these unique relations. Each singular being is related to God in a different way than its species and genera, and so it follows that God has unique ideas for these as well. This way of reasoning extends to imperfect beings. Each of these is uniquely related to God insofar as they have some minimal share in being, and so there are unique ideas for them as well. This line of reasoning also excludes that God has an idea of evil things. Evil has no share in being because evil is a privation. There can be no assimilation of privation as such. Therefore,

---

114. See *In I Sent.*, d. 35, a. un., q. 3 (Quaracchi, I.608a); *De scientia Christi*, q. 2, ad 11 (Quaracchi, V.10b).

there can be no divine idea of evil things. Yet, God can still know them because of the way that they fall short what they ought to be.

Most of the theories that come after Bonaventure's, and certainly all the Imitability Theories, take up one or other of the dichotomies that Bonaventure delineates. Divine ideas are likenesses, not the things themselves. They primarily perform a cognitive role and secondarily perform a causal role. They are one by signification and many by connotation. They are numerically infinite, not finite. They exist only as divine thoughts and not on their own. They extend to all possible singulars, species, genera, and imperfect things but not to evil things. Many will take issue with this or that aspect of Bonaventure's theory, but his general schema will remain unchallenged for about thirty years. It is not until Peter John Olivi in the 1280s and James of Viterbo in the early 1290s that some of the presuppositions of the Imitability Theory are questioned.[115] This questioning paves the way for Bl. John Duns Scotus to turn theories of divine ideas on their head and argue that divine ideas are not the means of knowing possible creatures, but rather the result of knowing them. The reader who is most interested in the progression theories of divine ideas, can skip ahead to these later thinkers. The authors treated in the next two chapters make significant refinements to the Imitability Theory, but they share Bonaventure's fundamental claim that divine ideas are the divine essence compared to a creature in such a way that the creature becomes known.

---

115. See Chapters V and IV, respectively.

Chapter II.
St. Thomas Aquinas
(ca. 1224/1225-1274)

THE PLACE OF DIVINE IDEAS IN ST. THOMAS AQUINAS'S THOUGHT

As we saw at the beginning of the last chapter, St. Bonaventure's understanding of metaphysics focuses on exemplarism. The metaphysician is most truly himself when he investigates the exemplary origin of things, so his primary task is to articulate a theory of divine ideas. No other task competes for primacy in Bonaventure's system. The same is not true for St. Thomas Aquinas's metaphysics. Exemplarism is an essential aspect for his metaphysics, but there are a host of other investigations that vie for the title of "primary inquiry."[1] Msgr. John Wippel singles out the real distinction between essence and existence, act and potency, the analogy of being, the primacy of the *actus essendi*, and the transcendentals as investigations that are each arguably primary in Aquinas's metaphysics.[2] Put up against this list, exemplarism pales in comparison. Aquinas's metaphysics cannot be understood fully without an appeal to exemplarism and divine ideas, but they are hardly the primary investigation.[3]

Some scholars have questioned whether Aquinas thinks a doctrine of divine ideas is even necessary. Aquinas includes a discussion of divine ideas as a nod to the venerable tradition of Augustine, but he tacitly undermines the need for them.[4] If these authors are right, Aquinas includes divine ideas only because others may accuse him of heresy if he omits them.[5] Proponents offer three reasons for embracing

---

1. Étienne Gilson, *Le Thomisme*, Sixth edition (Paris: Vrin, 1965), 86.
2. John F. Wippel, *The Metaphysical Thought of Thomas Aquinas: From Finite Being to Uncreated Being* (Washington, DC: The Catholic University of America Press, 2000), 94.
3. "My intention is not to present this doctrine as if it were *the* key to understanding his metaphysical thought; for, simply put, it is not" (Doolan, *Aquinas on Divine Ideas*, xiv. Emphasis original).
4. See, *inter alia*, A. D. Sertillanges, *S. Thomas d'Aquin, Somme Théologique, Dieu: Tome II (Ia 12-17)* (Paris: Éditions de la Revue de Jeunes, 1933), 403–5; Étienne Gilson, *History of Christian Philosophy in the Middle Ages* (London: Sheed and Ward, 1955), 71–72; R. J. Henle, *Saint Thomas and Platonism* (The Hague: Martinus Nijhoff, 1956), 359; Gilson, *Introduction à La Philosophie Chrétienne* (Paris: Vrin, 1960), 173–83; Gilson, *Le Thomisme*, 146; John Lee Farthing, "The Problem of Divine Exemplarity in St. Thomas," *The Thomist* 49, no. 2 (1985): 214; James Ross, "Aquinas's Exemplarism; Aquinas's Voluntarism," *American Catholic Philosophical Quarterly* 64, no. 2 (1990): 171–98; Armand Maurer, "James Ross on the Divine Ideas: A Reply," *American Catholic Philosophical Quarterly* 65, no. 2 (1991): 213–20; James Ross, "Response to Maurer and Dewan," *American Catholic Philosophical Quarterly* 65, no. 2 (1991): 235–43.
5. See Bonaventure, *In I Sent.*, d. 6, a. un., q. 3 (Quaracchi, I.130a): "qui negat ideas esse, negat Filium Dei esse." Thomas makes the same argument in *In I Sent.*, d. 36, q. 2, a. 1, s.c. 1 (Mandonet,

this position. First, since Aquinas's discussions of divine ideas always follow discussions of divine knowledge, divine ideas are an unnecessary addition. He can explain how God knows all things without an appeal to divine ideas. Second, if divine ideas were a necessary part of Aquinas's system, they would appear in all of his *ex professo* treatments of divine knowledge, but Thomas omits a discussion of divine ideas in the *Summa Contra Gentiles*. Therefore, they are not necessary. Third, a theory of divine ideas might be contrary to divine simplicity.

These arguments have some force. Although I was ignorant of the literature at the time, the first and third arguments struck me the first time I encountered the theory in the *De veritate* and *Summa theologiae* in graduate school. If memory serves, everyone except for the professor came to class with similar misgivings. It seemed contradictory that Aquinas would spend so much time emphasizing the unity and simplicity of divine knowledge in one question and then pluralize his knowledge in the next. Moreover, since Aquinas asks whether God knows things other than himself in the questions on divine knowledge, it was not clear what divine ideas were adding to the account. I have since changed my mind and think they are necessary for Aquinas's theory of divine knowledge. Still, this anecdotal evidence shows that it is not apparent how divine ideas fit into Aquinas's broader account of divine knowledge.

Many scholars have resisted this reading of divine ideas and argued that they do hold a principal place in Thomas's thought.[6] If the teaching is useless or dangerous, "why did Saint Thomas not see this?"[7] He was a careful reasoner who was not afraid to oppose Augustine's theories. Why would he leave in divine ideas simply because *Augustinus dixit*? Additionally, in the prologue to the *Summa theologiae*, Thomas states that his purpose is to instruct beginners and replace Peter Lombard's *Sentences* as the novice theologian's textbook. One reason students struggle with the *Sentences*, he says, is "because of the useless multiplication of questions, articles, and arguments."[8] Since keeping unnecessary questions is contrary to the text's stated goal, why would Thomas break that rule just fifteen questions into the text by asking about divine ideas if they were not necessary?[9] These considerations give us reason to think that divine ideas might be a necessary part of Aquinas's thought. However, a complete answer will only come through an investigation of

---

I.839). Since *In I Sent.* is one of his earliest writings, the most this statement could prove is that Thomas thought it was heretical to deny them early in his career. It might only show that he does not want to be accused of heresy.

6. See, most notably, Louis B. Geiger, "Les Idées Divines Dans l'oeuvres de S. Thomas," in *St. Thomas Aquinas, 1274–1974, Commemorative Studies*, ed. Armand Maurer, vol. 1, 175–209 (Toronto: Pontifical Institute of Mediaeval Studies Press, 1974); John F. Wippel, *Thomas Aquinas on the Divine Ideas* (Toronto: Pontifical Institute of Mediaeval Studies, 1993), 26n56; Boland, *Ideas in God*, 7; Doolan, *Aquinas on Divine Ideas*, 96–99 and 111–17.

7. Boland, *Ideas in God*, 7.

8. *ST*, prologus (Leonine, 4.5): "propter multiplicationem inutilium quaestionum, articulorum et argumentorum."

9. See Geiger, "Les Idées Divines," 181–82; Boland, *Ideas in God*, 213–14.

his theory. This question will not dominate the discussion, but adjudicating it is essential for the history of theories of divine ideas.

THE STATUS OF DIVINE IDEAS

Aquinas's theory of divine ideas develops throughout his career. As a result, it is difficult to give a systematic account of his theory, which is exacerbated by the fact that Aquinas does not offer a complete account every time he discusses ideas. If he discusses only a particular aspect of divine ideas and changes his theory on that aspect, what effect does that change have on the rest of his theory? In what follows, I will offer a systematic account of Aquinas's theory of divine ideas. I will examine the most critical changes in Aquinas's position in the text, and I will leave less critical changes for the notes. This method has the advantage of being more succinct. Readers who wish to delve more deeply into the development of Aquinas's thought should read Gregory T. Doolan's *Aquinas on the Divine Ideas as Exemplar Causes*.

What Is an Idea?

Idea

St. Thomas gives his most complete definition of the term "idea" in the *De veritate*: "an idea is a form that something imitates from the intention of an agent who predetermines the end for himself."[10] Aquinas is led to this definition in large part because the term 'idea' (*idea*) comes from Greek and is well-translated as 'form' (*forma*).[11]

The form of something can be said in three ways. First, a form is that by which (*a qua*) a thing is formed as the formation of the effect proceeds from the agent's form. Such a form is not the thing's idea. Second, a form is that according to which (*secundum quam*) something is formed, as the soul is man's form, and the statue's shape is its form. A form in this sense is part of the composite, and so truly called the thing's form. This sort of form is not a thing's idea because the name 'idea' seems to signify a form separated from the thing of which it is an idea. Third, a form is that to which (*ad quam*) something is formed, and this is an exemplar form to whose imitation something is formed. This third sense of 'form' is the common understanding of the term because an idea is a form that something imitates.[12]

Aquinas distinguishes two ways of understanding a form that something imitates. First, such a form is a principle of cognition, making something known. This

---

10. *De veritate*, q. 3, a. 1 (Leonine, 22/1.100:221–23): "idea sit forma quam aliquid imitatur ex intentione agentis qui praedeterminat sibi finem."
11. *In I Sent.*, d. 36, q. 2, a. 1 (Mandonnet, I.839); *De veritate*, q. 3, a. 1 (Leonine, 22/1.99:159–63); *Quodlibet* VIII, q. 1, a. 2 (Leonine, 25/1.53–55); *ST* I, q. 15, a. 1 (Leonine, 4.199a). Aquinas takes this translation from Augustine, *De div. qq. 83*, q. 46 (PL 40.30).
12. *De veritate*, q. 3, a. 1 (Leonine, 22/1.99:163–82), esp.: "forma alicuius ad quam aliquid formatur, et haec est forma exemplaris ad cuius imitationem aliquid consituitur"; Cf. *ST* I, q. 15, a. 1 (Leonine, 4.199a).

form exists in the knower and is a likeness of the thing known. Second, such a form is a thing's exemplar and a causal principle of its coming to be. Thus, like Bonaventure, Thomas posits two roles for divine ideas: a cognitive role and a causal role.[13] These two roles are one of the marks of an Imitability Theory.

The Cognitive Role: Speculative Cognition vs. Practical Cognition

In its cognitive role, an idea is a principle that makes a knower know. But is an idea a principle of speculative or practical knowledge? Aquinas changes his mind twice on this issue throughout his career. These changes are worth noting individually because Aquinas's position on speculative and practical cognition has a significant influence on what he understands an idea to be and the scope of divine ideas. As his career progresses, he begins to emphasize their role in practical cognition and narrows his understanding of practical cognition.

In *In I Sent.* (1252–1256) Aquinas makes a binary distinction between speculative cognition and practical cognition, without any further distinctions.[14] Given this distinction, ideas are equally principles of practical cognition and speculative cognition. An idea is a principle of knowing what proceeds from and is produced by the knower. An idea is also a principle by which the way things subsist in their proper natures are known. The common use of the term 'idea' is restricted to practical cognition, but ideas are principles of both speculative and practical cognition. Insofar as they are principles of speculative cognition, they are called contemplating forms, and insofar as ideas are principles of practical cognition, they are called exemplars.[15] Aquinas uses the example of an artist to explain further the distinction between speculative and practical cognition. In practical cognition, the artist's knowledge shows the end, his will intends that end, and his will commands the act through which the work will occur in conformity to a preconceived form.[16] Thus, production is an act of the will. The intellect's role in production is merely to show the end. In this text, Thomas does not specify whether any occasion of the intellect's showing the end qualifies as practical knowledge or whether the will's intending is also required.

When Aquinas returns to the question in the *De veritate* (1256–1259), he makes several distinctions not found in his earlier account. Following Aristotle, Aquinas notes that speculative cognition and practical cognition are distinguished by their ends. The end of speculative cognition is the truth, and the end of practical cognition is operation, that is, action or production. He then further distinguishes both speculative cognition and practical cognition for a total of four distinctions. At one extreme is purely speculative (*pure speculativa*) knowledge of inoperable things, that is, things that the knower could not produce. Man's knowledge of other

---

13. See pp. 22–24.
14. For the dating and chronology of Aquinas's works, see Jean-Pierre Torrell, *Initiation à saint Thomas d'Aquin*, Nouvelle édition profondément remaniée., vol. 1 (Paris: Les Éditions du Cerf, 2015).
15. *In I Sent.*, d. 36, q. 2, a. 1 (Mandonnet, I.839–40).
16. *In I Sent.*, d. 38, q. 1, a. 1 (Mandonnet, I.899).

animals and God's knowledge of himself fall into this category. Next, there is speculative knowledge of operable things, but not *qua* operable (*operabilis per scientiam, tamen non consideratur ut est operabilis*). In this case, the knower considers parts of a thing separately, even though they cannot exist separated from the rest of the thing, as when a builder considers the properties, genus, and differences of a house. These cannot exist separately, yet he can consider them separately. The other two sorts of cognition are practical. Sometimes the knower considers something that he can produce, but he does not intend to produce it. Such knowledge is habitually or virtually practical (*practica habitu vel virtute*). The builder who considers the whole house but does not intend to make that house has virtually practical knowledge. Finally, at the other extreme is actually practical (*actu practica*) knowledge, which occurs when the knower actually orders his knowledge to production.[17]

God has all four of these modes of cognition, but not all four equally deserve to be called 'ideas.' Since, as Augustine says, an idea is properly called a form, the term 'idea' extends only to cognition of things insofar as they are formable. Thus, strictly speaking, divine ideas are principles of actually practical (*actu practica*) or virtually practical (*practica virtute*) cognition. Nevertheless, the term can also be used broadly to refer to the reason (*ratio*) or likeness (*similitudo*) of a thing. According to this broader usage, an idea can pertain to purely speculative cognition. Thomas insists, however, that we ought to favor the strict use of the term.[18] In the strict use of the term, ideas are exemplar forms. The word 'exemplar' signifies a relationship to a cause, and this relationship is what justifies Aquinas's claim that an idea, properly speaking, is a principle of both actually practical and virtually practical cognition. Something can be called an exemplar from the fact that something *can be* made in imitation of it, even if the artist never makes it.[19] The builder's idea of a house he never builds is still the exemplar because he could make a house to its likeness.

Thomas's teaching in the *De veritate* is stricter and more refined about what qualifies as an idea. In *In I Sent.* Aquinas was willing to apply the term idea equally to speculative and practical cognition. He now distinguishes between a proper and broad sense of the term. Properly speaking, only principles of practical cognition should be called ideas, but since an idea implies a certain likeness, even principles of speculative knowledge can be called ideas.

---

17. *De veritate*, q. 3, a. 3 (Leonine, 22/1.107:85–121): "quandoque enim ad opus actu ordinatur ... et tunc est actu practica cognitio et cognitionis forma; quandoque vero est quidem ordinabilis cognitio ad actum non tamen actu ordinatur ... et tunc est practica habitu vel virtute non actu. Quando vero nullo modo est ad actum ordinabilis cognitio, tunc est pure speculativa, quod etiam dupliciter contingit: uno modo quando cognitio est de rebus illis quae non sunt nata produci per scientiam cognoscentis ... ; quandoque vero res cognita est quidem operabilis per scientiam, tamen non consideratur ut est operabilis." See Wippel, *Divine Ideas*, 21.

18. *De veritate*, q. 3, a. 3 (Leonine, 22/1.108:143–74), esp.: "Vel magis proprie dicamus quod idea respicit cognitionem practicam actu vel virtute, similitudo autem et ratio tam practicam quam speculativam."

19. *De veritate*, q. 3, a. 3, ad 3 (Leonine, 22/1.108:185–94).

Aquinas also refines what qualifies as practical cognition. In *In I Sent.*, Thomas is vague as to whether the intellect's showing the end is sufficient for practical cognition or whether the will's act of intending is also required. Thus, using the terminology of the *De veritate*, Aquinas does not specify whether virtually practical (*practica virtute*) knowledge qualifies as practical cognition or not. In the *De veritate*, Aquinas specifies that the will's intending is not required for knowledge to be practical. A form can be a principle of practical cognition even if it is only virtually practical—even if there is no intention to produce the thing. As a result, I think Gregory Doolan speaks too strongly when he says that in the *De veritate*, an idea "is something that is *imitated*."[20] Doolan is right to point out the greater emphasis on imitation in the *De veritate*, but the mark of an idea is imitability, not actual imitation.[21] Without this qualification, principles of virtually practical (*practica virtute*) knowledge would not be called 'ideas' in the strict sense since there is no intention to produce according to them, which means that nothing actually imitates them.

When Aquinas takes up the question of divine ideas in *Summa theologiae* I (1266–1268), he changes his mind again. This time Thomas makes a threefold distinction between speculative and practical cognition: knowledge can be speculative only (*speculativa tantum*), practical only (*practica tantum*), or partially speculative and partially practical (*secundum aliquid speculativa et secundum aliquid practica*). He arrives at this distinction by considering the ways that knowledge can be called 'speculative' and 'practical.'

Knowledge can be called 'speculative' in three ways (*tripiliciter*). First, knowledge can be speculative on the part of the things known, which cannot be produced by the knower. Man's knowledge of natural things is speculative in this way. Second, knowledge can be speculative in its mode of knowing. If a builder considers a house by defining and dividing and considering the universals predicated of it, his knowledge is speculative in its mode of knowing. Here, the builder is considering the genus and species of the house and perhaps various aspects of the house, such as the species 'quadrangular.' This sort of speculative knowledge considers something operable, but not *qua* operable. Third, knowledge can be speculative in its end because speculative knowledge is ordered toward a consideration of the truth. Knowledge is speculative in its end if the knower only wants to consider the truth. His knowledge is speculative because he does not order it to action.[22]

Turning to practical knowledge, Aquinas notes that the end of practical knowledge is operation, that is, action or production. Thus, if a builder considers how he could make some house but does not order it to the end of operation, then his

---

20. Doolan, *Aquinas on Divine Ideas*, 12. Emphasis original. My disagreement with Doolan is limited to his interpretation of the *De veritate*. I think his claim accurately represents Aquinas's mature thought.

21. While this claim follows from what Thomas says in *De veritate* q. 3, a. 3, it might not be consistent with the definition of ideas he gives in *De veritate*, q. 3, a. 1. See Carl A. Vater, "An Inconsistency in Aquinas's *De Veritate* Account of Divine Ideas," *Nova et Vetera* (2020): 639–52. I will not concern myself with this question except to say that if I am right, this inconsistency might be an additional reason for the differences between his account of divine ideas in the *De veritate* and the *ST*.

22. *ST* I, q. 14, a. 16 (Leonine, 4.196–97).

knowledge will be speculative. Since the builder is only thinking about the house and not intending to make it, his knowledge is speculative. If he does order his knowledge to build the house, his knowledge is practical. From these considerations of the ways that knowledge can be called speculative and practical, Aquinas concludes that knowledge is speculative only (*speculativa tantum*) if it is speculative in the first way—on the part of the things known—knowledge is practical only (*simpliciter practica*) if it is ordered toward operation, and knowledge is partially speculative and partially practical (*secundum quid speculativa et secundum quid practica*) if it is speculative in the second or third way, that is, in consideration of operable things but not *qua* operable or as not ordered to operation.[23]

This threefold division tightens the criteria for practical knowledge. Only knowledge that is actually ordered toward operation, which he calls actually practical (*actu practica*) in the *De veritate*, qualifies as practical cognition. Without such an ordering, knowledge is at least partially speculative. Thus, all things that God could create but never does fall into the middle category of partially speculative and partially practical. Only God's knowledge of what he actually creates is purely practical, although the parts of those things (e.g., an animal's heart) would still be known in a partially speculative and partially practical way.[24] This threefold distinction collapses the middle two distinctions that Thomas made in the *De veritate*. Thomas still acknowledges the distinction between knowledge of an operable thing but *qua* operable, and knowledge of an operable thing but not as ordered to production, but he does not find this distinction relevant to whether the knowledge is practical. Neither of these ways of knowing operable things results in production, so neither is actually practical, even if one is closer to being actually practical than the other. This change has a tremendous impact on Thomas's understanding of the cognitive role of ideas.

As he did in the earlier texts, Aquinas chooses terminology for ideas based on whether a form is a principle of speculative or practical cognition. Insofar as it is a cognitive principle, an idea is properly called a 'reason' (*ratio*) and can also pertain to speculative knowledge. Insofar as it is a principle of making things, an idea can be called an 'exemplar,' and it pertains to practical knowledge. He further specifies that 'exemplar' relates to all the things that God makes at some time. 'Reason' relates to all the things that God knows, even if they never come to be at any time, according to their proper reason, and insofar as he knows them through the mode of speculation.[25] All exemplars are reasons, but not all reasons are exemplars. Only the reasons according to which God makes at some time are also exemplars.[26]

---

23. *ST* I, q. 14, a. 16 (Leonine, 4.197), esp.: "Scientia igitur quae est speculativa ratione ipius rei scitae, est speculativa tantum. Quae vero speculative est vel secundum modum vel secundum finem, est secundum quid speculativa et secundum quid practica. Cum vero ordinatur ad finem operationis, est simpliciter practica."

24. The example of the animal's heart is mine.

25. *ST* I, q. 15, a. 3 (Leonine, 4.204), esp.: "Secundum ergo quod exemplar est, secundum hoc se habet ad omnia quae a Deo fiunt secundum aliquod tempus."

26. See M. J. F. M. Hoenen, *Marsilius of Inghen: Divine Knowledge in Late Medieval Thought* (Leiden: Brill, 1993), 122.

Although both exemplars and reasons can be called ideas, I do not think that Thomas has abandoned the distinction between a strict and a broad sense of the term 'idea.' In *Summa theologiae* I, q. 44, a. 3, Thomas declares, "an exemplar is the same as an idea."[27] Although reasons are ideas, they are not ideas in the primary sense. First and foremost, an idea is "an exemplar form existing in the mind of God."[28]

This articulation differs from the *De veritate* by restricting the scope of ideas in the strict sense, namely exemplars. In the *De veritate*, Aquinas calls anything God knows that he could create an 'exemplar.' Actual creation is irrelevant. If God knows that he *could* create according to it, it is an exemplar. In the *Summa theologiae*, Aquinas insists that the scope of exemplars is equal to the scope of creation. An idea is an exemplar only if God wills to create a creature to its likeness. This change means that an idea in the strict sense is not merely intellectual; an intention from the will is a necessary aspect of an idea. God must add, as it were, an act of will to that knowledge. I will discuss the aspect of intention more below in the section on The Character of Ideas.[29] This restriction of the scope of divine exemplars also highlights the causal role of divine ideas. By eliminating virtually practical (*virtute practica*) knowledge from the scope of divine exemplars, Aquinas emphasizes that divine ideas in the strict sense are about what God wills to do. What God could do still factors into his theory of divine ideas—Aquinas still calls these ideas 'reasons,' and the consideration of what God can do is logically prior to the consideration of what he does—but what God could do is less important than what he does.

This analysis of the cognitive role of divine ideas shows Thomas refining his understanding of ideas throughout his career. He is consistent in calling ideas 'reasons' or 'likenesses' insofar as they are principles of speculative knowledge and calling them 'exemplars' insofar as they are principles of practical knowledge. However, his understanding of these two sorts of knowledge develops dramatically. In his earliest writings, an idea was equally a principle of speculative knowledge and a principle of practical knowledge. As his career progresses, he begins to emphasize that ideas are principles of practical cognition. By the time he writes the *Summa theologiae*, he understands divine ideas to be almost entirely principles of practical knowledge. Ideas are still principles of speculative knowledge, but he seems to include this role merely for the sake of completeness. An idea is really something to the likeness of which God actually creates.

The Causal Role

As the preceding analysis makes clear, Aquinas places greater emphasis on the causal role of ideas than on the cognitive role of ideas. He consistently uses the term 'exemplar' for the causal role, which means we must investigate his theory of exemplars. Three aspects of Aquinas's theory of exemplarity stand out: the character

---

27. *ST* I, q. 44, a. 3, s.c. (Leonine, 4.460a): "exemplar est idem quod idea."
28. *ST* I, q. 44, a. 3 (Leonine, 4.460b): "ideas, id est formas exemplares in mente divina existentes."
29. See pp. 56–61.

of an exemplar, the two types of divine exemplarity that Aquinas identifies, and the relationship between exemplarity and the four causes. Thomas's definition of an idea is only explainable after these three aspects are understood.

The Character of Exemplars

"An exemplar," Thomas says, "is that to whose imitation a thing is made."[30] Under this general description, there are three types of exemplars.[31] The first sort of exemplar is an exemplar by nature, which has the form it imposes upon another according to natural being (*esse naturale*). They are the type of thing that they exemplify in another, as is clear from natural generation. Aquinas says that this sort of exemplarity is not true exemplarity because it is not intellectual. Natural generation involves a form to which a thing is made, but it lacks an essential aspect of exemplarity. An exemplar determines the end for itself, but no parent determines the end of its child's species.[32]

The other two types of exemplars are exemplars by intellect. They are distinguished according to the origin of the exemplar, that is, by the exemplar having its origin outside of the knower or within the knower. An exemplar is external when the artist seeks to recreate something that he has encountered in the world, as when the painter paints a landscape. This sort of exemplarity is intellectual exemplarity because the agent does not have the form he imposes according to *esse naturale*, but according to intellectual being (*esse intellectuale*). The painter is not a landscape. He is a man who knows a landscape. The painter also determines the end for himself because he alone decides that he will paint at all and that he will paint this landscape (as opposed to anything else).

Nevertheless, external exemplarity is imperfect. The ultimate standard or measure for the painter's artwork is not the form in his mind, but the extramental landscape that he imitates. The painting is judged insofar as it accurately depicts the landscape. Thus, external exemplarity entails a certain potency on the part of the artist who must receive the exemplar that he wishes to imitate on canvas.[33]

The third and most perfect kind of exemplar is the one that the artist thinks up for himself. When the artist invents the exemplar himself, there is no potency involved. Instead, having this sort of exemplar is a mark of perfection and actuality. It is not enough to think up the exemplar, however. The perfect exemplar must also

---

30. *In De div. nom.*, c. 5, lect. 3, n. 665 (Marietti, 249b): "exemplar enim est ad cuius imitationem fit aliud."

31. See *De veritate*, q. 3, a. 1 (Leonine, 22/1.100:209–22); *ST* I, q. 15, a. 1 (Leonine, 4.199); *ST* I, q. 44, a. 3 (Leonine, 4.460) for the following distinctions.

32. The requirement of determining the end for itself will be discussed below. See pp. 60–61.

33. Aquinas does not suggest this possibility, but it does not seem like the artist has to be entirely active or passive in his intellectual exemplarity. The exemplar might be partially external and partially invented by him, as we find in the case of a musician who plays an *ad libitum* adaptation on the theme of whatever piece he is playing. In this case, the artist is not passively replicating what he receives, but the exemplar of what he produces is not without external influence.

be a principle of practical cognition. The development in Thomas's thought on speculative and practical cognition comes into play here. According to the *De veritate*, an exemplar is anything that the artist knows he can produce, regardless of whether the artist ever intends to produce it. According to the *Summa theologiae*, an intention to create is indispensable for practical knowledge. Only those ideas that are, in the terminology of the *De veritate*, actually practical, qualify as exemplars. Thus, only those ideas according to which God produces a creature at some time in history are divine exemplars. All other ideas are merely *rationes*.

Two Types of Divine Exemplarity

An exemplar in the perfect sense is an intellectual exemplar that the artist thinks up for himself and wills to produce. Divine ideas must be exemplars in this sense because this sort of intellectual exemplarity does not entail any potency and implies a certain perfection instead. An external exemplar has no place in God because it implies a potency to receive the exemplar. Unlike Plato's Demiurge, God does not look beyond his essence for his ideas.[34] It might seem obvious that God is not a natural exemplar because he cannot generate another God. The word 'natural' might also imply a sort of necessity contrary to God's free act of creation. Nevertheless, Thomas does say that God is a natural exemplar. Therefore, God has a twofold exemplarity: perfect intellectual exemplarity and natural exemplarity.

Aquinas affirms the need for a twofold exemplarity because there are two ways in which names can express a mode of being that the word 'being' (*ens*) does not express. First, words express a special mode of *ens*, and second, words express a general mode of being that follows upon every *ens*. The special modes of *ens* are the division of being into the univocal categories of genera and species. The general modes of *ens* are the transcendental that all beings possess in varying degrees insofar as they are beings.[35] Aquinas's theory, then, needs to account for the fact that the categories do not admit of degrees, but the transcendentals do.

Aquinas explains this twofold exemplarity in *In I Sent.*, d. 19, q. 5, a. 2 in the context of a discussion of whether all things are true by uncreated truth. An objector argues that there is a problem with saying that all things are called true by uncreated truth in an exemplary way. The exemplar of each form is in God because the essence is creative. If it were enough to say that since uncreated truth exemplifies all things, all things are true by uncreated truth, then it would seem like all things could be called colored because color is in God in an exemplary way. Just as all things would be true because they are in God in an exemplary way, so too they would be colored because color is in God in an exemplary way. It is false that all things are colored. Therefore, it is also false that all things are true by uncreated truth.[36]

---

34. *In I Sent.*, d. 36, q. 2, a. 1, ad 2 and ad 3 (Mandonnet, I.840); *De veritate*, q. 3, a. 2 (Leonine, 22/1.104:158–74); *SCG* I, c. 46 (Leonine, 13.137); *ST* I, q. 15, a. 2 (Leonine, 4.202).
35. *De veritate*, q. 1, a. 1 (Leonine, 22/1.5:106–29); *In V Met.*, lect. 9, nn. 885–97 (Spiazzi, 237–40); *In III Phys.*, lect. 5, nn. 15–16 (Leonine, 2.114a–15a).
36. *In I Sent.*, d. 19, q. 5, a. 2, obj. 4 (Mandonnet, I.491).

Thomas argues that the objector has conflated two sorts of divine exemplarity. In one way, God is an exemplar by his intellect. Insofar as God has ideas in his intellect, the divine intellect exemplifies all the things that are from him, just as the artist's intellect exemplifies all artifacts through the form of art. In another way, God is an exemplar by nature. Since God is good by nature, he is the exemplar of all good things. The same holds for truth. Consequently, God is not an exemplar of color and of truth in the same way.[37]

This twofold exemplarity explains why, as we will see below, Thomas is so insistent that a divine idea is not the divine essence itself, but the divine essence as understood by God.[38] The divine essence *qua* essence is not the exemplar of a shark *qua* shark because God is not a shark. However, the divine essence *qua* essence is the exemplar of the shark *qua* being, true, and so on, because God has all transcendental perfections. It is only insofar as God understands his essence to be imitable that the various essences of things are distinguished. God is the exemplar of a shark *qua* shark because he knows his essence is imitable by the essence of a shark and wills to create according to it. Therefore, the divine essence is the natural exemplar of things insofar as they have a certain degree of transcendental perfection, and the divine essence is the intellectual exemplar of things insofar as God knows it to be imitable by various genera and species.

God's twofold exemplarity also explains why all finite beings imitate God deficiently but are perfect in their species. Every created being, in virtue of its finitude, participates in being imperfectly from God's being.[39] This imperfect imitation seems to be what Aquinas has in mind at the beginning of the Fourth Way: "We find in things that something is more and less good, and true, and noble, etc."[40] Thomas explicitly speaks of transcendentals being more or less. Everything that exists is a being, but "being" is said of creatures only analogously.[41] The existence of a more and less requires the existence of a most or absolute. Man can only judge that a dog has more being and perfection than a rock because he knows the absolute standard that both the dog and the rock approach.[42] God is the perfect measure and rule according to which all transcendental perfections are judged. He is perfect existence. All other things are a mixture of existence and tendency toward nothingness.[43]

Everything falls short of divine perfection, yet each thing is precisely the sort of thing that God intended it to be: "Each thing attains its perfect imitation of that which is in the divine intellect because such is how God disposed it to

---

37. *In I Sent.*, d. 19, q. 5, a. 2, ad 4 (Mandonnet, I.493).

38. See pp. 67–68.

39. *ST* I, q. 47, a. 1, ad 2 (Leonine, 4.486b): "nulla creatura repraesentat perfecte exemplar primum, quod est divina essentia."

40. *ST* I, q. 2, a. 3 (Leonine, 4.32a).

41. *In I Sent.*, d. 19, q. 5, a. 2, ad 1 (Mandonnet, I.492).

42. Aquinas's unnamed, remote source for this claim is Augustine, *De vera rel.*, c. 30, n. 56 and c. 39, n. 72 (PL 34.147 and 154); Augustine, *Conf.*, VII, cc. 11–12 (PL 32.742-43).

43. *ST* I, q. 104, a. 3, ad 1 (Leonine, 5.468b).

be."[44] Socrates imitates God imperfectly because he has finite being. Nevertheless, he is a perfect imitation of God's divine idea because God decreed that Socrates should have precisely the finite being that he has. God ordained that Socrates should fall short of divine perfection in precisely the way that he does.[45] Therefore, Socrates is simultaneously a perfect imitation insofar as he imitates his divine idea and an imperfect imitation insofar as he imitates the divine essence itself.

Exemplarity and the Four Causes

An idea is a form in the artist's mind that acts as a cause in the production of something, but what sort of causality does an exemplar exercise?[46] Aquinas seems comfortable saying the idea has exemplar causality, but this description is not particularly helpful. Aristotle, who does not have anything like a theory of divine ideas, argued that there are only four types of causes: material, formal, efficient, and final. Some authors, notably Seneca, argued that divine exemplarity is a fifth type of causality because it does not readily fit into Aristotle's fourfold division.[47] Seneca's conclusion seems reasonable since an exemplar seems to be a sort of formal, efficient, and final cause. It is a formal cause insofar as it is a form, an efficient cause as something intended, and a final cause insofar as "an exemplar form or idea has the notion of an end in a certain way."[48]

Aquinas never declares exemplarity to be a fifth sort of cause. He insists that an exemplar is a formal cause in his commentary on Aristotle's *Metaphysics*. A thing's formal cause can be intrinsic to the thing, and Thomas calls this sort of formal cause the thing's 'species.' Man's soul is an intrinsic formal cause. A thing's formal cause can also be extrinsic from the thing as that to the likeness of which the thing comes to be, and it is called a 'form.'[49] Aquinas further comments that Plato posited ideas to be exemplar forms. The same should be said about Aquinas's

---

44. *In II Sent.*, d. 16, q. 1, a. 2, ad 2 (Mandonnet, II.2.400): "unaquaeque res pertingat ad perfectam imitationem eius quod est in intellectu divino, quia talis est qualem eam esse disposuit."
45. See Doolan, *Aquinas on Divine Ideas*, 149.
46. The discussion that follows is greatly indebted to the discussion in Doolan, *Aquinas on Divine Ideas*, 33–41.
47. Seneca, *Ad Lucilium Epistulae Morales*, epist. 65, n. 7 (Gummere, I.448). Cf. David L. Greenstock, "Exemplar Causality and the Supernatural Order," *The Thomist* 16, no. 1 (1953): 4–5: "Unless we wish to claim that the exemplar forms a fifth class of causes all on its own, we are forced, it would seem, to reduce it to one of the four causes." Although Thomas quotes Seneca by name regularly, I have only been able to find one place where he mentions Seneca's position on ideas: *De veritate*, q. 2, a. 10, s.c. 1 (Leonine, 22/1.75:18–24). See pp. 240–41 for Ockham's engagement with Seneca.
48. *De veritate*, q. 3, a. 1 (Leonine, 22/1.100:254–55): "forma exemplaris vel idea habet quodam modo rationem finis."
49. *In V Met.*, lect. 3, n. 764 (Spiazzi, 211): "Alio autem modo dicitur causa, species et exemplum, id est exemplar; et haec est causa formalis, quae comparatur dupliciter ad rem. Uno modo sicut forma intrinseca rei; et haec dicitur species. Alio modo sicut extrinseca a re, ad cuius tamen similitudo res fieri dicitur; et secundum hoc, exemplar rei dicitur forma." Cf. *De veritate*, q. 3, a. 1, s.c. 3 (Leonine, 22/1.98:101–6).

theory of divine ideas. Divine ideas are the extrinsic formal causes to the likeness of which creatures are created.

Despite this explicit declaration, an objection arises that divine ideas cannot be formal causes. Thomas declares in *De principiis naturae* that a formal cause is an intrinsic cause. In that text, he first distinguishes causes into intrinsic and extrinsic. The intrinsic causes are the material cause and the formal cause and, the extrinsic causes are the efficient cause and the final cause.[50] Since an exemplar is an extrinsic cause, it seems impossible for it to exercise formal causality.

This objection is not convincing because it does not consider the context of the *De principiis naturae*. In that text, Thomas restricts the scope of his comments to material beings and their natural generation. Given this narrow scope, all formal causes are intrinsic, and there can be no such thing as an extrinsic formal cause for natural generation. However, it does not follow that there cannot be an extrinsic formal cause at all. In fact, Thomas seems to think that the intrinsic-extrinsic division of causes only holds when discussing natural generation. In his commentary on Aristotle's *Metaphysics*, Thomas does not even discuss causes as divisible by intrinsic and extrinsic. Instead, he says that causes are divided according to the species of causality and by their mode of causality.[51] Therefore, causes are not first divided into two and then each of those two into two for a total of four causes; "the *first immediate division* of the genus, cause, is the fourfold division into material, formal, efficient, and final."[52] When he divides the genus "cause" into intrinsic and extrinsic in the *De principiis naturae*, Thomas is using accidental differences, not specific differences. When the specific differences of the genus "cause" are considered, there is nothing inappropriate about positing an extrinsic formal cause.

Even if the objection against exemplars as formal causes fails, it still seems that exemplars are final causes because they attract the agent's action.[53] The final cause is the cause of causes. It causes the very causality of the efficient cause. The final cause of health is what causes a man to go for a walk or to see his doctor. Without the final cause, there is no efficient cause.[54] Likewise, without the exemplar, the artist would never produce.

This argument has a certain plausibility because an exemplar is a final cause "in a certain way" (*quoddam modo*). It is a final cause if we examine the production with respect to the efficient cause. In this respect, the exemplar moves the agent as a final cause. Nevertheless, an exemplar does not primarily entail the agent: "'exemplar,' if it is taken properly, conveys causality with respect to the things exemplified because an

---

50. *De prin. nat.*, c. 3 (Leonine, 43.42:42–52).

51. *In V Met.*, lect. 3, n. 783 (Spiazzi, 215).

52. Francis X. Meehan, *Efficient Causality in Aristotle and St. Thomas* (Washington, DC: The Catholic University of America Press, 1940), 179n40. Emphasis original.

53. Theodore J. Kondoleon, "Exemplar Causality in the Philosophy of St. Thomas Aquinas" (PhD diss., The Catholic University of America, 1967), 158–60.

54. See, *inter alia*, *De prin. nat.*, c. 4 (Leonine, 43.44:25–31).

exemplar is that to whose imitation another comes to be."[55] So, exemplarity primarily concerns the effect, not the cause. An exemplar exercises formal causality with respect to the effect because it is the measure of the effect produced in its likeness. This conclusion is strengthened by the fact that an exemplar is an intellectual cause, and so, exemplars do not have the same mode of being as what they exemplify. The exemplified thing cannot imitate the exemplar in every respect, but the exemplar measures the exemplified thing only because of the adequation of form to form.[56]

In sum, Aquinas argues that divine ideas exercise formal causality primarily, but they also exercise final causality secondarily because they cause the intelligent agent to produce something. However, this causality is secondary because motivating-the-agent is not what is characteristic of an exemplar. An exemplar is characterized by something being made like it. In the production of something, the exemplar makes the thing be what it is, which is the nature of a formal cause.

The Character of Ideas

The preceding discussion has prepared the way for a close examination of Aquinas's definition of an idea. "An idea," he says, "is a form that something imitates from the intention of an agent who predetermines the end for himself."[57] This definition has four aspects, each of which requires additional explanation: form, imitation, intention, and end.

Thomas continually asserts that 'form' is the proper translation of the term 'idea.' An idea is a form in the knower's mind that is a principle for both speculative and practical knowledge. Its role in practical knowledge is primary; ideas are forms because the forms of other things are known and preexist in an agent because of ideas. Ideas are that to which things are formed. Since they exist in the mind of the knower, an idea is an extrinsic exemplar form to the likeness of which a thing is formed.[58] It is a form "existing outside of the thing itself" in the mind of the efficient cause, numerically distinct from the exemplified thing.[59]

---

55. *De veritate*, q. 8, a. 8, ad 1 (Leonine, 22/1.247:157–60): "exemplar, si proprie accipiatur importat causalitatem respectu exemplatorum quia exemplar est ad cuius imitationem fit aliud."

56. See *ST* I, q. 18, a. 4, ad 2 (Leonine, 4.230): "Exemplata oportet conformari exemplari secundum rationem formae, non autem secundum modum essendi. Nam alterius modi esse habet quandoque forma in exemplari et in exemplato: sicut forma domus in mente artificis habet esse immateriale et intelligibile, in domo autem quae est extra animam, habet esse materiale et sensibile. Unde et rationes rerum quae in seipsis non vivunt, in mente divina sunt vita, quia in mente divina habent esse divinum." See also *ST* III, q. 24, a. 3, ad 3 (Leonine, 11.274). Both texts are cited in Doolan, *Aquinas on Divine Ideas*, 36n84.

57. *De veritate*, q. 3, a. 1 (Leonine, 22/1.100:221–23): "idea sit forma quam aliquid imitatur ex intentione agentis qui praedeterminat sibi finem."

58. Doolan, *Aquinas on Divine Ideas*, 25. Doolan cites *In III Sent.*, d. 27, q. 2, a. 4, ql. 3, obj. 1 and solutio 3, ad 1 (Moos, III.884.153 and 889–90.176–77); *De veritate*, q. 14, a. 5, obj. 4 (Leonine, 22/2.451:27–35); *ST* I, q. 5, a. 2, ad 2 (Leonine, 4.58).

59. *ST* I, q. 15, a. 1 (Leonine, 4.199a): "per ideas intelliguntur formae aliarum rerum, praeter ipsas res existentes." See Gregory T. Doolan, "Aquinas on the Divine Ideas and the Really Real," *Nova et Vetera* 13, no. 4 (2015): 1086: "The divine idea that God has of me is *not* me." Emphasis original. This point will be discussed in more detail on pp. 74–76.

Unlike an intrinsic form that forms through the mode of inherence, an exemplar form forms through the mode of imitation.[60] A form in the mind of the artist is an exemplar because some external thing imitates it. In this light, it is not surprising that Thomas describes divine ideas—in both early and late texts—as the ways God knows his essence to be imitable.[61] What sort of imitation or likeness is required for exemplar causality? The short answer to this question is that any manner of imitation suffices. Since God is the first exemplar cause of all things, any being, insofar as it has being, imitates God. As long as it is not a complete privation, even the least imitation is sufficient.[62]

This simple answer needs to be qualified because "art is not the principle or cause of some defect in the artifact but is the *per se* cause of their perfection and form."[63] Art itself is not to blame if a sculpture does not turn out as the artist intended. The root of the imperfection is either a defect in the matter that prevents it from receiving the form or the artist's imperfect possession of the art.[64] God suffers neither of these defects, so "God's creative idea is the model of things so efficiently that the creature can be only accidentally dissimilar to God's creative idea of it."[65] No defect in the world results from God failing to create as he wanted to create. Plato's dialogues frequently allude to the fact that Socrates was an ugly man. Given that God creates as he means to create, he created Socrates precisely as he intended to create him. It is not that God could not have created a physically beautiful Socrates. Instead, Socrates lacked physical beauty because the divine idea of Socrates did not exemplify physical beauty. If any given lack seems imperfect, it is because the way the imperfection fits into the divine plan for creation and how it

---

60. *De veritate*, q. 3, a. 3 (Leonine, 22/1.108:158–60): "sive talis formatio fiat per modum inhaerentiae, ut in formis intrinsecis, sive per modum imitationis ut in formis exemplaribus."

61. See, *inter alia*, *In I Sent.*, d. 36, q. 2, a. 2 (Mandonnet, I.841–42); *De veritate*, q. 3, a. 2 (Leonine, 22/1.104:200–105:219); *SCG* I, c. 54 (Leonine, 13.155a6–19); *ST* I, q. 15, a. 2 (Leonine, 4.201–2), esp.: "inquantum Deus cognoscit suam essentiam ut sic imitabilem a tali creatura, cognoscit eam ut propriam rationem et ideam huius creaturae." Here it is necessary to anticipate a point that will be made in greater detail below. There are, as it were, three moments in establishing a divine exemplar. First, the divine intellect knows the divine essence as imitable by each possible creature. Second, the divine will chooses to create some possible creatures. Third, the divine intellect knows what the divine will has freely elected to create. Divine exemplars are established in the third moment. Aquinas's distinction between divine ideas as exemplars and divine ideas as *rationes* does not apply to the first moment. Since the texts cited here concern the first moment, Aquinas's progressively increasing emphasis on divine ideas as principles of actually willed practical knowledge does not come into play. God can only have *rationes* and exemplars because he first knows his essence as imitable. See pp. 58–59.

62. See, e.g., *De veritate*, q. 3, a. 4 (Leonine, 22/1.110:75–80), esp.: "similitudo attendatur secundum formam aliquo modo participatam."

63. *In Ioan.*, c. 1, lect. 2, n. 87 (Cai, 18b): "ars non est principium sed causa alicuius defectus in artificiatis, sed per se est causa perfectionis ipsorum et formae." This text is likely corrupted and should read "principium seu causa" instead of "principium sed causa."

64. *In Ioan.*, c. 1, lect. 2, n. 87 (Cai, 18b–19a); *SCG* II, c. 2 (Leonine, 13.275a6–8).

65. Francis J. Kovach, "Divine Art in Saint Thomas Aquinas," in *Arts Libéraux et Philosophie au Môyen Age: Actes du Quatrième Congrès International de Philosophie Médiévale* (Montreal: Institut d'études médiévales, 1969), 668.

serves some greater perfection remains unknown.⁶⁶ Socrates lacked physical beauty, but his physical ugliness pointed to the beauty of his soul and the need to put the things of the soul ahead of things of the body.

The third aspect of the definition of 'idea' is intention. Aquinas says that something can imitate another in two ways: from the intention of an agent, or accidentally and by chance. Accidental imitation cannot be what is meant by 'idea.' An imitation by chance was not formed to that end because 'to' implies an order toward an end, but what occurs by chance was not ordered toward that end. If a painting happens to look like someone or something by accident, the painter did not *intend* to paint a likeness of that model. Therefore, the exemplified thing must imitate from the intention of an agent since an exemplar form or idea is that to which (*ad quem*) something is formed.⁶⁷ Intention implies agency and will, so the agent must know and will to assimilate something to the measure of it in his mind.⁶⁸ Knowledge alone is not enough for intention. Thus, if the word 'idea' is taken in the strict sense to refer to practical knowledge, then there are only ideas of those things that the agent actually produces.

Since an idea includes intention, it follows that God does not necessarily have exemplar ideas. Rather, God necessarily knows all the ways his essence could be imitated, but he does not necessarily create any of them. God only has exemplars because he intended to create. In the sense of reasons (*rationes*), God did necessarily have ideas because these refer only to cognition. Even if God did not will to create, he would still know his essence as imitable by every possible creature. Aquinas does not make this point explicitly, but it follows that God has *rationes* necessarily and exemplars contingently.⁶⁹ The divine will, then, is included in the complete definition of an idea.

From the necessity of divine *rationes* and the contingency of divine exemplars, it follows that the character of a divine idea is established in three moments, as it were.⁷⁰

---

66. See, *inter alia*, *ST* I, q. 25, a. 6, ad 3 (Leonine, 4.299); *ST* I, q. 48, a. 2, ad 3 (Leonine, 492b).

67. *De veritate*, q. 3, a. 1 (Leonine, 22/1.99:183–96).

68. Aquinas uses the term *intentio* in two distinct ways. The first way corresponds to the word 'intention' (without an article) as it is used in English. This sense is the primary sense of the term for Thomas, and it pertains to that which moves toward an end. The will moves all the other powers to their ends. Therefore, Thomas argues, *intentio* is properly an act of will, not intellect. See *In II Sent.*, d. 38, q. 1, a. 3 (Mandonnet, II.973–75); *De veritate*, q. 22, a. 13 (Leonine, 22/3.643:1–646:302); *ST* I-II, q. 12, a. 1 (Leonine, 6.94); *De malo*, q. 16, a. 11, ad 3 (Leonine, 23.330:241–331:257). The second way corresponds to the word "an intention" (with an article) as it is used in English. This sense comes from a translation of Avicenna's use of the term 'concept.' Aquinas uses the term in this way in the *De ente* especially. In the prologue of that work, Thomas announces that he will consider the way *ens* and *essentia* "se habeat ad intentiones logicas, scilicet genus, speciem et differentiam" (Leonine, 43.369:9–10).

69. See pp. 18–19 for the same point in Bonaventure.

70. Aquinas does not explicitly distinguish these three moments, but they are necessitated by his claim that intention is included in the character of a divine exemplar. They do not imply a temporal progression in God. They only entail that the acts of knowing the possibilities, choosing from the possibilities, and knowing what was chosen have a logical priority and posteriority. In short, Aquinas's theory of divine ideas seems to necessitate something like Scotus's theory of instants of nature. For Scotus's theory of instants, especially concerning divine ideas, see pp. 170–75.

First, the divine intellect knows itself to be imitable by every possible creature. Second, the divine will freely chooses to create some of those possible creatures. Third, the divine intellect knows what the divine will has freely willed. Given these three logically distinct moments, the complete definition of an idea in the strict sense of exemplar only occurs in the third moment, not the first, because an exemplar is a principle of practical knowledge, which occurs in the divine intellect in the third moment. If the character of a divine exemplar were complete before the third moment, God would not know according to which ideas he was creating. Nothing known by God, in the strict sense of an exemplar, has the character of an idea if we consider only the divine intellect in the first moment, when God has all ideas in the sense of reasons (*rationes*) of creatures, but has not yet willed them.

Notice that this entire discussion of intention is predicated on what God actually wills. The theory of exemplar that Aquinas endorses in *De veritate*, q. 3, a. 3 does not include the intention to produce. As a result, in this article's teaching, the character of an exemplar is complete in the first moment when God knows his essence as imitable. As soon as God knows his essence as imitable, he has virtually practical (*virtute practica*) knowledge, which Aquinas says is sufficient. Even though the complete definition of an idea explained here comes from *De veritate*, q. 3, a. 1, the understanding of exemplars used is the same as the understanding found in the later, *Summa theologiae* account of divine ideas.[71]

A discussion of imitation and intention would be incomplete without a discussion of how an imitation is measured. Thomas assigns measure and measured to knowledge and to the thing differently depending on whether the knowledge is speculative or practical. For practical knowledge, knowledge causes the thing and so measures of the external thing. A work of art is more perfect and complete to the extent that it attains a more excellent likeness of the artist's knowledge.[72] God's knowledge relates to everything other than himself in this way. For speculative knowledge, the thing known is the measure of the knowledge. Things cause our knowledge of them, and so our knowledge is true to the extent that it attains a greater likeness of the thing known.[73]

This distinction of moments also seems to support John Meinert's claim that exemplar causes are instrumental causes. Aquinas's theory of instrumental causality holds that "the secondary cause is moved by the primary [cause], causes by its own proper form, and thereby causes something higher or beyond its own proper form by the motion of the primary" (John Meinert, "*In Duobus Modis:* Is Exemplar Causality Instrumental According to Aquinas?" *New Blackfriars* 95, no. 1055 [2014]: 67). Instrumentality seems to hold even for divine ideas since they do not cause without the action of the divine will, are that to which a creature is made, and are numerically distinct from creatures.

71. For a defense of this claim, see Vater, "An Inconsistency," 639–52.

72. This claim requires qualification for the artist who fashions according to an external exemplar. In that case, the external exemplar is the measure of the artist's knowledge. Thus, when the artist's knowledge measures his artwork, it is ultimately measured by the external object that measures the artist's knowledge.

73. *De veritate*, q. 1, a. 2 (Leonine, 22/1.9:81–84); *ST* I, q. 22, a. 2 (Leonine, 4.259–60); *In X Met.*, lect. 2, n. 1959 (Spiazzi, 467). Cf. Doolan, *Aquinas on Divine Ideas*, 27.

The artist's knowledge is the rule and measure of his artwork, but only if he has willed to produce it. If the artist thinks up a possible exemplar but does not produce according to it, then there will never be an imitation. In that case, the form in his mind would be a cognitive principle, but not a causal principle. The intention to act from the will is the only thing that can make an idea be a causal principle.

The fourth aspect of Thomas's definition of 'idea' concerns the end. This aspect proves invaluable in determining Aquinas's account of ideas because not only does the agent have to intend that something imitate his intellectual exemplar, but he must also predetermine the end for himself. To understand what Aquinas means by "predetermine the end for himself," we must consider a distinction Aquinas makes in the *De principiis naturae* between the end of generation and the end of the generated thing, using the example of a knife. The end of the artist in generating the knife is the production of the knife itself, but merely being generated is not the end of a knife. A knife's end is its operation, to cut.[74]

When Aquinas says that the agent "predetermines the end for himself," he has both the end of generation and the end of the generated thing in mind, which is evident from his two examples. The first example is of an archer shooting an arrow. The archer determines the end of his operation since he shoots the arrow when and where he wants. As soon as the arrow is shot, the end of generation is complete because the arrow is in flight. The archer also determines the end of the arrow's flight since the arrow only flies in this direction (as opposed to another direction) because the archer determined that end for it.[75] Note that what is generated is this particular flight of the arrow, not the arrow itself. The archer determines the end of this flight because he determines in what direction and how forcefully he shoots the arrow. The archer has determined both the end of generation by shooting the arrow and the end of the thing that is generated by determining the target the arrow should hit.

Aquinas's second example is human procreation. When a man procreates, he predetermines his own end, but not the end of the child he generates. He determines whether he will procreate and when he will do so because he engages in the procreative act freely, but he does not determine the end of his child's humanity. As a result, the father's form of man is not the exemplar for the child's form of man.[76] It is not enough that the agent act intellectually and freely in producing some effect; he must establish the very end of the thing produced. If the agent does not predetermine the end of the thing produced, then neither the agent nor his knowledge is an exemplar. The knife maker's knowledge and the archer's knowledge are exemplars or ideas because they determine the end of what they produce. Neither the procreating man nor his knowledge is an exemplar or idea because he does not determine the end of his child's form.

---

74. *De prin. nat.*, c. 4 (Leonine, 43.45:104–113), esp.: "forma enim cultelli est finis generationis, sed incidere quod est operatio cultelli, est finis ipsius generati, scilicet cultelli."
75. *De veritate*, q. 3, a. 1 (Leonine, 22/1.99:196–100:209).
76. *De veritate*, q. 3, a. 1 (Leonine, 22/1.100:209–17).

The takeaway from Aquinas's distinction is that the primary agent gives the end to the generated thing. The agent's idea makes the thing to be what it is, including its end, and so, it follows that an agent can only have ideas of the things for which he can determine the end. This insight is at the heart of the distinction between natural things and artificial things. Man can determine the end of artificial things but never of natural things. Nature's artist determines the end of natural things. Since God—nature's artist—is the exemplar of all things, he predetermines the end of all things.[77] Each thing's divine idea determines its end.

Summary

Thomas's thought on the character of ideas and exemplars shows clear development. As his thought matures, he increasingly emphasizes the causal role of ideas. He always insists that the term 'idea' can be used for both speculative and practical cognition, but he insists that the proper sense of the term 'idea' is for practical cognition only. Strictly speaking, an idea and an exemplar are the same. His thought on exemplars also narrows to that in imitation of which an artist actually produces. That which the artist knows he could produce but does not intend to produce is not an exemplar. This emphasis on exemplarity and actually practical knowledge ensures that both intellect and will are part of the character of an idea. An exemplar must be both foreknown by the intellect and commanded by the will. Aquinas's earlier accounts of exemplar that include, in the *De veritate* terminology, virtually practical knowledge, do not include the will. On these accounts, the character of an idea is complete in the intellect. The exemplar serves as the final cause for the artist to produce, and, more fundamentally, it serves as the extrinsic formal cause of the thing that is produced. The exemplar measures what is produced in imitation of it and is so complete a measure of the imitation that it even determines the end of the imitation. The exemplar form or idea determines the thing's characteristic functions and determines whether any particular action will be good or bad for the exemplified thing.

Does God Have Ideas?

On several occasions, the previous section asserted without evidence that God has ideas, but Thomas is not content merely to assert the existence of divine ideas. He offers several arguments for the existence of divine ideas because while everyone attributes knowledge to God, many do so in ways that compromise his simplicity, limit his knowledge to actual causality, or speak only in metaphors.[78] It is necessary to give a precise account of God's knowledge of himself and of everything other than himself that avoids these errors. Thomas offers three types of arguments for God's knowledge of things other than himself, named by

---

77. *ST* I, q. 44, a. 3 (Leonine, 4.460a): "Deus est prima causa exemplaris omnium rerum."
78. *De veritate*, q. 2, a. 1 (Leonine, 22/1.39:109–10). Thomas corrects these errors in *De veritate*, q. 2, a. 2 (Leonine, 22/1.44:114–95).

Doolan the Argument from Natural Teleology, Argument from Similitude, and Argument from Divine Self-Knowledge.[79] The rest of this section will examine these three arguments.

The Argument from Natural Teleology

Aquinas uses the Argument from Natural Teleology most often in defense of the position that God knows things other than himself by exemplar forms.[80] Everything that tends determinately to some end either establishes that end for itself or the end is established for it by another. If neither of these were the case, then things would not tend to one end rather than another. But natural things tend toward determinate ends as is evidenced by the fact that they always (or for the most part) tend toward the same thing, which would not happen by chance. Therefore, since they do not establish the end for themselves (because they do not cognize that end), the end must be established for them by another, who is the institutor of nature. This institutor of nature is he who offers *esse* to all things and is the necessary being through himself, namely God. God could not establish the end of nature unless he understood it. Therefore, God is intelligent.[81]

The blacksmith could not make an ax unless he knew the act of cutting, what the ax would cut, the appropriate material out of which to make the ax, and the form of ax. Similarly, God must know everything that is ordered to him because they are ordered to him in the same way that they have *esse* from him. This argument concludes that creation is only possible because of a supremely intelligent being. So, it is not surprising to find Thomas cite the Aristotelian saying, "the work of nature is the work of intelligence," in some versions of the argument.[82] The very order of nature demands divine cognition of that order. Without divine cognition of creatures, unintelligent beings could not tend toward their ends.

It is telling that the Argument from Natural Teleology concludes, "Therefore, God is intelligent." God must know things other than himself intimately, but the argument does not show how God has this knowledge, nor why this knowledge is not contrary to his supreme simplicity. This argument is a good start, but it is incomplete by itself.

---

79. Doolan, *Aquinas on Divine Ideas*, 60.
80. Doolan, *Aquinas on Divine Ideas*, 61.
81. *SCG* I, c. 44 (Leonine, 13.130a14–b11). Cf. *In I Sent.*, d. 35, q. 1, a. 1 (Mandonnet I.809–10); *De veritate*, q. 2, a. 2 (Leonine, 22/1.50:214–51:234); *ST* I, q. 44, a. 3 (Leonine, 4.460); *In I Met.*, lect. 15, n. 233 (Spiazzi, 81).
82. *Auctoritates Aristotelis* (1) XII, nn. 281–82 (Hamesse, 138:84–184:139). See James A. Weisheipl, "The Axiom 'Opus Naturae Est Opus Intelligentiae' and Its Origins," in *Albertus Magnus, Doctor Universalis: 1280/1980*, ed. Gerbert Meyer and Albert Zimmerman (Mainz: Matthias-Grünewald-Verlag, 1980); L. Hödl, "'Opus Naturae Est Opus Intelligentiae.' Ein Neuplatonisches Axiom Im Aristotelischen Verständnis Des Albertus Magnus," in *Averroismus Im Mittelalter Und in Der Renaissance*, ed. F. Niewöhner and L. Sturlese, 132–48 (Zürich: Spur Verlag, 1994).

The Argument from Similitude

The Argument from Similitude works with the Argument from Natural Teleology to explain how God cognizes creatures. In all things not generated by chance, a form must be the end of its generation. An agent would not act because of a form except insofar as a likeness of the form is in him. Such a likeness could be in the agent in two ways. In one way, the form of the thing coming-to-be preexists in the agent according to *esse naturale*, as in agents that act by nature. Man generates man in this way. In some agents, however, the form preexists according to *esse intelligibile*, as in agents that act by intellect. A likeness of a house preexists in the mind of the builder in this way. Such intellectual likenesses are called 'ideas' because the artist intends to assimilate the house to the form conceived in his mind. The world did not come about by chance but was made by God as by an intelligent agent. Therefore, there must be a form to the likeness of which the world was made in the divine mind, and the *ratio* of an idea consists in this. Thus, God must have ideas.[83]

Although they are not stated explicitly in the above version, two of Aquinas's favorite metaphysical principles lay at the heart of this argument: every agent makes something like itself (*omne agens agit sibi simile*), and whatever is received is received according to the mode of the receiver (*quidquid recipitur ad modum recipientis recipitur*).[84] An agent cannot give what it does not have. Thus, the effect must always be like the cause in some way. The form of the effect must preexist in the agent in some way, either through the mode of inherence or through the mode of imitation.[85] He never draws the conclusion explicitly, but to say that God has the forms of possible creatures through the mode of inherence would be tantamount to pantheism. Thus, God must have the forms of possible creatures intellectually through the mode of imitation. They are the exemplar causes in whose imitation he intends to create.[86]

The Argument from Divine Self-Knowledge

The last sort of argument that Aquinas uses to show that God has ideas is the Argument from Divine Self-Knowledge. This argument is likely inspired, at least in part, by Albert the Great.[87] This argument becomes increasingly important for Thomas

---

83. *ST* I, q. 15, a. 1 (Leonine, 4.199), esp.: "Agens autem non ageret propter formam, nisi inquantum similitudo formae est in ipso. . . . Quia igitur mundus non casu factus, sed est factus a Deo per intellectum agente, ut infra patebit, necesse est quod in mente divina sit forma, ad similitudinem cuius mundus est factus. Et in hoc consistit ratio ideae." Cf. *De veritate*, q. 2, a. 3 (Leonine, 22/1.51:235–61); *SCG* I, c. 49 (Leonine, 13.142a11–19).

84. See John F. Wippel, *Metaphysical Themes in Thomas Aquinas II* (Washington, DC: The Catholic University of America Press, 2007), 152–71 and 113–22 for an in-depth look at each principle.

85. *De veritate*, q. 3, a. 1 (Leonine, 22/1.108:156–60). See pp. 56–57.

86. Cf. *Liber de causis*, prop. 7(8), n. 72 (Pattin, 152:6–8): "Omnis intelligentia scit quod est supra se et quod est sub se: verumtamen scit quod est sub se quoniam est causa ei." See pp. 15–16.

87. Albert the Great, *Quaestio de ideis divinis*, a. 2 (Aschendorff, 25/2.266:38–40): "ipse cognoscendo se cognoscit omnia, et ipse uno modo se est ad plura et pauciora et etiam infinite, si essent infinita."

as his career progresses. It does not appear in *In I Sent.* or the *De veritate*. It first appears in the *Summa Contra Gentiles*, and it is Thomas's primary argument in the *Summa theologiae*. Objections to God's knowledge of things other than himself arise because the objectors assume that if God knows things other than himself, that knowledge must originate *ab extra*. If the objectors' conditional is sound, then God's perfection and nobility would be compromised. However, the conditional is not sound. God's perfect knowledge of himself necessarily entails knowledge of all things other than himself. It is manifest that God perfectly understands himself because otherwise, he would not be perfect. If something is cognized perfectly, then its power must be cognized perfectly. Something's power cannot be cognized perfectly unless the things to which its power extends are cognized. Since divine power extends to things other than itself, in that he is the first efficient cause of all beings, he must cognize things other than himself.[88]

The crucial premise in this argument is that perfect knowledge of a being necessarily includes full knowledge of the extent of that being's power. If any of the being's possible effects are unknown, the being is not known perfectly.[89] Since God knows himself perfectly, he must have perfect knowledge of all his possible effects. God is pure act, and so his knowledge of himself is perfectly in act. Perfect knowledge of himself does not inhibit knowledge of things other than himself. His knowledge is not restricted to the universal or made indeterminate. His power extends not only to creatures in general or to the first creature only. Instead, his power extends to every possible creature and every possible aspect and act of those possible creatures. Therefore, he cognizes each thing distinctly.[90] The only source of God's cognition is God himself, but he knows all things other than himself because he knows himself.

Conclusions

Thomas offers three sorts of arguments for the conclusion that God knows things other than himself. The first two arguments, the Argument from Natural Teleology and the Argument from Similitude, form a certain unity for two reasons. First, they argue from the fact of creation. They are, in Thomas's terminology, demonstrations *quia*. They begin from an effect that is more known to us, and they argue to the

---

88. *ST* I, q. 14, a. 5 (Leonine, 4.172): "Si autem perfecte aliquid cognoscitur, necesse est quod virtus eius perfecte cognoscatur. Virtus autem alicuius rei perfecte cognosci non potest, nisi cognoscantur ea ad quae virtus se extendit. Unde, cum virtus divina se extendat ad alia, eo quod ipsa est prima causa efectiva omnium entium, ut supradictis patet; necesse est quod Deus alia a se cognoscat." Cf. *SCG* I, c. 49 (Leonine, 13.142a20–b8); *In XII Met.*, lect. 11, nn. 2602–16 (Spiazzi, 606–8), esp. n. 2615.

89. Both Scotus and Ockham object to this principle. See Scotus, *Rep. Par. I-A*, d. 36, qq. 1–2, n. 20 (Noone, 402:2–4) and Ockham, *Ord.*, d. 35, q. 2 (OTh IV.436:10–439:9). Knowledge of the full extent of a being's power, they claim, does not necessarily entail knowing its possible effects. Nevertheless, Ockham does think this is the strongest argument that reason can offer. See p. 237.

90. See *In Liber de causis*, prop. 1–3 (Saffrey, 4–25); *SCG* III, c. 67 (Leonine, 14.190); *ST* I, q. 105, a. 5 (Leonine, 5.475–76); *De potentia*, q. 3, a. 7 (Pession, II.55a–59b).

necessity of a cause.[91] Given the way the world is, it must be the case that God knows creatures through divine ideas. Divine ideas are the only way to account for the way the world is. Second, neither argument is sufficient to prove that God has ideas of possible creatures that God will never create. At best, these arguments can show that God must have exemplar forms of the things he does create at some time in history. Neither argument can show that God has ideas in the sense of reasons (*rationes*). It does not follow from the fact that God has exemplar forms of the things that he creates that he also has reasons of the things that he could have created but did not.

The Argument from Divine Self-Knowledge is unlike the other two arguments on both points. First, it argues from cause to effect, that is, it argues from the knowledge of divine power to possible effects of divine power. God's will to create is contingent, but that he can create is necessary.[92] Second, this argument shows that God has ideas of all possible creatures, not merely actual creatures. Put another way, it shows that God must have reasons in addition to exemplars. This argument defends the claim that God could have created otherwise than he did. The other two arguments do not defend this claim.

The Unity and Multiplicity of Divine Ideas

Aquinas faces a difficulty regarding the unity and multiplicity of divine ideas. It is not apparent how to reconcile a multiplicity of divine ideas with divine simplicity. It is also not clear how to reconcile numerically one divine idea with God's perfect knowledge. Like Bonaventure, Aquinas argues that there is just one divine idea and that there are many divine ideas using two crucial distinctions. The first distinction concerns the form that is the principle (*principium*) of God's knowledge and the forms that are the terms (*termini*) of God's knowledge.[93] The second distinction concerns types of relations and the way that they are known. This section will investigate Thomas's position on the unity and multiplicity of divine ideas, and then examine the theory of relations underpinning that position.

Note that Aquinas's discussion of ideas in this section concerns what I called the first moment in establishing the character of an idea.[94] The discussion about the unity and multiplicity of divine ideas is logically prior to the question of according to which ideas God creates. The question is whether God can have many *rationes* in the first place. As a result, Thomas speaks in terms of God's imitability, not how he is actually imitated. Aquinas's shift to emphasize divine exemplars does not affect the teaching in this section.

---

91. For the distinction between a demonstration *quia* and a demonstration *propter quid*, see *ST* I, q. 2, a. 2 (Leonine, 4.30).
92. See Doolan, *Aquinas on Divine Ideas*, 158. Recall that Bonaventure makes the same point. See p. 19.
93. He also expresses this distinction as the *quo* and the *quod* of divine knowledge.
94. See pp. 58–59.

The Multiplicity of Divine Ideas

Aquinas articulates his position in response to an error of Avicenna, who argues that God has one intention, namely, creatures in general. God knows creatures insofar as they are beings. Every distinction among creatures occurs through secondary causes, and as a result, God is only the immediate cause of one creature: the first intelligence. The first intelligence has three distinct acts of knowing: it knows God as its cause, itself as contingent through itself, and itself as necessary through another. These three acts of knowing result in the production of three creatures, namely, its soul, its celestial body, and another intelligence. This second intelligence has the same three acts and produces the third intellect, and so on until the tenth intelligence, the agent intellect, which produces the material world.[95] On this theory, God has only one general idea for all creatures. The proper ideas of singulars are in secondary causes.[96]

Aquinas says Avicenna's position is unsound for two reasons. First, it commits the metaphysical error of making the distinctions between creatures a result of chance. Second, it commits the epistemological error of making God's knowledge confused. As to the first, Thomas argues that the distinction among things cannot be by chance because they exhibit a certain order.[97] Moreover, if an agent's intention is drawn to one thing, then whatever else follows will be beyond his intention because it happens to the thing that is principally intended by him. If the agent's intention is only to something general, then however it is determined through something specific will be beyond his intention. If nature intended to generate only an animal, it would be beyond nature's intention for a man or horse to come to be. So, if God's intention in acting relates only to a creature in general, all distinctions among creatures happen by chance. It is unfitting to say that the distinction of creatures is *per accidens* for God, the first cause, yet *per se* for secondary causes because what is *per se* is prior to that which is *per accidens*.[98] Consequently, we must say that God predefines the whole distinction of things, and therefore it is necessary to posit proper reasons (*rationes*) of things. It further follows that we must posit many ideas in God.[99]

Concerning Avicenna's epistemological error, Thomas says that if God had but one idea, then his knowledge would be in potency and so imperfect. The intellect performs a perfect act of understanding when it knows the thing distinctly and determinately. In an imperfect act of understanding, which is imperfect knowledge, the intellect knows things indistinctly and under a certain confusion. To cognize a thing indistinctly is to understand a genus without also understanding the species. Thus, "to know *animal* indistinctly is to know it insofar as it is *animal*. But to know *animal*

---

95. Avicenna, *Met.*, IX, c. 8 (van Riet, II.476:40–488:95). See also Algazel, *Met.*, p. 1, tr. 5 (Muckle, 119–29).
96. *De veritate*, q. 3, a. 2 (Leonine, 22/1.103:108–21); *SCG* I, c. 50 (Leonine, 13.144a1–9).
97. *SCG* I, q. 50 (Leonine, 13.144a40–41).
98. For more on this principle, see *Liber de causis*, prop. 1, nn. 12–17 (Pattin, 136:39–137:62).
99. *De veritate*, q. 3, a. 2 (Leonine, 22/1.103:126–104:157); *SCG* I, c. 50 (Leonine, 13.144).

distinctly is to know it insofar as it is *rational animal* or *irrational animal*."[100] If God only knew creatures generally as beings and not in their distinctions, he would be most foolish.[101] Since nothing imperfect should be attributed to God, God should not be said to have merely general knowledge of creatures through just one idea.[102]

These arguments show that God must have many ideas, but they do not show how to account for such a multiplicity. At every stage of his career, Thomas insists as part of his answer to this question that a divine idea is not merely the divine essence, but rather the divine essence as understood.[103] The divine essence is the source of divine ideas, but divine ideas are not the divine essence qua essence. They are, as it were, the result of an act of divine knowledge. Knowledge occurs because there is a form in the intellect, which form Aquinas frequently calls an intelligible species (*species intelligiblis*).[104] The phrase "a form in the intellect" (*forma in intellectu*) has two meanings. First, the form is the principle (*principium; forma faciens* in the terminology of the *Summa theologiae*) of the act of understanding, the species by which the knower knows, the form making him understand in act. God's only form as principle is his essence. He does not acquire knowledge *ab extra*, otherwise, he would be in potency and so not be God. Second, the form is the term (*terminus; forma intellecta* in the terminology of the *Summa theologiae*) of the act of understanding; it is that which is understood. Such a form occurs when the artist thinks out (*excogitat*) or discovers (*adinvenit*) something, and the thing known is, as it were, brought about by the act.[105]

---

100. *ST* I, q. 83, a. 3 (Leonine, 5.336b): "Sicut cognoscere animal indistincte, est cognoscere animal inquantum est animal; cognoscere autem animal distincte, est cognoscere animal inquantum est animal rationale vel irrationale." See *In I Phys.*, lect. 1, n. 7 (Leonine, 2.5).

101. *SCG* I, c. 50 (Leonine, 13.145b1–3); *ST* I, q. 14, a. 6 (Leonine, 4.176a).

102. *De veritate*, q. 2, a. 4, s.c. 2 (Leonine, 22/1.56:104–9).

103. *In I Sent.*, d. 36, q. 2, ad 1 (Mandonnet, I.842); *De veritate*, q. 3, a. 2 (Leonine, 22/1.104:183–88); *ST* I, q. 15, a. 2 (Leonine, 4.202a).

104. *ST* I, q. 85, aa. 1–2 (Leonine, 5.330–35). The Aristotelian source for this teaching can be found, *inter alia*, in *De anima* III, cc. 4–8 and *Post. An.* II, c. 19. The most comprehensive account of intelligible species is Leen Spruit, Species intelligibilis: *From Perception to Knowledge*, 2 vols. (Leiden: Brill, 1994).

105. *De veritate*, q. 3, a. 2 (Leonine, 22/1.104:158–67), esp.: "Forma enim in intellectu dupliciter esse potest. Uno modo ita quod sit principium actus intelligendi, sicut forma quae est intelligentis in quantum est intelligens, et haec est similitudo intellecti in ipso; alio modo ita quod sit terminus actus intelligendi." See also *SCG* I, c. 53 (Leonine, 13.150–51); *ST* I, q. 15, a. 2 (Leonine, 4.202a); Quodlibet IV, q. 1, a. 1 (Leonine, 25/2/319–20). *Excogitat* appears in *In I Sent.*, d. 39, q. 1, a. 2, ad 1 (Mandonnet, I.923); *De veritate*, q. 2, a. 8; q. 3, aa. 2–3 (Leonine, 22/1.70:64, 104:165–67, and 107:97); *ST* I, q. 44, a. 3 (Leonine, 4.460). *Adinvenit* appears in *De veritate*, q. 3, a. 2, ad 6 (Leonine, 22/1.105:180–82).

There is a dispute over when Aquinas begins implementing this distinction between form as principle and form as term. Geiger and Farthing argue that while Thomas presents the distinction in the *De veritate*, he does not begin using it until the *SCG*. The distinction "is toyed with for just a tantalizing moment before Thomas proceeds to pursue the argument along quite different lines" (Farthing, "Problem of Divine Exemplarity," 205; Geiger, "Les Idées Divines," 197). Wippel argues that Aquinas uses the distinction in the *De veritate*. Thomas's emphasis on divine ideas as the divine essence being co-understood with the diverse proportions to things is evidence that he is using the distinction (Wippel, *Divine Ideas*, 19). I think Wippel is correct because Thomas emphasizes that knowing the divine essence

When God understands his essence, he does not merely understand the essence itself. He also understands it insofar as creatures can participate in it according to some mode of likeness.[106] God understands his essence to be imitable in a certain way and understands the creature by understanding that mode of imitation. No creature imitates God perfectly, and none of these modes of imitation suffices for perfect knowledge of another mode. God has distinct knowledge of all possible creatures only when he understands his essence along with all these modes. "The divine essence itself," Thomas says, "with the diverse proportions of things to it being co-understood, is the idea of each thing."[107] Aquinas explains God's understanding of these proportions in some detail in the *Summa Contra Gentiles*.

> The divine intellect can comprehend in its essence what is proper to each thing by understanding in what his essence is imitated and in what each one falls short of his perfection. For example, by understanding his essence as imitable through the mode of life and not the mode of cognition, he receives the proper form of *plant*; if by understanding his essence as imitable through the mode of cognition and not the mode of understanding, he receives the proper form of *animal*. And so on for other forms.[108]

Since there are many proportions, God has many ideas.[109] Therefore, divine ideas are both one and many. There is just one idea from the perspective of the divine essence because the divine essence is the only source of God's knowledge. There are many divine ideas from the perspective of the diverse proportions of creatures to the divine essence.

There are three points to make about Thomas's conclusion. The first point is that terms like *excogitat* and *adinvenit* might give the impression that God is discovering *de novo* the ways that the divine essence is imitable, but that is not what Thomas means. He means to emphasize that God knows all the ways he could be imitated before he wills to create according to some of those possible imitations. The character of a divine idea is completed by the divine will's choice to create according to this possible imitation (or not), but the divine will is not willing in the absence of knowledge. By saying that divine ideas are 'discovered,' Aquinas is

---

alone is insufficient to claim that there are many ideas. Only when God understands the divine essence and the various possible relations of imitation are there many divine ideas. Thomas can only refer to the divine essence along with the relation because he has distinguished two ways of understanding a form in the intellect.

106. *In I Sent.*, d. 36, q. 2, a. 2 (Mandonnet, I.842); *De veritate*, q. 3, a. 2 (Leonine, 22/1.104:188–93); *SCG* I, c. 54 (Leonine, 155a6–10); *ST* I, q. 15, a. 2 (Leonine, 4.202a).

107. *De veritate*, q. 3, a. 2 (Leonine, 22/1.105:213–15): "Et ideo ipsa divina essentia, cointellectis diversis proportionibus rerum ad eam, est idea uniuscuiusque rei."

108. *SCG* I, c. 54 (Leonine, 13.155a6–15): "Intellectus igitur divinus id quod est proprium unicuique in essentia sua comprehendere potest, intelligendo in quo eius essentiam imitetur, et in quo ab eius perfectione deficit unumquodque: utpote, intelligendo essentiam suam ut imitabilem per modum vitae et non cognitionis, accipit propriam formam plantae; si vero ut imitabilem per modum cognitionis et non intellectus, propriam formam animalis; et sic de aliis."

109. *SCG* I, c. 50 (Leonine, 13.155b1–19); *ST* I, q. 15, a. 2 (Leonine, 4.202a).

avoiding voluntarism. The divine essence and God's knowledge of it dictate the ways God is imitable. God does not have divine ideas merely because he wills to have them, but because he knows himself completely. Divine ideas are in the divine intellect, and then some are chosen by the divine will.[110]

Moreover, the term 'discovers' (*adinvenit*) is particularly critical for Aquinas. It brings together principles found in two of his arguments for the existence of divine ideas, namely the Argument from Similitude and the Argument from Divine Self-Knowledge.[111] In his Argument from Divine Self-Knowledge, Thomas emphasizes that a being is only known perfectly if the full extent of its power is known. When the divine intellect knows the divine essence, it discovers, as it were, the perfection of the divine essence. The divine intellect discovers the perfections of every possible creature in the divine essence because, as Aquinas emphasizes in his Argument from Similitude, whatever perfection is in an effect must be found in its efficient cause. Since God is the cause of every creaturely perfection, all those perfections must be in him.

In *Summa theologiae* I, q. 4, a. 2, Aquinas distinguishes two ways perfections preexist in their causes. In one way, a perfection exists according to the same character in a univocal cause, as when a man generates a man. In another way, a perfection exists more eminently in an equivocal cause.[112] A univocal agent is the sort of thing it generates. An equivocal agent is not the sort of thing it can generate. Instead, an equivocal agent has the power to produce the form in the first place. Edward Feser explains this distinction using the example of money. A univocal agent can give someone a $20 bill because he has a $20 bill in his wallet. An equivocal cause has $20 in a more eminent way because he can produce $20 in the first place.[113] In this example, the US Bureau of Engraving and Printing is an equivocal cause. Since God is the first efficient cause of things, the perfections of things must preexist in him more eminently. This distinction between univocal and equivocal causes is parallel to the distinction that Bonaventure draws between assimilation by essence and assimilation by likeness.[114] Univocal causes are the sorts of things they cause by essence. Equivocal causes have the likeness of what they cause.

The second point is that Thomas's conclusion that there are many ideas insofar as God knows his essence along with the diverse ways in which it can be imitated tacitly makes use of his theory of *esse*. When Thomas says that the divine essence

---

110. The fact that the divine will chooses some, not all, divine ideas raises the question of the status of the ideas that God does not choose. See pp. 76–78.

111. See pp. 63–64.

112. *ST* I, q. 4, a. 2 (Leonine, 4.51b–52a). See *ST* I, q. 104, a. 1 (Leonine, 5.464); *ST* I, q. 115, a. 1 (Leonine, 5.539–40); Doolan, *Aquinas on Divine Ideas*, 171–73.

113. Feser, *Scholastic Metaphysics: A Contemporary Introduction* (Heusenstamm: Editiones Scholasticae, 2014), 171–72. Feser includes a third distinction: having something virtually. Someone has a $20 bill virtually if he can get a $20 bill. Perhaps there is no $20 bill in his wallet, but he has at least $20 in the bank. He could write a check for $20. The recipient of that check could take it to the bank and exchange it for a $20 bill.

114. See p. 15.

is imitable in many ways, he refers to the ways finite beings can *exist*. "An idea," he says, "properly speaking, relates to the thing according as it is producible in *esse*."[115] As Boland emphasizes, "the uniquely proper *esse* of each single thing is the ultimate explanation of the plurality of ideas which are *creativae et productae rerum*."[116] Because the *esse*, understood as the *actus essendi*, of each singular thing is really distinct from the *actus essendi* of every other being, God has to know and produce each *actus essendi* distinctly.[117] This theory of *esse* explains why there have to be many divine ideas and, as we will see in detail below, it explains why, properly speaking, there are only divine exemplars of singulars.[118]

The third point is that Aquinas's theory of divine ideas differs from Bonaventure's theory only in emphasis. Since Bonaventure stresses that divine truth is expressive of itself, and Thomas stresses that the divine essence is imitated in diverse ways, many scholars argue that the two accounts are irreconcilably different.[119] The two accounts are not identical, but that conclusion makes Bonaventure and Thomas appear more dissimilar than they are. Thomas does prefer to speak of God's essence as opposed to truth, but he always emphasizes that he is speaking of the divine essence *as understood*. But the divine essence as understood *is* the divine truth.[120] So for Aquinas, the plurality of divine ideas is just as much a result of the supreme expressivity of divine truth as it is for Bonaventure. The difference is a matter of emphasis. Bonaventure's account emphasizes God's fecundity, which follows from his pure actuality, whereas Thomas's account emphasizes the fullness of the divine essence as containing eminently all possible creatures. Thomas's account also affords him an occasion to expound his theory of participation.

Divine Ideas as Rational Relations

Aquinas insists that divine ideas are many insofar as God understands his essence and the diverse ways in which possible creatures can imitate him. Possible creatures imitate (or participate in) the divine essence by having a certain real relation to God. When God knows how a particular creature could imitate him, what he knows is the relation of that thing to his essence. God is not really related to

---

115. *De veritate*, q. 3, a. 5 (Leonine, 22/1.112:43–44). See also, *De veritate*, q. 3, a. 8, s.c. and ad 2 (Leonine, 22/1.115:35–36 and 116:74–76). Recall that in the *De veritate*, an idea "properly speaking" is an exemplar known with *actu practica* or *virtute practica* knowledge. Thus, 'producible' is the right term in that text. In *Summa theologiae*, "produced at some time" would replace 'producible.'

116. Boland, *Ideas in God*, 209–10; See Vincent P. Branick, "The Unity of the Divine Ideas," *The New Scholasticism* 42, no. 2 (1968): 189–90: "To say that the ideas represent God, at least in some proportion, is to say the ideas represent the act of *to be*, for God is this act." Emphasis original.

117. See *In De Trinitate*, q. 4, a. 1 (Leonine, 50.121:118–23); *De veritate*, q. 2, a. 3, ad 16 (Leonine, 22/1.54:508–10). The teaching in these early texts coheres with his teaching in *ST* I, q. 15, a. 3, ad 4 (Leonine, 4.204b).

118. See pp. 78–81.

119. See, e.g., Bissen, *L'exemplarisme Divin*, 29–31; Cullen, "Semiotic Metaphysics," 163–65.

120. See, *inter alia*, *De veritate* q. 1, a. 7 (Leonine, 22.1.25:27–37); *De veritate* q. 1, a. 1 (Leonine, 22.1.5:159–161); Wippel, *Metaphysical Themes II*, 65–112.

creatures, yet "those respects are in him as understood by him."¹²¹ A divine idea, then, is fundamentally a known relation.¹²² It is the possibly real relation that God knows he could establish between himself and a possible creature. Such a relation is a rational relation on God's part—not a real relation—because the intellect establishes it. It will be necessary to examine Aquinas's theory of relations briefly to understand this position more fully. I will first examine the character of a relation. Then, I will distinguish three sorts of relations. Finally, I will apply these distinctions to divine ideas.

Relation is one of the nine accidental categories of being. Aquinas holds that relations exist in reality because "natural things have an order and relatedness to each other."¹²³ Relations are not merely the result of a mental act.¹²⁴ As he does with any accident, Aquinas distinguishes between the being (*esse*) and the character (*ratio*) of a relation. The *esse* of a relation is analogically the same as the *esse* of any other sort of accident: to be "a thing to which it belongs to exist in another."¹²⁵ It belongs to every accident, then, to exist in some substance or in some accident that exists in a substance. For Aquinas, real relations exist in the latter condition. Every real relation exists because of another accident existing in a subject. For example,

---

121. *De veritate*, q. 3, a. 2, ad 8 (Leonine, 22/1.106.300–301): "respectus illi sunt in Deo ut intellecti ab ipso." See also *De veritate*, q. 2, a. 9, ad 4 (Leonine, 22/1.74:258–66); *ST* I, q. 15, a. 2, ad 4 (Leonine, 4.202b).

122. Hoenen says that this is not St. Thomas's position (*Marsilius of Inghen*, 123). According to Hoenen, Aquinas thinks that God does not know creatures mediately through ideas. Instead, "As we saw in the previous chapter [sc. Chapter 4], Thomas believed that God has immediate knowledge of individual things in his essence" (123). However, Hoenen does not argue for this position in the previous chapter. He educes three of Aquinas's arguments that show *that* God knows creatures, but he does not discuss whether that knowledge of creatures is immediate in the essence or mediate through ideas (63–64). This claim is not enough to change my mind about how Aquinas's claim that "ipsa divina essentia, cointellectis diversis proportionibus rerum ad eam, est idea uniuscuiusque rei" should be understood (*De veritate*, q. 3, a. 2 [Leonine, 22/1.105:213–15]). Aquinas insists that it is the *proportions*, i.e., the *relations* of the things to God that are co-understood, not the creatures themselves that are co-understood.

In the absence of an argument for the position, all I can say is that if Hoenen is right, Aquinas does not hold the Imitability Theory. Instead, he holds the *Creatura Intellecta* Theory because the defining characteristic of that theory is that God's knowledge of possible creatures is logically prior to his knowledge of the rational relation that exists from God to the possible creature. See p. 147 and Chapter VII on Bl. John Duns Scotus.

123. *ST* I, q. 13, a. 7 (Leonine, 4.152b): "ipsae res naturalem ordinem et habitudinem habent ad invicem."

124. Mark Henninger calls Aquinas's position a "qualified realist" position. It is distinguished from the strongly realist position of someone like Scotus in that "one need not posit any further entity" that has "its own accidental reality really distinct from that of its foundation." (*Relations: Medieval Theories 1250–1325* [Oxford: Oxford University Press, 1989], 25). For a complete account of Aquinas's theory of real relations, see Henninger, *Relations*, 23–29.

125. *In IV Sent.*, d. 12, q. 1, a. 1, ql. 1, ad 2 (Moos, 4.499): "res cui debetur esse in alio." This description is not a proper definition because there is no higher genus to which we could refer when defining a category of being. See Wippel, *Metaphysical Thought*, 225–37, esp. 234–37; Étienne Gilson, "Quasi Definitio Substantiae," in *St. Thomas Aquinas, 1274–1974, Commemorative Studies*, ed. Armand Maurer, vol. 1, 111–29 (Toronto: Pontifical Institute of Mediaeval Studies Press, 1974).

the real relation "taller than" is founded upon the quantity of height existing in a subject relative to the quantity of height existing in another subject.

The *ratio* of a thing is "nothing other than what the intellect apprehends from the signification of some name."[126] If the thing can be defined, then the *ratio* is its definition. If it cannot be defined, as is the case with the categories, the *ratio* is just what our intellect grasps correctly about the thing.[127] The *ratio* of the category of relation is "only a respect (*respectus*) to another."[128] This category is unique in that it is characterized by mere relatedness, which does not necessarily inhere in something else, that is, the *ratio* of a relation can occur without the *esse* of a relation. A relation does not have to inhere in a subject. Categorical real relations must inhere in a subject, but rational relations and divine relations do not need to have such an inherence.[129]

The fact that the *ratio* of a relation can occur without its *esse* leads Thomas to distinguish between real relations and rational relations. A relation is real when it is founded upon some real accident in the subject of the relation. In a real relation, both the *esse* and *ratio* of relation are present. Furthermore, because the *esse* of relation is present, the relation exists independent of any intellectual activity. Conversely, a rational relation arises because of some intellectual activity. The *ratio* of relation is found in a rational relation, but not the *esse*.

Since each relation has two extremes (or terms), there are three possible ways that extremes can be related to one another. In one way, both extremes are rationally related to each other. In this case, the relatedness of the two can only exist by an intellectual act as when we say that something is the same as itself. Relations between being and non-being and between genus and species are always rational relations. In the second way, both extremes are really related to each other. Mutually real relations are found in all relations in the categories of quantity, and action and passion.[130] Relations between quantities are always real because they are founded in the quantities that both extremes have. Simmias is taller than Socrates because Simmias has more quantity of height than Socrates. Relations in the categories of action and passion are always real because both extremes are part of the action. The patient receives the action of the agent such that each has its character because of the other. The father is the father because of the son, and the son is son because of the father.[131]

---

126. *In I Sent.*, d. 2, q. 1, a. 3 (Mandonnet, I.66): "ratio, prout hic sumitur, nihil aliud est quam id quod apprehendit intellectus de significatione alicuius nominis."

127. See Henninger, *Relations*, 15.

128. *ST* I, q. 28, a. 1 (Leonine, 4.318b): "solum respectum ad aliud." See Jeffrey E. Brower, "Aristotelian vs Contemporary Perspectives on Relations," in *The Metaphysics of Relations*, ed. Anna Marmadoro and David Yates (New York: Oxford University Press, 2016), 40: "relations are that *in virtue of which* two (or more) things are related." Emphasis original.

129. *In I Sent.* d. 26, q. 2, a. 1 (Mandonnet, I.630).

130. *De potentia*, q. 7, a. 9 (Pession, II.208a); *In III Phys.*, lect. 1, n. 6 (Leonine, 2.102–3); *In V Met.*, lect. 17, nn. 1001–5 (Spiazzi, 226).

131. *ST* I, q. 13, a. 7 (Leonine, 4.152b–53a).

The third way the extremes can relate is when the relation is real for one extreme and rational for the other. Such relations occur when the extremes are not of the same order. Following Aristotle, Aquinas uses the example of the way the senses and knowledge are related to what is sensible and knowable.[132] The sensible and knowable exist in different ways in the thing and the knower. In the thing, they exist according to natural being. In the knower, they exist according to sensible or intelligible being (*esse sensibilis vel intelligibilis*).[133] The form of red is in the thing according to *esse naturale* such that the thing is red, but it is in the knower according to *esse sensibilis vel intelligiblis* such that he sees and knows red without becoming red. Natural being is not of the same order as sensible or intelligible being. Thus, the thing itself is only rationally related to the knower because the intellect understands the thing to be the term of the relation of its knowledge. The knower is really related to the thing because his knowledge depends upon the thing. The thing measures the knower's knowledge and is in no way measured by it.[134] There would be no real change in the thing if the knower ceased knowing it. Finally, the rational relation is not said to be in the thing known because it is related to other things, but rather because other things are related to it.[135]

Aquinas's theory of divine ideas uses the distinction between the *esse* and *ratio* of a relation and the distinction of a relation that is real for one extreme and rational for the other. God is subsisting being itself (*ipsum esse subsistens*), and creatures have created being. Since subsisting being itself cannot be created, God and creatures cannot be in the same order. Moreover, every creature depends entirely on God's intellect and will, and God's knowledge measures it. Therefore, creatures are really related to God, but God is not really related to creatures.[136] Divine ideas, then, are only rational relations in God.[137]

Since divine ideas are rational relations, they are not contrary to divine simplicity in any way. Divine ideas are many because many things are potentially related to God, not because God is really related to a creature. The multiplication of rational relations does not affect simplicity.[138] God can know an infinite number

---

132. Aristotle, *Met.* V, c. 15, 1021a27–b3 (AL XXV.3.2.112:573–114:629).

133. Aquinas occasionally prefers the term *esse spirituale* instead of *esse sensibilis* or *esse intelligibilis*. See, e.g., *In I Sent.*, d. 30, q. 1, a. 3 (Mandonnet, I.708); *ST* I, q. 78, a. 3 (Leonine, 5.254a). For a discussion of *esse spirituale*, see Han Thomas Adriaenssen, *Representation and Scepticism from Aquinas to Descartes* (New York: Cambridge University Press, 2017), 17–18.

134. *De veritate*, q. 1, a. 2 (Leonine, 22/1.9:81–120). Thomas notes that the thing measures knowledge only in cases of speculative knowledge. In the case of practical knowledge, knowledge measures the thing done or produced by the knowledge.

135. *ST* I, q. 13, a. 7 (Leonine, 4.153a), esp.: "est aliqua relatio . . . secundum rationem tantum, inquantum intellectus apprehendit ea ut terminus relationum scientiae et sensus."

136. *ST* I, q. 13, a. 7 (Leonine, 4.153a); *De potentia*, q. 7, a. 10 (Pession, II.209a–211b); *De potentia*, q. 7, a. 8, ad 3 (Pession. II.206b).

137. *ST* I, q. 13, a. 7 (Leonine, 4.153a), esp.: "in Deo non est aliqua realis relatio eius ad creaturas, sed secundum rationem tantum, inquantum creaturae referuntur ad ipsum." See *In I Sent.*, d. 30, q. 1, a. 3 (Mandonnet, I.707).

138. *De veritate*, q. 2, a. 9, ad 4 (Leonine, 22/1.74:264–66); *De veritate*, q. 3, a. 8, ad 1 (Leonine, 22/1.116:71–73). In both texts, Aquinas refers to Avicenna, *Met.* III, c. 10 (van Riet, I.182:80–82).

of possible real relations that creatures could have to him without becoming composite. Divine ideas are only logically distinct. While the possible creatures known by them have diverse real relations to God, God knows all these possible relations in the single act of knowing his essence.

As a final note, Thomas's articulation of divine ideas as rational relations also allows him to distinguish the multiplicity of divine ideas from the multiplicity of Divine Persons. Thomas argues that the four relations between the Persons of the Trinity (paternity, filiation, procession, and spiration) are real relations in God. If they were not really in God, then God would only be Father, Son, and Holy Spirit by our understanding alone, which is the Sabellian heresy.[139] The relations between the Divine Persons are real because each of the Persons is of the same order. Each has the same nature, and so the relations are real. Since divine ideas are neither of the same order as that to which they are related, nor are they real relations founded in the identity of the divine nature, they could not constitute additional Divine Persons.

The Existence of Things in God and Non-Existing Possibles

The last aspect of the status of divine ideas to consider is the question of the existence of things in God. Do things exist in God, namely, in their divine ideas? Do things exist more truly in their proper natures or their divine ideas? Do divine ideas have any existence other than being known by God? This topic is difficult because of those things that God could have made but never did—non-existing possibles. God knows them, but he never wills to create them. What sort of existence could such a possible being have?

The Existence of Things in God

Thomas begins his determination of the existence that things have in God by examining the preposition 'in.' To exist in God's knowledge (*in scientia Dei*), to exist in God (*in Deo esse*), and to exist in the divine essence (*esse in divina essentia*) are each distinct from the others. Concerning the first—to exist in God's knowledge—'knowledge' names a certain cognition. It follows that to exist in knowledge is nothing other than to be known through knowledge. Thus, everything that God knows, both the good and the evil, is said to exist in his knowledge. Concerning the third—to exist in the divine essence—'essence' is signified through the mode of form or nature. Consequently, to exist in the divine essence is nothing other than to subsist in the divine nature, or to be the same as the divine nature. Creatures cannot be in God as in his essence. Only the divine Persons, properties, and attributes exist in God's essence. Concerning the second—to exist in God—the name "God" signifies a subsisting thing whose being is also his operating. To be in God can be understood in two ways: (1) either that something is in his *esse*, or (2) that it is subject to his action. Creatures are not in God according to (1), but they are in God according to

---

139. *ST* I, q. 28, a. 1 (Leonine, 4.318a).

(2) in the same way that we say that works of which we are master are in us. According to (2), all the things that are from God are said to exist in him.[140]

The analysis of the word 'in' allows Thomas to draw two conclusions. First, whatever is in the divine essence is in God, but this claim is not convertible. For example, that which is subject to God's action exists in him, but not in his essence. The reason for this is that things are said to be in God insofar as they are contained and conserved by divine power. So even though a creature exists in its proper nature, it is still in God. However, it cannot be in its proper nature and in his essence at the same time. Second, whatever is in God is in his knowledge, but this claim is also not convertible. God knows everything in his essence, but he also knows evil things, which are not in his essence.[141]

God's knowledge extends beyond what is in God, and what is in God extends beyond what is in his essence. Thus, things exist in God, and "they exist in God through their proper *rationes*."[142] A divine idea is the *ratio* in God by which God knows a creature. Therefore, things exist in God precisely because God has a divine idea of them. Now everything that exists does so in the mode of that in which it is. It follows that a thing exists in God in the way that divine knowledge exists in God. God's understanding is his existence (*esse*), so things as they exist in God have God's existence. God's existence is his life, and so all things in God enjoy the divine life.[143] Creatures enjoy uncreated existence in God.

Creatures enjoy existence both in their proper natures and in God, but which sort of existence is truer? There is no straightforward answer to this question for Aquinas. On the one hand, uncreated existence is surely truer than created existence. On the other hand, it is truer for a thing to exist in its proper nature than in its likeness. The likenesses of things enjoying uncreated existence are in God; in themselves, the proper nature of things enjoy created existence. Thomas admits that if the *ratio* of natural things did not include matter and were form alone, then they would exist in a truer mode in every respect in the divine mind through their ideas than in their proper nature. This error in thinking about natures made Plato posit that the separated Form of Man is the true man, whereas a material man is a man by participation.

Since matter does belong to the character of natural things, Thomas makes a distinction between the natural thing's having *esse* and its having *this esse* (*esse hoc*). By *this esse*, he means the existence of a man or a horse. Natural things have truer *esse* absolutely in the divine mind than in themselves because they have uncreated being (*esse increatum*) in the divine mind and created being (*esse creatum*) in their proper natures. Concerning *hoc esse*, Thomas says that things have truer *esse* in

---

140. *In I Sent.*, d. 36, q. 1, a. 3 (Mandonnet, I.836). This paragraph follows Aquinas's order in considering the third point before the second point.
141. *In I Sent.*, d. 36, q. 1, a. 3 (Mandonnet, I.836). Cf. *ST* I, q. 18, a. 4, ad 1 (Leonine, 4.229b–30a).
142. *ST* I, q. 18, q. 4, ad 1 (Leonine, 4.230a): "sunt in Deo per proprias rationes."
143. *De veritate*, q. 4, a. 8 (Leonine, 22/1.135:36–136:75); *ST* I, q. 18, a. 4 (Leonine, 4.229b).

their proper nature than in the divine mind because material existence (*esse materiale*) pertains to the truth of man's nature. However, man does not exist materially in God's mind. The same is true for the existence of a house. It has a more noble existence (*esse*) in the builder's mind, but the house is still more truly called a house when it is in matter than in the mind because it is a house in act when it exists in matter and a house in potency when it exists in the builder's mind.[144] Here it is worth recalling that divine ideas are not the things themselves. As Doolan says, "The divine Idea that God has of me is *not* me."[145] Since the divine idea of me is not really me, not everything predicable of me is predicable of the divine idea of me, especially material existence.

The last thing to note before turning to the question of non-existing possibles is that divine ideas do not have any existence independent of their being thought by God. Thomas insists that "whatever is cognized has to exist in some way, at least in the one knowing it."[146] Being thought is a sort of being, so the objects of God's thought have to have some sort of being, and that being is uncreated. God bestows uncreated existence upon divine ideas because of his supreme simplicity. From the fact that divine ideas enjoy God's very existence, it does not follow that they have any existence of their own. If they did, then that existence would have to have some sort of finite, created existence. Since divine ideas initially arise because of the action of the divine intellect, independent of any action of the divine will, if divine ideas had any created existence of their own, then they would be created without the election of the divine will. Creation would be a necessary emanation from God, not a free act of love.[147]

Possibles

The question of the way non-existing possibles exist in God raises a particular difficulty. Given that such possible beings do not actually exist, it would seem like they should not exist in God. Since such creatures do not exist, James Ross argues that "the 'maximum degree of reality' for a thing before its creation, I say, is *none* at all (*De potentia Dei* 3,5 ad 2). The possibility 'before creation' is not the reality of me, but of God's ability to make things. God sees what might be '*not in themselves but*

---

144. *ST* I, q. 18, a. 4, ad 3 (Leonine, 4.230), esp.: "in mente divina habent esse increatum, in seipsis autem esse creatum.... ad veritatem hominis pertinet esse materiale, quod non habent in mente divina." Cf. *De veritate*, q. 4, a. 6, co and ad 1 (Leonine, 22/1.133:51–134:85), where Aquinas expresses the same teaching in terms of the distinction between ontological truth (*veritas rei*) and logical truth (*veritas propositionis*). Doolan defends that these two texts have the same teaching ("The Really Real," 1078–81). For Aquinas's theory of truth, see Wippel, "Truth in Thomas Aquinas," *Metaphysical Themes II*, 65–112.

145. Doolan, "The Really Real," 1086. Emphasis original.

146. *In I Sent.*, d. 38, q. 1, a. 4 (Mandonnet, I.905): "quidquid cognoscitur, aliquo modo oportet esse, ad minus in ipso cognoscente."

147. *In I Sent.*, d. 35, q. 1, a. 3 (Mandonnet, I.814); *In I Sent.*, d. 43, q. 2, a. 1 (Mandonnet, I.1007–9); *De veritate*, q. 23, a. 4 (Leonine, 22/3.660–65); *De potentia*, q. 1, a. 5 (Pession, 17–20); *ST* I, q. 19, a. 3 (Leonine, 4.234–35). The traditional reading of Henry of Ghent falls into this error. See pp. 182–87.

in himself (*ST* I,14,5c).”¹⁴⁸ Before God creates them, possible beings themselves have no ontological status. Ross, therefore, denies that non-existing possibles have any ontological status.

Ross's objection rightly points out that divine ideas are God's knowledge of a relation, not the creature itself. As a result, the creatures themselves that God creates according to divine ideas do not have any existence independent of God before God wills to create them. Nevertheless, the objection misses the point for two reasons. First, it ignores that possible creatures are in God's understanding. Second, it ignores an important distinction that Thomas makes in the term "possible."

First, God's understanding is identical to his existence and his living. God's understanding includes knowing all the possible real relations that creatures could have to him. By knowing the relation, God's knowledge extends to the creature, meaning the creature is included in God's understanding. Thus, the creature, as known by God, must share God's existence. If creatures have no ontological status prior to creation, God would not know creatures, which Aquinas expressly denies. Since possible creatures have uncreated existence, they must be one with their divine ideas. Although actual creatures have their own existence, distinct from the uncreated existence, possible creatures have no such distinct existence. Their only existence is uncreated existence. Thus, Wippel concludes, "from an ontological standpoint, one may say that a possible is identical with its appropriate divine idea."¹⁴⁹ The non-existing possible has some existence because God knows it, but it does not have any other existence than its being known by God. He knows it in its idea and so it is one with its idea.

Second, Aquinas says that something can be possible in two ways. In one way, something is called "possible" according to some potency. This potency can be either active or passive. Something is in active potency when an agent can actualize the potency. There is an active potency in the builder to build. Something is in passive potency when there is a preexisting potentiality in the thing to be actualized by an agent. There is a passive potency in the wood to be burned. In another way, something is called "possible" not because of some potency, but absolutely. Something is possible absolutely when the terms of the proposition are not contradictory.¹⁵⁰ Having made these distinctions, it is clear that possibles do not have passive potency because they do not already exist. However, they are possible

---

148. Ross, "Aquinas's Exemplarism," 185. Emphasis original.
149. John F. Wippel, *Metaphysical Themes in Thomas Aquinas* (Washington, DC: The Catholic University of America Press, 1984), 168. Wippel admits a logical distinction between a possible and its idea can be made "from the psychological side" because "a divine idea also implies that God understands that he understands that he understands his essence as being imitable in a given way" (168). However, the multiplication of logical distinctions does not affect the ontological unity between a possible and its idea, even if these distinctions were multiplied *ad infinitum*.
150. *De potentia*, q. 3, a. 14 (Pession, II.80b). Thomas also says that something can be possible not because of some potency but metaphorically, as when some line is said to be potentially rational in geometry. This metaphorical potency is not important for our purposes. See also, *SCG* II, c. 37 (Leonine, 13.354b3–9); *ST* I, q. 25, a. 3 (Leonine, 4.293).

absolutely and God does have an active potency to create them.[151] It follows that non-existing possibles are necessarily possible and enjoy uncreated existence. Each creature is necessarily possible, but God remains free to create or not create any possible creature.

THE SCOPE OF DIVINE IDEAS

Now that it is clear what Thomas thinks divine ideas are, what does he think about the scope of divine ideas? His distinction between divine ideas as exemplars and as reasons (*rationes*) is central to his understanding of the scope of divine ideas. Since a divine exemplar is an idea of something that God wills to produce and since creation is finite, there are a finite number of divine exemplars. A divine reason is an idea of something that God could create. Since God's infinite essence is imitable in an infinite number of ways, there are an infinite number of divine reasons. The question is where the line should be drawn between divine exemplars and divine reasons. This section will investigate what Aquinas says about divine ideas of singulars, species, genera, evil, possibles, and accidents to see where he draws the line.

Singulars, Species, and Genera

Aquinas insists that "without a doubt, God has cognition of all things, both universals and singulars."[152] He has this cognition because he is the total cause of every being, that is, he is the cause of their forms and their matter. As a result, he does not merely cognize the universal natures of things, but rather as they are individuated by matter.[153] Plato argued that there were ideas of species only and not of singulars for two reasons. First, he thought that matter was uncreated and so did not have an origin from an idea. Since matter is the principle of singularity, there were no ideas of singulars. Second, he thought that there were only ideas of what is *per se* intended. The intention of nature is principally to conserve the species. Thus, he posited ideas only of species and not of singulars. This second reason also explains why Plato denied that there are ideas of genera. Nature's intention does not stop at the production of the form of a genus but at the form of a species.[154]

Aquinas opposes Plato's first argument by claiming God creates matter. As a result, divine ideas must account for the complete and entire existence of things. Ideas are ordered to the *esse* of things. Singulars have truer existence than universals since universals do not subsist except in singulars. Therefore, singulars ought to have ideas more than universals.[155] Indeed, if the term 'idea' is taken as 'exemplar,'

---

151. Wippel, *Metaphysical Themes*, 165.
152. *In I Sent.*, d. 36, q. 1, a. 1 (Mandonnet, I.830): "Deus absque dubio omnium, et universalium et singularium, cognitionem habet."
153. *In I Sent.*, d. 36, q. 1, a. 1 (Mandonnet, I.829–32); *De veritate*, q. 2, a. 5 (Leonine, 22/1.62:246–313); *ST* I, q. 14, a. 11 (Leonine, 4.183b).
154. *De veritate*, q. 3, a. 8 (Leonine, 22/1.115:40–116:63); *ST* I, q. 15, a. 3, ad 4 (Leonine, 4.204b).
155. *De veritate*, q. 3, a. 8, s.c. 2 (Leonine., 22/1.115:35–39), esp.: "ideae ordinantur ad esse rerum." See *De veritate*, q. 3, a. 5 (Leonine, 22/1.112:43–44).

then there is but a single idea for the singular, species, and genus because Socrates, *man*, and *animal* are not distinguished according to being (*esse*) in Socrates.[156] Thus, Doolan argues that "there are properly speaking only ideas of individuals because only individual things can actually be produced."[157] Genera and species only exist in singulars, and so a single divine exemplar of the singular is sufficient for God to create the singular, species, and genus.

Antoine Côté has argued that this interpretation strains Aquinas's thought.[158] His biggest objection is that there is little textual evidence for this claim. Côté is right that the only place Aquinas explicitly draws this conclusion is in *De veritate*, q. 3, a. 8. He is incorrect, however, when he says that the textual evidence is limited to a single *sed contra*. Aquinas explicitly draws the same conclusion in his reply to the second objection of q. 3, a. 8, and he refers to the principle that ideas relate to things insofar as they are producible in existence in *De veritate*, q. 3, a. 5.[159] Moreover, Aquinas consistently holds that universals, namely, species and genera, do not have substantial existence. They exist only in singulars.[160] Strictly speaking, only the primary substance—the singular—is produced. Since divine ideas, strictly speaking, refer only to what is produced, it follows that God does not have distinct divine exemplars for the singular, species, and genus.

This conclusion is not affected by Aquinas's increased emphasis on exemplars as actually created in later works. In fact, I think Aquinas's greater emphasis strengthens Doolan's conclusion. If a divine exemplar is what God actually creates, and what he creates is singulars and never species or genera independently of singulars, then God only has divine exemplars of singulars. Aquinas makes this exact point in *Summa theologiae* I, q. 15, a. 3, ad 4 to deny that God has exemplars of genera: "genera cannot have an idea other than the idea of the species according as

---

156. *De veritate*, q. 3, a. 8, ad 2 (Leonine, 22/1.116:74–79).

157. Doolan, *Aquinas on Divine Ideas*, 127. This point is also made, though not as strongly, by Mark D. Jordan, "The Intelligibility of the World and the Divine Ideas in Aquinas," *The Review of Metaphysics* 38, no. 1 (1984): 21.

158. Antoine Côté, "Review of Gregory T. Doolan, Aquinas on Divine Ideas as Exemplar Causes," *Journal of the History of Philosophy* 47, no. 4 (2009): 624.

159. *De veritate*, q. 3, a. 5 (Leonine 22/1.112:43–44): "idea proprie dicta respicit rem secundum quod est productibilis in esse." See also, *De veritate*, q. 3, a. 8, ad 2 (Leonine, 22/1.116:74–79): "si loquamur de idea proprie secundum quod est rei eo modo quo est in esse productibilis, sic una idea respondet singulari, specie et generi, individuatis in ipso singulari, eo quod Socrates, homo et animal non distinguuntur secundum esse."

160. See, e.g., *In I Sent.*, d. 19, q. 5, a. 1 (Mandonnet, I.484–90); *In II Sent.*, d. 17, q. 1, a. 1 (Mandonnet, II.411–15); *De ente* c. 2 (Leonine, 373:243–59 and 292–308); *In II De anima*, c. 12 (Leonine, 45.1.115:95–116:151); *In VII Met.*, lect. 11, n. 1536 (Spiazzi, 370b). See Jorge J. E. Gracia, "Cutting the Gordian Knot of Ontology: Thomas's Solution to the Problem of Universals," in *Thomas Aquinas and His Legacy*, ed. D. Gallagher, 16–36 (Washington, DC: The Catholic University of America Press, 1994); Paul Vincent Spade, "Degrees of Being, Degrees of Goodness: Aquinas on Levels of Reality," in *Aquinas's Moral Theory: Essays in Honor of Norman Kretzmann*, ed. Scott MacDonald and Eleonore Stump, 254–75 (New York: Cornell University Press, 1999); Gabriele Galluzzo, "Aquinas on Common Nature and Universals," *Recherches de Théologie et Philosophie Médiévales* 71, no. 1 (2004): 131–71; Jeffrey E. Brower, "Aquinas on the Problem of Universals," *Philosophy and Phenomenological Research* 92, no. 3 (2016): 715–35.

'idea' signifies an exemplar, because a genus never comes to be except in some species."¹⁶¹ Doolan's statement still stands because it is based on Aquinas's theory of *esse* and what God actually produces. If Aquinas argued that God makes species or genera independently of singulars in his later works, then the claims of the *De veritate* might be overturned. As it is, Aquinas did not change his mind on this point, and so, Doolan's point stands. Strictly speaking, there are only divine ideas of singulars. The difference between the *De veritate* and the *Summa theologiae*, then, is whether there are divine exemplars for non-existing possible singulars. Aquinas affirms such exemplars in the *De veritate* and denies them in the *Summa theologiae*.

To Plato's second reason—nature *per se* intends only the species—Aquinas agrees that nature primarily intends to preserve the species. However, he still insists that divine ideas are of singulars. An exemplar is that in imitation of which something comes to be. Consequently, the character of an exemplar requires that the agent intends to assimilate the work to the exemplar. Thus, the agent's intention is part of the character of the exemplar. It follows that the exemplar is first related to what the agent primarily intends. Now any agent intends what is more perfect in his work. Species are the most perfect thing in an individual because it perfects an imperfection on the part of the individual and an imperfection on the part of the genus. Relative to the singular, the species perfects the imperfection of matter, which is the principle of singularity and is in potency to the form of the species. Relative to the genus, the species perfects the potency to a variety of specific differences. Thus, nature does not primarily intend to produce Socrates or an animal; it intends to produce a man. The exemplar in God's mind relates first to the species in every creature.¹⁶²

At first glance, Thomas's agreement that divine exemplars relate first to the species, not the singular, seems contrary to his claim that there are only divine exemplars of the singulars, but there are two reasons to think that there is no conflict. First, what is first in the order of intention is last in the order of execution. Nature intends *man*, but *this* man is generated first because *man* does not exist except in singular men. Since everything arises by divine ideas, the order of execution is from divine ideas. There are, indeed, divine ideas of singulars.¹⁶³ Second, Thomas insists that God's providence extends to singulars. His providence could not extend to singulars unless his divine idea of the creature exemplified the creature as singular, not merely at the level of the lowest species.¹⁶⁴

Ultimately, the apparent tension between the claim that there is only one divine exemplar for the singular, species, and genus and the claim that divine exemplars are first related to the species is the result of approaching the issue from two different perspectives. The claim that the divine exemplar is of the singular takes the

---

161. *ST* I, q. 15, a. 3, ad 4 (Leonine, 4.204b): "genera non possunt habere ideam aliam ab idea speciei, secundum quod idea significat exemplar: quia nunquam genus fit nisi in aliqua specie."

162. *Quodlibet* VIII, q. 1, a. 2 (Leonine, 25/1.54:40–74).

163. *Quodlibet* VIII, q. 1, a. 2, ad 1 (Leonine, 25/1.55:75–83). For more on the principle that what is first in the order of intention is last in the order of execution, see *ST* I-II, q. 1, a. 1, ad 1 (Leonine, 6.6b); *In II Phys.*, lect. 5 (Leonine, 2.70a).

164. *De veritate*, q. 3, a. 8 (Leonine, 22/1.116:64–68); *ST* I, q. 15, a. 3, ad 4 (Leonine, 4.204b).

divine perspective. Since God has an idea of what he produces and he produces the singular, his idea is of the singular. The claim that divine exemplars are first related to the species takes the creaturely perspective. Divine ideas are related to the singular creature as singular, as species, and as genus, but the primary way a singular creature is related to its divine idea is as species.¹⁶⁵

For Thomas, the scope of divine ideas extends to singulars. God does not have distinct exemplars for species or genera. Moreover, since he specifies in the *Summa theologiae* that God has exemplars of what he produces, God only has divine exemplars of the singulars that he actually makes, not of non-existing possibles.¹⁶⁶

Philosophically, the restriction of divine exemplars to actually created singulars does not entail a finite number of divine exemplars. Divine exemplars could be numerically infinite because Aquinas teaches that reason cannot exclude the possibility of an eternal world. The propositions "The world is created by God" and "The world has always existed" are mutually possible because a creative, efficient cause does not have to precede its effect temporally. The nonexistence of an effect need not precede its existence temporally.¹⁶⁷ In theory, the world could be eternal, in which case an infinite number of individuals would exist that would have to be exemplified by an infinite number of divine exemplars. Theologically, however, Thomas teaches that the number of divine exemplars is finite. It is possible that the world existed from eternity, but it is false. The duration of time from the beginning of the world until the end is finite. In a finite amount of time, only a finite number of creatures can exist. Therefore, God does have a finite number of divine exemplars.

Neither the restriction to singulars nor the restriction to a finite number of ideas holds if we consider divine ideas in the sense of *rationes*. There is a distinct divine reason for each diverse consideration of a thing. The considerations of Socrates as Socrates, Socrates as man, and Socrates as animal are diverse. Therefore, God has a distinct divine reason for each consideration.¹⁶⁸ Divine reasons are in no way restricted by whether God creates a creature. Therefore, God has an infinite number of distinct divine reasons corresponding to the infinite number of singulars, species, and genera that he knows he could create.

Evil

Aquinas argues that evil is the privation of a good that ought to be present.¹⁶⁹ It does not exist in reality. Evil can only be called a being insofar as it can be involved

---

165. See Doolan, *Aquinas on Divine Ideas*, 129–30.
166. *ST* I, q. 14, a. 16; q. 15, a. 3 (Leonine, 4.196–97 and 204). Recall that in *De veritate*, q. 3, a. 3, Aquinas argued that divine practical cognition extended to both actually practical and virtually or habitually practical knowledge (Leonine, 107:85–174). Thus, according to the teaching in the *De veritate*, God would have exemplars of every possible singular being that he could produce, regardless of whether he ever willed to produce any of them.
167. *De aeternitate mundi* (Leonine, 43.86:82–87). See Wippel, *Metaphysical Themes*, 191–214.
168. *De veritate*, q. 3, a. 8, ad 1 (Leonine, 22/1.116:80–84).
169. *ST* I, q. 48, a. 3 (Leonine, 4.493b).

in a true proposition, like "blindness is in the eye."[170] Evil *qua* evil is nothing and does not imitate God. Since an idea is an exemplar that a creature imitates, there cannot be a divine exemplar of evil in God. Moreover, divine exemplars are the principles of the formation of things. God cannot be the principle of evil. Therefore, he cannot have an exemplar of evil.[171]

Even if we consider ideas in the sense of reasons, God does not have a proper idea of evil. Since evil is a privation, it lacks form, which is required for knowledge, and so, not even God can know it through its proper character (*ratio*).[172] God only knows evil through the *ratio* of the good, and how a given creature recedes from participating in his divinity, and as such, he knows the way it suffers evil. Early in his career, Thomas is willing to call this indirect knowledge of creatures an idea in God, but as his career progressed, he became less willing to say that God has an idea of evil.[173] This tendency reached its pinnacle in the *Summa theologiae* where Aquinas rejects that God has an idea of evil, regardless of whether 'idea' is understood as exemplar or reason.[174]

Prime Matter

The question of a divine idea of prime matter is similar to the question of a divine idea of evil in the sense that prime matter is entirely devoid of form and actuality. It is pure potency. Since definition and knowledge come from form, there can be no definition or direct cognition of prime matter. Prime matter is known only by analogy in that existence is prime matter in the way proper to prime matter as existence is to a worm in the way proper to worms. Nevertheless, prime matter must be a real and intrinsic principle of every material being because it accounts for substantial change. It is neither generated nor corrupted, and it is numerically one in all things because it lacks the necessary dispositions that would make it differ in number. Since everything that exists is in act, prime matter cannot exist *per se*, but only exists through the composite.[175]

Aquinas states on many occasions that God creates prime matter.[176] It follows that there must be a divine exemplar of prime matter, but Aquinas is quick to

---

170. *ST* I, q. 48, a. 2, ad 3 (Leonine, 4.492b): "malum non est sicut in subiecto in bono quod ei opponitur, sed in quodam alio bono: subiectum enim caecitatis non est visus, sed animal."
171. *In I Sent.*, d. 36, q. 2, a. 3, ad 1 (Mandonnet, I.844); *De veritate*, q. 3, a. 4 (Leonine, 22/1.110:66–72); *SCG* I, c. 71 (Leonine, 13.205–7); *ST* I, q. 15, a. 3, ad 1 (Leonine, 4.204b).
172. See p. 67.
173. *In I Sent.*, d. 36, q. 2, a. 3, ad 1 (Mandonnet, I.844).
174. *ST* I, q. 15, a. 3, ad 1 (Leonine, 4.204b): "malum non habet in Deo ideam, neque secundum quod idea est exemplar, neque secundum quod est ratio."
175. For more on Aquinas's position on prime matter, see Wippel, *Metaphysical Thought*, 312–27. Two of the seminal texts for Aquinas's teaching on prime matter are *De prin. nat.*, c. 2 (Leonine, 43.41:70–119) and *Quodlibet* III, q. 1, a. 1 (Leonine, 25/2.241–42).
176. *In I Sent.*, d. 36, q. 2, a. 3, ad 2 (Mandonnet, I.844–45); *In II Sent.*, d. 1, q. 1, a. 4 (Mandonnet, II.25); *In II Sent.*, d. 12, q. 1, a. 4 (Mandonnet, II.315); *De veritate*, q. 3, a. 5 (Leonine, 22/1.112:35–36); *SCG* II, c. 16 (Leonine, 13.300b); *SCG* II, c. 42 (Leonine, 13.365b4–14); *SCG* II, c. 44 (Leonine, 13.370a4–8);

specify that the divine exemplar of prime matter is not distinct from the divine exemplar of the composite.[177] Properly speaking, a divine exemplar relates to a thing that is producible in *esse*. What is produced, strictly speaking, is the composite. Therefore, the divine exemplar is of the composite and includes the substantial principles of the composite.

In his earlier works, Aquinas allows that God could have a divine reason of prime matter, saying that even though prime matter cannot exist apart, nothing prevents it from being considered by itself.[178] By the time he wrote the *Summa theologiae*, however, he had changed his mind. God cannot have a divine reason of prime matter "for matter in itself neither has *esse* nor is cognizable."[179] By this later work, Aquinas had thought through the consequences of prime matter as pure potency. A thing is intelligible to the extent that it is in act. Since matter of itself is not in act in any way, not even God can know it directly. Since God cannot know it directly and distinctly, there cannot be a divine reason of prime matter.

Accidents

Given Aquinas's position on divine ideas of species and prime matter, we might expect him to answer that while God has a distinct divine reason (*ratio*) for each accident, the one divine exemplar of the singular includes all its accidents. He defies this expectation. He does so for philosophical reasons and because of a concern about the true presence of Christ in the Eucharist. When the priest says the words of consecration over the bread and wine, the accidents of bread and wine remain, but their substance is removed. If there were one divine exemplar for both the substance of the bread and the accidents of the bread, then it seems impossible for God to cause the accidents to remain without their substance.

An accident is "a thing to which it belongs to be in another."[180] In his discussions of divine ideas, Aquinas distinguishes two types of accidents: proper accidents and separable accidents. The principles of the subject cause proper accidents. They are never separated from their subject in being (*esse*) because they are produced in

---

De potentia, q. 3, a. 5, ad 3 (Marietti, 49b); *ST* I, q. 15, a. 3, ad 3 (Leonine, 4.204); *ST* I, q. 44, a. 2 (Leonine, 4.257–58); *ST* I, q. 44, a. 4, ad 4 (Leonine, 4.262); *ST* I-II, q. 9, a. 6 (Leonine, 6.82b).

177. *In I Sent.*, d. 36, q. 2, a. 3, ad 2 (Mandonnet, I.844–45); *De veritate*, q. 3, a. 5 (Leonine, 22/1.112:43–50); *ST* I, q. 15, a. 3, ad 3 (Leonine, 4.204).

178. *De veritate*, q. 3, a. 5, ad 3 (Leonine, 22/1.112:68–71). In *In I Sent.*, d. 36, q. 2, a. 3, ad 2 (Mandonnet, I.845), Aquinas says prime matter has an idea in God imperfectly.

179. *ST* I, q. 15, a. 3, ad 3 (Leonine ed., 4.204): "habet quidem materiam ideam in Deo, non tamen aliam ab idea compositi. Nam materia secundum se neque esse habet, neque cognoscibilis est." That Aquinas changes his mind on this point has been known since at least the early 16th century. See Thomas de Vio (Cajetan), *Comentaria in Summam theologiam* I, q. 15, a. 3, n. 4 (Leonine, 4.205). For a contemporary discussion of this question, see Wippel, *Divine Ideas*, 42; Wippel, *Metaphysical Thought*, 323 and 326.

180. *In IV Sent.*, d. 12, q. 1, a. 1, ql. 1, ad 2 (Moos, 4.499): "res cui debetur esse in alio." For a discussion of this definition, see Wippel, *Metaphysical Thought*, 228–37; Gilson, "Quasi Definitio Substantiae," 111–29.

being (*esse*) with their subject by a single operation. As a result, since an idea properly speaking is the operable form of a thing, there are not distinct divine exemplars of proper accidents. Every proper accident shares an idea with its subject. Separable accidents do not follow their subject inseparably, nor do they depend upon their subject's principles. Thus, a distinct operation produces such accidents. Thomas uses the example of grammar: just because a man comes into existence does not mean that something grammatical does. Since distinct operations are required to bring about the subject and the separable accident, Aquinas concludes that there are distinct divine exemplars for each separable accident God creates. If divine ideas are understood in the broader sense of reasons, then God has distinct ideas of all proper and sensible accidents because each of them can be considered distinctly *per se*.[181]

Possibles

The last aspect of Aquinas's account of the scope of divine ideas concerns non-existing possibles. God could have made these beings, but he did not choose to do so. Once again, Aquinas's thought on this subject changes as his career progresses. Specifically, his opinion on whether there are divine exemplars of non-existing possible beings changes as his view of an exemplar narrows from both actually practical (*actu practica*) knowledge and virtually practical (*practica virtute*) knowledge in the *De veritate* to only actually practical knowledge in his later writings.

In the *De veritate*, St. Thomas argues that an idea in the proper sense relates not only to actually practical knowledge but even virtually practical knowledge. Consequently, it is proper to say that God has divine exemplars even of those things that he does not will to make.[182] Aquinas thinks this position is justifiable because although God never willed to produce a non-existing possible being, he still wills himself to be able to produce them. His knowledge relates to them under the aspect of production.[183]

By the time Aquinas writes the *Summa theologiae*, he has restricted his understanding of an exemplar to those ideas that are actually imitated at some point in time. Since God never creates non-existing possible beings, he does not have divine exemplars of them, but he does have divine reasons of them.[184]

---

181. *De veritate*, q. 3, a. 7 (Leonine, 22/1.114:66–93); *In I Sent.*, d. 36, q. 2, a. 3, ad 4 (Mandonnet, I.845); *ST* I, q. 15, a. 3, ad 4 (Leonine, 4.204).

182. *De veritate*, q. 3, a. 6 (Leonine, 22/1.113:35–47). See also *De veritate*, q. 2, a. 8 (Leonine, 22/1.69:28–70:91); *SCG* I, c. 66 (Leonine, 13.184–85).

183. *De veritate*, q. 3, a. 6, ad 3 (Leonine, 22/1.113:60–67). See Boland, *Ideas in God*, 255n108.

184. *ST* I, q. 15, a. 3, ad 2 (Leonine, 4.204); *De potentia*, q. 1, a. 5, ad 11 (Marietti, 2.20b). In *Quodlibet* IV, q. 1, a. 1, written in 1271, Aquinas does not explicitly articulate the position of the *ST*. However, it can reasonably be inferred that he means to articulate the same position. See Wippel, *Divine Ideas*, 37; Doolan, *Aquinas on Divine Ideas*, 142–43.

RECAPITULATION AND CONCLUSIONS

St. Thomas Aquinas defines an idea as "the form that something imitates from the intention of an agent who predetermines the end for himself."[185] Ideas play a twofold role in Aquinas's thought. First, they are principles of cognition insofar as they are forms in the intellect called divine reasons (*rationes*). Second, they are causal principles insofar as they are the exemplars according to which things are made called divine exemplars. Aquinas places a greater emphasis on the second, causal role of divine ideas. He argues that God has ideas because all things make something like themselves; it is the only way to account for the fact that all things seek an end, and because God knows the full extent of his power.

Aquinas further argues that God has many divine ideas because he must know all things distinctly. If God had a single idea, then his knowledge would be too universal and confused to know individual beings distinctly. When God knows his essence, he knows all the ways that essence can be imitated. He knows the unique real relation that any possible creature would bear to him if it were created. Each of these possible real relations is a divine idea, and God knows the possible creatures through knowing these relations.

Aquinas's distinction between divine ideas in the sense of exemplar and the sense of reason looms large in his account of the scope of divine ideas. Except for prime matter, God has a distinct divine reason of every possible creature and every aspect of every possible creature. Divine reasons are so plentiful because each possible creature and each of its aspects is intelligibly distinct from every other possible creature and every other aspect of any possible creature. There is no divine reason of prime matter because it lacks any actuality by which it could be distinctly known. However, the scope of divine exemplars is limited to singular beings that exist at some point in history and their separable accidents. Species, genera, prime matter, proper accidents, and possible are excluded from the scope of divine ideas either because God does not create them or because he produces them in the same operation as the singular being.

---

185. *De veritate*, q. 3, a. 1 (Leonine, 22/1.100:220–23): "idea sit forma quam aliquid imitator ex intentione agentis qui praedeterminat sibi formam."

Chapter III.
Henry of Ghent (before 1240–1293)

THE PLACE OF DIVINE IDEAS IN HENRY OF GHENT'S THOUGHT

Divine ideas play a central role in Henry of Ghent's metaphysical thought. The subject of metaphysics for Henry is the simple concept *ens simpliciter*, which prescinds from the question of existence or nonexistence. Thus, the subject of metaphysics is essences, not existence.[1] Henry habitually argues that essences are things (*res*) in two ways corresponding to the two ways the term *res* is derived. In one way, an essence is *res* derived from *reor, reris* (I think, you think). Anything thinkable qualifies as a *res a reor*. In another way, an essence is a *res* derived from *ratitudo* (ratification or verification). Only what is apt to exist is a *res a ratitudine*. *Res a ratitudine* is further distinguished into those *res* whose essences include *esse* and those whose essences do not include *esse*. Only God's essence includes *esse*. Essences that do not include *esse* are the ideas according to which God knows and produces everything other than himself.[2] Divine ideas, then, are an essential aspect of metaphysical inquiry. Moreover, since Henry holds a theory of divine illumination, it follows that divine ideas are metaphysically and epistemologically central for Henry: "No scholar would ever raise the question whether 'the internal logic' of Henry's thought 'really requires a theory of divine ideas at all,' as did Gilson about Aquinas."[3] Divine ideas are philosophically indispensable.

Henry of Ghent left two major works: his *Summa quaestionum ordinarium* and fifteen *Quaestiones quodlibetales*.[4] Henry intended these two works to be read together because in each text he frequently refers to a prior discussion in the other.

---

1. *Summa*, a. 34, q. 3 (Leuven, 28.190); *Summa*, a. 21, q. 3 (Badius, I.138rD); *Summa*, a. 24, q. 3 (Badius, I.138vP). See Martin Pickavé, "Henry of Ghent on Metaphysics," in *A Companion to Henry of Ghent*, ed. Gordon A. Wilson (Leiden: Brill, 2011), 156.

2. See *Quodlibet* V, q. 2 (Badius, 154rD); *Quodlibet* V, q. 6 (Badius, 161rK); *Quodlibet* VII, qq. 1–2 (Leuven, 9.26:46–28:87). See Jan A Aertsen, *Medieval Philosophy as Transcendental Thought*, Studien und Texte zur Geistesgeschichte des Mittelalters Bd 107 (Leiden: Brill, 2012), 286–97.

3. Roberto Plevano, "Divine Ideas and Infinity," in *Henry of Ghent and the Transformation of Scholastic Thought: Essays in Memory of Jos Decorte*, ed. Guy Guldentops and Carlos Steel (Leuven: Leuven University Press, 2003), 191. He is quoting Wippel, *Divine Ideas*, 1.

4. For the dating of the *Quaestiones quodlibetales*, see Gordon A. Wilson, "Henry of Ghent's Written Legacy," in *A Companion to Henry of Ghent*, ed. Gordon A. Wilson (Leiden: Brill, 2011), 6. For the dating of the *Summa*, see José Gómez-Caffarena, "Cronología de la *Suma* de Enrique de Gante por relación a sus *Quodlibetos*," *Gregorianum* 38 (1957): 133.

Henry's *Summa* is the redacted edition of his classroom disputations. He planned for the work to have two sections: one on God and one on creatures, but he was only able to complete the section on God.[5]

The Status of Divine Ideas

What Is an Idea?

Henry of Ghent's most complete account of divine ideas is found in his *Quodlibet* IX (Lent 1286). He begins this account with a close look at the object and manner of divine knowledge. Nothing understands something except the per se object of the power by which it knows, or that of which the per se object is an intellectual means of knowing (*ratio cognoscendi*), but the object of the intellect can be understood in two ways: In one way, it is the object of the intellect by informing the intellective power, making it to understand in act by its power. In another way, it is the object of the intellect by terminating its knowledge by its act.[6]

In the first sense, the only per se object of the divine intellect is the divine essence. If the divine intellect had any other per se object, then it would be in potency to receive knowledge *ab extra*, making God imperfect. Thus, his substance would not be the noblest of all.[7] In the second sense, the object of the intellect is further distinguished into the primary and secondary terminating objects of the divine intellect. The primary terminating object of the divine intellect is the object informing the divine intellect to its act of understanding, that is, the divine essence itself. God's primary object knowledge is himself. The secondary terminating object of the divine intellect is something other than God, which must be the case because otherwise God would be the most foolish of knowers.[8]

The secondary terminating object of the divine intellect can be understood in two ways: by knowing what the creature is in God or by knowing the *esse* the creature has in itself other than God (although it does not have this existence outside of God's knowledge). Henry uses the example of a statue of Hercules to explain this

---

5. For the general plan of the works, see *Summa*, a. 21, *intro*. (Badius, I.123r). For a discussion of the work's incompleteness, see Mário S. De Carvahlo, "On the Unwritten Section of Henry of Ghent's Summa," in *Henry of Ghent and the Transformation of Scholastic Thought: Studies in Memory of Jos Decorte*, ed. Guy Guldentops and Carlos Steel, 327–70 (Leuven: Leuven University Press, 2003). Note especially the appendix of places where Henry refers to the section *de creaturis* at the end of de Carvalho's article.

6. *Quodlibet* IX, q. 2 (Leuven, 13.26:20–27): "obiectum autem intellectus, convenienter sumendo rationem obiecti, potest aliquid esse dupliciter: uno modo potentiam intellectivam informando actu intelligendi sua actione; alio modo ipsum actum intelligendi terminando sua cognitione." This distinction between the object as informing and as terminating is taken from Aquinas. See p. 114–15.

7. *Quodlibet* IX, q. 2 (Leuven, 13.27:28–36). See Averroes, *In XII Met.*, c. 51 (Iunctina, VIII.157va25–37) and pp. 4–5.

8. *Quodlibet* IX, q. 2 (Leuven, 13.27:37–44), esp.: "Secundo modo contingit aliquid esse obiectum intellectus dupliciter: uno modo primarium, alio modo secundarium. Obiectum primarium non est nisi obiectum informans ad actum intelligendi, et non est nisi ipsa divina essentia .... Obiectum vero secundarium est aliud a se."

distinction. The first way of understanding the secondary terminating object is like understanding the image of Hercules insofar as the image is a certain thing, and not as an image. Insofar as it is a thing, the statue is a hunk of marble that has been shaped in a certain way. Understood in this way, God knows things other than himself as they exist in his essence and are the same as his essence. They are one simple thing with him in every way. The second way of understanding the secondary terminating object is as an image. The statue of Hercules *qua* image is understood insofar as it is a depiction of Hercules. As such, Hercules himself is known. In this second way, God understands things other than himself truly because he understands the existence that they have in themselves. In this sense, God understands his essence as a reason (*ratio*) that has the character of a respect (*respectus*) by which he relates to things other than himself. He does this as they are something by essence in divine cognition, namely in that which the divine essence is the reason and exemplar form of those things, and as form, cause, and formal principle of the exemplified things.[9]

Henry then looks more closely at how God's essence is the reason by which he knows things other than himself. He concludes that it is nothing other than an imitability by which other things imitate the divine essence, and we call this reason of imitability an "idea." An idea is not the divine essence in itself and absolutely because the divine essence in itself is the primary object of the divine intellect. In keeping with his predecessors, then, Henry argues that a divine idea is a secondary object of the divine essence upon the divine intellect. God's primary object is himself absolutely, but secondarily he knows himself under the aspect of imitability. Henry concludes this argument with a definition of an idea: "an idea, in its formal definition (*ratio*), is nothing other than a *respectus* of imitability from a consideration of the intellect on the divine essence itself."[10] In his slightly earlier *Quodlibet* V (Advent 1280 or Lent 1281), Henry offers another definition of an idea that helps flesh out his whole account of divine ideas: "insofar as it is a thing and certain essence, every perfection in a creature has the character (*ratio*) of an idea in God."[11]

From these two definitions of divine ideas, six aspects of divine ideas emerge: Divine ideas are (1) something relative and not absolute, specifically (2) relations of imitability (3) of the perfections (4) of complete natures, that are (5) nothing other than the divine essence (6) as known by the divine intellect. Each aspect will be treated in turn.

---

9. *Quodlibet* IX, q. 2 (Leuven, 13.27:45–28:65), esp.: "Sed aliud a se, ut obiectum secundarium suae cognitionis, potest cognoscere dupliciter: uno modo cognoscendo de creatura id quod est in Deo, alio modo cognoscendo de ipsa id quod ipsa habet ese in se ipsa, aliud a Deo, quamvis non habeat esse extra eius notitiam."

10. *Quodlibet* IX, q. 2 (Leuven, 13.29:80–81): "idea nihil aliud sit de ratione sua formali quam respectus imitabilitatis ex consideratione intellectus in ipsa divina essentia." Cf. *Quodlibet* VIII, q. 1 (Badius, 300rB): "idea nihil aliud sit quam ipsa divina essentia sub ratione respectus imitabilitatis qua alia a se nata sunt eam imitari."

11 *Quodlibet* V, q. 1 (Badius, 151rF): "omnis perfectio in creatura inquantum ipsa est res et essentia quaedam, habet in Deo rationem ideae."

First, the genus term of the definition from *Quodlibet* IX is respect (*respectus*). A divine idea is nothing other than a certain relatedness; it is not something absolute. This aspect of divine ideas will be explained in further detail in the section on a plurality of divine ideas, but what matters for now is that at its core an idea is an image that points beyond itself. Divine ideas are the possible relations that God knows creatures could bear to him. In fact, an idea is "nothing but a respect to a creature."[12] Just as the statue of Hercules is an image through which we acquire knowledge of Hercules, so divine ideas are "means of understanding the perfections that are in the creatures themselves."[13] Divine ideas are not absolute things; they point to that of which they are an idea.

Second, divine ideas are respects of imitability. Like Bonaventure before him, Henry argues that there are two ways things can be like each other. The first sort of likeness is called a likeness of similitude, which is found when two things participate in one and the same form. Two white things have a likeness of similitude because they both participate in whiteness. Likeness of similitude in no way exists between God and any creature. The other kind of likeness is a likeness of imitation, which is universally found in makers and things made; causes and effects. There is a likeness of imitation because the effect is just like the cause since every agent makes something like itself.[14] Since God and creatures are related as exemplifier and exemplified, the ideas by which God knows creatures are the various degrees by which a possible creature can have a likeness of imitation to God.

Third, creatures imitate God by sharing the supreme divine perfection in a limited way. When God knows divine ideas, he knows the degrees to which possible creatures can be perfect as God is perfect. An idea "is nothing other than the conception of determinate perfection in God with respect to the determinate perfection corresponding to him in a creature."[15] It follows that all creaturely perfections are found in God in a more excellent way.[16] Henry will occasionally play on the verbal relation between the words *idea* and *idealis* to emphasize that a divine idea is a creature's ideal against which the creature is measured.[17] The creature, especially the rational creature who acts with free choice, is most perfect when it imitates its divine idea most perfectly.

Fourth, divine ideas are of complete essences. This aspect of divine ideas greatly affects Henry's take on the scope of divine ideas. By declaring that divine ideas are only of complete essence, he limits the scope of divine ideas to the lowest species of creatable things.[18]

---

12. *Summa*, a. 42, q. 2 (Leuven, 29.46:77–78): "idea, non dicit nisi ex respectu ad creaturam."
13. *Quodlibet* V, q. 1 (Badius, 151rG–H): "sunt rationes intelligendi ipsas perfectiones quae sunt in ipsis creaturis."
14. *Summa*, a. 21, q. 2 (Badius, I.124rF). See p. 16.
15. *Quodlibet* V, q. 1 (Badius, 151rE): "nihil aliud est nisi perfectionis conceptio in Deo determinatae ex respect ad determinatam perfectionem ei correspondentem in creatura."
16. *Summa*, a. 32, q. 3 (Opera, 27.38:82–85); *Summa*, a. 42, q. 2 (Leuven, 29.46:60–85).
17. *Quodlibet* V, q. 1 (Badius, 151rG).
18. See *Quodlibet* VII, qq. 1–2, s.c. 2 and solutio (Leuven, 11.4:30–32 and 8:5–6) and pp. 114–19.

Fifth, divine ideas are nothing other than the divine essence. Divine ideas are not Platonic Forms that God comes to know by turning his intellectual gaze toward them. If divine ideas were something other than the divine essence, God would not be the perfection of all creatures. Since divine ideas are the ideal and exemplars of creatures, creatures would have a final cause other than God.

Finally, although divine ideas are nothing other than the divine essence, they are not the divine essence *qua* essence. God only has ideas because he knows his own essence.[19] If, *per impossibile*, God did not have an intellect, there would be no divine ideas. Divine ideas are in the divine intellect because God knows the respects in which possible creatures can imitate his supreme perfection. Divine ideas extend God beyond his own essence because his knowledge extends to things that can exist beyond his essence.[20] Since divine ideas are the ways that God knows a creature can imitate him, God only has ideas insofar as he is a principle and cause of creatures.[21]

Divine Ideas as Principles of Cognition

Divine ideas are, for Henry, both principles of cognition and principles of production, that is, exemplars. Henry places greater emphasis on the cognitive role of divine ideas than their causal role. Henry's emphasis is a result of his historical circumstances, his understanding of the intellect as a natural power, and the way he distinguishes between speculative and practical knowledge, which he thinks is both the truth and the best reading of Aristotle. On December 10, 1270, Stephen Tempier, the bishop of Paris, condemned thirteen propositions and excommunicated anyone who taught or held them. The third condemned propositions was "that man's will wills or chooses out of necessity."[22] Some at the University of Paris were teaching that man's intellect could issue a command that a certain action be performed such that his will was not free to choose otherwise. If this account of the relationship between the intellect and will is correct, then the will is, at least sometimes, not free. In light of this condemnation, Parisian authors scrambled to emphasize that they likewise condemn the proposition.[23] The technical vocabulary that arose concerned whether the intellect could determine whether something was to-be-done or not to-be-done (*fiendum vel non fiendum*).

Although Tempier's condemnation specifically concerned man's will, the condemnation was quickly applied to God and the angels because it is characteristic of every will to will freely. This inference from the condemnation to the freedom

---

19. *Summa*, a. 32, q. 3 (Leuven, 27.38:82–85).
20. *Summa*, a. 42, q. 2 (Leuven, 29.46:74–85).
21. *Summa*, a. 37, q. 2 (Leuven 28.151:3–155:99).
22. CUP I.487: "Quod voluntas hominis ex necessitates vult vel eligit." For a discussion of this proposition, especially regarding Henry, see Tobias Hoffmann, *Free Will and the Rebel Angels in Medieval Philosophy* (New York: Cambridge University Press, 2021), 58–84.
23. Most notably, Aquinas interrupted his classroom disputations to ask a question on the relationship between the intellect and the will. See *De malo*, q. 6 (Leonine, 23.145–53).

of the divine will had a great impact on Henry. In *Summa*, a. 36, q. 4 (1279–1281), Henry insists that God does not have practical cognition or practical ideas except accidentally because if he did, then his cognition would have *fiendum* or *non fiendum*. Thus, his knowledge would coerce his will into creating this and not creating that. Creation would be an act of necessary emanation rather than a freely chosen act of love. By the time he wrote *Quodlibet* VIII (Advent 1284), Henry was more willing to admit that God has practical knowledge and practical ideas, but he was still hesitant. Since Henry's thought changes in this area, the teachings from both texts will be examined.

In *Summa*, a. 36, q. 4, Henry asks whether God's intellect is a speculative or practical power. He begins his answer by clarifying what makes our intellect speculative or practical. If God's intellect really were practical, then in addition to considering things as operable, his intellect would determine their operation (or lack thereof) as the end of its cognition. Since the determination *fiendum* or *non fiendum* would belong to the divine intellect of itself prior to any action of the will, the divine will would have to follow the determination of the intellect. The problem is exacerbated by the fact that God's intellect is a purely natural power. God necessarily knows all that he knows in the way that he knows it. Thus, like Bonaventure, Henry argues that God necessarily has divine ideas.[24] If the divine intellect determined *fiendum* and *non fiendum*, then the divine intellect would determine the set of things created and the set of things not created necessarily and independently of the divine will. If creation is to be a free act, therefore, it must be the case that God's intellect determines nothing about what is to be done.[25]

Since God's intellect does not determine what is to be done or not done, it cannot be practical. No practical intellect could be so indifferent. A practical intellect considers what is to be done *qua* to be done. God knows that some object of his understanding *can* be done and may be better to do, but this knowledge does not determine *fiendum* and *non-fiendum*. His knowledge remains entirely speculative. Even his knowledge of how his will has chosen remains just as speculative as his knowledge of what his will has actually not elected to do.[26]

He applies this conclusion to divine ideas in his reply to the first objection. Since God's intellect is entirely speculative, it follows that divine ideas are purely speculative as well.[27] His reason for this conclusion is that knowledge has a twofold end: the end of the knowledge itself (*finis scientiae*) and the end of the knower (*finis scientis*). The end of the knowledge is that because of which the knowledge is and the end of the knower is what the knower intends from the knowledge. The end of

---

24. Catherine König-Pralong, *Être, essence et contingence* (Paris: Belles lettres, 2006), 65. For Bonaventure, see p. 19.

25. *Summa*, a. 36, q. 4 (Leuven, 28.108:67–110:00). On the divine intellect as purely natural power, see *Summa*, a. 36, q. 5, ad 2 (Leuven, 28.129:80–82): "Necessitas autem in intelligibilibus circa divinam essentiam est absoluta necessitas intelligendi ipsa in divino intellectu."

26. *Summa*, a. 36, q. 4 (Leuven, 28.110:01–113:76).

27. *Summa*, a. 36, q. 4, ad 1 (Leuven, 28.114:92–99).

the knowledge can be further distinguished into the principal end and the nonprincipal end. The principal end is the end to which the knowledge is ordered essentially, while the nonprincipal end of the knowledge is the end to which the knower's intention can order it. Only the principal end of the knowledge is relevant for determining whether the knowledge is speculative or practical. Geometry could be put to some practical use, but the end of the knowledge itself is speculative. The end of ethical knowledge is for operation and is purely practical. The fact that someone might make a speculative inquiry of ethics without any intention to act does not change its primary end. Thus, God's knowledge is speculative and can only be called practical accidentally (*per accidens*) in the same way that a geometer's knowledge can be accidentally practical.[28]

Henry revisits the question whether God has practical ideas in *Quodlibet* VIII, q. 1 (Advent 1284). He reaffirms that God knows things other than himself as the secondary object of his essence. Thus, the divine essence contains the truth of every limited being (*esse*) and essence.[29] He understands the distinctions among limited beings because he knows his essence as imitable by them. Divine ideas, then, are the divine essence considered under various respects of imitability.[30]

God understands these respects of imitability (or ideal reasons) in two ways: according as they are certain essences or existences in themselves, or according as they are certain things operable by God. In the first way, God's cognition is purely speculative and the ideas themselves are purely speculative ideas. In the second way, God cognizes some things with practical knowledge and through practical ideas insofar as the ideas are *rationes cognoscendi* of those things. Henry qualifies that God understands ideal *rationes* in the second way because, strictly speaking, practical and speculative knowledge only differ according to different *rationes* of ends to which the knowledge is ordered, not according to the *rationes* understood. The fact that knowledge is of something operable does not make the knowledge practical. The end of practical knowledge is work, and so operable things, like moral matters, can be considered in two ways: In one way, as when it is known precisely what virtue and vice are, how virtue consists in the mean, how vice diverts from the mean, and so on. These considerations are always speculative. In the other way, the speculative knowledge is extended beyond cognition of the true. It seeks to know so that the will acts according to the true. This knowledge is immediately practical.[31]

---

28. *Summa*, a. 36, q. 4, ad 2 (Leuven, 28.115:10–118:92).

29. *Quodlibet* VIII, q. 1 (Badius, 299vA), esp.: "quia propter suam illimitationem eminenter continet [divina essentia] in se omnis esse et essentiae limitatem veritatem." When Henry says that the divine essence eminently contains all limited truth, he means that the perfections of creatures preexist in the divine essence. Every agent makes something like itself because it cannot give what it does not have. This principle is tacitly present in each of his four arguments for the existence of divine ideas. See pp. 162–67.

30. *Quodlibet* VIII, q. 1 (Badius, 299vB–300rB).

31. *Quodlibet* VIII, q. 1 (Badius, 300rD–vD), esp.: "Secundo autem modo secundum aliquos cognoscit illa scientia practica: et per ideas practicas: ut sunt rationes cognoscendi illorum."

Applying this distinction to divine knowledge, Henry argues that the divine intellect can be practical in a speculative way. His intellect does not pass judgment about what is to be done or not done even though he knows these things and what is more fitting to be done in all circumstances. To show how the divine intellect's indeterminacy is possible, Henry distinguishes two ways of understanding *fiendum*: In one way, the thing ought to be made only insofar as the agreement of things is concerned. In another way, a thing ought to be made insofar as the fittingness of the agent is concerned. The second way is properly practical but does not apply to God because it entails that it would be unfitting for the agent not to make the thing. If God's intellect were practical in this way, it would coerce his will to making this thing and not making that thing. The first way is less properly practical insofar as it only considers the quality of things to be done and proposes various *modi operandi* to the will. It is fitting on the part of the object that it be done, but the divine will is not in any way determined to act or not.[32]

God's intellect is practical, then, insofar as he knows what is to be made is from the fittingness of things. Henry does not offer an example, but we can imagine that there is a fittingness on the part of the object that if herbivores exist, then so should plants. It would be unfitting for herbivores to be made without their sole source of nutrition. God's intellect is practical in this way. The divine intellect proposes certain ways of operating to the will, but the divine will is free to create what it will. Thus, divine ideas are speculative insofar as they are mere *rationes cognoscendi* of things in their essences, and they are practical insofar as they are *rationes producendi* things in their existence.[33]

Henry's argument in *Quodlibet* VIII is in continuity with the argument of *Summa*, a. 36, but it shows development. He still insists that if God's intellect determined *fiendum* or *non-fiendum*, then the divine will would be coerced into acting in a certain way. Since God necessarily has all the knowledge he has, he would be constrained to create in exactly the way he has. Creation would be necessary, not free. Nevertheless, Henry is more willing to admit divine practical knowledge and practical divine ideas in the *Quodlibet* than in the *Summa*.

I think the position of *Quodlibet* VIII is superior for two reasons: First, it better captures God's knowledge of all possible combinations of creatures, and his knowledge of which combinations are better. The divine intellect proposes some options to the divine will as better without coercing a choice. Second, the argument of *Quodlibet* VIII recognizes the indispensable role of divine ideas in creation. Divine ideas are not merely how God knows possible creatures; they play a causal role insofar as God creates according to them. They are divine exemplars; the perfect models of created things.

---

32. *Quodlibet* VIII, q. 1 (Badius, 300vE).
33. *Quodlibet* VIII, q. 1 (Badius, 300vF–301rF).

Does God Have Ideas?

Henry offers four distinct arguments for positing divine ideas in God. In most places in his corpus, he only offers one or a few of the arguments, but in *Quodlibet* IX, q. 2, he declares that these four arguments perfectly explain the necessity of positing divine ideas. The implication is that this list is exhaustive. The arguments that Henry offers are from God's perfect self-knowledge, his exemplar causality, his efficient causality, and from God as the final cause and measure of things.

Argument from Divine Self-Knowledge

Henry's Argument from Divine Self-Knowledge is concise. Since God's knowledge is perfect, he must cognize things other than himself precisely as other. If he did not cognize them as other, then he could not be wise.[34] This argument is a quick *reductio ad absurdum*. Since it is contradictory to deny God's perfection, the antecedent is false. God's knowledge is perfect.

By itself, this argument is not entirely convincing because it does not rule out the possibility that God's perfect knowledge consists in knowing only himself and not things other than himself. This argument bears a certain resemblance to Aquinas's Argument from Divine Self-Knowledge, but it is missing the premise that God would not know himself perfectly unless he knew the full extent of his power.[35] Henry does attempt to supply this premise in *Quodlibet* VIII, q. 1 when he says that God's understanding of his own essence is the reason why he knows whatever is after his essence.[36] This premise tacitly assumes that all the perfections of creatures are contained in a higher way, that is, eminently, in God's essence. If creaturely perfections were not contained in the divine essence in some way, God would not know them simply by knowing his essence. Even with this added premise, however, Henry leaves it unstated that God is the cause of everything other than himself. So, while the argument seems salvageable, Henry does not articulate it as such.

Argument from Formal and Exemplar Causality

In his second argument, Henry argues that God must have divine ideas because his knowledge is the exemplar cause of things as they are something in themselves essentially. Henry offers two versions of this argument: In *Quodlibet* IX, q. 2 he argues from the divine perspective concerning the origin of finite essences, and in *Summa*, a. 42, q. 2 (1281) he argues from the creaturely perspective using the language of participation. In both cases, Henry's insight is that God's knowledge

---

34. *Quodlibet* IX, q. 2 (Leuven, 13.33:9–14): "Primo enim oportet eas ponere ad cognoscendum alia a se perfecte secundum rationem qua alia, et plures ideas in Deo secundum dictum modum ut omnia alia a se perfecte cognoscat." See Augustine, *De div. qq.* 83, q. 46, n. 1 (PL 40.29); *Quodlibet* VIII, q. 1 (Badius, 299vA).

35. See pp. 63–64.

36. *Quodlibet* VIII, q. 1 (Badius, 299vA): "Hoc igitur quod intelligit suam essentiam causa est intelligendi id quod est post suam essentiam."

establishes the essences of possible creatures as essences. If, *per impossibile*, God did not know his own essence, then there would be no essences of finite beings.

In *Quodlibet* IX, q. 2, he argues that there are many ideas in God as in an archetypal world, singularly present from eternity. As their exemplar cause, God establishes essences in quidditative being (*esse quidditativum*). God would not know himself perfectly from eternity unless he cognized himself as the constitutive principle of other things. Such essences do not actually exist—do not have existential being (*esse existentiae*)—until God wills to create them, but the divine essence as known according to ideal notions is an exemplar form by which the essences of creatures are what they are.[37]

In *Summa*, a. 42, a. 2, Henry argues that essential perfections existing in creatures must preexist in God. Since *esse* is the formal act in a created thing, the essential perfection of a thing in its nature and essence consists in its first *esse*, which it has formally from its essence. Each creature participates *esse* from God, who is his *esse* essentially. Nothing can be in the participated being in act unless it were first in the being which is essentially such. Therefore, whatever has participated *esse* has *esse* in that which is *esse* essentially. Therefore, any perfection found in a being that participates *esse* must be found in the unique and simple *esse* of God, who is subsistent *esse* itself. Thus, the perfections of all things are in God.[38]

These two arguments bear a certain similarity to Aquinas's Argument from Similitude since they employ the principle that everything produces something like itself.[39] Every effect is like its cause because nothing can give what it does not have. Henry takes it for granted that creaturely perfections are eminently contained in the divine essence, which could not serve as the formal exemplar of creatures if it did not contain in some way what it was to exemplify. Since finite essences have a certain perfection, that perfection must preexist in their divine cause. If it did not, God could not create it. Henry argues that the divine essence is able to have all the perfections of creatures because it is unlimited.[40] Since there is no limit to the divine essence's perfection, there is no finite and limited perfection that it does not have. That divine cause, since it is perfect and unlimited, establishes all finite perfections simply by knowing itself. Moreover, the divine intellect causes the essences that it does because it knows the ways the divine essence can be imitated. Knowing all the

---

37. *Quodlibet* IX, q. 2 (Leuven, 13.34:15–37:06), esp.: "talis scientia de rebus ex parte Dei est causa exemplaris rerum ut sint ad se aliquid per essentiam." See *Quodlibet* III, q. 9 (Badius, 150vO–151vO); *Summa*, 22, q. 6 (Badius, I.135vK–N); *Summa*, a. 33, q. 3 (Leuven, 27.154:30–157:04). Henry's theory of quidditative or essential being, as opposed to existential being, is one of Henry's most controversial and misunderstood theories. See pp. 105–13 for a detailed discussion of it.

38. *Summa*, a. 42, a. 2 (Leuven, 29.40:02–41:35), esp.: "cum Deus secundum praedeterminata sit ipsum esse subsistens per essentiam, et a quo omne esse creaturae participatur in quocumque gradu perfectionis participetur quidquid est perfectionis, in quocumque esse participato, et per consequens in quacumcue creatura, necesse est illud ponere essentialiter in ipso esse Dei unico et simplici. Et ita in Deo sunt omnium rerum perfectiones."

39. See p. 63.

40. *Quodlibet* VIII, q. 1 (Badius, 299vA). See pp. 23–24 for a similar claim in Bonaventure.

limited ways in which finite creatures can participate in the unlimited perfection of the divine essence establishes the essences of finite things.

Argument from Efficient Causality

Henry's third argument is from the actual existence of finite beings. The existence of many, specifically diverse, finite beings is evidence that God has divine ideas and that there are many of them. If God did not have divine ideas, then he could not produce creatures intelligibly. He can only produce as many creatures as he knows, which is why Avicenna, who did not posit a plurality of ideas in God, argued that God could only produce numerically one creature immediately.[41] Since an agent only acts insofar as it is in act, whatever it produces in act in an effect must be in act in the agent. But since the perfection of each thing consists in its being in act and according as it is in act, the perfection of the effect is from the perfection of the agent.[42]

Once again, Henry's argument is indebted to Aquinas's Argument from Similitude, and it is also influenced by Bonaventure's third *fundamentum* from reason.[43] God could not be the efficient cause of creatures without some likeness of them in him. That likeness is found in divine ideas, whereby God knows his essence as imitable. This argument is, as Henry says in *Summa*, a. 42, q. 2, intimately tied to the previous Argument from Exemplar Causality. For this Argument from Efficient Causality to be sound, the perfections of creatures must be in divine wisdom.

Argument from Final Causality

The Argument from Final Causality leans heavily on God as the proper measure of things. A measure is a type of relation whereby things are judged against a standard. All ordered measures, he says, are reduced to some first measure that is simplest and best with the result that it ought to be the measure of the others. Henry explains this last claim by distinguishing three types of measure: The first type of measure is always exceeded and measures only by replication of itself. The number one measures all other numbers by adding itself to itself. The second type of measure is sometimes exceeded by what it measures, sometimes equal to it, and sometimes exceeds it. The motion of the planets is of this type. Their uniform motion exceeds things below them, is equal to themselves, and is exceeded by its continual orbits. The third type of measure always exceeds what it measures and is proper to God. The measured is in him virtually, and it only exists from the consideration of the intellect.[44]

This argument can be understood either with regard to human knowing or with regard to final causality, but only the latter is relevant here.[45] Just as God is the

---

41. *Quodlibet* IX, q. 2 (Leuven, 13.44:18–29). See Avicenna, *Met.*, IX, c. 8 (van Riet, II.476:40–488:95); Algazel, *Met.*, p. 1, tr. 5 (Muckle, 119–29).
42. *Summa*, a. 42, q. 2 (Leuven, 39.39.71–85).
43. See pp. 23–24 and 63.
44. *Quodlibet* IX, q. 2 (Leuven, 13.37:00–41:20).
45. Marrone, *The Light of Thy Countenance*, II.259–390.

first agent by his power and his *esse*, so too he is the ultimate end by his goodness. In fact, his *esse*'s perfection consists in his goodness. Thus, just as all agents participate in their ability to act from God, so all things have goodness from God insofar as they are ordered to an end. Just as God's power contains the powers of all others, his goodness includes the goodness of all others. Therefore, he contains essentially their perfections and all their desires are for his goodness insofar as they are capable of it. Their incomplete goodness is perfected by his perfect goodness.[46] Each thing seeks to live up to its perfect exemplar in God. God is the measure of the perfection that a thing has, both insofar as it exists and insofar as it has achieved the virtue proper to it.

Henry sees the last three arguments—from formal/exemplar, efficient, and final causality—working together. At the heart of these arguments are the related principles that everything makes something like itself and nothing can give what it does not have. If the perfections of creatures did not preexist eminently in God, he could not create them. Since creaturely perfections preexist in God, creatures are like God.

The Unity and Multiplicity of Divine Ideas

Henry holds that divine ideas are one and many. They are one insofar as they are one with the divine essence, which accords with God's simplicity, and they are many insofar as they are rationally distinct in the divine intellect, which accords with God's perfect knowledge. Henry gives two arguments for the multiplicity of divine ideas: The first argument is taken from the side of creatures and the second is taken from the side of the Creator.

Arguments for a Multiplicity of Divine Ideas

Henry's argument from the side of creatures is found in *Quodlibet* V, q. 1. There are many divine ideas because every perfection in a creature, insofar as the creature is a thing and essence, has a certain *ratio* of an idea in God. Thus, the perfection and idea of donkey, a stone, and all other perfections in creatures, both substances and accidents, are in God.[47] Henry argues for this conclusion from the real distinctions between essences and the names given to them. Names are imposed to signify the essences of things according to the determinate perfection's mode of being by which each creature differs from God. Consequently, everything and every perfection existing in creatures, whether substantial or accidental, insofar as it is a thing and nature having a determinate grade of perfection in its essence, has the *ratio* of perfection in God and an idea in his wisdom (like man, sweet, and wisdom).[48] Each

---

46. *Summa*, q. 42, a. 2 (Leuven, 39.43:80–89), esp.: "sicut in virtute sua continent essentialiter virtutes omnium aliorum, ita et in bonintate sua continet essentialiter bonitates omnium aliorum."

47. *Quodlibet* V, q. 1 (Badius, 151rF).

48. *Quodlibet* V, q. 1 (Badius, 151rH): "illa nomina imponuntur ad significandum rerum essentias secundum modum essendi determinatae perfectionis qua qualibet creatura differt a Deo et a quolibet alio."

creature has a limited perfection, and its limited perfection differs from the limited perfection of other kinds of creatures. Thus, there are diverse ideas in God according to the diverse grades of limited perfection in creatures.[49]

Henry's argument from the side of the Creator is found in *Quodlibet* IX, q. 2. Henry defines an idea as "a respect [*respectus*] of imitability from a consideration of the intellect on the divine essence."[50] The plurality of divine ideas follows immediately upon the realization that there is not just one way in which the divine essence is imitable by a creature simply and in general. If God had but one divine idea, he would not cognize things other than himself except by a universal cognition and as one thing since that respect would be one. He would only know singular beings in potency. The imitability of God is multiplied according to the absolute essences of things according to their lowest species by the divine intellect's work. The divine intellect can discern this plurality of essences because it is infinitely perspicacious and penetrates the whole power of the divine essence. As an example, Henry quotes Averroes's statement that "he who knows the nature of heat according as it is heat simply, is not said not to know, rather to know, the nature of heat existing in hot things."[51] By knowing *ens simpliciter*, God knows all the ways beings could fall short of *ens simpliciter*. Thus, he has many ideas that are the *rationes intelligendi* of things. And, as the definition of an idea makes clear, these ideas are certain respects in which God is related to the essence of external things as an exemplar form.[52]

Henry's quoting of Averroes here is the closest he comes to arguing against Averroes's claim that God does not have determinate knowledge of things other than himself.[53] Henry presumably thinks that the quotation is effective against Averroes because Averroes seems to admit that knowing heat simply is sufficient for determinate knowledge of all possible heats. Thus, Averroes has the intellectual principles in place to conclude that God has determinate knowledge of all things other than himself.

These two arguments, and especially the second, bear a striking resemblance to Aquinas's arguments for the multiplicity of divine ideas.[54] For both authors, divine ideas are many because God knows the many limited ways creatures can

---

49. *Quodlibet* V, q. 1 (Badius, 151vL).
50. *Quodlibet* IX, q. 2 (Leuven, 13.29:79–81): "idea nihil aliud sit de ratione sua formali quam respectus imitabilitatis ex consideratione intellectus in ipsa divina essentia." Recall that since Henry distinguishes between *respectus* and *relatio*, I translate *respectus* as 'respect' and *relatio* as 'relation'. See p. 46n62.
51. *Quodlibet* IX, q. 2 (Leuven, 13.29:89–91): "qui scit naturam caloris secundum est calor simpliciter, non dicitur nescire, immo scire, naturam caloris existentis in rebus caldis." See Averroes, *In XII Met.*, com. 51 (Iunctina, VIII.158rb12–14).
52. *Quodlibet* IX, q. 2 (Leuven, 13.29:82–30:26), esp.: "Deus, cognoscendo naturam entis in eo quod est ens simpliciter, quod est ipse, cognoscit naturam entis in qualibet extra quod est in illis participatum."
53. See pp. 4–6.
54. See pp. 67–68.

imitate the divine essence's perfection. Henry departs from Aquinas in focusing on relatives rather than on participation. This emphasis on divine ideas as a *respectus* is not surprising since Henry argues that finite beings are fundamentally the real relation that they bear to God: "A creature's *esse* is nothing other than a *respectus* to God in the creature."[55] Since creatures are fundamentally relations to God, it is unsurprising that Henry would articulate God's knowing them in terms of relation.

Henry of Ghent on Relation

Henry's emphasis that divine ideas are fundamentally respects demands a more detailed examination of his theory of relation. Relations are central to Henry's metaphysics in general and to his theory of divine ideas in particular, but it is difficult to study Henry's theory of relations because he seems to have changed his mind twice. Jos Decorte identifies three 'periods' in Henry's account of relations: (1) before 1278, which includes *Quodlibets* I–II and *Summa*, aa. 1–25; (2) 1278–1284, which includes *Quodlibets* III–VIII and *Summa*, aa. 26–54; (3) 1285–1292, which includes *Quodlibets* IX–XV and *Summa*, aa. 55–75.[56] In the first period, relation plays almost no role in Henry's thought. It begins to play a larger role in the second period when he realizes that relation is useful for certain Trinitarian problems. Henry fully develops his theory of relation in the third period. Since his most complete treatment of divine ideas appears in *Quodlibet* IX, much of the following exposition will focus on aspects of Henry's third period.

Henry argues that divine ideas are rational respects. In order to understand what he means by a rational respect, three aspects of his theory of relation must be understood: (1) Henry's account of a relation in general, especially his distinction between the *res* and the *ratio* of a relation, (2) his distinction between a relation (*relatio*) and a respect (*respectus*), and (3) his distinction between a real respect and a rational respect.

The *Res* and *Ratio* of a Relation

Similar to Aquinas, Henry argues that every category of being has a *res* and a *ratio*.[57] The *res* of each category is whatever is contained in the order of that category through its essence and nature. The *ratio* of the category is the mode of being of

---

55. *Summa*, a. 29, q. 1 (Badius, 171vF): "esse creaturae nihil aliud est in creatura quam respectus ad Deum."

56. Jos Decorte, "Relatio as Modus Essendi: The Origins of Henry of Ghent's Definition of Relation," *International Journal of Philosophical Studies* 10, no. 3 (2002): 310–11. For a similar, but not identical, division of Henry's thought, see Steven P. Marrone, *Truth and Scientific Knowledge in the Thought of Henry of Ghent* (Cambridge, MA: Medieval Academy of America, 1985); Stephen P. Marrone, "Henry of Ghent in Mid-Career as Interpreter of Aristotle and Thomas Aquinas," in *Henry of Ghent: Proceedings of the International Colloquium on the Occasion of the 700th Anniversary of His Death (1293)*, ed. W. Vanhamel, 193–209 (Leuven: Leuven University Press, 1996).

57. See pp. 70–72.

the things contained in the category.⁵⁸ For example, the *ratio* of the category *substance* is to subsist or to stand under, and the *res* of the category *substance* is everything that agrees with the *ratio*.⁵⁹

Henry denies that there are ten categories of being. Only three categories of being have a distinct *res*: substance, quality, and quantity.⁶⁰ The other seven traditional categories of being are reduced to the category of relation, which he also denies has a distinct *res* from the *res* of the absolute category on which it is based.

Relation does not have a distinct *res*, but it does have a distinct *ratio*. The *ratio* of a relation is being-toward-another (*ad aliud esse* or *habitudo nuda*).⁶¹ Since he admits a proper *ratio* for relation, Henry has to contend with the objection from Aristotle and Averroes that relation is the weakest sort of being and necessarily entails dependence.⁶² Both are supposed to be true of relation because a relation could come to be or be destroyed without any change in the quality in which the relation is founded or in the substance in which the quality is affected. For example, if a door and the adjacent wall were both painted the same shade of white, then the door would have the relation as-white-as relative to the wall. If we paint the wall black, the door will lose the relation as-white-as the wall without any change in the door or its whiteness.⁶³ Thus, the relation is both weak and dependent upon the constancy of other term of the relation.

Henry grants that relations in creatures are weak and entail dependence, but weakness and dependence are not characteristic of relation as such. The weakness of relations in creatures stems from the weakness of creaturely substances. The relation inherits the weakness of the *res* in which it inheres, but "the *ratio* of respect

---

58. *Summa*, a. 32, q. 5 (Leuven, 27.79:15–18), esp.: Res praedicamenti est quidquid per essentiam et naturam est contentum in ordine alicuius praedicamenti; ratio praedicamenti est proprius modus essendi eorum quae continentur in praedicamento." Notice that Aquinas's distinction between the *esse* and *ratio* of a category corresponds to Henry's *ratio* and *res*, respectively. The authors do not use the term *ratio* in the same way.
59. *Summa*, a. 32, q. 2 (Leuven, 27.36:37–40). See Aristotle, *Met*., V, c. 13 (AL 25.3.2.110–111).
60. *Quodlibet* V, q. 6 (Badius, 161vO).
61. See, *inter alia*, *Summa*, a. 32, q. 5 (Leuven, 27.91:44) and *Quodlibet* IX, q. 3 (Leuven 13.55:52). In *Quodlibet* V, q. 1, ad 1 (Badius, 155rN), from his second period, Henry offers a different definition of relation: "in creaturis praedicamentum relationis est res cui convenit in alio esse non absolute, sed in respectu ad aliud." This definition seems to claim that category of relation does have a *res*, and not merely a *ratio*, which would mean that it has its own accidental being. Scotus points out this tension and argues that the two accounts are incompatible (*Ord*., II, d. 1, q. 5, n. 169 [Vatican ed., VII.96:4–6]). See Jos Decorte, "'Modus' or 'Res': Scotus's Criticism of Henry of Ghent's Conception of the Reality of a Real Relation," in *Via Scoti: Methodologica Ad Mentem Joannis Duns Scoti*, ed. Leonardo Sileo, vol. 1, 407–29 (Rome: Edizioni Antonianum, 1995).
62. Aristotle, *Met*., X, c. 4, 1055a35–b1 (AL 25.2.3.205); Averroes, *In X Met*., com. 28 (Iunctina, VIII.312G-H).
63. I owe this example to Jos Decorte, "Relation and Substance in Henry of Ghent's Metaphysics," in *Henry of Ghent and the Transformation of Scholastic Metaphysics: Studies in Memory of Jos Decorte*, ed. Guy Guldentops and Carlos Steel (Leuven: Leuven University Press, 2003), 4. In contemporary analytic philosophy, such changes are known as "Cambridge changes." See Peter T. Geach, *God and the Soul* (London: Routledge and Kegan Paul, 1969), 71–72.

simply does not have weak being, but rather strong being: for there is as much true being in its beings being-toward-another, as there is in absolute being-in-itself in its genus."[64] If a relation were founded upon a strong *res*, it would not suffer weakness and dependence because the more absolute and independent a being is, the more other beings depend on it.[65]

Relatio and *Respectus*

Most of Henry's contemporaries use the terms *relatio* and *respectus* synonymously. Henry admits that generally the two terms both mean being-toward-another such that every relation is a respect and every respect is a relation. Yet, Henry identifies an important distinction between them when used according to their proper significations. In its proper sense, a *relatio* is the subject of the relatedness, but a *respectus* may or may not be the subject. The relational terms 'father' and 'fatherhood' make the distinction clear. Both names are respects because they imply a being-toward-another, but in the proper sense, only 'father' is a relation, not 'fatherhood.' 'Father' is the name of a subject such that we can say that a father is the father of the son. 'Fatherhood' is not a subject in this way; we cannot say that fatherhood is the fatherhood of sonship. Thus, Henry concludes, terms like 'father' are both respects and relations, but terms like 'fatherhood' are respects only. So, a *respectus* is characterized by a bare relatedness to something, even if it is not the subject of the relatedness.[66]

This distinction matters because Henry defines a divine idea as a *respectus*, not a *relatio*. A divine idea has being-toward-another, namely, the possible creature, but a divine idea is not the subject of that being-toward. This insight is crucial both with respect to the relation of the creature to God and the relation of God to the creature. Concerning the creature's relation to God, the creature's divine idea is not the subject of the relatedness of a creature to God. It is the mere relatedness. The subject of the relatedness of a creature to God is the creature itself. Concerning God's relation to the creature, again there is no *relatio* because God is not the subject of any real relation to a creature. All that divine idea implies is a *respectus* from God to the creature, not a *relatio* from God to the creature. By denying that God is the subject of a real relation to any creature, Henry ensures that God is not dependent upon creatures.

---

64. *Summa*, a. 32, q. 5 (Leuven, 27.120:41–44): "Ratione autem respectus simpliciter non habet esse debile, sed forte: est enim ita verum esse in genere suo ad aliud esse, quantum in genere suo secundum se absolute esse." See *Quodlibet* IX, q. 3 (Leuven, 13.56:85–89); *Summa*, a. 55, q. 6 (Leuven, 31.396–414).

65. *Summa*, a. 32, q. 5 (Leuven, 27.121:52–54).

66. *Summa*, a. 35, q. 8 (Leuven, 28.81:34–82:60), esp.: "Sistit enim ratio respectus in aliquo quod non dicitur ad aliud per ipsum, et ideo non est respectus ille relatio, proprie loquendo de nomine relationis. Non est enim proprie respectus aliquis relatio, nisi per quam subiectum suum ad aliud dicitur. E converso autem omnis relatio est respectus, quia includit respectum in se, cum superadditione alicuius alterius relationis, licet non ipsa secundum se dicatur ad illud ad quod est, sed subiectum eius." See Decorte, "'Modus' or 'Res,'" 411.

Real Relations and Relations of Reason

The mention that God is not really related to creatures brings up the question of real versus rational relations. Henry declares five conditions for a real relation, and he distinguishes five types of rational relations. First, for a relation to be a real relation, there must be being-toward-another in both extremes of the relation, which is common to every respect and relation. Second, both extremes of the relation must have being-in-something, which ensures that each extreme has a real dependence of that-which-is to that-in-which-it-is, but not vice versa. Third, each extreme must be said mutually of the other. Fourth, when the extremes are said of each other, they must be said of each other with consequentiality, by which Henry means that one must be the consequence of the other. Yet, as Henry notes in the fifth condition, neither extreme is the cause of the other. Taken together, the last three conditions ensure that relations like same and diverse, one and many, and so on, are real mutual relations, but relations between knower and known, generator and generated, and action and passion are not real mutual relations.[67]

Since the relation of knower and known is not a real mutual relation, Henry can claim that divine ideas are not real relations. Divine ideas imply a real relation on the creature's part, but not on God's part. For God, they are only rational respects. A rational respect is a relatedness that is posterior to an act of the intellect and depends upon that intellectual act for its existence. The consideration of the intellect can occur in two ways: (I) First, it occurs by causing a *relatio* in both extremes. (II) Second, it occurs by causing a *respectus* in one of the extremes and a real relation in the other. The first way can be further distinguished into two: (I-a) In one way, the intellect makes diverse relations having a diversity in reality (*ex natura rei*), as when one considers the distinction between the species and genus of a thing. (I-b) In another way, the distinction occurs from the consideration of the intellect alone, as when the intellect considers something to be identical with itself.[68]

The second way, which results in a mixed relation, can also be distinguished into two: (II-a) In one way, when the thing being related does not present any relatedness (*habitudo*) of itself. In this case, the intellect imposes, rather than draws out, the relation, as when the left side of a column is distinguished from the right side. There is nothing about the column itself that makes one side left and the other side right. (II-b) In another way, that which is being related has some relatedness (*habitudo*) of itself such that the intellect would make the relation concerning it. This way is twofold: (II-b-1) In one way, a real relation preexists in one of the extremes and the rational relation is formed in it according to its correspondence. The real relation is the cause of the rational relation, which happens universally in relations of measure to measured. (II-b-2) In a final way, the rational relation is naturally prior to the real relation. The real relation exists in one extreme because of the rational respect in the other extreme. This happens universally in relations that are

---

67. *Summa*, a. 35, q. 8 (Leuven, 28.82:62–87:99).
68. *Quodlibet* IX, q. 1, ad 1 (Leuven, 13.6:72–7:85).

in God to creatures from eternity and occurs on the part of the divine intellect and the divine will.[69]

The fifth type of rational respect (II-b-2) is unique to divine ideas. The real relation that a creature bears to God only exists because God foreknew that a creature could be related to him in just that way. A divine idea is the rational respect that God knows himself to have to a (possible) creature from eternity. It is the rational respect by which God knows his essence to be imitable. The creature's relation to God is a real relation because it really depends on him, but it is rational on God's part because God does not depend upon God.

As a final point, it is worth re-emphasizing that a divine idea is the rational respect by which God knows a possible creature. God knows divine ideas directly and creatures only indirectly. God knows creatures only by knowing the relation they could bear to them. His knowledge of the relation is (at least logically) prior to his knowledge of the creature, which means that God knows the relation before he knows both extremes that the relation relates. Henry does not think it is a problem for God to know the relation before knowing the creature because "cognizing one of the relatives, he necessarily also cognizes the other."[70] By knowing his essence as imitable in such a way, God necessarily knows the possible creature. This point is important to keep in mind because criticism of this theory of knowing relations is the ground for a major shift in theories of divine ideas.[71]

The Finitude of Divine Ideas

One of the hallmarks of Bonaventure's theory of divine ideas is that they were numerically infinite. Aquinas's emphasis on divine ideas as exemplars according to which God creates at some point in history caused him to say that divine exemplars are finite, but God still has an infinite number of divine reasons. Since Bonaventure

---

69. *Quodlibet* IX, q. 1, ad 1 (Leuven, 13.7:86–[1]07), esp.: "relatio illa secundum rationem quoquomodo est ratio causandi illam quae est secundum rem, ut contingit universaliter in relationibus quae ab aeterno sunt in Deo ad creaturas, et ex parte divini intellectus et divinae voluntatis."

A consideration of the intellect can:
(I) Cause a *relatio* in both extremes.
    (I-a) The intellect makes diverse relations having a diversity *ex natura rei* (genus and species)
    (I-b) The intellect makes diverse relations not found *ex natura rei* (identity of a thing to itself)
(II) Cause a *respectus* in one extreme and a real relation in the other extreme.
    (II-a) The thing being related does not present any relatedness (*habitudo*) of itself, so the intellect imposes it (left-side and right-side of a column).
    (II-b) The thing being related presents some relatedness that would make the intellect make the relation as it does.
        (II-b-i) A real relation preexists in one of the extremes and the rational relation is formed in it according to its correspondence. The real relation causes the rational relation.
        (II-b-ii) A rational relation is naturally prior to the real relation and makes the real relation exist. Divine ideas.

70. *Quodlibet* IX, q. 2 (Leuven, 13.30:28–29): "Cognoscens enim distincte unum relativorum, necessario simul cognoscit et aliud."

71. See pp. 124–25, 152–53, and 164–66.

agrees that what God actually creates is finite, he and Aquinas are in fundamental agreement on the number of divine ideas and differ only in emphasis. Henry of Ghent's theory of divine ideas is opposed to Bonaventure's and Aquinas's because he thinks that divine ideas, even in principle, are finite in number.[72]

Henry arrives at the conclusion that divine ideas are numerically finite in two steps: In the first step, Henry limits the scope of divine ideas to the lowest species of things. "Individuals," he says, "do not have proper ideas in God."[73] This point will be treated more thoroughly in the section on the scope of divine ideas, but for now it suffices to say that for Henry an infinite number of divine ideas would entail an infinite number of finite essences.[74]

Second, Henry denies that an infinite number of creatable essences is possible. He argues from the finitude of creatable essences. Each finite essence contains a greater or lesser degree of perfection to the extent that it imitates divine perfection. Since the perfection of an essence comes from its form, an essence is more perfect to the extent that it has, as it were, more form or the addition of more forms. If there were an infinite number of finite essences, then one of them would have an infinite degree of perfection, which would require an infinite addition of forms. In that case, some finite essence would be infinite, which is impossible. Therefore, there is, even in principle, a finite number of creatable essences, and, by extension, a finite number of divine ideas.[75]

At the heart of Henry's arguments that divine ideas are finite in number is the claim that there is an inherent contradiction in saying that finite essences be numerically infinite. Since not even God can do what is impossible, finite essences and the divine ideas of them must be numerically finite. God's knowledge of possible creatures is vast but not infinite. Just as any number we can think, regardless of how large it is, is finite, so too every creatable essence, no matter how perfect it is, is finite. And the sum total of all finite essences, although it would be a practically unfathomable number, would still be a finite number.

The Existence of Things in God

Henry's theory of the existence of things in God is fraught with controversy. Henry frequently distinguishes between essential being (*esse essentiae*) and existential being (*esse existentiae*).[76] He is clear that divine ideas, prior to any act of the divine will, have essential being, and actually created beings have existential being.

---

72. For a more complete account of Henry's theory on this point, see Plevano, "Divine Ideas and Infinity," 192–97. See pp. 32–34 and 81 for Bonaventure and Aquinas.

73. *Quodlibet* V, q. 3 (Badius, 155vO): "individua proprias ideas in Deo non habent."

74. *Quodlibet* V, q. 3 (Badius, 155vO), esp.: "idea respectum dicit ad essentias rerum: ita quod infinitas idearum necessario ponit infinitatem essentiarum creaturae secundum speciem." See pp. 114–16.

75. *Quodlibet* V, q. 3 (Badius, 155vR).

76. See, *inter alia*, *Quodlibet* I, q. 9 (Opera, 5.48:34–56:36); *Summa*, a. 21, q. 4 (Badius, I.127rN–vQ); *Quodlibet* V, q. 4 (Badius, 158vO); *Quodlibet* IX, q. 2 (Leuven, 13.30:30–31:52); *Quodlibet* X, q. 7 (Leuven, 14.145–97).

Essential being is what makes an essence naturally suited to be created, and so, it is not merely an object of thought. What is not clear is what essential being is.

There are two main interpretations of essential being: The first camp is the traditional interpretation of Henry inaugurated by Giles of Rome and Godfrey of Fontaines, codified by Scotus, and given its clearest contemporary articulation by Msgr. John Wippel.[77] According to this interpretation, essential being is a strange sort of existence over and above divine cognitive being, yet it is not the full-blown existential being of actually existing creatures. The second camp is the more recent interpretation, which has been articulated most clearly by Richard Cross.[78] According to this interpretation, essential being is nothing other than divine cognitive being. Henry does not intend to say that essences have any existence independent of God's mind. Rather, an essence in itself necessarily includes cognitive being in God's intellect.

Since scholars are so divided on the issue, I will examine each interpretation, and judge which one coheres better with Henry's texts. I think Cross's interpretation is textually superior, but both interpretations create unresolvable tensions in Henry's theory.

The Traditional Interpretation

The traditional interpretation begins from Henry's interpretation of Avicenna's theory of essence. Henry argues that essences can be considered in three ways and a distinct mode of existence corresponds to each consideration. An essence can be considered (1) in itself absolutely without any reference to existence in singulars or an intellect, (2) as existing in singulars, and (3) as existing in an intellect. According to Avicenna, only (2) and (3) are also modes of existence, and certain accidents that are not part of the essence accrue to the essence from existing in these modes. For example, when an essence exists in singulars, the accidents *many* and *particular* accrue to it, even though they are not part of the essence itself. The first consideration—the absolute consideration—prescinds from the accidents that accrue from existence in singulars or an intellect. It considers only what is essential. In this consideration, "horseness in itself is just horseness."[79]

Henry departs from Avicenna in declaring that the absolute consideration of an essence has an existence proper to it.[80] This proper being, which he calls essential

---

77. Giles of Rome, *De esse et essentia*, q. 12 (Venice ed., 17va); Godfrey of Fontaines, *Quodlibet* II, q. 2 (PB I.53–68), *Quodlibet* VII, q. 3 (PB II.285–87), *Quodlibet* IX, q. 2 (PB III.189–208); Scotus, *Lect.* I, q. 36, a. un., n. 6 (Vatican ed., 17.462–63); Scotus, *Ord.*, I, d. 36, a. un., n. 13 (Vatican ed., 6.276); Wippel, *Metaphysical Themes*, 163–89, esp. 173–84 and the appendix on 189.

78. José Gómez Caffarenta, *Ser Participado y Ser Subsistente En La Metafísica de Enrique de Gante* (Rome: Universitas Gregoriana, 1958), 32–33; Tobias Hoffmann, *Creatura Intellecta: Die Ideen Und Possibilien Bei Duns Scotus Mit Ausblick Auf Franz von Mayronis, Poncius Und Mastrius* (Münster: Aschendorff, 2002), 120; König-Pralong, *Être,* 64–70 and 81–82; Richard Cross, "Henry of Ghent on the Reality of Non-Existing Possibles—Revisited," *Archiv für Geschichte der Philosophie* 92, no. 2 (2010): 115–32.

79. Avicenna, *Met.* V, c. 1 (van Riet, II.229:42): "Equinitas ergo in se est equinitas tantum."

80. Wippel, *Metaphysical Themes*, 175–76. Although it is not the best reading of Avicenna, Henry's reading can be found in the text. In *Met.* I, c. 5, Avicenna argues that each quiddity has an *esse proprium*

being, is distinguished from the essence's existential being.[81] An essence receives essential being from God insofar as God is its formal exemplar by the act of the intellect. Since it has essential being, an essence is naturally suited to have existential being. Existential being depends entirely upon the divine will.

According to the traditional interpretation, essential being is some sort of real being that has "a strange and intermediate kind of reality."[82] Essential being cannot be reduced to divine cognitive being for two reasons: First, Henry says that anything with essential being is really related to God. Second, Henry declares that what has essential being is essentially something in itself.

Henry makes the first point in two places. He declares in *Quodlibet* V, q. 4 that what has essential being cannot fail to have the notion of ideal perfection in God. God, from the necessity of his perfection, has the notion of ideal perfection and of imitability to everything that has essential being. Such a reason (*ratio*) is only in God from a *respectus* and comparison to a creature. The respect of God to creatures is according to reason only, but the relation of a creature to God is real (*secundum rem*).[83] When Henry speaks of a creature here, he must be speaking of the divine idea itself because, as we saw above in the section on the plurality of divine ideas, divine ideas do not arise because God is actually comparing himself to a creature. Instead, God can only know the creature by knowing himself and the relation that could exist between him and a creature. His knowledge of the creature is (at least logically) posterior to his knowledge of the respect which is a divine idea. So, the essence, which has essential being, is both called a "creature" here and declared to have a real relation to God. It makes sense that Henry would call these essences "creatures" since, other than the real relations between the Divine Persons, everything that is really related to God is a creature.[84] Thus,

---

(van Riet, I.35:58). Henry references this text in *Quodlibet* III, q. 9 (Badius, 60vO). See Jean Paulus, *Henri de Gand: Essai sur les tendances de sa métaphysique* (Paris: Vrin, 1938), 98; Catherine König-Pralong, *Avènement de l'aristotélisme en terre chrétienne: L'essence et la matière: entre Thomas d'Aquin et Guillaume d'Ockham* (Paris: Vrin, 2005), 53–58; Jules Janssens, "Henry of Ghent and Avicenna," in *A Companion to Henry of Ghent*, ed. Gordon A. Wilson (Leiden: Brill, 2011), 69.

81. Specifically, he argues that they are intentionally distinct. As König-Pralong notes, "le critère en est que l'un des deux termes peut être conçu sous l'opposé de l'autre" (*Avènement de l'aristotélisme*, 55). For more on this distinction, see *Quodlibet* I, q. 9 (Leuven, 5.55); *Quodlibet* X, q. 7 (Leuven, 14.157–68); *Quodlibet* XI, q. 3 (Badius, 441r-v). See also Paulus, *Henri de Gand*, 220–36, 284–91; Gómez Caffarenta, *Ser Participado*, 65–92; Raymond Macken, "Les Diverses Applications de La Distinction Intentionnelle Chez Henri de Gand," in *Sprache Und Erkenntnis Im Mittelalter*, ed. W. Kluxen, 769–76 (Berlin: De Gruyter, 1981); König-Pralong, *Avènement de l'aristotélisme*, 84–88; Roland J. Teske, *Essays on the Philosophy of Henry of Ghent* (Milwaukee: Marquette University Press, 2012), 93–115, 126–34.

82. Wippel, *Metaphysical Themes*, 179. See Armand Maurer, "Ens Diminutum: A Note on Its Origin and Meaning," *Medieval Studies* 12 (1950): 220.

83. *Quodlibet* V, q. 4 (Badius, 158vO), esp.: "habet enim de necessitate perfectionis suae rationem perfectionis idealis et imitabilitatis ad omne illud quod est aliquid in esse quiditativo et essentiae: et quod potest esse aliquid in esse existentiae."

84. *Quodlibet* IX, q.1, ad 1 (Leuven, 13.14:78–85). See *Summa*, a. 53, q. 1 (Leuven, 31.5–14); *Summa*, a. 55, q. 5, ad. 2 (Leuven, 31.393:84–394:101). Henry is so serious that the relations between

as a result of their essential being, these essences have some sort of creaturely existence independent of God.[85]

This position is problematic because this strange creaturely existence arises from the divine intellect's necessary act, not the divine will's voluntary act.[86] Thus, Henry seems to be guilty of making creatures necessary and positing a necessary emanation from the divine intellect. Since creatures would exist in some way independent of the divine will, when the divine will did establish essences in existential beings, it would not be *ex nihilo*. God would be creating out of already existing essences.[87]

Henry makes the second point—what has essential being is something in itself—especially in *Quodlibet* IX, q. 2. There he argues that because divine ideas have essential being and are naturally suited to exist, they have a diminished being (*ens diminutum*) that is not merely cognitive being. Henry likens this to the way our intellect constitutes the beings made by it in cognitive being. The cognized beings in our intellect have diminished being relative to natural things, which our intellect does not make. They do not have being simply, since that is from God alone, and they do not have cognitive being only. They do not have mere cognitive being because they are present in our intellect as the acting and making objects of the intellect, making our intellects to be in act. They could not make the intellect to be in act unless they were themselves in act. In the same way, the essences in God's intellect are diminished with respect to God's being. But the essences in God's intellect are not as diminished as the essences known by our intellects. The diminished beings in our intellects are in no way naturally suited to have true existence outside the intellect beyond cognitive being. The diminished beings in God's intellect are something of themselves essentially that are naturally suited also to exist outside of the divine intellect by God's will. They are naturally suited to have existential being which is true and perfect being.[88]

---

the Divine Persons are the only real relations in God that he does not even allow relations like the equality of the Persons to be real relations. See *Summa*, a. 55, q. 6 (Leuven 31.398:41–400:83).

85. See *Quodlibet* IX, q. 1, ad 1 (Leuven, 13.7:8–8:14). Wippel argues that this essence as really related to God is the basis for Henry's distinction between things as thinkable (*res a reor*) and things as naturally suited to exist (*res a ratitudine*). Essences are naturally suited to exist precisely because they are already really related to God. See Wippel, *Metaphysical Themes*, 177–78.

86. König-Pralong, *Être*, 65: "Aussi indifférentes soient-elles, les essences ne peuvent pas ne pas exister."

87. This objection is raised against Henry in his lifetime by Giles of Rome, Godfrey of Fontaines, and James of Viterbo. Giles, *De esse et essentia*, q. 12 (Venice, 17va); Godfrey, *Quodlibet* II, q. 2 (PB I.53–68); *Quodlibet* VII, q. 3 (PB II.285–87); *Quodlibet* IX, q. 2 (PB III.189–208); James, *Quodlibet* I, q. 5 (Ypma, 63). See E. Hocedez, "Gilles de Rome et Henri de Gand Sur La Distinction Réelle (1276–1287)," *Gregorianum* 8, no. 3 (1927): 360; John F Wippel, *The Metaphysical Thought of Godfrey of Fontaines: A Study in Late Thirteenth-Century Philosophy* (Washington, DC: The Catholic University of America Press, 1981), 130–45.

88. *Quodlibet* IX, q. 2 (Leuven, 13.31:34–52), esp.: " Ista autem non sunt sic diminuta respectu entis quod Deus est, et existentia in esse cognito, quin in illo esse sint aliquid ad se per essentiam, quod natum est, Deo efficiente, etiam existere extra divinum intellectum praeter esse cognitum, in esse existentiae."

Divine ideas do not have merely cognitive being but are something of themselves essentially. Wippel explains the way divine ideas have both cognitive being and yet do not have merely cognitive being by recalling Henry's teaching in *Quodlibet* IX, q. 2 that divine ideas are secondary objects of divine cognition. A secondary object can be considered either as it is a certain thing (as the statue of Hercules is a statue) or as image (as the statue of Hercules is a sign of Hercules). Divine ideas considered as things are entirely one and simple with the divine essence. Divine ideas considered as images "may be also viewed as enjoying some reality in themselves from eternity."[89] The essences of things, which enjoy essential being, are not merely objects of divine cognition, but they are also something of themselves.

The More Recent Interpretation

The more recent interpretation of Henry's theory of essential being holds that essential being does not entail any extramental reality. There is no "'ghostly' realm of things distinct both from all really existing items and from all merely mental items."[90] Instead, as König-Pralong puts it, "essential being is the mode of being according to which the creature formally imitates God, who thinks himself diversely imitable by the ensemble of creatures."[91] Essential being is Henry's way of referring to divine cognitive being. Essential being is just the sort of cognitive being characteristic of the objects of divine thought.

Cross argues that the traditional interpretation misreads the texts central to its interpretation. Specifically, the traditional interpretation ignores Henry's insistence that essences with essential being do not exist outside of the intellect. In *Quodlibet* V, q. 4, Henry insists that what is something essentially and by nature cannot not have the character of ideal perfection in God, "even though it is not in some existence (*existentia*) outside of the intellect."[92] Someone may object that the term *existentia* is vague. If *existentia* is meant to refer to existential being, then we could not conclude about essential being. This interpretation is ruled out, however, in *Quodlibet* IX, q. 2. Henry again insists that essences do not exist outside of the divine intellect, but this time he uses the term *esse* instead of *existentia*: God "can know something other than himself, as a secondary object of cognition, in two ways: in one way by knowing what the creature is in God; in the other way, by knowing what it is in itself, other than God, although it does not have *esse* outside of his knowledge."[93] The essence has no *esse* whatsoever other than being known by God. Since he uses *esse*, there is no mistaking that

---

89. See Paulus, *Henri de Gand*, 87–92; Wippel, *Metaphysical Themes*, 180–81.
90. Cross, "Non-Existing Possibles," 122. See also Gómez Caffarenta, *Ser Participado*, 32–33; Hoffmann, *Creatura Intellecta*, 120.
91. König-Pralong, *Être*, 82.
92. *Quodlibet* V, q. 4 (Badius, 158vO): "licet non sit in existentia aliqua extra intellectum."
93. *Quodlibet* IX, q. 2 (Leuven, 13.27:45–48): "potest cognoscere dupliciter: uno modo cognoscendo de creatura id quod ipsa est in Deo, alio modo conoscendo de ipsa id quod ipsa habet esse in se ipsa, aliud a Deo, quamvis non habeat esse extra eius notitia."

Henry intends say that the essential being of the essence does not entail any existence outside of the divine intellect.[94]

Cross sees the rest of *Quodlibet* IX, q. 2 as confirmation of this reading against the traditional interpretation. The traditional interpretation reads Henry's claims about God establishing essences with an act of intellect as a formal exemplar as evidence of its reading of essential being, but, Cross argues, that is not the case. When speaking of God's understanding as a formal exemplar, Henry says that it is by this knowing that "the exemplified things have being-something-essentially according to the character of a formal cause in its cognitive being. And this is just as our intellect constitutes beings made by it in cognitive being."[95] The only being that Henry ascribes to the essences of which God is a formal exemplar is cognitive being. As Cross notes, "these imitations are themselves merely mental objects of divine thoughts, things with *esse cognitum*, and it is these divine mental objects that are the bearers of *esse essentiae*."[96] Essential being, then, is merely shorthand for divine cognitive being.

Henry's account of diminished being in *Quodlibet* IX, q. 2 becomes more intelligible from this account of essential being. God's intellect bestows being upon its objects of cognition just as man's does, and in both cases the mode of existence of these cognized beings is inferior to the mode of existence of the knower. God's existence is so great, however, that he can make other things exist in true and perfect existential being in a way that man cannot. The essences known by God are diminished with respect to God's infinite existence, but not so diminished that they could not be established in existential being. The essences in man's intellect are too diminished to be so established. Thus, the traditional interpretation misreads the word 'diminished.' It "is not a marker of a degree of reality, but, as it were, of a degree of possibility."[97] The objects of divine cognition can exist outside his intellect in ways that the objects of our intellects simply cannot. The diminished beings in God's intellect are diminished in the sense that they are only possibly existent, but they are still naturally suited to exist.[98] The traditional interpretation errs in reading Henry metaphysically instead of semantically. Ultimately, it comes down to the fact that "we can, and God cannot, think of *impossibilia*."[99] None of the essences that God thinks are uncreatable, but man can think things that could only be objects of thought, like "gold mountain."

This account handles the traditional interpretation's second objection, namely, that the essences are something of themselves, but the first objection—that the

---

94. Cross, "Non-Existing Possibles," 122–23.
95. *Quodlibet* IX, q. 2 (Leuven, 13.30:31–31:34): "secundum rationem causae formalis habent esse aliquid per essentiam ipsa exemplata in esse suo cognito. Et hoc quemadmodum intellectus noster entia facta ab ipso constituit in esse cognito." See Pasquale Porro, "Universaux et Esse Essentiae: Avicenna, Henri de Gand et Le «troisième Reichs»," in *Le Réalisme Des Universaux*, 10–50 (Caen: Presses Universitaires de Caen, 2002).
96. Cross, "Non-Existing Possibles," 124. See *Summa*, a. 59, q. 5 (Badius, 150rO).
97. Cross, "Non-Existing Possibles," 128.
98. König-Pralong, *Avènement de l'aristotélisme*, 58.
99. Cross, "Non-Existing Possibles," 128.

essences are really related to God—remains. Henry argues that a real relation "is founded in the thing (*res*), and precisely from the necessity of the nature upon which it is founded without any consideration or work of the intellect or will concerning the thing, since it is already present."[100] The word *res*, Cross argues, is being used loosely. Instead of referring to items with existential being, Henry is using *res* "to cover anything possible: i.e., to include compossible mental contents as well as real extramental items."[101] A divine idea can be the subject of a real relation because the essence of which it is a *ratio intelligendi* entails a relation to a real item, namely, the divine essence. In fact, the relation is logically prior to the essence and constitutive of it: "The being (*esse*) of each and every creature is, in the creature, nothing other than a respect to God insofar as it is his effect under the notion of a likeness, such that just as the truth in a creature is nothing but a respect in to God, as to a formal exemplar cause."[102] It becomes a *res* by having a real relation to God, but the real relation does not imply something above and beyond the divine essence as thought. Since the thing is naturally suited to exist, it has essential being, but essential being leaves the divine idea indifferent to creation.[103]

Evaluation

I think that the more recent interpretation makes better sense of Henry's texts, but the resulting theory of essential being is still problematic for Henry's overall thought. If the traditional interpretation be true, then Henry has, for all intents and purposes, denied that God creates *ex nihilo*. This conclusion follows inexorably from the traditional interpretation, and it is the basis for a strong objection against a Catholic thinker. Henry frequently defends *creatio ex nihilo*, so if his theory of essential being truly denies *creatio ex nihilo*, then even Henry would want to reject it.[104]

Moreover, Henry knew the objection. Giles of Rome raised the objection in his ordinary questions *De esse et essentia* prior to 1285, and Godfrey of Fontaines declared it publicly in his second *Quodlibet*, which occurred no later than Easter 1286.[105] Henry responds to these accusations, especially the accusation from Giles,

---

100. *Quodlibet* IX, q. 1, ad 1 (Leuven, 13.14:70–73): "[Relatio realis] in re fundata est, et hoc praecise ex necessitate naturae ipsius super quam fundatur, absque omni consideratione aut opere intellectus vel voluntate circa ipsam ut iam praeexistentem."
101. Cross, "Non-Existing Possibles," 125.
102. *Summa*, a. 29, q. 1 (Badius, 171vF): "ciuslibet enim esse creaturae nihil aliud est in creatura quam respectus ad Deum, inquantum sub ratione similis, est eius effectus, ut sicut veritas in creatura non est nisi respectus in ea ad Deum, ut ad causam formalem exemplarem." See *Summa*, a. 27, q. 1 (Badius, 162rN).
103. Teske, *Henry of Ghent*, 130.
104. Henry defends *creatio ex nihilo* in *Quodlibet* I, q. 7–8 (Leuven, 5.37:41); *Quodlibet* X, q. 7 (Leuven, 14.145–197).
105. Giles, *De esse et essentia*, q. 12 (Venice, 17va); Godfrey, *Quodlibet* II, q. 2 (PB I.53–68). For the dating of Giles's work, see Hocedez, "La Distinction Réelle," 360–61. For the dating of Godfrey's work, see Wippel, *Godfrey of Fontaines*, xxiii–xxviii. For a more in-depth discussion of this debate, see König-Pralong, *Avènement de l'aristotélisme*, 62–88.

in *Quodlibet* X, q. 7, which is dated Christmas 1286. In this question, Henry is asked whether positing that the essence of a creature is really the same with its *esse* can save the doctrine of creation. The implication in the question is that Henry's position cannot be saved, and so Henry finds himself on the defensive.

Henry begins his answer to the question with a lengthy account—92 lines in the critical edition—of Giles's own position in *De esse et essentia*, q. 9, from which "it is manifest that this question is a direct response to Giles's treatise."[106] Henry knows that Giles is behind the question (if not the questioner himself), and he does not take kindly to the accusation. He initially refers to Giles using the customary anonymous 'some' (*aliqui*), but he then refers to Giles as "our adversary" (*adversans nobis*).[107] Henry is so upset that his tone becomes combative and polemical.

When Henry begins to explain his own position, he explicitly refers to *Quodlibet* I, q. 9 and reaffirms the position.[108] A creature's *esse* is not something absolute in reality other than its essence. Creaturely essences have essential being, not insofar as they are in themselves and absolutely considered, but in comparison to the divine essence, which is their formal cause. In fact, essential being cannot even be said to be added to an essence because an essence is not even an essence properly unless it has essential being. Henry's position on essential being has not changed, and the charges leveled against him astonish him. If Henry persists in his theory of essential being, then either he does not think it entails a denial of creation *ex nihilo*, or he has abandoned creation *ex nihilo*. Henry affirms creation *ex nihilo* in the same *Quodlibet* X, q. 7, right after affirming essential being.[109] Henry does not think that essential being entails a denial of creation *ex nihilo*, which implies that he does not interpret his own work according to the traditional interpretation.

The fact that Henry says that essences have essential being, not in themselves and absolutely considered, but in comparison to the divine essence, points toward the more recent interpretation. The comparison of God's essence to the creaturely essence is done by the divine intellect, so the creaturely essence is established precisely because it has essential being, which is nothing other than divine cognitive being. The divine intellect is the formal exemplar of creaturely essences by making them be what they are in its act of thinking about them. The essence has essential being, but it has no being independent of God's intellect.[110]

The more recent interpretation, then, is the better interpretation of Henry's theory of essential being, yet it still suffers two major flaws: First, it does not adequately address Henry's claim that essences have some being of their own such that

---

106. Hocedez, "La Distinction Réelle," 365. See *Quodlibet* X, q. 7 (Leuven, 14.147:50–151:42).

107. *Quodlibet* X, q. 7 (Leuven, 14.152:64). See Hocedez, "La Distinction Réelle," 365. For a general account of Henry's polemics in *Quodlibetal* disputes, see Porro, "Doing Theology (and Philosophy) in the First Person," in *Theological Quodlibeta in the Middle Ages: The Thirteenth Century*, ed. Christopher Schabel, 201–6 (Leiden: Brill, 2006).

108. *Quodlibet* X, q. 7 (Leuven, 14.151:46–47): "determinata in nostro primo Quodlibet, ubi diximus et adhuc dicimus."

109. *Quodlibet* X, q. 7 (Leuven, 14.168:53–56).

110. *Quodlibet* V, q. 4 (Badius, 158vO); *Quodlibet* IX, q. 2 (Leuven, 13.27:45–48).

they have a real relation to God prior to their receiving existential being.[111] Second, the more recent interpretation requires holding that a lower power can do what a higher power cannot do.

Regarding the first flaw, if essences with essential being are really related to God, then, since essential being is nothing other than divine cognitive being, there would be additional real relations in God. But Henry insists that the only real relations in God are those pertaining to the Divine Persons.[112] He does not even allow that relations like goodness, truth, and equality be real relations in God.[113] If essences with essential being are really related to God, then in God there will be, not a small handful of real relations, but a vast (though finite) number of real relations. It would not help to say that the relations are merely mixed relations, real on the part of the essence but rational on the part of God, because the essence is in God. The foundation of the real relation would not be a creature with an existence distinct from God's. The foundation would be in God himself and have divine cognitive being.

Even if the first flaw can be avoided, the second flaw—that a lower power could do what a higher power cannot do—is more devastating. When Cross argues that the term 'diminished' in "diminished being" concerns possibility, not reality, he explicitly says that "we can, and God cannot, think of *impossibilia*."[114] Men can think of chimera like the goatstag, but God cannot. At first glance, this claim seems like a defense of God's perfect knowledge. Perhaps thinking of fantastical beings is an imperfection because they cannot exist and being able to think them is evidence of a weak intellect, so denying that God can think of *impossiblia* is proper, not problematic.[115]

Closer examination shows that denying God can think of *impossibilia* is problematic. If God cannot know *impossibilia* and we can, then God cannot know all our thoughts. God's knowledge will not extend to everything thinkable, but only a subset of what is thinkable. This consequence is contrary to Henry's own claims that God is omniscient. While the more recent interpretation of Henry's theory of essential being seems a better reading of the texts, it still entails difficulties in other parts of Henry's thought, namely, his theory of relations in God and divine omniscience.

Since Henry's theory of essential being entails either a denial of creation *ex nihilo* or a denial of divine omniscience, the theory seems problematic regardless of which interpretation is a better reading of the text. Still, I say we should prefer the more recent interpretation because of Henry's continued insistence that essences with essential being do not exist outside of God's intellect. Essential being is divine cognitive being. There are still problems, but they are the right problems.

---

111. *Quodlibet* IX, q. 2 (Leuven, 13.31:49–50); *Quodlibet* IX, q. 1, ad 1 (Leuven, 13.7:8–8:14).

112. See *Summa*, a. 54, q. 3 (Leuven, 31.160:128–135); *Summa*, a. 54, q. 6 (Leuven, 31.302:1235–303:1257); *Summa*, a. 55, q. 5, co. and ad 2 (Leuven, 31.391:44–392:64, 393:84–394:101).

113. *Summa*, a. 55, q. 6 (Leuven, 31.400:82–83): "Et ideo personarum aequalitas in divinis ex utraque parte est relatio secundum rationem."

114. Cross, "Non-Existing Possibles," 128.

115. This defense is reminiscent of Averroes's second argument against God's knowledge of things other than himself. See pp. 4–5.

THE SCOPE OF DIVINE IDEAS

Henry of Ghent's account of the scope of divine ideas is consistent throughout his career. He expresses it succinctly: "these eight modes of beings do not have proper ideas in God: second intentions, relations, artificial things, genera, differentiae, individuals, privations, and numbers. Therefore, it remains that the specific essences of things alone have proper ideas."[116] Henry's theory of the scope of divine ideas is as sparse as possible. Since Henry thinks that divine ideas must be numerically finite, it is not surprising that he would limit the scope of divine ideas, although the extent of the limitation might be surprising because it contradicts his own theory of divine knowledge. He posits divine ideas as the only source of divine knowledge of creatures, but his account of the scope of divine ideas does not result in perfect divine knowledge of creatures. I will explain Henry's reasons for limiting divine ideas to the most specific species of the essences of things. Henry's theory on divine ideas of singulars, species, and genera will be considered first, accidents second, numbers third, and lastly, form and matter. Once these arguments have been presented, I will show the inconsistency of his account.

Singulars, Species, Genera

Henry of Ghent offers two main arguments to show that the scope of divine ideas extends only to the most specific species, and not to singulars, genera, or differentiae. The first argument is based on the individuation of an essence in singulars. The second argument is based on the principle that there are only ideas of what is *secundum se* and *ad se ipsas* essentially.

The first argument comes from *Quodlibet* II, q. 1 (Advent 1277). Henry argues that diverse individuals of the same species imitate God according to the same grade of perfection. God knows creatures insofar as their perfections are in him, which perfections imitate him according to their grades. The same grade of perfection corresponds to the same character (*ratio*) of perfection in God. Therefore, God knows diverse individuals of the same species by the same *ratio* of perfection. Since a creature's *ratio* of perfection in God is its idea in him, there are no divine ideas of individuals.[117]

As proof of the major premise, Henry argues that two things need to be considered in every created essence, namely, the essence *qua* essence, and its actual existence or subsistence. The character of the essence *qua* essence has a twofold indifference: In one way, the essence is indifferent to actual, existential being and to nonbeing

---

116. *Quodlibet* VII, qq. 1–2 (Leuven, 11.18:31–35): "isti octo modi entium proprias ideas in Deo non habent: intentiones secundae, relations, artificialia, genera, differentiae, individua, privations et numeri. Restat igitur quod proprias ideas solummodo habent specificae rerum essentiae." See Tobias Hoffmann, "Ideen Der Individuen Und Intentio Naturae: Duns Scotus Im Dialog Mit Thomas von Aquin Und Heinrich von Gent," *Freiburger Zeitschrift für Philosophie Und Theologie* 46, no. 1/2 (1999): 142.

117. *Quodlibet* II, q. 1, arg. (Leuven, 2.3:11–17). Recall that Bonaventure uses this argument with the contrary minor premise. See p. 37.

because there is nothing about the essence that requires it to exist or not exist. In another way, the essence is indifferent to universal being and particular being because it only receives these determinations when it is receives substantial being in a determinate supposit or when it is abstracted from supposits by an intellect.[118]

Applying this distinction to divine ideas, Henry says that the essence of a thing can be considered in two ways: as in itself, and as in one or many supposits. It follows that an idea according to which God cognizes the thing, of which he is a likeness, can be considered in two ways: First, as it is an absolute essence. Second, as it is an essence related to supposits. In the first way, there is only one idea in God according to each species of creature. In this one idea he cognizes the whole power of the essence and that its possible multiplication comes to be through various supposits. In the second way, God's idea is one with respect to his essence and many with respect to the multiplication of supposits under the essence. Just as the essence is one in itself and many with respect to many supposits, so the idea of the same essence is one absolutely and many insofar as it relates to the supposit under the essence's identity.[119] At the heart of this distinction between essence and supposits is Henry's theory of individuation. According to Henry, individuation is a double negation that accrues to the essence from another such that there is no formal distinction between individuals. Thus, no distinct idea is required for God to know each individual.[120]

This way of viewing the scope of divine ideas makes the relationship between divine ideas and individuals parallel to the relationship between the divine essence and divine ideas. Just as the divine essence remains one despite many divine ideas, so the divine idea of the most specific species remains one despite many possible supposits.

Henry's second main argument is found in *Quodlibet* VII, qq. 1–2 (Christmas 1282). Henry offers his most complete account of the scope of divine ideas in these two questions, which he treats together. He arrives at the scope of divine ideas by making a series of distinctions among created things. First, created things are either natural things or not things, but only second intentions or artifacts. The latter can be derived from the ideas of natural things and so have no proper ideas of their own. Among natural things, some are *secundum se* and *ad se ipsas*, which fall into

---

118. *Quodlibet* II, q. 1 (Leuven, 6.4:24–5:53). Henry defends the major premise in part because Aquinas denied it. Aquinas holds that each individual has its own, distinct *esse* by which it imitates God and so there must be a distinct idea for each individual. Aquinas, *De veritate*, q. 3, a. 8, s.c. 2 (Leonine, 22/1.115:35–39). See pp. 78–80.

119. *Quodlibet* II, q. 1 (Leuven, 6.5:54–71), esp.: "secundum quamlibet speciem creaturae in Deo est tantum una idea, qua cognoscit totam virtutem essentiae et eius multiplicationem possibilem fieri per varia supposita." Henry offers similar arguments in *Quodlibet* V, q. 3 (Badius ed., 155vR–156rT) and *Quodlibet* IX, q. 2 (Leuven, 13.33:91–99). See Hoffmann, "Ideen Der Individuen," 143–44.

120. For Henry's theory of individuation, see *Quodlibet* II, q. 8 (Leuven, 6.47); *Quodlibet* V, q. 8 (Badius, 166rM); Stephen F. Brown, "Henry of Ghent (b. ca. 1217; d. 1293)," in *Individuation in Scholasticism: The Later Middle Ages and the Counter Reformation 1150-1650*, ed. Jorge J.E. Gracia, 195–219 (Albany, NY: State University of New York Press, 1994).

the categories of substance, quantity, and quality, and others are to another and in respect to another only, which fall into the other seven categories.[121] There are not divine ideas of the second sort. Among natural things that are *secundum se* and *ad se ipsas*, some are such essentially and others are such accidentally only. Only the quiddities and specific essences of the most specific species are such essentially. Genera, differentiae, and individuals are *secundum se* and *ad se ipsas* only accidentally. Henry concludes that the scope of divine ideas is limited to those natural things that are *secundum se* and *ad se ipsas* essentially.[122]

There are not divine ideas of genus and differentia because they do not differ from the species except as complete and incomplete, and so they are known by knowing the complete essence. He rules out ideas of individuals since they do not add anything real to the species.[123] Individuals exist *per se* in a certain way, but they do not imitate the divine *esse* as individuals. Peter does not imitate God as Peter, having in himself this humanity, but according as he is man.[124] Peter qua Peter is just a determination of the divine idea of man because Peter does not add anything formally to the idea. If he did, then he would be of a difference essence than *man*. Thus, God has ideas of the most specific species only.

Accidents

Given what has already been said about the scope of divine ideas, it is not surprising that Henry limits the scope of divine ideas of accidents. Since natural beings in the accidental categories of quantity and quality are *secundum se* and *ad se ipsas* essentially, there are divine ideas of the most specific species in these two categories. There are no ideas of the genera, differentiae, or individuals in these accidental categories. God has an idea of *scarlet* but not of *red*, *color*, or this scarlet. When it comes to the category of quantity, Henry is even more restrictive, arguing that it does not have a proper idea except as the form of continuity.[125] As we will see in the next section, he does not even allow there to be divine ideas of discrete quantities. The remaining seven categories of accidents are *secundum se* and *ad se ipsas* accidentally only, and so Henry denies divine ideas of them.

Henry does not make any distinction between proper and separable accidents as Aquinas does. Nevertheless, it seems safe to conclude that Henry, like Thomas, would admit distinct ideas of separable accidents, but not of proper accidents. Since proper accidents follow upon the species, they do not have complete

---

121. For Henry's derivation of the last seven categories, see *Summa*, a. 32, q. 5 (Leuven, 27.87:26–96:90).
122. *Quodlibet* VII, qq. 1–2 (Leuven, 11.6:52–8:2).
123. *Quodlibet* VII, qq. 1–2 (Leuven, 11.8:3–9).
124. *Quodlibet* VII, qq. 1–2, ad 1 (Leuven, 11.21:20–23): "Petrus enim, licet quodam modo per se, non tamen per se et primo habet esse secundum imitationem divini esse secundum quod est Petrus, habens in se hanc humanitatem, sed secundum quod homo simpliciter, habens in se humanitatem simpliciter."
125. *Quodlibet* VII, qq. 1–2 (Leuven, 11.9:47–49).

essences. They are included in the divine idea of the most specific species from which they follow.¹²⁶

Numbers

Numbers are a particular source of difficulty for Henry. He cannot allow there to be divine ideas for discrete numbers because discrete numbers are infinite. If there were an idea for each discrete number, then, as Augustine and Bonaventure argue, divine ideas would be infinite in number.¹²⁷ Since Henry holds that divine ideas are numerically finite, he cannot allow divine ideas of all discrete numbers.

Henry's solution to this conundrum is to take refuge in the form of continuity. God has an idea of the form of continuity because it contains every number. Properly speaking, number is nothing but a multitude through the division of the continuous. Number and discrete quantity do not add anything to the continuous except the notion of negation or respect of the parts to each other. A discrete quantity is nothing but a negation or privation of a continuous quantity. Since there are no ideas of negations and privations, there are no ideas of discrete quantities and numbers.¹²⁸ In knowing continuous quantity, God has perfect knowledge of all discrete quantities and numbers without needing additional divine ideas.

Form and Matter

Henry's denial of divine ideas of second intentions, artifacts, relations, genera, differentiae, individuals, privations, and numbers might lead us to think that God does not have ideas of form and matter.¹²⁹ Form and matter are not most specific species and complete essences, but principles of material individuals. However, Henry does hold that there is a proper idea of form and matter. Although matter is not entirely (*omnino*) makeable on its own independent of the composite being, it has a proper idea in God other than the idea of form, through which matter is makeable in the composite. This idea of matter is one for all parts of matter which are naturally suited to be joined in the unity of a material singular, as the idea of the form of the continuous is one to all continuous things that are naturally suited to be joined in the unity of a continuous singular.¹³⁰

---

126. See pp. 83–84.
127. See pp. 32–33.
128. *Quodlibet* VII, qq. 1–2 (Leuven, 9:47–10:76). He references Aristotle, *Met.* VIII, c. 3 (AL XXV.2.162:22–163:6) and *Met.* V, c. 6 (AL XXV.2.91:10–27).
129. *Quodlibet* VII, qq. 1–2 (Leuven, 11.18:31–35).
130. *Quodlibet* VII, qq. 1–2 (Leuven, 11.20.97–21:3), esp.: "[materia] habet tamen propriam ideam in Deo aliam ab idea formae, per quam est factibilis in compositio." In *Quodlibet* I, q. 10 (Leuven, 5.63–74), Henry argues that prime matter has a certain nature of its own such that God could make it subsist without any form. Again, in *Quodlibet* X, q. 8, he argues that "in quolibet composito per se ex materia et forma, sicut sunt duae essentiae, sic sunt duo esse utroque modo" (Leuven, 14.205:70–71). For an account of Henry's position, see König-Pralong, *Avènement de l'aristotélisme*, 151–56.

Henry insists that a divine idea of matter does not mean that the there are two principal ideas in material things, one for the matter and one for the specific essence. The *esse* of the composite is principally from the form, and there are not two beings, one of the form and another of the composite. These beings are the same being.[131]

By articulating an idea of matter in this way, Henry makes it clear that the idea is not of prime matter or of *this* matter in any given singular. It is the idea of the passive principle of any composite whatsoever. If Henry were to posit a divine idea of prime matter, then he would be committing himself to saying that prime matter has an essence. Matter would thus have essential being yet have being without form. If Henry meant that the idea of matter were of *this* matter, then God would seem to be able to have an idea of at least one individual, which he consistently denies.

An Inconsistency in Henry's Account

Henry of Ghent's theory of the scope of divine ideas is minimalistic. There are only as many ideas as there are most specific species of complete essences. God does not have ideas of second intentions, relations, artifacts, relations, genera, differentiae, individuals, privations, or numbers. There is something elegant about the account's simplicity, but what it gains in simplicity, it loses in efficacy. Divine ideas are the *rationes cognoscendi* by which God knows things other than himself. They are his only source of knowledge of possible creatures.

> If there were not an idea in God, then he could not know something outside of himself as other than him, and as a result neither could he produce something entirely outside himself in being. And if there were not many ideas in God, he could not know many things outside himself, nor as a result, produce them.[132]

The multiplicity of divine ideas is the only safeguard of God's perfect knowledge. If God had but one idea, his knowledge of things other than himself would not be distinct. He would have universal knowledge only, which would be imperfect and in potency. Thus, there must be an idea for each most specific species.

Henry's theory that there are ideas of the most specific species seems to allow perfect divine knowledge of the genera and differentiae, but Henry's own words show that the theory cannot account for perfect knowledge of individuals. It could work for genera and differentiae because they are included in the intelligible content of the species. If we were to know the essence of a most specific species fully, then we would know its genera and differentiae all the way to its category of being. If God knows all such essences perfectly, then he can know the categories perfectly.

---

131. *Quodlibet* VII, qq. 1–2 (Leuven, 11.21:3–15).
132. *Quodlibet* IX, q. 2 (Leuven, 13.44:30–45:34): "si in Deo non esset idea, non posset aliquid extra se, ut aliud est ab ipso, cognoscere, et per consequens nec aliquid omnino extra se in esse producere, et si in Deo non essent plures ideae, non posset scire plura extra se, nec per consequens producere."

The case is different for individuals. Henry consistently affirms that individuals "do not add form upon the form of the most specific species, but only its determination."[133] Just as the builder makes many houses by the same form, so God makes many individuals of the same species by the same divine idea. But if we inspect the analogy more closely, Henry says, we find that the builder is not making according to the form of house, but rather the form of circular house, quadrangular house, and so on. It might be natural to assume that for Henry *house* is a genus and *circular house* is a most specific species, but instead he says that circular and quadrangular are "*quasi* differences in species."[134] Circular and quadrangular do not result in completely different species of house the way that rational and nonrational do for animal. Circular and quadrangular are not essential differences in house, yet it would be impossible to know *this* house without knowing whether it be circular or rectangular.

I submit that such nonessential differences are found in individuals. The essence of the most specific species *man* is neither intrinsically male nor intrinsically female, but every individual of the species is either male or female. From the essence of *man* alone, it is impossible to know whether this individual is male or female. Even perfect knowledge of the essence would only yield the knowledge that the individual is either male or female. If perfect knowledge of the essence is insufficient to judge whether the individual be male or female, then by Henry's own principles, the most specific species would have to be further distinguished into two ideas, one for males and one for females. Further examples could be multiplied such that a distinct idea would be required for each individual. If God's only *rationes cognoscendi* are the essences of the most specific species, then he could not have perfect cognition of individuals nor produce them. But God has produced such individuals, so the scope of his divine ideas must extend to the individuals. Henry's limitation of the scope of divine ideas does not preserve God's perfect knowledge.[135]

RECAPITULATION AND CONCLUSIONS

According to Henry of Ghent, a divine "idea, in its formal *ratio*, is nothing other than a respect of imitability from the consideration of the intellect on the divine essence."[136] Divine ideas are the only means by which God can know and produce things other than himself. God has perfect knowledge of things. He is their formal exemplar, the measure of all things, and their efficient cause through divine ideas. When he knows himself, he knows all the ways in which possible creatures could

---

133. *Quodlibet* IX, q. 2 (Leuven, 13.33:91–92): "individua non addunt formam super formam speciei specialissimae sed solummodo determinationem eius."
134. *Quodlibet* IX, q. 2, ad 2 (Leuven, 13.45:47): "plures domnus sunt quasi specie differentes sicut circularis, quadrata et huiusmodi."
135. Scotus offers a similar internal criticism of Henry's account in *Rep.* I-A, d. 36, qq. 3–4, n. 39 (Noone, 438:25–439:8).
136. *Quodlibet* IX, q. 2 (Leuven, 13.29:79–81): "idea nihil aliud sit de ratione sua formali quam respectus imitabilitatis ex consideratione intellectus in ipsa divina essentia."

imitate him. He does this by knowing the real relation that a possible creature could bear to him. God's knowledge of the real relation is not real on his part, but merely rational. If God were really related to (possible) creatures, then he would be dependent on them.

Since God's knowledge is perfect, he knows all relations that creatures could bear to him. As a result, he has many divine ideas. If he had but one divine idea, his knowledge would be imperfect and in potency. The multiplicity of divine ideas is not infinite, however. Since the distinction among creaturely essences occurs because the essences occupy various grades of perfection, an infinite number of ideas of essences would result in the impossible situation of an infinitely perfect creaturely essence. The inherent limitations of creatures make it impossible for there to be an infinite number of divine ideas.

Although there has been much controversy on this point, I argued that the essential being that Henry ascribes to divine ideas is just divine cognitive being. Divine ideas do not have any existence independent of their being known by God. To say otherwise is to deny, at least tacitly, creation *ex nihilo*, which Henry would never do. This interpretation of essential being still leaves problems in Henry's overall system, but it is the best reading of his texts.

Henry minimizes the scope of divine ideas to the essences of the most specific species only. There are no ideas of relations, artifacts, genera, differentiae, individuals, privations, or numbers. There are, however, ideas of form and matter.

Henry's account of divine ideas is indebted to both Bonaventure and Thomas, although he sharply disagrees with both on many points. Like Bonaventure, Henry emphasizes the cognitive role of divine ideas, but he uses Thomas's language of imitability. In a perceived conflict with Aquinas, Henry argues that divine ideas are not principles of cognition except accidentally. If they were practical, then they would coerce the divine will and predetermine with absolute necessity what God would and would not make. Like both Bonaventure and Aquinas, Henry argues that divine ideas are secondary objects of the divine intellect upon the divine essence. Divine ideas are the essence as *understood* to be imitable in certain ways.

The biggest points of disagreement between the three thinkers concerns the number of divine ideas and the scope of divine ideas. Both Bonaventure and Aquinas argue for an infinite number of divine ideas (at least in Aquinas's sense of *ratio*). Henry, however, argues that divine ideas are finite, even in principle. Henry parts ways with the other two in claiming that divine ideas are of the most specific species only, while Bonaventure and Thomas argue that God has ideas of individuals, and, in the sense of *ratio*, every genus, differentia, accident, and so on.

Part II.
The Infinite Intellect Theory of Divine Ideas

I call the second theory of divine ideas covered in this study the Infinite Intellect Theory. As far as I can tell, it was only held by Peter John Olivi and his student Petrus de Trabibus. The Infinite Intellect Theory was developed in opposition to the Imitability Theory, which Olivi thinks is contrary to faith and reason. In particular, he argues that it entails an irrational account of how relations are known. Imitability Theorists argue that divine ideas are relations between God and creatures. By knowing himself and the relations, God knows creatures. Put another way, God knows one term of the relation by means of the other term and the relation itself. Infinite Intellect Theorists argue that it is impossible to know the relation before knowing both terms of the relation. This line of argumentation is decisive for later authors. In particular, it is one of the motivating factors for the development of the *Creatura Intellecta* Theory of divine ideas.[1] I emphasize both the argument and its influence because, as I said in the introduction, I think that reflection upon what a relation is and how it functions is a major cause for the changes in theories of divine ideas.[2]

The positive account of the Infinite Intellect Theory emphasizes God's unity and simplicity. God's intellect, object understood, and act of understanding are identical. Divine ideas are thus God's very act of understanding because he is his understanding of any particular thing. Insofar as he understands a creature, he has an idea and exemplar of it. Unlike the created artist who exists by a natural form and knows by an intellectual form, God has but one form by which he exists and knows. His nature and knowledge are only distinct according to reason. In reality, his form is his knowledge.

---

1. See pp. 147–48.
2. See p. 7. There has not been an occasion to emphasize this point much in the prior three chapters since Bonaventure, Thomas, and Henry all have sufficiently similar accounts of relations.

Chapter IV.
Peter John Olivi (ca. 1248–1298) and Petrus de Trabibus (fl. 1290s)

Peter John Olivi was a controversial Franciscan figure. He began to study theology at Paris in about 1267, but he never became a master. The Franciscan order established a commission to study Olivi's work in 1283 because some of his teachings "seemed to sound badly."[1] The seven-man commission included Richard of Mediavilla, who would become *magister regens* at Paris beginning in 1284 and whose own thought on divine ideas was influenced by Olivi's criticisms. Among the errors that the commission condemned and forced Olivi to recant publicly were errors concerning divine ideas.[2] Olivi's teachings after the recantation continued to be a source of scandal and so he was dismissed from Paris.[3] Not all of Olivi's arguments are fully fleshed out, so we will also have recourse to the thought of Olivi's student, Petrus de Trabibus to finish and explain some of Olivi's theory.

CRITIQUE OF THE IMITABILITY THEORY

The controversy over divine ideas seems to have originated from Olivi's *Quaestio de ideis* (*Summa* I, q. 6 bis). In *Summa* I, q. 6, Olivi asks about the invariability of the divine will. The sixteenth objection argues that God's will is uniformly related to the things orderable to it as to a final end just as his intellect is uniformly related to understanding those things that are represented by the divine exemplar.[4] The mention of the divine exemplar gives Olivi the occasion to discuss divine ideas. In one of the manuscripts of this question, Olivi's discussion of divine ideas appears as a separate question appended to *Summa* I, q. 6. As a result, in his recent edition of the text, Sylvain Piron published the discussion of divine ideas separately under the title *Quaestio de ideis* (*Summa* I, q. 6, bis), rather than publish it as a lengthy reply to the sixteenth objection.[5]

---

1. *Chronica XXIV Generalium* (*Analecta franciscana*, III.374–75), esp.: "male videbantur sonare."
2. *Chronica XXIV Generalium* (*Analecta franciscana*, III.376). See Olivi, "Tria scripta sui ipsius apologetica" (Laberge, 115–55, 374–407).
3. *Chronica XXIV Generalium* (*Analecta franciscana*, III.382).
4. Olivi, *Quaestio de divino velle et scire*, arg. 16, n. 34 (Piron, 5).
5. Prior to this edition, no complete edition of this question existed in print. Portions of Olivi's reply to the objection relevant for his influence on Scotus were found in Appendix A of Timothy B. Noone and Carl A. Vater, "The Sources of Scotus's Theory of Divine Ideas," in *Divine Ideas in Franciscan Thought*, 91–96, used with permission. A more complete French translation of the text was published in Sylvain Piron, "Pierre de Jean Olivi," in *Sur La Science Divine*, ed. J.-C. Bardout and O. Boulnois, 204–25 (Paris: Presses Universalitaires de France, 2002). An earlier version of the portion of this chapter

To understand the relationship between the divine intellect and the divine will, Olivi says, it is necessary to understand what the terms "divine exemplar" and 'idea' signify in God. He immediately summarizes five positions, the last of which is his, and then he critiques the other four. The first two positions are especially pertinent.[6] The first is Aquinas's position that 'exemplar' signifies the divine essence as it can be participated in diverse ways and imitable by diverse creatures. One reason (*ratio*) of imitability entails one idea and especially with respect to those things that has disposed (*disposuit*) or willed to create.[7]

Olivi declares that this theory "seems to be contrary to faith and reason."[8] He offers many objections to Aquinas of which four are pertinent for our purposes. First, on Aquinas's account, the divine act of understanding cannot know possible creatures immediately or as they are in themselves. Instead, it apprehends creatures as absent from God. Creatures are represented to him as in an exemplar, not as they are in themselves. So, it seems that God does not even understand them except with a certain comparison, namely, by comparing them to the divine essence and to the mode of its ability to participate.[9]

Second, Aquinas's theory misunderstands how relations are known. On the Imitability Theory, knowledge of a relation is (logically) prior to knowledge of one of the terms of the relation. God knows the relation that a certain creature can bear to him and through that relation he comes to know the creature as the term of that relation. The relation is known before both terms are known. As Henry of Ghent says, "knowing one of the relatives distinctly, he necessarily knows the other at the same time."[10] On this model, God knows himself as one term of the relation, the relation itself, and then knows the possible creature.

Olivi objects that relations are not known this way. Both terms of the relation must be known before any relation between them can be known. Therefore, God must know the terms of the relation first and then the relation.[11] Imitability Theorists make it seem like the knowledge of the term '2' and the relation "is half of" automatically yields knowledge of the other term, '4.' Mathematics problems seem

---

dealing with Olivi's and Petrus's critique of the Imitability Theory can be found in Noone and Vater, "Sources of Scotus's Theory," 78–82.

6. The second position is Bonaventure's, which Olivi tries to interpret as agreeing with him. It will be discussed in the next section beginning on p. 126.

7. Olivi, *Quaestio de ideis*, n. 4 (Piron, 2). See Aquinas, *ST* I, q. 15, a. 2 (Leonine, 4.201-2); Aquinas *De veritate*, q. 3, a. 2 (Leonine, 22/1.102-6), and pp. 56–61.

8. Olivi, *Quaestio de ideis*, n. 9 (Piron, 3): "videtur esse contrarius fidei et rationi."

9. Olivi, *Quaestio de ideis*, n. 9 (Piron, 3). See Olivi, *Quodlibet* III, q. 2 (Defraia, 174).

10. Henry, *Quodlibet* IX, q. 2 (Leuven, 13.30:28-29): "Cognoscens enim distincte unum relativorum, necessario simul cognoscit et aliud." See pp. 103–4.

11. Olivi, *Quaestio de ideis*, n. 12 (Piron, 3): "Oportebit ergo prius intelligere ipsa extrema seu terminos huius respectus." See also, Olivi, *In II Sent.*, q. 55 (Jansen, II.346); Olivi, *Quodlibet* III, q. 2 (Defraia, 174). See Alain Boureau, "Le Concept de Relation Chez Pierre de Jean Olivi," in *Pierre de Jean Olivi (1248–1298)*, ed. Alain Boureau and Sylvain Piron, 41–55 (Paris: Vrin, 1999). Boureau points out that Olivi's theory of relation is important in the transition from the realism of earlier authors to the nominalism of later authors.

to be solved in exactly this way, but the example is misleading because the solver of the problem already knows the discrete number '4.' The relation "does not suffice to make the imitable thing known because it presupposes that it is in fact already known."[12] A proper example would have to result in knowledge of what was previously unknown. To Olivi's mind, the Imitability Theory begs the question.

At this point, one of the main claims of this book begins to emerge, namely, that the transition in theories of divine ideas is driven primarily by disagreements over relations.[13] The Imitability Theorists examined in Part I all argue that God knows creatures through the relation that a divine idea is. Olivi is challenging that claim, and his objection posits an account of relations that becomes almost universally accepted. Richard of Mediavilla, Scotus, and early Thomists and Scotists argue that relations cannot be known before both terms of the relation.[14] These thinkers still claim that divine ideas are relations, but they are not relations that make God know. The Nominalist Theorists take the objection even further and argue that divine ideas are not relations.[15]

Third, Olivi declares that positing divine ideas as diverse grades of participating does not suffice to apprehend the diversity of all creatable or created things. It is not clear how God can understand all things fully in this way.[16] Olivi does not explain this assertion, but his student, Petrus de Trabibus, does. Petrus admits that nothing is done or can be done by God unless he has some likeness with the creature he creates, and the creature imitates him in some way. Imitability Theorists are right to say that a divine idea entails the divine essence's imitability by a creature, but imitability is not the nature or character of an idea.[17] For Petrus, an idea is a cognitive, causative, and determinative reason (*ratio*) of makeable things. Imitability seems to touch on the cognitive *ratio*, but the causative and determinative aspects come from the divine will.[18]

Imitability touches on one of the aspects of a divine idea, but it does so incompletely. Imitability cannot account for distinct knowledge of each creature because imitability does not distinguish one possible creature from another. Being an imitation of God is characteristic of every creature, and what is common to every creature does not distinguish them.

This third objection seems incomplete because it misrepresents the arguments of the Imitability Theorists. They do not argue that creatures are distinguished

---

12. Sylvain Piron, "La Liberté Divine et La Destruction des Idées chez Olivi," in *Pirre de Jean Olivi (1248-1298)*, ed. Alain Boureau and Sylvain Piron (Paris: Vrin, 1999), 83.
13. See p. 7.
14. See pp. 152-53, 164-66, and 195-206, respectively.
15. See pp. 216-20 and 238-39, respectively.
16. Olivi, *Quaestio de ideis*, n. 13 (Piron, 3-4), esp.: "Diversus autem gradus participandi istas, aut diversus gradus participandi rationes generales entis non sufficiat ad apprehendendum diversitatem omnium specierum creabilium, aut creatarum."
17. Petrus, *In I Sent.*, d. 35, p. 1, a. 2, q. 2 (Noone-Vater, 99:60-63): "verum est quod idea dicit divinae essentiae imitabilitatem a creatura. Hoc tamen non videtur ratio ideae."
18. Petrus, *In I Sent.*, d. 35, p. 1, a. 2, q. 2 (Noone-Vater, 98:36-99:60).

because they imitate God, but rather because they imitate God *in diverse ways*. It is the degree to which a creature imitates God that distinguishes it, not mere imitation. The argument ignores Aquinas's emphasis that a divine idea, strictly speaking, is an exemplar that God has willed to create at some time in history.

Olivi seems to have anticipated this sort of objection and offers the fourth argument in reply. He asks how and through what the divine essence represents diverse possible imitations since the divine essence cannot be participated by some creature univocally and it is not numerically identical to the creature. In particular, how does seeing the divine essence as capable of being participated in diversely results in the knowledge of some other essence than the divine essence? Imitability of this kind, he says, does not posit something in the divine essence except God's very essence.[19]

I am not quite convinced by the fourth argument because it seems to assert rather than argue that God could not know creaturely essences by knowing himself as imitable in diverse ways. It has an advantage over the third argument in explicitly including the diversity of possible imitations, but it does not show how seeing God's essence as able to be participated in is not to see other essences. What is needed is an argument like the one Scotus will offer that the imitation or even a particular degree of imitation is the specific difference of any creature.[20]

This critique of the Imitability Theory is Olivi and Petrus's most important contribution to the history of theories of divine ideas. First and foremost, they argue that the Imitability Theory rests on a faulty theory of relation. Relations cannot be known directly before both terms of the relation are known. Moreover, imitability itself does not seem sufficient to distinguish one creature from another. As we will see below in Chapter VII, Richard of Mediavilla tacitly accepts these criticisms, and, as we will see in Chapter VIII, Scotus strengthens them and declares them to be decisive against the Imitability Theory.

THE INFINITE INTELLECT THEORY OF DIVINE IDEAS

The theory of divine ideas that Olivi articulates—and Petrus clarifies in certain respects—is far less influential than the critiques they offer of what I call the Imitability Theory. Scotus examines the theory, but he quickly dismisses it as erroneous.[21] Olivi arrives at his theory—the Infinite Intellect Theory—by explaining Bonaventure's theory because he thinks that he has the proper and faithful interpretation of Bonaventure.

Bonaventure holds that the light of the divine intellect, since it is beyond every genus, can express all things in all genera. Therefore, it is the exemplar of all things

---

19. Olivi, *Quaestio de ideis*, n. 14 (Piron, 4), esp.: "Videre enim divinam essentiam et, ut ita dicam, totam intensionem eius in quantum tale, non est videre aliquam aliam essentiam."

20. See pp. 162–63.

21. Scotus, *Rep.* I-A, d. 36, qq. 1–2, nn. 33–37 (Noone, 407:33–409:15). Scotus does not examine Olivi's opinion in either the *Lectura* or *Ordinatio*. See pp. 164–66.

as it is the expressing light of all things. Its determinate expressions are the notions of determinate things that, with respect to things that will come to be, some call 'ideas.' Since the divine light is its expression, the determinate expressions themselves thus express each thing. Yet, they are not many lights (*lumina*), but only one light (*lux*), which would be like the light of the sun if the sun were its rays. In that case, it could be said that there are, as it were, many rays only with respect to the diversity of the terms or places, but in itself and its essence, there is but one light.[22]

Olivi thinks this theory is understood poorly if it is interpreted the way I interpreted it in Chapter I, which closely aligns Bonaventure with Aquinas. Understood in this way, Bonaventure's theory falls to the same criticism as Aquinas's theory, Olivi says. Bonaventure's theory is understood well if "divine light" is understood as the actuality and clarity of divine understanding (*intelligere*). Thus, when Bonaventure speaks of 'expressions,' he intends only God's very *intelligere* as it is the actual expression of each object's proper *ratio*.[23]

This interpretation of Bonaventure aligns with Olivi's own position. Divine *intelligere* can be called a representative *ratio* or actual representation of certain things, but more properly it should be called their adjudicative (*diiudicativa*) and affirmative or negative reason, or rather the actual adjudication or affirmation. Olivi uses the human intellect to explain what he means. In man, simple apprehension of quiddities or terms is through or with a certain representation of them. But to attribute *esse* or *non-esse* to them is to affirm and deny their actual existence, not to represent something, which is clear from the fact that it is the same representation of both terms. It is the same representation of the quiddity itself and of its existence. The representation remains entirely uniform in the act of affirmation and in the act of negation.[24]

The divine intellect, he says, works in a similar way. Insofar as it is of quiddities or terms, the divine intellect is the reason or representation of quiddities or terms without a relation to *esse* or *non-esse*, or without affirmation or negation. But as it affirms one of the alternatives or sees the verification or true affirmation of one of the alternatives, it should rather be called their judgment or judicial discretion (*iudicialis discretio*). It follows, Olivi says, that God of himself absolutely understands all knowable terms and quiddities. God's *intelligere*, by its nature and necessarily, was understanding (*fuit intelligere*) these objects. God always knows—and could not not know—what each knowable or possible thing is and what existence (*existere*) that he could give to them. Nevertheless, he could not know the affirmation or negation of one of the alternatives, but this is not to know it as actual. Thus, he did not know that alternative from himself as necessarily as true and actual. It is only an act of the divine will that makes the divine intellect affirm or deny *esse*

---

22. Olivi, *Quaestio de ideis*, n. 5 (Piron, 2). See Bonaventure, *De scientia Christi*, q. 2 (Quaracchi, V.9) and pp. 15–17.

23. Olivi, *Quaestio de ideis*, n. 19 (Piron, 5), esp.: "potest sane intelligi si 'lux divina' sumatur pro actualitate et claritate divini intelligere."

24. Olivi, *Quaestio de ideis*, n. 20 (Piron, 5).

of a possible creature.[25] Olivi is quick to affirm that while this affirmation or negation requires two acts in man, it is just one act in God.

Like the Imitability Theorists, Olivi affirms that God necessarily has all the ideas that he has. God necessarily knows every possible creature, and his knowledge of them is called their 'reason' (*ratio*) or 'representation' (*representatio*).[26] His knowledge at this stage prescinds from affirming or denying *esse* of the possible creature. Once the divine will acts, the divine intellect affirms that this possible creature exists and denies that that one does. At this point, the divine intellect is called the "judgment" (*diiudicatio*) or "judicial discretion" (*iudicalis discretio*). There is, as it were, a three-step process by which the divine intellect arrives at complete knowledge of possible and actual creatures.

Olivi applies this conclusion to divine exemplarity. The divine act is the exemplar of things. By divine act, Olivi means the act of understanding (*intelligere*) insofar as it is actual intelligence (*intelligentia*) or actual understanding (*intelligere*) of all possible things in God and even of things that will come to be (*fiendarum*). The divine act is properly the *ratio* or idea of a thing insofar as God actually understands it because it is completely determined by God to be what it is. The divine essence is not properly an exemplar or idea of things in any other way.[27] For Olivi, divine ideas are God's very *intelligere* and not to be distinguished into reified respects of imitability. The divine idea or divine exemplar of a thing is just God's understanding it.[28]

Although this position is opposed to any version of the Imitability Theory in many respects, Olivi still insists that divine ideas are divine understanding, and not the divine essence itself. Divine ideas are still the essence as understood. The difference is that they are not the divine essence as understood to be imitable. Divine ideas are just the act of understanding as directed to this or that thing. This position, Olivi says, seems consonant with faith and reason.

Once again, Petrus de Trabibus can help clarify Olivi's position. "God understands himself and things other than himself" can be said if it means that God's knowledge of himself comes from the same means and in the same act and intuition. It cannot mean that God understands himself and others entirely in the same *ratio* and comparison. This understanding fails to recognize that God's cognition of other things connotes a respect to something makeable and implies a certain imitability. A divine idea entails a certain connotation and implication that is not

---

25. Olivi, *Quaestio de ideis*, n. 20 (Piron, 5), esp.: "divinus intellectus, prout est ipsarum quiditatum seu terminorum, sine relatione ad esse vel non esse, seu sine affirmatione vel negatione, est earum ratio seu representatio."

26. See, e.g., p. 19.

27. Olivi, *Quaestio de ideis*, n. 8 (Piron, 2), esp.: "in quantum vero est actuale intelligere huius vel illius rei . . . est illius rei ratio, vel ydea."

28. See Olivi, *Quaestio de ideis*, n. 88 (Piron, 18): "Quando ergo dicit quod rationes ydeales omnium fiendarum ad hoc sufficiebant, si loquatur de sufficientia per quam res in se ipsa sufficienter existit et que exigitur ad rei existentiam, concede, quia ille non sunt aliud, etiam secundum rationem, quam ipse actus intelligendi quo Deus intelligit res, nec rationes causales aliud dicunt quam actu volendi quo Deus vult res."

present when God knows himself.²⁹ Borrowing terminology from Bonaventure, Petrus affirms that creatures do not have a likeness of univocity (*similitudo univocitatis*) to God, and so a divine idea includes a likeness of imitation (*similitudo imitationis*) by which the creaturely effect imitates the divine cause.³⁰

Petrus's references to Bonaventure strengthen Olivi's claim that his theory is the same as Bonaventure's theory properly understood. The reference to connotation emphasizes that the divine idea is not other than the divine act of understanding itself because God's understanding expresses all the possible ways that creatures can be like God and imitate him. The very act of divine *intelligere* necessarily expresses every creature that God could make.

Petrus further argues that the example of the artist deployed by Imitability Theorists is misleading. The analogy is helpful insofar as it emphasizes that God acts by art and not by nature. The natural agent has a natural form by which it exists, but the artist has an artificial form or species by which he knows and according to which he acts. The analogy breaks down insofar as it does not capture the simplicity of God. In the created agent, the natural form by which he exists is other than the artificial form by which he knows and acts. Since God is simple, he lacks this distinction between natural and artificial form, as well as any real distinction between his nature and his knowledge since his form is his knowledge.³¹ Since these are not really other, Imitability Theorists speak misleadingly, and they reify divine ideas by making them out to be distinct from the divine act of understanding.

God has divine ideas for Olivi and Petrus because he has perfect cognition. Olivi makes use of Bonaventure's claim that God can comprehend and act in every genus whatsoever precisely because he transcends every genus.³² With regard to things other than himself, his knowledge is perfect because of divine ideas. An idea,

---

29. Petrus de Trabibus, *In I Sent.*, d. 35, p. 1, a. 1, q. 1, ad 2 (MS Assisi, Bibl. Communale 154, f. 93va): "Ad secundum dicendum quod cum dicitur 'Deus eodem modo cognoscit se et alia', potest intelligi dupliciter: aut particulariter, quia eodem est medio et eodem actu et intuit, et sic habet veritatem; aut univeraliter, quia omnino eadem ratione et comparatione, et sic est falsa. Unde simpliciter potest positio prima negari quoniam cognition sui non connotat respctum ad aliquid factibile nec importat aliquam imitabilitas. Cognitio autem creatorum seu creabilium connotate et importat, et ideo se non cognoscit Deus per ideam. Creata autem per ideam cognoscit." See pp. 28–29.

30. Petrus de Trabibus, *In I Sent.*, d. 1, p. 1, a. 1, q. 1, ad 3 (MS Assisi, Bibl. Communale 154, f. 93va): "Ad tertium dicendum quod est similitudo univocitatis quae dicit convenientiam in aliqua essentiali communi vel natura; et talis non est inter Deum et creaturam. Et est similitudo imitationis qua effectus imitantur causam; et talis similitude est inter Deum et creaturam." See p. 16.

31. Petrus de Trabibus, *In I Sent.*, d. 35, p. 1, a. 1, q. 1 (MS Assisi, Bibl. Communale 154, f. 93rb): "omne agens habet speciem et formam aliquo modo effectus sui, cum effectus sit quaedam similitudo agentis; sed agens per naturam habet formam naturalem qua exsistit; agens per artem et scientiam habet formam seu speciem artificialem qua cognoscit et secundum quam agit. Productio autem creaturarum a Deo non est per modum naturae sed per modum artis et scientiae. Ergo necesse est ponere species vel formas rerum factibilium in Deo quae ideae dicuntur.... Non enim est in eo [sc. in agente increato] alia forma naturalis qua exsistit et alia forma artificialis seu scibilis qua cognoscitur, sicut nec aliud est natura et scientia nisi secundum rationem quoniam sua forma est sua scientia."

32. Olivi, *In II Sent.*, q. 3, ad 1 (Jensen, I.57). See pp. 26–27.

Petrus says, entails a cognitive, causative, and exemplative reason (*ratio*). A cognitive *ratio* in God is not other than his cognition and his cognition is not other than his understanding. A causative and exemplative *ratio* adds a potency to produce and the notion of determinate perfection, to which a producible thing can be assimilated. The cognitive *ratio* is from the divine intellect alone, and the causative and exemplative *rationes* are from the divine will.[33] Divine ideas are just the divine act of understanding to which the divine act of willing accrues, from which it follows that God makes some of the things he knows, but not everything. Since Petrus emphasizes that divine ideas are not just cognitive reason, but causative and exemplative reasons, it is reasonable to conclude that he thinks God has ideas only of those things that he wills to make at some time.

Olivi and Petrus argue for the plurality of divine ideas in the same way as Imitability Theorists. Olivi emphasizes that there are many *rationes* because the truth of all things is there, even though there is no real plurality that would violate God's simplicity.[34] Petrus argues that it is most absurd to judge that God has just one idea. God creates singulars most properly. Since an idea is a creative and exemplative *ratio* of a creatable thing, if God had just one idea, he could only produce one thing. He would produce one thing with his one idea, and there would not be any plurality or diversity in things.[35]

The plurality of ideas is according to reason (*secundum rationem*), not in reality (*secundum rem*). God's essence is simple and so all things are one and the same in it, including God's perfections and ideas. Nevertheless, the divine intellect's composing and dividing all things that are in its power and will to make result in a plurality of ideas and distinctions. This plurality is a plurality of *rationes*, not a plurality of things.[36]

---

33. Petrus de Trabibus, *In I Sent.*, d. 35, p. 1, a. 1, q. 2 (MS Assisi, Bibl. Communale 154, f. 93va–b): "Dicit enim idea rationem cognitivam causativam et exemplarativam rei dispositae seu determinatae ad fiendum. . . . Ratio autem cognitiva in Deo non est aliud quam sua cognitio et sua cognitio non est aliud quam suus intellectus. Ratio autem causativa et exemplarativa addit super rationem cognitivam potentiam ad producendum et rationem determinatae perfectionis, cui potest res producibilis assmilari."

34. Olivi, *Quaestio de ideis*, n. 129 (Piron, 25).

35. Petrus de Trabibus, *In I Sent.*, d. 35, p. 2, a. un., q. 1 (MS Assisi Bibl. Communale 154, f. 94ra): "Hoc enim absurdissimum est aestimare. Singula igitur propriis sunt creata rationibus; ratio atuem huiusmodi unica est, quoniam cum idea dicat rationem factivam et exemplativam rei factibilis, ad cuius imitationem res extra producitur, si in Deo non esset nisi idea una, non produceret nisi unum. Nam quidquid produceret, produceret ad similitudinem ideae unius; sed quantumcumque uni et eidem sunt similia, necesse est <add. interlin. A> inter se esse similia; ergo cum omnia producta assimilarentur uni ideae sine omni pluralitate et diversitate et ita omnia essent unum et idem et non esset aliqua pluralitas in rebus in rebus. Quod cum sit manifeste falsum, manifeste verum est in Deo plures ideas esse." Olivi offers similar reasoning at *Quaestio de ideis*, nn. 130–31 (Piron, 26).

36. Petrus de Trabibus, *In I Sent.*, d. 35, p. 2, a. un., q. 3 (MS Assisi Bibl. Communale 154, f. 95ra): "Dicendum igitur quod ideae dupliciter possunt considerari: aut in ratione entis seu essentiae—et sic nullam habent omnino distinctionem vel pluralitatem, quia omnes sunt una et eadem essentia simplex, sicut et omnes perfectiones Deo attributae—aut in ratione ideae. Quare in Deo <idea> non est ratio entis vel essentiae sed respectus rationis, quoniam idea, ut visum est prius, habet rationem cognitivam rei factibilis; et sic habent <ideae> pluralitatem et distinctionem ab intellectu divino componente et

Petrus argues that divine ideas are both numerically infinite and numerically finite depending on whether 'idea' refers to the *rationes* of all possibles or in its proper meaning and intention since there are only ideas of things disposed to come to be. God's possibilities are infinite and so there are an infinite number of ideas corresponding to the infinite number of creatures he could create. But since only things that God makes properly have ideas, there is a finite number of ideas.[37]

Olivi does not have much to say about the scope of divine ideas. In an argument against Aquinas's theory, Olivi says that individuals of the same species imitate God in the same way.[38] Thus, on this theory, there would not be ideas of individuals. Since Olivi rejects Aquinas's theory, not much can be inferred from this statement about Olivi's own position. He seems to think divine ideas are numerically infinite, so we can at least infer that the scope of ideas is wide ranging.[39]

Petrus argues that God has ideas for all the things he makes, including prime matter. Divine ideas are the means by which God knows and wills creatures. If God did not have an idea for something that he makes, then he would produce something unknowingly and unwillingly. He insists that God even has ideas of things produced by secondary causes. God produces these things mediately because the secondary cause must be reduced to the first agent as in its cause. There is an idea of prime matter because it exists; it is being in potency (*esse materiae est esse in potentia*). The only thing for which there is not a divine idea is evil, and that is because evil is not a thing. The evil act has some being (*entitas*) as an act and there is an idea of this, but there is not an idea of the act insofar as it is malicious and deprived of being.[40]

---

disponente omnia quae sunt in potestate et voluntate ad fiendum. Unde ideae non sunt plures res, sed sunt plures rationes, non secundum considerationem intellectus nostri creati, sed intellectus divini." In the same place, Petrus also refers to the position rejected by Bonaventure that forms have distinction, composition, and opposition in matter, distinction and composition in the intellect, and distinction in God. See p. 26.

37. Petrus de Trabibus, *In I Sent.*, d. 35, p. 2, a. un., q. 4 (MS Assisi Bibl. Communale 154, f. 95rb): "Rationes autem in Deo constat esse infinitas, quoniam habet rationes omnium possibilium sibi. Si idea communiter pro ratione accipiatur, potest concedi ideas in Deo esse infinitas; si autem idea in propria acceptione et intentione accipiatur, cum ideae non sint nisi dispositorum fieri et haec non sint infinita, dicendum ideas esse finitas, quoniam ideae non sunt eorum quae non fuerunt, nec sunt, nec erunt." Olivi references Augustine and Dionysius's claims that divine *rationes* are many and infinite, but he brings it up in the context of rejecting a plurality of ideas in reality. Olivi seems to endorse an infinite number of divine ideas, but the context makes it difficult to determine definitively. Olivi, *Quaestio de ideis*, n. 108 (Piron, 22). See p. 78.

38. Olivi, *Quaestio de ideis*, n. 13 (Piron, 3).

39. Olivi seems to approve of Augustine and Pseudo-Dionysius, "qui huiusmodi rationes divinas dicunt esse plures et infinitas," but the context of this quotation is reprimanding his interlocutors for misunderstanding the plurality as a real plurality (*Quaestio de ideis*, n. 108 [Piron, 22]). As a result, his thought on the infinity or finitude of divine ideas remains obscure.

40. Perus de Trabibus, *In I Sent.*, d. 35, p. 3, a. un., q. 1 (MS Assisi Bibl. Communale 154, f. 95va–b): "Responsio: dicendum quod rem creari vel produci a Deo in naturae diversitate est causa sufficiens quod res potest habere ideam, quoniam Deus non producit aliquid nesciens neque nolens. Ex hoc autem quod producit sciens sequitur quod habeat rationem rei productae seu ideam secundum Augustinum

It seems clear that Petrus is speaking of divine ideas in the more restricted sense of what God actually wills and creates, but his theory could apply just as well to what God knows he could create. Thus, while Petrus accepts a distinction similar to Aquinas's distinction between *rationes* and exemplars, that distinction does not reduce the scope of ideas for Petrus. His theory is thus closer to infinite plenitude posited by Bonaventure.[41]

RECAPITULATIONS AND CONCLUSIONS

In certain respects, Olivi's and Petrus's Infinite Intellect Theory is very traditional. Divine ideas are the divine essence as known, distinct from God's act of self-cognition, and so qualify as a certain secondary consideration of the divine essence. God has ideas only of things other than himself. He has no idea of himself because divine ideas are not merely cognitive principles, but causal principles as well. An idea includes a certain likeness of imitation by which the creature is like God. The divine act of understanding necessarily results in cognition of all possible creatures other than God, but it is only the will of God that completes the character of an idea.

These similarities belie a radically different account of divine ideas. Olivi's theory of divine ideas is incompatible with the Imitability Theory for two reasons: First, they rely on contrary theories of relations. The Imitability Theory requires that God know a relation prior to knowing both terms of the relation, but Olivi objects that relations cannot be known in this way. The relation can only be known after the terms of the relation are known. Second, Olivi insists divine ideas must be identical to the divine act of understanding, not some relation or respect. He comes to this conclusion because of an emphasis on divine simplicity; God's understanding and the objects of his knowledge are not really distinct. Thus, the objects of his knowledge are one with his act of understanding. There is no need to refer to anything intermediary like Imitability Theorists do.

XI De civitate Dei cap. 10. . . . Dupliciter autem contingit aliquid esse productum a Deo: immediate ut in creatione vel in his quae super naturam et artem fiunt; et mediate ut illa quae secundum naturam et artem fiunt—et omnia talia habent ideam in Deo, quoniam ea quae natura vel arte fiunt, fiunt secundum causarum institutionem et secundum quod eorum causae concordant et continuantur cum Primo agente, quoniam talia in Primum agens ut in causam suam primariam /A=95vb/ reducuntur, sed in quantum a Primo agente discordant et ab eo discontinuantur, quia, in quantum huiusmodi non possunt reduci in Primum agens ut in causam suam, non dicuntur fieri ab ipso, et ideo talia, licet dicant aliquid privationis, ut actus malus per et habitus malus non habent ideam in Deo nisi quantum ad rationem privationis. Quoniam igitur materia prima a Deo facta est et producta immediate, accidentia autem naturaliter vel artificialiter producta reducuntur in Deum, sicut in suam causam primariam, ideo omnia ista necesse est habere ideam in Deo. Malus autem actus sive malus habitus, quantum non procedit a Primo agente, secundum quod <autem> illa procedunt a Primo agente et cum eo concordant et continuantur, non est a Deo simpliciter, sed quantum ad hoc quod habet entitatis, et ideo non habet ideam in ipso per se quantum ad rationem malitiae sed quantum ad rationem entitatis."

41. See pp. 36–40.

Although he attempts to position his theory as the proper interpretation of Bonaventure's theory, Olivi's theory of divine ideas departs from Bonaventure's. For Bonaventure, cognition necessarily makes use of likenesses. Even if man's intellect were pure act, it would still have likenesses as *rationes cognoscendi* because it would use itself as a likeness to know things other than itself.[42]

The Infinite Intellect Theory of divine ideas is not influential, but Olivi's criticisms of the Imitability Theory mark a decisive turning point in theories of divine ideas. Prior to Olivi, everyone holds some version of the Imitability Theory, but after, almost no one does, and the transition is primarily a result of new thinking about relations.

---

42. Bonaventure, *De scientia Christi*, q. 2, ad 7 and 10 (Quaracchi, I.9b and 10b). For Olivi's position on the role of divine ideas in the beatific vision, see Stève Bobillier, "Divine Ideas and Beatific Vision by Peter John Olivi," in *Divine Ideas in Franciscan Thought*, 51–73.

Part III.
The *Obiectum Cognitum* Theory of Divine Ideas

The third theory of divine ideas in this study is what I call the *Obiectum Cognitum* Theory. James of Viterbo is the only adherent to the theory I have found. Its name comes from James's emphasis on creatures as the *obiecta cognita*. It is closer to the Imitability Theory than the Infinite Intellect Theory because it uses the language of *ratio cognoscendi*, distinguishes the unity and plurality of divine ideas in a way that is reminiscent of the Imitability Theory (especially Bonaventure's version), emphasizes that ideas are exemplars, and insists that every idea entails a real respect to the *ideatum*.

The *Obiectum Cognitum* Theory departs from the Imitability Theory by its greater insistence on the (possible) creature. James uses the language of *ratio cognoscendi*, but he applies the term to the divine essence, not the divine idea. Since a cause and *ratio cognoscendi* are always a cause and a means of knowing *something*, James insists that the divine essence is the *ratio cognoscendi* of the creature itself. Divine ideas are thus not relations, as the Imitability Theory holds, but the creatures themselves.

James quietly signals his abandonment of the Imitability Theory by failing to uphold its central tenet: the knowledge of a creature through a relation, to which relation is the divine idea. Much of what James says could be interpreted as a further development of the Imitability Theory, but this similarity belies a significant difference between the two theories. James's theory is the first step toward divine ideas being defined as creatures themselves, which will be a hallmark of the last two theories expounded in the study: the *Creatura Intellecta* Theory and the Nominalist Theory.

Chapter V.
James of Viterbo (ca. 1255–1308)

James of Viterbo was the second Augustinian master at the University of Paris. He succeeded Giles of Rome as Master of Theology in 1292.[1] Like Olivi, James departs from the Imitability Theory, and he argues instead that a divine idea is the object known (*obiectum cognitum*), not the relations through which the objects are known. James's theory is not particularly influential, and as far as I can tell, he is the only one who held it. It is not influential, at least in part, because it is immediately criticized by Godfrey of Fontaines, and it is soon eclipsed by Scotus's theory of divine ideas.[2] Scotus thinks that James's theory of divine ideas is more acceptable than both the Imitability and Infinite Intellect Theories, and he even offers a defense of James's theory. Nevertheless, Scotus thinks the theory is still fatally flawed and subjects it to fierce criticism.[3] James's account of the scope of divine ideas is not especially novel or influential, so this chapter will pass over it.[4] To understand James's theory of divine ideas, it is necessary first to see his conception of an idea in general, and then his application of ideas to God. After these initial investigations, we will turn to his account of the plurality of divine ideas, the existence of things in God, and finally, his account of the scope of divine ideas.

DIVINE IDEAS AS *OBIECTA COGNITA*

Much of James's initial reflection on ideas is reminiscent of Aquinas.[5] An idea, he says, is the same as a form or a species, but not every form is an idea. Only a form to the imitation of which something is made is called an idea. He further specifies the character of an idea by making two distinctions: The first distinction is between

---

1. For an account of James's life, see Eric L. Saak, "The Life and Works of James of Viterbo," in *A Companion to James of Viterbo*, ed. Antoine Côté and Martin Pickavé, 11–32 (Leiden: Brill, 2018). The date of James's inception is debated in the secondary literature. Saak, drawing on the work of Wippel, argues for 1292 (20n36). See John F. Wippel, "The Dating of James of Viterbo's Quodlibet I and Godfrey of Fontaine's Quodlibet VIII," *Augustiniana* 24, no. 1 (1974): 348–86. E. Ypma had placed James's inception in 1293. See E. Ypma, "Recherches Sur La Carrière Scolaire et La Bibliothèque de Jacques de Viberbe †1308," *Augustiniana* 24, no. 1 (1974): 247–92.

2. For Godfrey's criticisms, see especially *Quodlibet* VIII, q. 3 (PB 4:48–50). See also Wippel, *Godfrey of Fontaines*, 115–45; Antoine Côté, "James of Viterbo on Divine Ideas and the Divine Cognition of Creatures," in *A Companion to James of Viterbo*, 86–95. Côté also considers the criticisms of Bernard of Auvergne and William of Alnwick.

3. Scotus, *Ord.* I, d. 35, q. un., nn. 12–13, 24–26 (Vatican, VI.248–49 and 254–55); Scotus, *Rep.* I-A, d. 36, qq. 1–2, nn. 32, 34–38 (Noone, 407:1–8 and 407:20–409:29). Scotus's defense of James's theory can be found at *Rep.* I-A, d. 36, qq. 1–2, nn. 39–49 (Noone, 410–15). See pp. 164–66.

4. See Antoine Côté, "James of Viterbo on Divine Ideas," 78–82.

5. See pp. 51–52 and 56–61.

the two ways things come to be: by nature (*ab agente naturali; naturaliter*) and by intellect (*per intellectum*).[6] Both ways of coming to be involve imitation, but ideas concern what comes by intellect, not in what comes to be by nature. A son imitates the nature of his father, but the father's nature is not an idea. Only that to the imitation of which something comes to be by an agent acting by intellect is properly called an idea. Thus, an idea is also called an exemplar according to which and toward which the intellect makes something.[7]

James's second distinction is between types of exemplars: An exemplar can be external, as in the case of the artist who paints a landscape, or it can be conceived by the artist's intellect. Although the external exemplar is mediated by the artist's intellect, it is not truly an exemplar because it is not thought up (*excogitatum*) by the artist. These two distinctions allow James to conclude that an idea is the concept of a form that is called an exemplar or the very form that is an exemplar as conceived.[8]

James says that an idea is called a reason (*ratio*) insofar as it is something conceived by the intellect, and it is called an exemplar insofar as it represents an extrinsic form.[9] He appropriates Aquinas's language of *ratio* and exemplar, but he uses the terms differently.[10] The divine will's choice to create or not create does not determine the distinction for James. Instead, the distinction is between viewing the idea from the part of the knower and from the part of the content of the idea. An idea is a *ratio* because it informs the knower's intellect. It is an exemplar because the intelligible content of the *ratio* points to an external form that the knower could bring about.

James further distinguishes his theory of ideas from Aquinas's and even from Henry of Ghent's theory when he considers the relationship between the idea and the thing ideated (*ideata*).[11] There must be some relationship between the idea and the thing ideated because an idea entails imitation. It turns out that they have a threefold relationship: First, the ideated is like the idea according to the *ratio* of unity since it imitates the idea. Second, an idea is the cause and active principle of the ideated according to the *ratio* of causality. Finally, the two are related according to the notion of knowability since the idea is the that-which-is (*quod quid est*) or quiddity of the ideated. The third relation between the idea and the ideated requires

---

6. James says that by "*per intellectum*" he means to include the will since the intellect performs no external actions without the will (*Quodlibet* III, q. 15 [Ypma, 194:21–22]). This caveat ensures that James's theory cannot be classified as intellectualist. For James's theory of the will, see Stephen D. Dumont, "James of Viterbo on the Will," in *A Companion to James of Viterbo*, 249–305. See pp. 19–20 and 45–52 for the same distinction in Bonaventure and Aquinas, respectively.

7. *Quodlibet* III, q. 15 (Ypma, 195:17–196:26), esp.: "[idea est] illa forma ad cuius imitationem fit aliquid." Cf. *Quodlibet* I, q. 5 (ed. Ypma, 65:107–8): "Completive autem et formaliter est idea, quae nihil est aliud quam divina essentia ut imitabilis intellect ab ipso Deo."

8. *Quodlibet* III, q. 15, (Ypma, 196:26–47).

9. *Quodlibet* III, q. 15 (Ypma, 196:48–52).

10. See pp. 46–50.

11. See pp. 70–74 and 103–4.

additional explanation, James says, because there are two ways of predicating 'quiddity,' which is the very essence as signified by the definition. Since a definition signifies the concept of an intellect, it follows that a quiddity is the thing's essence as conceived. The essence can be conceived either as it is something according to itself (*secundum se*) or as it is caused or causable. Insofar as it is something in itself, the thing's essence as conceived by the intellect is called the "essential quiddity" (*quidditas essentialis*). Insofar as it is conceived as caused or causable, it is called the "causal or exemplar quiddity" (*quidditas causalis vel exemplaris*). A causal quiddity is understood in its cause because when the cause is understood, the effect is understood in it. The causal quiddity is proper to an idea because an idea denotes the very quiddity of the ideated as caused or causable.[12]

James emphasizes the distinction between essential quiddities and causal quiddities because he does not want to fall prey to the traditional interpretation of Henry's understanding of formal exemplars.[13] By emphasizing that ideas are causal quiddities and not essential quiddities, James distances himself from Henry, insisting that an idea is the essence that a being could have.[14] A causal quiddity is a real possibility, but it has no actuality independent of being thought.

James applies this general theory to divine knowing. He emphasizes that God's only source of cognition is the divine essence. Regarding his means of knowing, God does not understand anything outside of himself. He knows only through himself. Regarding the objects that God knows, James says that God knows both himself and things outside of himself, that is, creatures as distinct from him. Although these objects of cognition are many, James insists that there is a sense in which the objects are one known object. They can be one because God understands that the divine essence as cause is the formal and principal object, and creatures are known secondarily through the principal object. God's simplicity and perfect mode of cognition are preserved.[15]

God knows creatures by knowing his own essence, which can be considered in two ways: as it is an essence, or as it is a power (*potentia*) and cause. Created beings are in God in both ways. Insofar as the essence is considered as an essence, creatures are in God because they are God and they are not considered distinct from God. They are identical to the divine essence because everything in God is

---

12. *Quodlibet* III, q. 15 (Ypma, 197:68–198:102): " res aliqua dupliciter intelligi potest. Uno modo ut est aliquid secundum se; et hoc modo essentia ipsius rei ut concepta per intellectum dicitur quidditas eius essentialis. Alio modo ut est causata vel causabilis; et sic intelligitur in sua causa. Dum enim intelligitur causa, intelligitur effectus in ipsa. Quod verum est, cum intelligitur causa non solum ut est aliquid in se, sed etiam ut est causa. . . . Et quia idea dicit formam quae est causa exemplaris in quantum est causa, et exemplar ut est ab intellectu concepta, ideo ipsa idea dicitur quod quid est, sive quidditas ideati . . . quia per ipsam et in ipsa intelligitur ideatum sicut effectus in sua causa."

13. See pp. 106–9.

14. Mark D. Gossiaux, "James of Viterbo and the Late Thirteenth-Century Debate Concerning the Reality of Possibles," *Recherches de théologie et philosophie médiévales* 74, no. 2 (2007): 514.

15. *Quodlibet* I, q. 5 (Ypma, 68:218–69:235). James is borrowing this account from Henry of Ghent. See pp. 88–89.

identical to the divine essence. Insofar as the essence is considered as a power and cause, creatures are in the essence because God can produce and cause them. In this way, creatures are taken as distinct from God because power and cause entail a respect to something external. This way of understanding creatures is the proper way.[16]

This distinction in consideration of the divine essence seems to serve two purposes for James: First, it shows that James holds a twofold divine exemplarity similar to the twofold divine exemplarity that Aquinas posits.[17] God's consideration of his essence as an essence results in knowing creatures as identical to the divine essence. In this way, God is a sort of natural exemplar; all creatures imitate God's essential perfection in certain ways common to all beings. When God considers his essence as a cause, he knows creatures properly in their own natures. Here, God is the intellectual exemplar of creatures. He is the exemplar of creatures not because he too possesses their creaturely perfections, but rather because he knows them. He is the exemplar of a shark's goodness because he is himself good, but he is the exemplar of the shark *qua* shark because he knows himself to be able to cause the shark's essence. James never makes this twofold exemplarity explicit, but, as these brief reflections make clear, the theory can reasonably be inferred from his texts.

The second purpose this dual consideration serves is for the unity and plurality of divine ideas. When God considers his essence as it is an essence, divine ideas are one and identical to the divine essence, and when he considers his essence as it is a cause, divine ideas are many and point to creatures distinct from God.

James's initial characterization of divine ideas seems like a straightforward articulation of the Imitability Theory, which he notes is the common theory.[18] A divine idea, properly speaking, is established when God knows his essence as a cause. James never makes this point explicit, but if, *per impossibile*, God did not know himself, there would be no divine ideas. James even employs the language of *ratio cognoscendi* in this context, but the way he uses it shows his departure from Imitability Theorists, for whom the divine ideas themselves are relations that serve as the *rationes cognoscendi* of creatures. James insists that the divine essence is the *ratio cognoscendi* insofar as it is understood as a cause, but it is always the case that when something is the means of knowing as a cause, the result is that something

---

16. *Quodlibet* I, q. 5 (Ypma, 62:23–63:47), esp.: "Essentia vero divina potest dupliciter considerari. Uno modo ut essentia est, alio modo ut potentia et causa est. Et secundum hanc duplicem considerationem entia creata dupliciter sunt in Dei essentia. Sunt enim in ipsa ut essentia est, quia Deus illa est. Et sunt in ipsa ut est causa et potentia, quia Deus illa producere et causare potest."

17. James argues in this way in *Quaestiones de divinis praedicamentis*, q. 4 (Ypma, 99–101). See pp. 52–54.

18. Côté describes James's theory this way: "James sides with the dominant view within scholasticism in believing that divine ideas are nothing other than the divine essence itself insofar as it is cognized by God as *imitable* by creatures" ("James of Viterbo on Divine Ideas," 72. Emphasis original). Broadly speaking, Côté is correct, but this appraisal does not take into consideration that James does not argue that God's knowledge is through knowledge of a relation. See *Quodlibet* I, q. 5 (Ypma, 64:85–86 and 65:107–8).

else is known. Since, something else has to be the object cognized by means of the divine essence, the only option is the creature.[19] Divine ideas are the objects cognized by means of the divine essence, and the objects cognized are the creatures.[20]

James clarifies his position saying that to be cognized includes two aspects, namely, the thing cognized and the *ratio cognoscendi*, which is twofold: In one way, it holds on the part of the knower and is not the object cognized, but the concept of the intellect itself. In another way, it holds on the part of the thing known and is principally the means of knowing the object known. In this sense, the object is sometimes something other than the knower and sometimes it is the same as the knower. Applying this distinction to God, James says that on the part of the knower, God's *ratio cognoscendi* is the Divine Word. On the part of the thing known, God's *ratio cognoscendi* is his very essence as a cause, which is called an idea. The object known in this case is the creature itself.[21] James breaks with the Imitability Theory in declaring that God knows the creature, not a relation of imitability, by knowing his essence as cause.

THE UNITY AND MULTIPLICITY OF DIVINE IDEAS

James's theory of the unity and multiplicity of divine ideas follows the Imitability Theory closely. James recognizes that the common view is that an idea is the divine essence understood as imitable.[22] The multiplicity of divine ideas follows from the fact that the divine essence can be imitated in diverse modes and grades. The shift from an Imitability Theory to the *Obiecta Cognita* Theory might raise concerns that James's account of the multiplicity of divine ideas is not compatible with the simplicity and unity of God. The difficulty is that, according to James, God knows the creature itself as distinct from himself. How can this knowledge be reconciled with his unity?

James seeks to reconcile the two claims in *Quaestiones de divinis praedicamentis*, q. 4 (1293–1294). Divine unity is compatible with two types of plurality: one which has its foundation in God and one which is caused by God. The first is the divine attributes and Divine Persons; the second is the multiplicity of creatures. The Divine Persons can only be known through revelation, but the multiplicity of divine attributes can be known by reason. They are discovered through the principle that the perfections in the effect must preexist in the cause. The multiplicity of perfections in creatures must preexist in God and in nobler way (*nobilior*).[23] This same reasoning can be applied to the multiplicity of creatures to discover the multiplicity of divine ideas.[24]

---

19. See Côté, "James of Viterbo on Divine Ideas," 73; *Quodlibet* I, q. 5 (Ypma, 64:68): "nam quod nullo modo est et omnino nihil est, non intelligitur."

20. *Quodlibet* I, q. 5 (Ypma, 64:63–65:102), esp.: "Si igitur Deus cognoscit creaturas per suam essentiam ut causa est, oportet ponere aliquid aliud a divina essentia esse obiectum cognitum. Hoc autem non est nisi creatura. Quare creatura, antequam sit in effectu, est res aliqua ut obiectum cognitum, ut est a Deo alia et distincta."

21. *Quodlibet* I, q. 5 (Ypma, 70:291–302).

22. *Quodlibet* I, q. 5 (Ypma, 64:85–86 and 65:107–8).

23. See p. 69.

24. *Quaestiones de divinis praedicamentis*, q. 4 (Ypma, 96–98).

James distinguishes divine attributes and divine ideas according to the distinction of natural and intellectual exemplars. Some perfections in creatures exist in God naturally, like goodness. Since they exist in him naturally, these perfections are the divine attributes. Other perfections in creatures exist in God only intelligibly, that is, in his intellect. These perfections are the divine ideas. This distinction between perfections yields a further distinction. Divine attributes imply no limitation since they are in God naturally, but divine ideas are limited perfections in God because they properly belong to creatures. James also distinguishes the way that divine attributes and divine ideas are predicated of God. What divine attributes' names signify (*res significatae*) are predicated properly of God, but their mode of signifying (*modi significandi*) is predicated only imperfectly. The distinction between *res significatae* and *modus significandi* is a recognition that we can speak of the same thing in different modes. Irène Rosier-Catch explains this phenomenon using the example of 'pain.' 'Pain' can be both a noun (*dolor*) and a verb (*doleo*). Each word refers to a certain pain in the body, but they do so in different ways. In particular, the verb signifies that the pain is experienced at a certain time.[25] Again, the proposition "Socrates is not men" is true with respect to its *modus significandi* (since Socrates is not multiple individuals in the species), but false with respect to the *res significatae* (since he is in the species).[26] The various divine names, such as goodness, truth, and wisdom, each point to the same thing, namely God, but the way they are predicated entails certain creaturely imperfections. So, if the predications were taken in terms of their *modus significandi*, then God would be called imperfect. As a result, the divine names are predicated in terms of what they signify only. They are not predicated according to man's imperfect *modus significandi*. The names of creatures that correspond to divine ideas can only be predicated of God metaphorically because their perfections are limited.[27]

In sum, there is a three-fold distinction between divine attributes and divine ideas. Divine attributes are natural exemplars that imply no limitation in God. Man predicates these attributes of God properly, even if the way he does so is imperfect. Divine ideas are intellectual attributes that imply only a certain degree of perfection in a creature. Since divine ideas imply limited perfection, the names of the creatures that correspond to the divine ideas are predicated of God metaphorically.

---

25. Irène Rosier-Catch, "Grammar," in *The Cambridge History of Medieval Philosophy*, ed. Robert Pasnau and Christina Van Dyke (New York: Cambridge University Press, 2010), I.207.

26. Irène Rosier-Catch, "*Res significata* et *Modus significandi*: Les enjeux linguisitques et théologiques d'une distinction médiévale," in *Sprachtheorien in Spätantike und Mittelalter*, ed. S. Ebbensen (Tübingen: Gunter Narr Verlag, 1995), 145.

27. *De divinis praedicamentis*, q. 4 (Ypma, 99–101), esp.: "Idea vero dicit perfectionem secundum gradum limitatum.... Intellectus autem divinus potest intelligere perfectionem limtatum. Ex hoc autem sequitur tertia differentia, quod nomina creaturarum quae respondent attributis, dicuntur de Deo proprie quantum ad rem significatam, nam proprie dicitur sapiens et huiusmodi, licet non quantum ad modum significandi. Nomina vero creaturarum quae respondent rationibus idealibus, non dicuntur de Deo, nisi translative, non autem proprie, quia dicunt perfectionem cum limitationem." See Gossiaux, "James of Viterbo," 510–11.

Neither the plurality of divine attributes nor the plurality of divine ideas is contrary to divine unity. The divine attributes are actually one, and only many according to the limitations of man knowing and predicating. James articulates the plurality of divine ideas using the solution found in Bonaventure.[28] Divine ideas are only many if we speak of them in relation to creatures because each of the many possible creatures imitates God in a distinct way. This is not, James says, an actual multiplicity, but a virtual multiplicity. If we consider the divine idea for what it is, not what is known by it, however, then each divine idea is identical to the divine essence, and, as a result, identical to every other divine idea. Divine ideas are one because they are the divine essence, but they are many because they are the divine essence as known to be imitated in many diverse ways.[29]

THE EXISTENCE OF THINGS IN GOD

James's theory of the existence of things in God seems to carve out a middle position between Aquinas's theory, which holds that things in God have merely cognitive being, and the traditional interpretation of Henry's theory, which ascribes to things in God some manner of real being independent of divine cognitive being.[30] His solution holds that the essences, which are divine ideas, have cognitive being and yet are distinct from God potentially; "possibles are real only in a qualified sense."[31]

James's theory hinges on his distinction between understanding the divine essence as an essence and as a cause. Insofar as God's essence is considered as an essence, created things exist in the divine essence as identical to it. Insofar as his essence is considered as a cause, however, created things are other than God and distinct from him because the terms "power" (*potentia*) and "cause" (*causa*) entail a respect to something external. God understands creatures in both ways. In the first way, he understands creatures as identical to himself and his knowledge of creatures is nothing other than contemplating his own perfections. In the second way, he understands creatures as existing in his power and as distinct from himself. This second way is the proper way of understanding creatures and the focus of the question of existence of things in God.[32]

A creaturely essence that God understands, even before it exists, must be called a 'thing' (*res*), not absolutely but with a certain qualification (*cum determinatione*), namely, as an *obiectum cognitum*.[33] It is something because God knows it, and it enjoys divine cognitive being. The only requirement to be an object of God's knowledge is possibility.[34] Although James does not spell out the relationship between

---

28. See p. 29.
29. *De divinis praedicamentis*, q. 4 (Ypma, 104).
30. See pp. 74–76 and 106–9.
31. Gossiaux, "James of Viterbo," 507. This section follows Gossiaux's line of thinking.
32. *Quodlibet* I, q. 5 (Ypma, 63:33–55). See Côté, "James of Viterbo on Divine Ideas," 73.
33. *Quodlibet* I, q. 5 (Ypma, 63:59–61): "creatura vel essentia creaturae antequam sit in actu, est res aliqua non simpliciter sed cum determinatione, scilicet ut obiectum cognitum."
34. *Quodlibet* I, q. 5 (Ypma, 64:63–69 and 65:113–15).

cognitive being and possibility explicitly, "it is safe to assume that James held, as did Scotus, that God does not cognize anything that is not possible (i.e., that there is no *esse cognitum* that is not an *esse possibile*), and conversely that there is no possible that is not cognized by God."[35] Essences need not exist in reality to be known, and this point is especially true for God because things only exist in reality because God foreknew them.

James distinguishes two ways in which something can be called possible: First, a thing can be called possible because of a potency existing in it. In this sense, something is possible because there is a passive potency in the thing to be actualized, as air can be ignited by fire. Second, a thing can be called possible by means of a potency existing in another. A creature was possible before creation through God's power, but not through its own potency since it did not exist yet.[36] Thus, possible essences are known by God because it is within God's power to create them. There is no potency on the side of the possible essence itself.

It follows that before being created, possible essences do have some being as objects of God's power and knowledge that is not merely reducible to God's existence. Indeed, a possible essence is somehow distinct from God; it is a real, true being (*verum ens reale*). It deserves to be called 'true' both through a comparison to its cause because it is something possible through some cause and through a comparison to the intellect because it is something cognized or at least cognizable. Thus, James has no qualms about conceding that a creature's essence, even before creation, is something true absolutely speaking. Again, the creaturely essence deserves to be called a 'being,' even though strictly speaking 'being' ought not be predicated of 'essence' since the concrete is not predicated of the abstract. It is a being in some sense, provided we understand 'being' as possible and as cognized. Finally, the creature's essence is real and a thing in a qualified sense—real as possible and as cognized. Possible essences, then, are real, true beings, but only with the restrictions as possible and as cognized.[37]

The fact that possible essences in God are real, true beings only in a qualified and restricted sense allows James to insist that they are not really related to God prior to their actual existence. Here, we recall James's claim that an idea and the ideated have a threefold relationship:[38] First, they are related by unity since the ideated is said to imitate the idea. Second, they are related by causality since an idea is the cause and active principle of the ideated. Finally, the two are related according to the notion of knowability since the idea is the *quod quid est* or quiddity of the ideated. James explains the third relation in greater detail because there are two

---

35. Côté, "James of Viterbo on Divine Ideas," 75. Côté references Scotus, *Ord.* II, d. 1, q. 2, n. 93 (Vatican, 7.49).

36. *Quodlibet* II, q. 10 (Ypma, 127:166–80). See Gossiaux, "James of Viterbo," 498.

37. *Quodlibet* I, q. 5 (Ypma, 66:149–67:171): esp.: "Si tamen aliquo modo possit concedi essentia est ens, tunc essentia creaturae, antequam sit in effectu, potest dici et est en cum determinationibus supradictis, scilicet ut possibile et ut cognitum." See also, *De divinis praedicamentis*, q. 11.

38. See p. 142.

ways of predicating 'quiddity': essential quiddity and causal quiddity. An essential quiddity is the essence understood as it is something itself and conceived by the intellect. A causal quiddity is the essence understood as caused or causable.[39] As Gossiaux points out, the first and second sort of relations "concern the *ideatum* as it exists actually, while the third relation holds whether the *ideatum* exists actually or potentially."[40] The essence relates to God as known and knowable regardless of whether it exists actually, and so possible essences are not caused by God as by an exemplar cause: "the divine idea expresses actually the perfection which a possible essence displays only potentially."[41] Possible essences are not real beings as exemplified and caused unless God has willed to create them in actual existence.

James's insistence that God is not the exemplar cause of possible essences (unless he has willed to create according to them) is important because, like his predecessors, he thinks that the possible essences are necessarily possible. God necessarily has the divine ideas that he has. He does not will to have some ideas and not others. He necessarily has the divine ideas that he has because he necessarily understands his own power and each thing to which his power could extend. God can even be said to will the possible essences in the sense that he necessarily wills that they are in his power to produce.[42] None of this necessity coerces God into making any creature or set of creatures, but it does make it necessary that he could create them. If possible essences were really related to God, then something other than God would be really related to him, and James's theory would fall prey to the criticisms that creation is necessary and not *ex nihilo*.

RECAPITULATIONS AND CONCLUSIONS

James of Viterbo's theory of divine ideas has much in common with the Imitability Theory, yet he is the second figure in this study to break with the Imitability Theory. He agrees that God's only source and principle of knowledge is the divine essence and that a divine idea is a way in which God knows his essence to be imitable. He agrees that the plurality of divine ideas follows from the plurality of ways that God can be imitated. He even agrees that God necessarily has each divine idea such that the essences of possible creatures are necessarily possible. Yet, James denies that a divine idea is a *ratio cognoscendi*. A divine idea is not a relation through which a creature is known. Instead, a divine idea is the *obiectum cognitum*. Divine ideas are real, true beings, but only as possible and as cognized. Thus, James's theory of the existence of things in God shows that they enjoy more than mere cognitive being, but they do not have the sort of being traditionally ascribed to Henry of Ghent's essential being.

---

39. *Quodlibet* III, q. 15 (Ypma, 197:68–198:102).
40. Gossiaux, "James of Viterbo," 514.
41. Gossiaux, "James of Viterbo," 514.
42. *Quodlibet* II, q. 10 (Ypma, 126:134–144), esp.: "Deus necessario intelligit alia a se hoc modo, quia necesario intelligit potentiam suam." Note that he makes use of Aquinas's argument from divine self-knowledge. See pp. 63–64.

James of Viterbo's *Obiectum Cognitum* Theory is not historically influential, primarily because Scotus's theory of divine ideas offers a blistering critique of each of the three theories that have been discussed so far: the Imitability Theory, the Infinite Intellect Theory, and the *Obiectum Cognitum* Theory. James abandons the claim that divine ideas are relations, but he does not abandon the account of knowing relations that marks the Imitability Theory. Scotus's critique and his own theory of divine ideas are so thorough that, as we will see, even the early Thomists were Scotists on divine ideas. Before we turn to Scotus, however, it will be helpful to examine the theory of Richard of Mediavilla because in attempting to defend the Imitability Theory against Olivi's objections, he anticipates Scotus's theory.

Part IV.
The *Creatura Intellecta* Theory of Divine Ideas

I call the fourth theory in this study the *Creatura Intellecta* Theory. Its name comes from Scotus, who argues that a divine idea is the understood creature (*creatura intellecta*). This theory is hinted at in Richard of Mediavilla's account of divine ideas and emerges fully in Scotus's writings. In many ways this theory of divine ideas is similar to the Imitability Theory. Like Imitability and *Obiecta Cognita* Theorists, Scotus insist (1) that divine ideas are the secondary terminating object of the divine intellect, (2) that the character of a divine idea necessarily includes a rational respect (*respectus rationis*) from God to a creature, and (3) he connects his account of the scope of divine ideas to Bonaventure's theory. Scotus goes out of his way to emphasize his continuity with the Imitability Theory on these points, especially the first two.

The *Creatura Intellecta* Theory departs sharply from the Imitability and *Obiecta Cognita* Theories in how it uses rational respects. Richard and Scotus accept Olivi's and Petrus's arguments about the way relations are known. As a result, they deny the fundamental tenet of the Imitability Theory, namely, that divine ideas are the relations by means of which God knows possible creatures. Instead, they argue that God must have direct knowledge of the creature. As will be seen below, Scotus uses his theory of instants of nature to explain the logical process that must be at work for God to have an idea.[1] In the first instant, God knows his essence. In the second instant, God knows the creature directly. In the third instant, a rational respect is established from God to the possible creature. In the fourth and final instant, God knows that rational respect, and the *ratio* of a divine idea is complete.

In the final analysis, the *Creatura Intellecta* Theory looks a lot like the Imitability Theory. A divine idea is a known relation of reason according to which God knows he can create a creature and the exemplar according to which he actually creates some creatures. Thus, the *Creatura Intellecta* Theory retains a cognitive and a causal role for divine ideas. Nevertheless, the two theories are diametrically opposed in that the Imitability Theory holds that God knows possible creatures through relations, and the *Creatura Intellecta* Theory holds that God knows relations because he knows possible creatures.

---

1. See pp. 170–75.

Chapter VI.
Richard of Mediavilla
(ca. 1249–1302)

Richard of Mediavilla (Middleton) was *magister regens* in the chair of theology at the University of Paris from 1284 to 1287. As I noted in the chapter on Peter John Olivi, Richard was on the commission that investigated Olivi in 1283.[1] As a result, Richard knew Olivi's criticism of the Imitability Theory thoroughly. Richard rejected Olivi's conclusion that the Imitability Theory was contrary to faith and reason, but he accepted Olivi's criticism concerning the knowledge of relations. In response, Richard seems to try to articulate a version of the Imitability Theory that does not fall prey to Olivi's critiques, but he becomes the first to articulate the *Creatura Intellecta* Theory. Richard published his Commentary on the *Sentences* sometime between 1285 and 1295.[2]

Much of Richard's theory of divine ideas reads like an endorsement of the Imitability Theory. Divine ideas are both principles of speculative cognition and practical cognition, although properly, they are principles of practical cognition.[3] Divine ideas are intrinsically one with the divine essence, yet they are many insofar as many possible creatures can imitate the divine essence. Divine ideas are distinguished from each other by respects of reason.[4] Against Henry of Ghent's potentially dangerous claims, Richard holds that there is an infinite number of divine ideas, and they enjoy divine cognitive being.[5] Nevertheless, Richard's theory is a bridge from Olivi's critiques of the Imitability Theory to Scotus's *Creatura Intellecta* Theory. It is strong evidence that Olivi's criticisms, especially as articulated by Scotus, are decisive against the Imitability Theory. For the sake of space, only the part of Richard's theory pertinent to the debate over the Imitability Theory and the *Creatura Intellecta* Theory will be examined.

---

1. See p. 123. For an account of Richard's involvement in Olivi's condemnation, see E. Hocedez, *Richard de Middleton: Sa Vies, Ses Oeuvres, Sa Doctrine* (Louvain: Spicilegium Sacrum Louvanienses, 1925), 79–92.

2. For the dating of Richard's *Sentences* commentary, see Hocedez, *Richard de Middleton*, 49–55.

3. *In I Sent.*, d. 35, a. 1, q. 5 (Brexiae, I.304a–305a). Richard specifies that if divine knowledge is compared to the will, then it is not *plene practica* because then the divine will would be determined to will in a certain way.

4. *In I Sent.*, d. 36, a. 2, q. 3 (Brexiae, I.314a–315a), esp.: "intellectus [divinus] intelligit essentiam suam ut diversarum creaturarum repraesentativam et ut ab eis imitabilem."

5. *In I Sent.*, d. 36, a. 2, q. 5 (Brexiae, I.316b–317b) and *In I Sent.*, d. 35, a. 1, q. 4 (Brexiae, I.302a–304a), respectively. See pp. 104–5 for Henry on the number of divine ideas.

"Ideas," Richard says, "are called forms, that is, the likenesses of intelligible things in the intellect."[6] However, this formulation is a little too broad because it allows an idea for any object of knowledge. God would have an idea of himself. Richard cuts off this conclusion by noting that the ways God knows himself and creatures are rationally distinct. The divine essence, he says, is God's intellectual means of knowing (*ratio cognoscendi*) himself and creatures. Nevertheless, insofar as it is the *ratio cognoscendi* of God himself, the divine essence does not have the character of an idea. What is exemplified through an idea—the *ideatum*—is a thing differing from its idea. Since the divine essence is not a thing differing from the divine essence, God does not have an idea of the divine essence. Insofar as the divine essence is the *ratio cognoscendi* and the means of producing (*ratio operandi*) creatures, it has the character of an idea. God knows both himself and things other than himself through the same thing in reality—his essence—but he knows them through different reasons.[7]

Richard's disambiguation adds two aspects to the character of an idea: First, an idea must be a likeness of something other than the knower. This aspect ensures that God does not have an idea of himself, but it seems ad hoc. Thus, Richard adds the second additional aspect of an idea: An idea is both a *ratio cognoscendi* and a *ratio operandi*. Ideas are not merely cognitive principles; they are also causal principles. Richard does not explain how this second aspect supports the first, but the implication is that ideas are principles of practical knowledge. Practical knowledge concerns what the knower could produce. Nothing can produce itself—not even God. Thus, there can be no divine idea of God.

Richard's clarification also emphasizes that God has but one source of knowledge, namely, his essence.[8] Like his predecessors, Richard thinks that divine ideas are secondary objects of the divine intellect.[9] Through a single principle of knowledge, God knows an infinite number of things.

How does God have these likenesses in his intellect? Do they belong to the divine intellect insofar as it is known as imitable by creatures? Richard takes up this question in the first book of his *Commentary on the Sentences*, d. 36, a. 2, q. 2. No earlier author in this study devoted an entire question to this issue because none of them had to respond to Olivi, whose claims were condemned, but still merited a response. Richard says that the term 'idea' can be taken in three ways: In one way,

---

6. *In I Sent.*, d. 36, a. 2, q. 1 (Brexiae, I.312a): "Ideae vocantur formae, hoc est similitudines intelligibilium in intellectum."

7. *In I Sent.*, d. 36, a. 2, q. 1, ad 2 (Brexiae, I.312a), esp.: "divina essentia inquantum est ratio cognoscendi seipsam non habet rationem ideae, quia ideatum est res differens ab idea sua." Richard's distinction is indebted to Aquinas's and Henry's distinction between the principle and term of knowledge. See pp. 56 and 101, respectively.

8. *In I Sent.*, d. 35, a. 1, q. 3 (Brexiae, I.301b): "per essentiam suam cognoscit creaturam." Cf. ad 3 (Brexiae, 302a): "Deus non intelligit per aliquid extra se."

9. *In I Sent.*, d. 36, a. 2, q. 2 (Brexiae, I.313a), esp.: "[essentia hominis ab aeterno] fuit secundarium obiectum divini intellectus." See pp. 67 and 88–89 for the same claim in Aquinas and Henry, respectively.

'idea' means separately existing Platonic forms, which do not belong to the divine essence. In a second way, 'idea' can be taken as naming a creature's essence insofar as the divine intellect understands it. Such an idea is an exemplar of the creature as it is in its real essence and produced in actual existence. Ideas in this sense do not belong to the divine essence, Richard says. Although the divine intellect from eternity understood the essence of man, man's essence was not the divine essence because it did not intrinsically exist in God. It was a secondary object of the divine intellect.[10] Man's essence indeed exists in God, but it does not exist according to its natural existence. It was not the real flesh and blood of man, but the essence as understood in an intellect. There is a veiled critique of Henry of Ghent here. Divine ideas do not have their own existence; they are just the secondary objects of the divine intellect.[11]

In a third way, 'idea' entails a cognitive and operative reason (*ratio*) of creatures intrinsically in God. There are two ways to take this understanding: First, an idea is the divine essence insofar as it is imitable by a creature. Second, an idea is the divine essence insofar as it is understood as imitable by a creature. At stake is whether the divine intellect's act of understanding establishes ideas or not. Following Richard, I will call these two understandings the first way and the second way, respectively. The first way is prior to the second way because God can *understand* the divine essence as imitable by a creature precisely because it *is* imitable by a creature. The act of the divine intellect does not make the divine essence imitable; the divine essence is already imitable, and the divine intellect knows that imitability.[12]

Richard treats the two ways of understanding an idea as a cognitive and operative reason in God in turn. In the first way—the divine essence as imitable—an idea entails in God a respect of reason (*respectus rationis*) as in potency to a creature, and it connotes in the creature a real respect in potency to God. Richard does not explain why the respects are in potency, but his reason must be that a *respectus rationis* is the result of an act of the intellect.[13] Since an idea in this first way is logically prior to God's knowing his essence as imitable, there cannot be any *respectus rationis* in act yet. The divine intellect could not make such a *respectus* be in act if it were not possible, so the *respectus rationis* is present in the divine essence in

---

10. *In I Sent.*, d. 36, a. 2, q. 2 (Brexiae, I.313a).

11. Richard critiques the traditional understanding of Henry's theory of essential being at *In I Sent.*, d. 35, a. 1, q. 4 (Brexiae, I.302–4). See pp. 106–9.

12. *In I Sent.*, d. 36, a. 2, q. 2 (Brexiae, I.313a), esp.: "quia enim divina essentia est imitabilis a creatura: ideo Deus intelligit eam, ut imitabilem a creatura, non e converso." This point is reminiscent of Aquinas's claim that the divine essence discovers (*adinvenit*) the divine ideas. See pp. 67–69.

13. *In I Sent.*, d. 30, a. 1, q. 4 (Brexiae, I.269a): "Quandoque vero est relatio in uno extremorum secundum rem et in alio secundum rationem tantum, et hoc quando duo extrema non sunt unius ordinis, ut scientia et scibile." Richard's account of mixed relations in this question is very close to Aquinas's. See pp. 72–73. However, Richard's overall theory of relations departs from Aquinas's theory because Richard thinks that relations are *res*. In short, whereas Aquinas thinks that if *a* and *b* are related, *a* is not really changed by a change in *b*, Richard holds that *a* is changed by a change in *b*. For a discussion of Richard's account of relations, see Henninger, *Relations*, 59–67.

potency. Since ideas in this sense are *respectus* in potency, Richard concludes that the plurality of ideas is a plurality according to reason in potency. Thus, God knows a creature through an idea (*per ideam*) insofar as he is the form of his understanding expressing for himself those things by which he is imitable.[14]

When Richard describes the respects entailed by the second way—the divine essence understood as imitable—his debt to Olivi becomes clear. An idea entails a *respectus rationis* in act in the divine essence to a creature, and it connotes a respect of reason in act in the creature to God as well as a real respect in potency. Thus, the plurality of ideas is a plurality according to reason in act, and thus, God does not know creatures through an idea (*per ideam*) in this way because an idea taken in this way presupposes knowledge of both the divine essence and the creature according to its mode of understanding (*rationem intelligendi*).[15]

Once again, Richard does not explain why these respects are entailed, but the reason for the first respect from God to a creature should be clear from the previous paragraph. When God knows his essence as imitable, he knows the *respectus rationis* he bears to a possible creature, and since he knows that *respectus* in act, the *respectus* is in act. Richard's account of the respects from the possible creature to God requires more explanation. The creature has a real respect to God in potency and a rational respect to God in act. The real respect to God must be in potency because the creature does not actually exist. Since it does not exist, it cannot be the subject of a real relation in act. Creatures only exist if God wills them to exist; an act of the divine intellect alone does not create. The real respect in potency cannot be the only relation connoted by God's rational respect in act, however, because then the transition, as it were, from potency to act in God's rational respect would result in no change on the side of the creature. A change in a relation requires a change in both extremes.[16] God's *respectus rationis* in act relative to a creature requires something in act on the part of the possible creature. Since the creature does not exist and cannot have a real respect in act to God, it must have a rational respect in act. The relationship in act between God and the possible creature is a *respectus rationis* for both extremes. Such relations only arise when a knower knows the extremes of the relation (in this case, God and the possible creature).[17]

This fact about knowing relations that are rational for both extremes explains why Richard says God cannot know creatures through ideas in the second way of understanding 'idea'. In order for God's *respectus rationis* to be in act with respect to the creature, the creature has to be known. Therefore, when God knows his

---

14. *In I Sent.*, d. 36, a. 2, q. 2 (Brexiae, I.313b), esp.: "idea dicit in Deo respectum rationis, ut in potentia ad creaturam, et connotat in creatura realem respectum in potentia ad Deum ... et sic Deus cognoscit creaturam per ideam inquantum est forma sui intellectus sibi exprimens ea a quibus est imitabilis."

15. *In I Sent.*, d. 36, a. 2, q. 2 (Brexiae, I.313b), esp.: "Deus per ideam non cognoscit creaturam, quia idea hoc modo accepta praesupponit secundum rationem intelligendi divina essentia, et creaturae cognitionem."

16. *In I Sent.*, d. 30, a. 1, q. 4, ad 6 (Brexiae, I.269b); *In I Sent.*, d. 26, a. 3, q. 1, ad 4 (Brexiae, I.239b–40a).

17. *In I Sent.*, d. 30, a. 1, q. 4 (Brexiae, I.269a).

essence as imitable, he knows both himself and the creature before he has an idea of the creature.

In his explanation of both ways of understanding 'idea'—the divine essence insofar as it is imitable by a creature and the divine essence insofar as it is understood to be imitable—Richard says that divine idea names a respect in God and *connotes* a respect in a creature. His use of connotation is reminiscent of Bonaventure.[18] To say that a divine idea connotes a respect to a creature means that it refers first and foremost to God, but it also entails a creature secondarily. More specifically, a divine idea refers to the respect in God first and foremost, and it entails the respect in the possible creature secondarily. So, in both ways of taking the term 'idea,' the term includes both God and a possible creature, but it includes them as primary and secondary.

One of Peter John Olivi's main objections to the Imitability Theory is that the extremes of a relation must be known before the relation can be known. Richard grants the truth of this objection and relocates the Imitability Theory to the divine essence itself rather than the divine essence as known. God knows through an idea if the 'idea' means the divine essence as imitable. God does not know through divine ideas if we take an idea to mean the divine essence understood as imitable by a creature.

God knows a creature in an idea taken in the second way insofar as he intuits himself to be the exemplar of the creature; he sees the creature shine forth again (*refulgere*) in himself. God knows a creature in himself, but to know through something (*per aliquid*) and in something (*in aliquid*) are not the same. If God knew through ideas in this second way, creaturely essences and not just the divine essence would be the immediate object of God's knowledge.[19] God can know through an idea taken as the divine essence as imitable because the *respectus rationis* present is in potency. In this case, God does not know through a relation. The creature is known directly as a possible imitation of the divine intellect because the divine essence expresses the creatures directly. Since a divine idea in the second way is a *respectus rationis* in act, not an expressing form, it depends on the expression already to have occurred. It is only because the divine essence expresses the possible creature that the respects of reason can be known.

Richard does not seem to have a problem saying that God knows the creatures directly, but he notes that it makes many people nervous. Thus, it seems more common to say that it only belongs to the divine essence to be an idea insofar as it is understood as imitable by a creature. They hold this position because God does not know a creature through his essence except as he understands it as imitable by a creature. Consequently, God truly knows a creature through an idea and in an idea. The divine essence under the character (*ratio*) of an idea does not know the *ratio* of the cognition by which God knows a creature with the same act of

---

18. See pp. 28–29.
19. *In I Sent.*, d. 36, a. 2, q. 2 (Brexiae, I.313b).

knowledge that he knows himself. Nevertheless, there is a *ratio* through which the knowledge by which God knows relates to the creature as a secondary object.[20]

Richard concludes that there are divine ideas, both insofar as divine essence is imitable by creatures and as the divine intellect knows it to be imitable by creatures. In the first way, God knows creatures *through* ideas, and he knows creatures *in* ideas in the second way. Divine ideas cannot be how God knows creatures in the second way because ideas in this sense are actual relations of reason, not merely potential relations of reason. As an actual respect of reason, the idea can only be known if both terms related by it are known. In the second sense of 'idea,' God knows creatures in the divine idea, but ideas are not the means by which God knows creatures; his knowledge of the creature is logically prior. He can know creatures through ideas taken in the first sense because, in this sense, the divine essence is expressive of the creature, and so it is through knowing his essence as expressive of the creature that he knows the creature.

It is hard to know what to make of this account. It seems to be an attempt to save the Imitability Theory. Divine ideas are the ways the divine essence is imitable, and God knows creatures through this imitability. Moreover, divine ideas are respects of reason on God's part and potential real respects on the creature's part. Divine ideas are many because each creature has a unique respect to God. However, he readily grants Olivi's account of knowing relations, which presents a serious objection to the Imitability Theory.

The key to Richard's theory seems to be relocating divine ideas from the divine intellect to the divine essence itself, such that divine ideas are at least in part logically prior to the act of the divine intellect. The divine essence is inherently expressive of the potential respects and relations between itself and creatures. The divine essence's imitability is not a result of God knowing it but rather, as it were, discovered in it. Richard's use of the term 'expressing' (*exprimens*) and my interpretation with the term 'discover' make it clear that Richard sees his theory as authentically Bonaventurean and Thomistic.[21] If divine ideas are located first in the essence itself, then we can speak of divine ideas in the second sense as the actually known respects and relations between God and possible creatures.[22]

---

20. *In I Sent.*, d. 36, a. 2, q. 2 (Brexiae, I.313b).

21. See pp. 16 and 67–68.

22. Richard is one of the first to ask whether the origin of creaturely intelligibility is the divine essence or the divine intellect. On the Imitability Theory, the answer is the divine essence: "all the divine intellect has to do is cognize the essence and in doing so it realizes that it can be imitated in various ways" (Garrett R. Smith, "*Esse Consecutive Cognitum*: A Fourteenth-Century Theory of Divine Ideas," in *Contemplation and Philosophy: Scholastic and Mystical Modes of Medieval Philosophical Thought*, ed. Roberto Hofmeister Pich and Andreas Speer [Leiden: Brill, 2018], 492–93). That Richard asks whether the origin of creaturely intelligibility is in the divine essence is further evidence that he accepts the criticism of the Imitability Theory. Scotus seems to hold both theories, but early Scotists William of Alnwick and Petrus Thomae argue that the origin of intelligibility is the divine essence. See Garrett R. Smith, "The Origin of Intelligibility according to Duns Scotus, William of Alnwick, and Petrus Thomae," *Recherches de Théologie et Philosophie Médiévales* 81, no. 1 (2014): 37–74.

Despite his efforts to remain faithful to his predecessors, his relocation of the divine ideas from the divine intellect to the divine essence is decidedly a departure from Bonaventure and Thomas. Bonaventure does indeed speak of expression, but he is always describing divine *truth*, not the divine essence. Divine truth is found in the divine intellect, which means that divine ideas are, as it were, not in the divine essence but rather in the divine intellect. Aquinas consistently refers to the divine essence as imitable, but he always does so in the context of the divine essence as *known*. For both Bonaventure and Aquinas, if, *per impossible*, God did not know his essence, then there would be no divine ideas. The same is not true for Richard. If God did not know his essence, Richard would still hold that there are divine ideas. Divine ideas are cognitive and operative reasons of creatures. These reasons would be present in the divine essence as imitable even if that imitability were unknown. God would not know creatures through ideas, but God's act of understanding does not establish or create divine ideas.

Richard seems to endorse both ways of taking the term 'idea' as working together. Divine ideas are both the divine essence as imitable and the divine essence understood as imitable. Both positions hold that imitability and a rational respect on God's part are integral to the character of a divine idea. He seems to think that these two accounts work together because 'idea' in the sense of the divine essence as imitable is prior to 'idea' in the sense of the divine essence as understood as imitable. In the first way, God can know through ideas, but he can only know in ideas in the second way. Richard posits this distinction between knowing through ideas and knowing in ideas because he denies that God could know a relation without already knowing both terms of the relation. According to the first view of divine ideas, an idea is a relation that is already present in potency, ready to be known by the divine idea. Thus, God can know through the idea because the terms of the relation in potency are already present. If divine ideas are considered according to the second view, however, since the various respects and relations are already known in act, the knowledge of them presupposes that both terms of the relations are already known.

This understanding of divine ideas is contrary to the Imitability Theory. That God knows the possible creature through the relation, which is the idea, is central to the Imitability Theory. It follows that Richard of Mediavilla holds that God has direct knowledge of possible creatures. He is, then, the first to hold the *Creatura Intellecta* Theory of divine ideas. His account masquerades as a defense of the Imitability Theory because he emphasizes that the character of an idea includes God knowing the rational respect that he bears to a creature and knowing the real relation that a creature could bear to him. However, as we will see more explicitly in the next chapter on Scotus, known rational relations are characteristic of the *Creatura Intellecta* Theory.[23]

Richard's account of divine ideas shows just how much agreement there is between the Imitability Theory and the *Creatura Intellecta* Theory. Divine ideas still

---

23. See pp. 164–65.

play a cognitive and causal role in this theory, and the character or nature of a divine idea includes a rational relation. Despite this overwhelming agreement, the two theories are incompatible. Scholastic authors introduce a theory of divine ideas to explain *how* God knows and produces creatures. The Imitability Theory and *Creatura Intellecta* Theory take opposing views of *how* God knows possible creatures. An Imitability Theory claims that God knows the creature through the relation, and a *Creatura Intellecta* Theory claims that God cannot know the creature through the relation and that God knows the creature directly. Richard breaks from the Imitability Theory in holding that God has divine ideas because he knows possible creatures, not in order that he may come to know possible creatures.

Chapter VII.
Bl. John Duns Scotus
(ca. 1265–1308)

Bl. John Duns Scotus's theory of divine ideas is simultaneously traditional and innovative. His account is traditional insofar as he insists that divine ideas are a secondary object of the divine intellect upon the divine essence, and they entail a known relation of reason. Moreover, Scotus resists the incremental restriction of the scope of divine ideas and recovers Bonaventure's theory which posits a divine idea for every possible being and every possible aspect of each of those possible beings.

Scotus's theory is also innovative insofar as we find the full-blown conclusion of Peter John Olivi's objections to the Imitability Theory. As was noted in Chapter IV, some of Olivi's objections are not fully formed.[1] In Scotus's theory of divine ideas, those critiques have been rearticulated and strengthened. Olivi was formally rebuked for saying that the Imitability Theory is contrary to faith and reason.[2] Scotus's versions of Olivi's objections show that the Imitability Theory—or at least the Thomistic and Henrician versions of it—is, in fact, contrary to reason.[3] Scotus is keenly aware of how controversial this claim is, so he emphasizes on three occasions in the discussion that he is not denying that divine ideas include relations.[4] The character of a divine idea is complete only when God knows the rational relation from him to the possible creature, but the rational relation is not the means by which God knows the creature. Rather, God's direct knowledge of the creature allows him to have the rational relation. In this sense, I second Jacopo Francesco Falà's claim that "Scotus is a true revolutionary."[5] What this means for Scotus is that the *Creatura Intellecta* Theory of divine ideas is very similar to the Imitability Theory of divine ideas, and the former corrects certain errors about relations found in the latter.

---

1. See pp. 125–26.
2. Olivi, *Quaestio de ideis*, n. 9 (Piron, 3). For the formal condemnation, see Olivi, "Tria scripta sui ipsius apologetica," n. 3 (Laberge, 126:20–23).
3. I will argue in the Conclusion that Bonaventure's metaphysics of finite beings saves his version of the Imitability Theory from Scotus's critiques.
4. *Rep.* I-A, d. 36, qq. 1–2, nn. 27, 29, 64 (Noone, 404:11, 404:27–405:1, 422:6–9).
5. See Jacopo Francesco Falà, "Divine Ideas in the *Collationes Oxonienses*," in *Divine Ideas in Franciscan Thought*, 114; Allan B. Wolter, "Scotus on the Divine Origin of Possibility," *American Catholic Philosophical Quarterly* 67, no. 1 (1993): 95–107, esp. 105–6; Timothy B. Noone, "Scotus on Divine Ideas: *Reportatio Paris.* I-A, d. 36," *Medioevo* 24, no. 1 (1998): 389–90.

Divine ideas are central to Scotus's thought in general and his thought on divine knowledge in particular.[6] For Scotus the subject of metaphysics is being qua being as Avicenna and Aquinas had argued, not an immaterial substance as Averroes had argued.[7] The primary distinction of being qua being is the transcendental disjunction of finite being and infinite being.[8] God alone is infinite being, which means that God falls under the subject of metaphysics. Scotus's proof for God's existence concludes that an Infinite Being exists and is the source and principle of all finite being. God performs this role through intellect and will, which means that he knows and loves creatures into existence. His knowledge of creatures as creatable is only by means of ideas, so his theory of divine ideas plays an important role in his overall metaphysical theory and his theory of divine knowledge.

Scotus leaves us three commentaries on Peter Lombard's *Sentences*: the *Lectura*, *Ordinatio*, and *Reportatio Parisiensis*. In the first two commentaries, which are from his time in England in the 1290s, Scotus focuses exclusively on questions concerning the status of divine ideas.[9] In the *Reportaio Parisiensis*, however, which he disputed ca. 1302–1303, Scotus treats both the status and the scope of divine ideas.[10] It is difficult to account for the difference. It is unlikely that Scotus was not aware of the discussion at Paris even though it seems Scotus did not travel to Paris before 1300 or 1301.[11] This theory is unlikely because the *Lectura* and *Ordinatio* give

---

6. Olivier Boulnois, "Jean Duns Scot," in *Sur La Science Divine*, ed. J.-C. Bardout and O. Boulnois (Paris: Presses Universalitaires de France, 2002), 245.

7. *In VI Met.*, q. 4, nn. 10–12 (OPh IV.87–88); *Rep.* I-A, prol., q. 3, a. 1 (Wolter-Bychkov, I.75–77). See Avicenna, *Met.*, I, c. 1 (van Riet, I.4–6); Aquinas, *In De Trinitate*, q. 5, a. 4 (Leonine, 50:153–54); Averroes, *In XII Met.*, com. 5 (Iunctina, VIII.293rb).

8. For Scotus's theory of the univocity of being, see *In De anima*, q. 21, nn. 25–32 (OPh V.218–221); *In VI Met.*, q. 1, nn. 47–48 and q. 4, n. 11 (OPh IV.19–20 and 87–88); *Lect.*, I, d. 3, p. 1, qq. 1–2, nn. 97–113 (Vatican, 17.261–67); *Ord.*, I, d. 3, p. 1, qq. 1–2, nn. 26–55 and q. 3, nn. 131–66 (Vatican, 3.18–38 and 3.81–103). See Allan B. Wolter, *The Transcendentals and Their Function in the Metaphysics of Duns Scotus* (St. Bonaventure, NY: Franciscan Institute, 1946), 41–57; Ludger Honnefelder, *Ens Inquantum Ens: Der Begriff Des Seienden Als Solchen Als Gegenstand Der Metaphysik Nach Der Lehre Des Johannes Duns Scotus*, Beiträge zur Geschichte der Philosophie und Theologie des Mittelalters—Neue Folge 16 (Münster: Aschendorff, 1989); Stephen P. Marrone, *The Light of Thy Countenance*, 2:489–536; Stephen D. Dumont, "Henry of Ghent and Duns Scotus," in *Medieval Philosophy*, ed. J. Marenbon, Routledge History of Philosophy 3, 291–328 (New York: Routledge, 2003); Peter King, "Scotus on Metaphysics," in *The Cambridge Companion to Duns Scotus*, ed. Thomas Williams, 18–21 (New York: Cambridge University Press, 2003); Garrett R. Smith, "The Analogy of Being in the Scotist Tradition," *American Catholic Philosophical Quarterly* 93, no. 4 (2019): 638–43.

9. Scotus continued to revise the *Ordinatio* into the 1300s and at Paris, but he still did not add any comments on the scope of divine ideas.

10. William Duba and Chris Schabel, "Remigio, Auriol, Scotus, and the Myth of the Two-Year Sentences Lecture at Paris," *Recherches de Théologie et Philosophie Médiévales* 84, no. 1 (2017): 165–73.

11. Ignatius Brady, "Prooemium," in *Fr. Rogeri Marston O.F.M., Quodlibeta Quatuor*, ed. Gerald J. Etzkorn and Ignatius Brady, 36*–38*(Quaracchi: Ex typographia collegii S. Bonaventurae, 1968); William J. Courtenay, "Scotus at Paris," in *Via Scoti: Methodologia Ad Mentem Joannis Duns Scoti.*, ed. Leonardo Sileo, vol. 1, Atti del 244 Duns Scotus Bibliography Congresso Scotistico Internazionale Roma 9–11 Marzo 1993 (Rome: Edizioni Antonianum, 1995), 157; Allan B. Wolter, "Scotus at Oxford," in *Via Scoti: Methodologia Ad Mentem Joannis Duns Scoti. Atti Del 244 Duns Scotus Bibliography Congresso*

conclusive evidence that Scotus was intimately aware of Henry of Ghent's thought on divine ideas.[12] It stands to reason that Scotus knew Henry's claim that divine ideas are finite and yet did not address it.

Two more likely scenarios involve Scotus's change of milieu in traveling to Paris. First, perhaps it is the case that the scope of divine ideas was not a burning issue in England, so Scotus did not have to address it until he arrived in Paris, where the issue was more hotly debated. Second, the way Scotus organizes his material in the *Lectura* and *Ordinatio* differs from that of the *Reportatio*. In the earlier texts, Scotus takes up the questions of relations in divine ideas and the plausibility of Henry's theory of essential being in Book I, dd. 35–36.[13] In the *Reportatio*, Scotus takes up the question of God's knowledge in general in Book I, d. 35 and the question of the status and the scope of divine ideas in Book I, d. 36. The work of two distinctions in the *Lectura* and *Ordinatio* is accomplished in half of a distinction in the *Reportatio*. The way Scotus organizes his material in the *Reportatio* is more closely aligned with the organization found in Parisian authors, especially Aquinas and Richard of Mediavilla. It seems likely enough that Scotus changed his division of the text to conform to what his Parisian colleagues were doing. This change afforded him an opportunity to visit the topic afresh and expand his account.

The *Reportatio* is Scotus's most influential writing on divine ideas. As Timothy Noone shows, the earliest Scotists, such as William Alnwick, have a clear preference for these Parisian lectures over the *Ordinatio* on divine ideas.[14] Since the *Reportatio* is Scotus's most complete, most mature, and most influential treatment of divine ideas, I will focus exclusively on the account Scotus gives in the *Reportatio*, noting important parallel treatments from the *Lectura* and the *Ordinatio* in the footnotes.[15]

THE STATUS OF DIVINE IDEAS

In the *Reporatio Parisiensis*, Scotus asks four questions about divine ideas. The first two, which he answers together, concern the status of divine ideas, and the second two, which he also treats together, concern the scope of divine ideas. Scotus does not follow the usual pattern of asking what an idea is, whether God has them, whether they are one or many, and so on. Instead, he asks (1) whether something other than

---

Scotistico Internazionale Roma 9–11 Marzo 1993, ed. Leonardo Sileo, vol. 1 (Rome: Edizioni Antonianum, 1995), 183; Brady argues that the political climate between England and France in the 1290s positively rules out an earlier trip to Paris for Scotus.

12. See *Lect.*, I, d. 35, q. un., n. 9 (Vatican, 17.446:18–25); *Ord.*, I, q. un., n. 12–13 (Vatican, 6.248–49). Scotus even uses the discussion of divine ideas to critique Henry's account of essential being. See *Lect.*, I, d. 36, q. un. (Vatican, 17.461–76); *Ord.*, I, d. 36, q. un., nn. 13–25 (Vatican, 6.246:5–281:4).

13. See pp. 106–9.

14. Noone, "Scotus on Divine Ideas," 360. See William of Alnwick, *Determinationes*, 22 (Civitas Vaticana, Palatini lat. 1805, f. 148r). For more contrasting accounts of Scotus and Alnwick, see Étienne Gilson, *Jean Duns Scot: Introduction a Ses Positions Fondamentales* (Paris: Vrin, 1952), 248n2; Armand A. Maurer, *The Philosophy of William of Ockham: In the Light of Its Principles* (Toronto: Pontifical Institute of Mediaeval Studies, 1999), 220n38.

15. See Boulnois, "Jean Duns Scot," 245.

God and the divine essence is in the divine intellect as a per se intelligible object for it, and (2) whether the things that the divine intellect cognizes other than himself by a simple intellect require distinct relations to be understood distinctly. The first question is a standard question and Scotus gives the ubiquitous Scholastic answer. The second question shows that his main goal is to uproot the Imitability Theory and replace it with the *Creatura Intellecta* Theory.[16] Scotus answers all the standard questions in the course of answering these two questions, but the ordering of these questions is at the service of arguing for the *Creatura Intellecta* Theory over and above the Imitability Theory. As a result, this chapter will follow Scotus's ordering.

What Is a Divine Idea?

Scotus begins his response to *Reportatio Parisiensis* I-A, d. 36, q. 1 by offering a version of the set of distinctions Henry proposed regarding God's object of cognition. The intellect's object can have one of two relations to the intellect: (1) First, it is related as a mover to something mobile such that the intellect is moved by the intelligible. (2) Second, the object of the intellect can relate to the intellect as terminating the act of the power. This second relation can be further distinguished because (2a) the object can terminate the potency's act primarily according to a proper *ratio* as the sensible terminates the act of the sense power primarily, or (2b) it can terminate the potency's act secondarily insofar as it is included in the character of what terminates the potency's act primarily. A common sensible like quantity secondarily terminates the act of sensing with respect to the proper sensible in this sense.[17]

Scotus applies these distinctions to God's intellect. The only object that moves God's intellect is the divine essence—(1) from above. Scotus's position is common, but his reason is unique.[18] Every divine intellection is formally infinite. Nothing created moves what is formally infinite to act because nothing moves or actualizes something nobler than itself, regardless of whether that motion is equivocal or univocal. A created being is formally finite regardless of whether it exists in extramental reality (*in re extra*) or in the divine intellect. Therefore, the divine essence alone has the character of intelligibility for the divine intellect.[19]

Scotus judges that (2a) the object terminating God's intellect primarily is God himself. This judgment is again common but supported by a unique argument. The object that primarily terminates some potency's act is necessarily required for that act. Since vision would be caused in the seer, even by God, it would necessarily

---

16. For an overview of the Imitability Theory, see pp. 11–12.
17. *Rep.* I-A, d. 36, qq. 1–2, n. 10 (Noone, 398:5–21). See pp. 88–89 for Henry's account. Scotus cites Aristotle as his authority, but Henry's text is surely influencing him. It is worth noting that Scotus does not further distinguish (2b) like Henry does. See Aristotle, *De anima* III, c. 1, 429a13–17 (Leonine, 201); Aristotle, *Met.* XII, c. 7 (AL XXV.3.257).
18. See Gilson, *Jean Duns Scot*, 286.
19. *Rep.* I-A, d. 36, qq. 1–2, n. 11 (Noone, 398:22–399:4), esp.: "si quaestio intelligatur de obiecto primo modo secundum rationem motivi ad mobile, sic dico quod nihil aliud ab essentia sua est sibi obiectum intelligibile."

corequire something in the notion of the primary terminating act of vision. Nothing created or finite is necessarily required for an infinite act, because then that act would not be infinite but possible without it. Therefore, no finite thing primarily terminates an infinite act.[20] To say otherwise is to say that "God's eternal understanding somehow depended on thinking about creaturely being and that His blessedness, logically consequent on His supreme act of self-understanding, also depended on His awareness of creaturely being."[21] When God knows his essence, he primarily knows himself.

When Scotus considers (2b) the object terminating God's intellect secondarily, he says that something other than God and the divine essence can be the object of the divine intellect because that other thing is included eminently in what primarily terminates that act and it terminates by reason and power of the primary object terminating the divine act primarily. This is possible because such an object is not required for the act but more follows upon and depends upon the act. Such objects are not related to the divine intellect's act as measure to measured, but the other way around.[22]

Scotus offers many arguments to justify that God knows things other than himself. Three arguments that both support his conclusion and attack the Imitability Theory stand out: First, Scotus gives an argument from the part of the object that is indebted to Olivi and Petrus.[23] Each specific difference names a certain grade of being and a determinate perfection with respect to the perfection of all being (*totum ens*). Therefore, since each thing is related to being known as to existence (*esse*), every such specific difference names a determinate species of imitability. The divine intellect relates to all being. Therefore, God cognizes each being according to its grade of entity and intelligibility.[24]

Scotus's second and third arguments are taken from the part of the divine intellect. Both these arguments involve correcting his predecessors' poor understanding. The first argument has its roots in Pseudo-Dionysius and Alexander of Hales, and it is familiar to us from Bonaventure, Aquinas, and Petrus.[25]

---

20. *Rep.* I-A, d. 36, qq. 1–2, n. 13 (Noone, 399:11–20).

21. Noone, "Scotus on Divine Ideas," 362. See Timothy B. Noone, "Aquinas on Divine Ideas: Scotus's Evaluation," *Franciscan Studies* 56, no. 1 (1998): 309.

22. *Rep.* I-A, d. 36, qq. 1–2, n. 14 (Noone, 399:21–29).

23. For an investigation of the influence of Olivi and Petrus de Trabibus on Scotus's theory of divine ideas, see Noone and Vater, "The Sources of Scotus's Theory of Divine Ideas," 85–111. See pp. 123–26 for Olivi's arguments.

24. *Rep.* I-A, d. 36, qq. 1–2, n. 18 (Noone, 401:4–10). See Olivi, *In I Sent.*, q. 6, ad 16 (Noone-Vater, 95:102–6); Petrus, *In I Sent.*, d. 35, p. 1, a. 2, q. 2 (Noone-Vater, 99:60–63). Recall that Henry says that an idea "is nothing other than the conception of a determinate perfection in God with respect to the determinate perfection corresponding to him in a creature." (*Quodlibet* V, q. 1 [Badius, 151rE]). See pp. 89–91 for a discussion of Henry's definition of divine ideas.

25. Ps.-Dionysius, *De div. nom.*, c. 7, §2 (PG 3.883A); Alexander of Hales, *Summa theologica* I, inq. 1, tract. 5, sect. 1, q. 2, c. 2, n. 165 (Quaracchi, I.248b); Bonaventure, *In I Sent.*, d. 35, q. un., a. 1 (Quaracchi, I.601a); Aquinas, *ST* I, q. 14, a. 5 (Leonine, 4.172); Petrus de Trabibus, *In I Sent.*, d. 35, p. 1, a. 1, q. 2 (MS Assisi 154, f. 93va). For Bonaventure, Aquinas, and Petrus's arguments, see pp. 24, 63–64, and 128–29, respectively.

The intellect, comprehending something as a cause, comprehends all things to which its causality extends. But the divine essence is the cause of all things. Therefore, the divine intellect comprehending and understanding his essence, understands and comprehends all intelligible things causable by it. But all intelligible things other than it are such. Therefore, he understands all intelligible things.[26]

If the argument is taken to mean that the effect is understood in the same act of the intellect by which the cause is comprehended, then it is false. It would follow that cognition of something other than God (namely, a creature) would be included in the same act by which God understands himself. Thus, just as God's beatitude formally is in cognition of himself, so it would be found in cognition of a creature, which is repugnant.[27] However, if the argument is taken to mean that he who comprehends a cause to the extent that it is knowable can know those things to which its causality extends, then it is true. The power (*potentia*) to comprehend all things caused by the cause follows in the intellect comprehending the cause.[28]

Scotus's other argument from the part of the intellect is the argument from God's knowledge of the ways he can be imitated or participated.[29] God perfectly cognizes his essence, which can be participated by a creature in an infinite number of ways, although it is not participated in all such ways. Therefore, he cognizes every way according to which he can be participated or imitated, and he knows all creatures because a creature does not exist except through participation.[30]

Like the previous argument, this argument can be understood well or poorly. If, like Aquinas and Henry, we understand that knowing something under the notion of its imitation with respect to the First Intelligible is knowing that thing quidditatively, then the argument is false. Scotus's reasoning is from Petrus: imitation is not the specific difference of this or that being.[31] It is not necessary that someone knowing all colors insofar as they imitate whiteness knows all colors quidditatively. He could know that colors can participate in whiteness according to more

---

26. *Rep.* I-A, d. 36, qq. 1–2, n. 19 (Noone, 401:11–16): "Intellectus, comprehendens aliquid ut causam, comprehendit omnia ad quae illius causalitas se exendit. Sed essentia divina est causa omnium. Ergo intellectus divinus comprehendens et intelligens essentiam suam, intelligit et comprehendit omnia intelligibilia causabilia ab eo. Sed talia sunt omnia intelligibilia alia ab eo. Ergo etc."

27. See Augustine, *Conf.*, V, c. 4, n. 4 (PL 32.708): "Licet te et illa videas, non tamen propter illa sed propter te beatior."

28. *Rep.* I-A, d. 36, qq. 1–2, n. 20 (Noone, 401:17–402:16).

29. See pp. 68 and 95–97 for a discussion of this argument in Aquinas and Henry, respectively. Noone suggests that Scotus takes the argument from Roger Marston, *Quodlibet* IV, q. 4, ad arg. in opp. (Etzkorn-Brady, 372) because the argument from imitability had become commonplace by that time (Noone, "Scotus on Divine Ideas," 364). I think Scotus had Henry in mind. Having just borrowed the set of distinctions about the object of the intellect from Henry's *Quodlibet* IX, q. 2, we reasonably conclude that Scotus would be thinking of the argument from imitability that Henry offers just paragraphs later.

30. *Rep.* I-A, d. 36, qq. 1–2, n. 21 (Noone, 402:17–22), esp.: "cognoscit omnem modum secundum quem est participabilis sive potest participari vel imitari."

31. Petrus, *In I Sent.*, d. 35, p. 1, a. 2, q. 2 (Noone-Vater, 99:60–63). See p. 125.

or less, and yet not know their absolute specific differences.³² The argument can only be true if we understand it to mean that God perfectly understands his imitable essence, and therefore perfectly knows every way in which it can be imitated, meaning both the imitations and the foundations of the imitations as entities that are imitated. Scotus insists God must know the foundations of the imitations because an imitation is not perfectly known unless the foundation of the imitation is known.³³

This argument is Scotus's first strike at the Imitability Theory. There can be no doubt that Aquinas, at least, interprets the argument in the way Scotus critiques. In the *Summa Contra Gentiles*, Thomas says that when God understands his essence as imitable through the mode of life and not the mode of cognition, he understands (*accipit*) the proper form of a plant, and if he understands it as imitable through the mode of cognition and not the mode of intellect, he has the proper form of animal, and similar with the others.³⁴ Scotus's example of whiteness receiving more or less is even found in *Summa Contra Gentiles*.³⁵ No one has determinate knowledge of a red fox (*Vulpes vulpes*) simply by knowing that it imitates the divine essence more than a tulip but less than a man. Again, assuming the following example is true, no one has determinate knowledge of the arctic fox (*Vulpes lagopus*) by knowing that it imitates God more than the kit fox (*Vulpes macrotis*) and less than the red fox (*Vulpes vulpes*). "To imitate the divine essence more than *Vulpes macrotis* and less than *Vulpes vulpes*" is not the specific difference of *Vulpes lagopus*; *lagopus* (hare-foot) is its specific difference.³⁶ God, or any knower, must know the specific difference of *Vulpes lagopus* to know it determinately. Knowing the relation of imitability it has to God does not suffice.³⁷ A knower knows the object determinately only if he knows if the foundation of the imitation along with the relation of imitability.

Scotus insists that the foundation of the imitation must be known precisely because he accepts Olivi's argument that both terms of the relation must be known in order for the relation itself to be known.³⁸ The relation and one term of the relation are not sufficient.³⁹ Knowledge of both terms of the relation is (at least logically) prior to knowledge of the relation. God must know himself and the foundation of the imitation—the creature itself—as terms of the relation before he can know the relation of imitability itself.

Scotus's discussion thus far gives a partial answer to the question "What is a divine idea?" and sets the stage for his opposition to the Imitability Theory. A divine

---

32. *Rep.* I-A, d. 36, qq. 1–2, n. 22 (Noone, 402:23–403:8).
33. *Rep.* I-A, d. 36, qq. 1–2, n. 23 (Noone, 403:9–17), esp.: "non perfecte cognoscitur imitatio nisi cognoscatur fundamentum imitationis." See Ward, *Divine Ideas*, 24–25.
34. Aquinas, *SCG* I, c. 54 (Leonine, 13.155a6–15). See p. 68.
35. Aquinas, *SCG* I, c. 50 (Leonine, 13.144b30–40).
36. Assuming the biologist's taxonomy has arrived at the specific difference.
37. This example is an expansion on Noone and Vater, "Sources of Scotus's Theory," 94.
38. See pp. 212–13 for Olivi.
39. Henry, *Quodlibet* IX, q. 2 (Leuven, 13.30:28–29). See pp. 103–4.

idea is a secondary object terminating the divine intellect's act, which object is included in the divine intellect's primary terminating object, the divine essence. On this point, Scotus is in full agreement with his predecessors.[40] Scotus breaks with some of his predecessors in his defense of divine ideas as secondary terminating objects, which is clearly indebted to Olivi and Petrus.[41] A relation of imitability cannot be the means by which God knows possible creatures. Ultimately, Scotus takes issue both with the relation and with the imitability, but here his arguments focus on the problems with imitability. Imitability is not the specific difference or determinate perfection of any creature at all. In fact, being an imitation of the divine essence unifies each creature since all creatures have imitating-the-divine-essence in common.

If this were Scotus's only objection to the Imitability Theory, then he would be attacking a strawman since the Imitability Theory does not merely hold that God knows himself as imitable. He knows himself as imitable in varying degrees. It is the knowledge of these various degrees that yields intimate knowledge of each creature in all its singularity. Even still, this qualification does not help because the knowledge that something is imitable to a greater or lesser extent does not yield the determinate, quidditative knowledge that Imitability Theorists claim. Knowing that white is imitable more or less perfectly is not the same as knowing the essences of red, blue, and so on, never mind the more specific essences of scarlet, crimson, periwinkle, and arctic. Scotus's underlying reason for denying quidditative knowledge in this case depends upon his first argument. The specific difference of a quiddity or essence is not a relation, not even a relation to the divine essence. It is something absolute about the quiddity or essence itself.[42]

The Plurality of Divine Ideas

In addition to Scotus's concerns about saying that God can have perfect knowledge through degrees of imitability, he is also concerned about saying that God can know possible creatures by means of a relation. The question before Scotus in *Reportatio* I-A, d. 36, q. 2 is whether distinction relations in God are required for distinctly knowing distinct intelligibles. Imitability Theorists say yes. Divine ideas are nothing but the rational relations of God to possible creatures and God knows the possible creatures through knowing these relations.

Scotus is more hesitant. One part of the question is certain for him, but another part of the question is doubtful. It is certain that there are distinct relations and distinct ideas in God for knowing distinct intelligibles when speaking of God's simple knowledge of distinct quiddities like rock, man, and so on. Scotus agrees

---

40. See, for example, pp. 67–68 and 88–89.
41. See pp. 123–26.
42. As I will point out in the final chapter, I think Scotus's argument is only effective against thinkers who follow Avicenna in holding a strong account of essence. A thinker like Bonaventure, who argues that the essences of things are semiotic, can dodge this criticism precisely because he thinks that essences are fundamentally relational. See pp. 271–73.

with a central tenet of the Imitability Theory: divine ideas are relations; the character of a divine idea necessarily includes a rational relation from God to the possible creature. Scotus holds this position because a higher power can do everything a lower power can do in a higher way. A created intellect can compare the divine essence to every created, intelligible thing. Therefore, God can through his comparative act cause diverse rational relations in himself.[43]

But this issue is not what is at stake. The question is not whether the character of divine ideas includes rational relations, but whether those rational relations are the means by which God knows possible creatures. It is doubtful—and to Scotus's mind, false—that God knows possible creatures though rational relations. Before arguing his own position, however, Scotus identifies three theories which posit that God must have such relations so that he can know creature distinctly. These three theories are the Imitability Theory, the *Obiectum Cognitum* Theory, and the Infinite Intellect Theory.[44]

Of these three theories, Scotus thinks James of Viterbo's *Obiectum Cognitum* Theory is most probable and even offers a defense of the theory.[45] Yet, this theory fails, and Scotus offers serious objections to all three theories. Despite explicit claims to the contrary, both the Imitability Theory and Infinite Intellect Theory entail that the relations to the divine intellect are real relations, not rational relations. A *ratio intelligendi* precedes the act of understanding. But no second act precedes a rational relation. A rational relation always follows a discursive act. For an object known through another is never understood except through discursion, and every notion or rational relation happens through the intellect's activity (*per intellectum negotiantem*).[46] But to know an object is not to know a means, that is, a species. An object is known nondiscursively.[47]

Moreover, every intellection (*intellectio*) in us that relates to a thing as a thing in itself has a real respect to the object. A real respect does not occur if the intellection relates to the thing as through the act of another comparing the intellection to it because then the intellection would not be related to it except as a rational relation. When the intellect knows something by knowing itself, comparing itself to it, it only causes a rational relation to the thing in itself. But for God to know creatures it is not necessary that he compare himself to them by reflecting upon his act. Therefore,

---

43. *Rep.* I-A, d. 36, qq. 1–2, nn. 26–28 (Noone, 404.8–26), esp.: "Certum enim est quod in Deo sunt relationes distinctae et distintae ideae ad distincta cognoscibilia cognoscenda." See *Lect.*, I, d. 35, q. un., n. 15 (Vatican, 17.449:14–27)

44. *Rep.* I-A, d. 36, qq. 1–2, nn. 29–30 (Noone, 404.26–406:7), esp.: "omnes concedunt tales rationes ideales in Deo, sed quaerit quaestio utrum istae rationes ideales sint necessario ponendae in Deo ut habeat per eas distinctam cognitionem de distinctis cognitis."

45. *Rep.* I-A, d. 36, qq. 1–2, nn. 34, 39–49 (Noone, 407:20–21, 410:4–415:23).

46. The term *negotio* here refers to intellectual activity beyond simple apprehension. In us, it would refer to the acts of comprehension and division and acts of discursive reasoning.

47. *Rep.* I-A, d. 36, qq. 1–2, nn. 35–36 (Noone, 408:26–409:4), esp.: "Nam ratio intelligendi praecedet intellectionem sive actum intelligendi; sed nullum actum secundum praecedet relatio rationis, sed semper relatio rationis sequitur actum discursus."

if this ideal relation is included in his act of understanding by which he understands external things and is not caused through a collective act, it will be a real relation.[48] Since the only real relations in God are among the Divine Persons, if divine ideas are also real relations, then God is not a Trinity, but an infinity.[49]

James of Viterbo's *Obiectum Cognitum* Theory is not subject to this criticism, but it still holds an impossible view of knowing relations. On the *Obiectum Cognitum* Theory, the ideal relations are in the essence as it is a cognized object (*obiectum cognitum*).[50] Since they are in the object known from the fact that it is cognized and not in itself, the relations are rational relations. But how can they be known reasons in this way and yet be the means of knowing (*rationes intelligendi*) of others determinately? These relations in the essence come after (*sequuntur*) a comparative act of the intellect by which the essence is compared to other things. The divine intellect does not compare the divine essence to something unknown because a comparison of things to each other presupposes knowledge of both extremes. Just as nature does not compare except to a preexisting thing, so it seems that the intellect does not compare the essence to those other things through such relations unless it already knows the other things. Therefore, these relations are not necessary to know other things determinately because the relations presuppose knowledge of them.[51]

The influence of Olivi could not be more obvious.[52] The *Obiectum Cognitum* Theory fails because it fundamentally misunderstands how relations are known. The relation only arises because the extremes or terms of the relation are related to each other. The relation does not exist before one of the terms; instead, the relation is "logically consequent upon God's knowledge of creatures."[53] As a result, Scotus concludes that no such relation is necessarily required to have distinct and determinate cognition.

He educes two ways of declaring this conclusion: The first way begins from Aristotle's three modes of relations. The first mode occurs when one extreme contains the other many times, as in the relation double to half. The second mode occurs when the extremes are related as active to passive, as in the case of heat to what is heated. The third mode occurs when one of the extremes is related to the other only because the other is related to it, as in the case of the measurable to the measure and the knowable to the knower.[54] Scotus comments that relations of the third mode of relatives differ from the others because the relation is not mutual in the third mode.

---

48. *Rep.* I-A, d. 36, qq. 1–2, n. 37 (Noone, 409:5–15), esp.: "Si igitur in suo intelligere quo intelligit res extra includatur ista relatio idealis et non causetur per actum collativum, erit relatio realis."

49. Since Henry of Ghent holds the numerical finitude of divine ideas, he would only be committed to a great multiplicity. See pp. 104–5.

50. See pp. 139–41.

51. *Rep.* I-A, d. 36, qq. 1–2, n. 38 (Noone, 409:16–29). See also, nn. 40–42 (Noone, 411:10–412:14).

52. See pp. 224–25.

53. Noone, "Aquinas on Divine Ideas: Scotus's Evaluation," 315. See *Lect.*, I, d. 35, q. un., n. 16 (Vatican, 17.450:6–9).

54. Aristotle *Met.* V, c. 15, 1020b26–1021b11 (AL 25.3.2.112:579–114:629).

One term is not related to the other except that the other is related to it. He borrows Aristotle's example of knowledge. The intelligible object is only related to the knower because the knower is related to it. Universally, the measure is only related to the thing measured because the measured is already related to it. The intelligible object is the cause and measure of our knowing and does not depend upon our knowing. The intelligible object is denominated 'relative' from the real relation that it terminates. It is not called 'relative' according to some relation because then it would not be our understanding's measure nor would it be a relation in the third mode but a relation in the second mode, where mutuality is required. Therefore, it terminates the relation according to its bare, absolute character.[55]

This account of the relation between the knower and the object known is true for man's finite way of knowing, but divine knowing works the other way around. The very divine act of understanding (*ipsum divinum intelligere*) is the measure of all intelligible things, just as the artist is the measure of the work of art, the art of which is not taken from things but is the cause of things. And therefore, each thing other than God is related to the divine intellect as what is measured to its measure, and the divine act of understanding terminates the relation of each intelligible thing through a bare, absolute notion and not through some relation in God corresponding to the relation of the measured thing to it.[56]

The second way of declaring Scotus's conclusion is to say that no relation in God is required for him to understand things other than himself, nor is a relation of the intelligible object to God required, nor a real relation since there is no such relation from God to a creature, nor a rational relation because it is impossible that a rational relation be simultaneous with or precede divine intellection of the other. It is impossible because no comparative intellection precedes simple intellection. If some relation were simultaneous or preceded divine intellection, then that relation would be a real relation independent of the divine intellect (*ex natura rei*).[57] But if a rational relation follows the intellection of the creature, then it is not necessary for knowing the creature.[58]

The first of these ways of understanding the conclusion is closer to the sort of argumentation we have seen in earlier authors.[59] It argues from Aristotle's third mode of relations and emphasizes that the rational relation on the part of the measure does not hold because of some further relation but merely because of the measure itself. The rational relation in the measure is posterior to the real relation of the measured to the measure. It arises only because of some further analysis. The real relation of the measured to the measure occurs because of what the measure is

---

55. *Rep.* I-A, d. 36, qq. 1–2, n. 50 (Noone, 416:1–12).

56. *Rep.* I-A, d. 36, qq. 1–2, n. 50 (Noone, 416:12–20). See *Rep.* I-A, d. 35 (Wolter-Bychkov, II.351–80).

57. As Garret R. Smith explains, "An *ex natura rei* distinction is one that obtains apart from the operation of the intellect" ("Origin of Intelligibility," 49n27).

58. *Rep.* I-A, d. 36, qq. 1–2, n. 51 (Noone, 416:21–417:2).

59. See pp. 72–74 and 100–102.

absolutely: its absolute character. Since God is the measure of every intelligible thing, he terminates the relation of those things to himself through something absolute, not an additional relation. The rational relation of God to the thing only arises, as it were, later. As we will see, Scotus uses his ubiquitous theory of instants of nature to account for this logical posteriority.

Scotus's second argument is more extreme. No relation whatsoever is required for God to know every possible creature distinctly. On its face, the claim does not even seem intelligible. It had long been standard to say that truth and knowledge is a certain rectitude, conformity, or adequation of the intellect and the thing known.[60] How can there be a rectitude without some sort of relationship between the knower and the thing known? We just saw that Aristotle uses knowledge as a paradigmatic case of a relation. How can we understand Scotus's claim? Even if the claim is intelligible, what does it mean for the existence of things in God? Earlier authors argued that possible creatures have divine cognitive being because existing in the mind entails at least a sort of relative being.[61] But if God does not require a relation to know possible creatures, then do they have any being at all? The rest of this section will deal with the question of relation. The question of the being of possible creatures will be handled in the next section.[62]

The Subtle Doctor was keenly aware of how baffling his claim was, and so immediately after expounding his second argument, he responds to those who say that it is not intelligible that the divine act of understanding is related to some object and yet there is no relation in either extreme. He distinguishes between things that are really distinct (*distincta realiter*) and things that are eminently distinct (*distincta eminenter*).[63] For Scotus, things are really distinct when they are separable as thing and thing (*res et res*). Two dogs are really distinct from each other because each dog can exist separately without the other.[64] Things are eminently (or virtually,

---

60. See, *inter alia*, Anselm, *De veritate*, c. 11 (Schmitt, I.191); Grosseteste, *De veritate* (Baur, 134–35); Bonaventure, *In I Sent.*, d. 8, p. 1, a. 1, q. 1, ad 4 et 7 (Quaracchi, I.151b); Aquinas, *De veritate*, q. 1, a. 1 (Leonine, 22/1.5:162–6:176).

61. For Bonaventure, Aquinas, Henry of Ghent, and James of Viterbo on divine cognitive being, see pp. 34–36, 74–78, 109–11, and 143–45.

62. See pp. 295–308.

63. *Ord.* I, d. 2, p. 2, qq. 1–4, n. 402 (Vatican, 2.355–56), esp.: "potest vocari 'differentia virtualis', quia illud quod habet talem distinctionem in se non habet rem et rem, sed est una res, habens virtualiter sive praeeminenter quasi duas realitates, quia utrique realitati ut est in illa una re competit illud quod est proprium principium tali realitati, ac si ipsa esset res distincta: ita enim haec realitas distinguit et illa non distinguit, sicut si illa esset una res et ista alia." Note that this passage gives insight into both a real distinction and an eminent distinction for Scotus.

64. For more on the real distinction for Scotus, see M. J. Grajewski, *The Formal Distinction of Duns Scotus: A Study in Metaphysics* (Washington, DC: The Catholic University of America Press, 1944), 55–62; Michael Joseph Jordan, "Duns Scotus on the Formal Distinction" (Ph.D. diss., Rutgers University, 1984); Alan B. Wolter, *The Philosophical Theology of Scotus: Writings of Alan B. Wolter, OFM*, ed. Marilyn McCord Adams, 27–41 (Ithaca, NY: Cornell University Press, 1990); Stephen D. Dumont, "Duns Scotus's Parisian Question on the Formal Distinction," *Vivarium* 43, no. 1 (2005): 7–62; Antoine Vos, *The Philosophy of John Duns Scotus* (Edinburgh: Edinburgh University Press, 2006), 254–55.

virtualiter) distinct where the subject includes the predicate.[65] An artist and his knowledge of his work of art is an example of an eminent distinction. The term 'artist' entails knowledge of his work of art, but an artist and his knowledge are not two distinct things; they are one thing and cannot be really distinct from each other. There is no real distinction (and consequently no relation) between the artist and his knowledge, even though his knowledge is of something that (when it exists) is really distinct from him. They are only eminently (or virtually) distinct.

Scotus continues that wherever some things are really distinct, they are really related. But where they are eminently distinct, not really distinct, they are not really related. In us, the act of understanding and an infinite object are really distinguished, and so there is a real relation between them, namely, the relation of measure to measured. But it is not this way in God because the object of his intellect and his act of understanding are really the same, not really distinguished. Nevertheless, the divine act of understanding is not related to its understood object by a rational relation because the objects are there from the nature of an eminent thing, although they are not really distinguished. And whatever is characteristic of perfection in these objects that is thus really distinguished and really related, is more perfectly in God where they are not really distinguished or related. Consequently, just as the act of understanding is knowledge declarative and manifesting of the object of which mode it is in creatures where they are really distinguished and related, in the same way the divine act of understanding is knowledge and a manifestation of any object whatsoever without any such distinction or relation because of their true identity. And therefore, it is not necessary to posit a relation because of the intellection of some object, neither in one extreme, the other, nor in both at the same time.[66]

There does not have to be a relation involved for God to know possible creatures because he is identical to the possible creatures as known and only eminently distinct from them as known. Prior thinkers thought that God's knowledge required a relation because they thought God's knowledge is too much like our own. They overplayed the analogy between the finite artist and the divine artist. Scotus is willing to accept the analogy, but the ways the knower and the known are distinct must be understood properly.

Scotus further cuts off the possibility that a relation is necessary because the possible creature—a rock—depends on God. Perhaps someone will grant that the divine act of understanding is not related to the rock since the measure never depends upon the measured, but he might think that the rock's dependence upon God requires a relation on its part to God. Nevertheless, a relation does not follow upon the dependence because the rock in cognitive being is nothing in reality (*tantum nihil est secundum rem*). There is no dependence because what is nothing does not depend. Moreover, if the rock is something it is not only a respect but something absolute.

---

65. *Rep.* I-A, d. 36, qq. 1–2, n. 52 (Noone, 417:8–9). Scotus's most famous discussions of eminence are from his proof for the existence of God. See, *inter alia*, *Lect.* I, d. 2, n. 61 (Vatican 16.133).

66. *Rep.* I-A, d. 36, qq. 1–2, n. 52 (Noone, 417:3–26).

Therefore, the rock, as something absolute, can be understood to the divine act of understanding before something related. Dependence is no justification for saying that God's act of understanding a possible creature is by means of a relation.[67]

This line of argument, which grants that no relation is required for God to know possible creatures, seems to destroy the very character of a divine idea as articulated by Scotus's predecessors and even Scotus himself at the beginning of the question. As Falà writes, it seems that Scotus is "definitively rejecting the consideration of ideas as relations of imitability."[68] Every eternal relation in God to creatures seems severed. If there be no real or rational relations from God to creatures as known or creatures as known to God, then he does not seem to be able to compare himself to creatures.

Scotus begins to respond to this concern by defining a divine idea: "An idea is an eternal reason (*ratio*) in the divine mind in accordance with something formable according to its proper *ratio*."[69] This definition solidifies Scotus's adherence to the *Creatura Intellecta* Theory of divine ideas. There is no obvious reference to relation in the definition, and the idea is the proper reason or character of the creature itself. Scotus affirms this in the sentence following the definition: "an idea is not some relation but the object cognized in the divine mind, in which creatures exist (*sunt*) objectively."[70] If divine ideas are just the creatures as known, then "the idea of a stone is nothing but the stone as known."[71] Since God does not make a man and a donkey by the same *ratio*, there are many ideas. These many ideas are not outside of God because he does not need anything other than himself, and since everything in God is eternal, these many *rationes* in God's intellect are eternal.[72]

There are, I think, two ways of interpreting Scotus's definition:[73] First, Scotus could be read as denying that the character of a divine idea includes any sort of relation. This reading seems correct, but it does not help Scotus show that God can compare himself to creatures. Since the definition focuses on God's knowledge of possible creatures, it is not surprising that it seems to be of little help since it emphasizes that God does not know possible creatures through some relation.

Second, Scotus could be read as endorsing the necessity of a rational relation in the character of a divine idea. A rational relation is necessary because the

---

67. *Rep.* I-A, d. 36, qq. 1–2, n. 54 (Noone, 418:12–25).

68. Falà, "Divine Ideas in the *Collationes Oxonienses*," 125.

69. *Rep.* I-A, d. 36, qq. 1–2, n. 57 (Noone, 419:17–19): "Dico igitur quod idea est ratio aeterna in mente divina secundum aliquid formabile secundum propriam rationem eius."

70. *Rep.* I-A, d. 36, qq. 1–2, n. 57 (Noone, 419:19–21): "idea non est relatio aliqua sed obiectum cognitum in mente divina in qua sunt creaturae obiective." What it means for creatures to exist objectively will be explored in the next section. See pp. 175–82.

71. *Rep.* I-A, d. 36, qq. 1–2, n. 58 (Noone, 420:11): "idea lapidis non sit nisi lapis ut intellectus." See Jan P. Beckmann, "Entdecken Oder Setzen? Die Besonderheit Der Relationstheorie Des Duns Scotus Und Ihre Bedeutung Für Die Metaphysik," in *John Duns Scotus: Metaphysics and Ethics*, ed. Ludger Honnefelder, Rega Wood, and Mechthild Dreyer (Leiden: Brill, 1996), 372.

72. *Rep.* I-A, d. 36, qq. 1–2, nn. 58–62 (Noone, 419:22–421:6).

73. Henry of Harclay holds the first theory in his early writings and the second theory later in his career. See pp. 202–6.

definition of an idea includes that the possible creature is *formable*. God only knows the creature as formable if he knows a rational relation. This point becomes clear when we consider how Scotus applies his theory of instants to divine ideas. Scotus's theory of instants of nature relies on his so-called *propositio famosa*: "whatever real order there would be among things if they were really distinct, such is the order of those things according to reason, where they are distinct according to reason."[74] Although the things in question are not really distinct and there is no temporal progression in them, they can still have a natural priority and posteriority that is discovered by the order of explanation. As Fr. Alan Wolter explains, "If B presupposes A logically, but not vice versa, then A may be said to be prior by nature to B."[75] In this case, God's knowledge of his essence is logically prior to his knowledge of creatures, so the instant of nature at which God knows himself is prior to the instant of nature at which he knows creatures.[76]

Since, as we saw above, Scotus allows two ways of understanding that God does not need a relation to know creatures, he similarly allows two possible sets of instants of nature that result in a divine idea: In the first set of instants, God knows his own essence. In the second instant, he knows and understands creatures by the mediation of his essence. This knowledge occurs directly and without any rational relation. According to this way of taking the instants, the intelligible object depends upon the divine intellect for its *esse cognitum* in this second instant because the object is constituted in *esse cognitum* by that act of understanding. Further, at the second instant, God, under a merely absolute *ratio*, terminates the relation of the creature having *esse* outside of God. He is denominated by a certain relation to the possible creature and is called the creature's Lord. In the third and final instant, God can compare his essence to that intelligible object and understands the rational relation between the thing known and the divine essence.[77]

---

74. Rep. I-A, prol., q. 1, a. 4, n. 111 (Wolter-Bychkov I.42): "Qualis order realis esset inter aliqua si essent distincta realiter, talis est ordo eorum secundum ration, ubi sunt distincta secundum rationem." See Stephen D. Dumont, "The *Propositio Famosa Scoti*: Duns Scotus and Ockham on the Possibility of a Science of Theology," *Dialogue* 31, no. 3 (1992): 415–29.

75. Wolter, "Scotus on the Divine Origin of Possibility," 106. Calvin G. Normore formulates the same claim slightly differently: "A is naturally prior to B if and only if mention of A is required in giving an explanation of B" ("Duns Scotus's Modal Theory," in *The Cambridge Companion to Duns Scotus*, ed. Thomas Williams [New York: Cambridge University Press, 2003], 134).

76. For a close look at Scotus's theory of instants of nature and divine ideas, see Ernesto Dezza, "Giovanni Duns Scoto e gli *Instantia Naturae*," in *Divine Ideas in Franciscan Thought*, 135–59.

77. Rep. I-A, d. 36, qq. 1–2, n. 63 (Noone, 421:7–24), esp.: "Deus in primo instanti cognoscit essentiam suam et in secundo instanti cognoscit et intelligit creaturas mediante essential sua. Et tunc secundum illam viam dependet obiectum cognoscibile ab intelligere divino in ese cognito, quia per illud intelligere constituitur in esse cognito . . . . In tertio autem instanti potest comparare essentiam suam ad illud obiectum intelligibile extra secundum relationem rationis." Note that Scotus claims that the intelligible being of creatable essences is constituted by the divine intellect in the second instant. In other texts, Scotus argues that the divine essence constitutes intelligible being. See Garrett R. Smith, "Origin of Intelligibility," 39–50, especially 42n16 and 43n23 for a list of texts supporting each position. Ward offers a sustained defense of the position that the divine essence constitutes intelligible being, which he calls the "Containment Theory" (*Divine Ideas*, esp. 39–44).

Before turning to the second set of instants, I note that Scotus is not definitively rejecting ideas as relations. The character of a divine idea is complete only after the third instant. Scotus makes this claim explicit in the *Lectura*. In the last instant, "God reflects upon that comparison and upon the act of comparing, and thus the idea is known."[78] God does not need a rational relation to know the possible creature, but he does need one to have a divine idea. He needs a relation to have an idea precisely because an idea is of a possible creature "in accordance with something formable."[79] God knows the creature itself directly, but he knows it as formable (makeable) only when he knows the rational relation that he bears to it. If this point is omitted, Scotus's theory of divine ideas would be identical to the theory of William of Ockham, which denies any relation at all in divine ideas.[80]

In the second set of instants, God knows his essence in the first instant. In the second instant, God understands the stone and the stone is constituted in a cognitive being not related to God. The stone does not depend on God at this instant because at this point it is nothing in reality (*nihil est in re*). God understands the stone without any dependence of the stone on him. In the third instant God compares himself to the stone as it is understood, and thus has a rational relation to it. In the fourth instant God can understand the rational relation. Once again, the character of the divine idea is not complete until God knows the rational relation that exists from him to the possible creature, which allows Scotus to reaffirm again that he does not deny that there are rational relations to creatures in God. He only denies that relations are necessary for God to know the creatures.[81]

By granting two sets of instants, Scotus admits two ways of understanding God's direct knowledge of creatures and each way allows and necessitates rational relations for the complete character of a divine idea. As Noone points out, "[o]f these two alternative replies, there can be no doubt that Scotus tends to prefer the second one."[82] The easiest way to see that he prefers the second reply, which entails no relation whatsoever in God's cognition of possible creatures, is that Scotus only introduces this option in the *Reportatio*. In both the *Lectura* and *Ordinatio*, he

---

Hoenen notes that the third instant in the *Reportatio*, which corresponds to the third and fourth instants in the *Ordinatio*, is distinguished from the first two because Scotus introduces possibility. In the first two instants, God does something and something happens to the possible creature. In the third instant God *can* (*potest*) compare his essence. See Hoenen, *Marsilius of Inghen*, 83 and 125–26.

78. *Lect.*, I, d. 35, q. un., n. 22 (Vatican, 17.452:27–28): "in quarto autem instanti reflectitur supra illam comparationem et supra actum comparandi, et sic cognoscitur idea." Scotus expresses the same position, although less explicitly, in an *adnotatio* to the fourth and last instant in the *Ordinatio* treatment of this issue. See *Ord.* I, d. 35, q. un., n. 32 and *Adnotatio Duns Scoti* (Vatican, 6.258:4–23).

79. *Rep.* I-A, d. 36, qq. 1–2, n. 57 (Noone, 419:18): "secundum aliquid formabile."

80. Ockham, *Ord.* I, d. 35, q. 5 (OTh IV.487:4–489:8). See pp. 238–45.

81. *Rep.* I-A, d. 36, qq. 1–2, n. 64 (Noone, 421:25–422:9), esp.: "in secundo instanti quo Deus inteligit lapidem et constituitur in esse cognito non refertur lapis ad Deum nec dependet, quia sic adhuc nihil est in re et in omni illo sive in toto instant intelligit Deus lapidem sine omni dependentia lapidis ad ipsum. Et tunc, sicut prius, Deus comparat se at lapidem ut intelligitur, et sic habet relationem rationis ad ipsum."

82. Noone, "Scotus on Divine Ideas," 372.

endorses the position he identifies as the first position in the *Reportatio*. If he had considered the new position after the *Lectura* and *Ordinatio* and found it inferior to the first position, he would not have included it at all in the *Reportatio*.

Again, that he prefers the second *Reportatio* explanation can be seen by a comparison of the sets of instants of nature he educes in the *Lectura* and *Ordinatio* compared to the two sets of instants he educes in the *Reportatio*. In both the *Lectura* and *Ordinatio*, Scotus educes one set of four instants. The sets of instants from the *Lectura* and *Ordinatio* are as follows: In the first instant, the divine intellect understands his essence under a merely absolute *ratio*. In the second instant, God produces and understands a stone (or any other creature) in intelligible being, not by a comparative act, but by a direct act such that there is a relation in the understood stone to divine intellection according to the third mode of relations. In the third instant, God compares his essence to the stone in intelligible being from which a certain ideal relation or rational relation is caused in him. In the fourth instant, God, as it were, reflects upon the rational relation produced in the third instant and upon his act of comparing, and thus he knows an idea.[83]

The sets of four instants in the *Lectura* and *Ordinatio* become the set of three instants in the *Reportatio*, which is evident because the second instant in each of these three sets includes God establishing the stone in intelligible being which initiates a relation from the known stone to God. The *Lectura* and *Ordinatio* do not specify why the relation occurs, but the *Reportatio* makes it clear that the stone as understood is related precisely because it depends upon the divine act of under-

---

83. *Lect.*, I, d. 35, q. un., n. 22 (Vatican, 17.452:12–28); *Ord.*, I, d. 35, q. un., n. 32 (Vatican, 6.258:4–18). The sets of instants in the *Lect.* and *Ord.* are not identically worded, but they express the same position.
For the sake of clarity, I list the sets of instants together.
Lectura and *Ordinatio*
1. The divine intellect understands his own essence
2. God understands the creature in *esse intelligibile*, not in a comparative act but the stone by a direct act, which a relation to the divine intellect according to the third mode follows.
3. The divine intellect compares its essence to the stone in *esse intelligibile* from which a certain ideal relation is caused.
4. The divine intellect reflects upon the comparison of the third instant and the act of comparing and thus an idea is known.
Reportatio: First Set of Instants
1. God knows his essence
2. God knows and understands creatures by the meditation of his essence. The knowable object depends on the divine act of understanding in *esse cognito* because through that act of understanding it is constituted in *esse cognito*.
3. God can compare his essence to that external intelligible object according to a rational relation
Reportatio: Second Set of Instants
1. God knows his essence.
2. God understands the stone and constitutes it in *esse cognito*, but it is not referred to God nor depends on him.
3. God compares himself to the stone as understood and thus has a rational relation to it
4. God can know the rational relations.

standing. Thus, this relation of dependence on the part of the possible creature makes God its Lord.

If the sets of instants from the three texts align this way, what explains the reduction from four instants to three? Why does Scotus combine the third and fourth instants of the earlier texts into a single instant in the *Reportatio*? I think Scotus rethought the requirements of a relation in the third mode and how it comes to be known. In the *Lectura* and *Ordinatio*, Scotus argues that each term of the relation requires its own instant to be established. The second instant establishes the relation on the part of the creature as known and the third instant establishes the relation on the part of God. But the two terms of the relation should not be established in two separate instants. In a relation of the third mode, a rational relation is established in the measure at the same moment that what is measured depends upon the measure. When I come to know some stone, the rational relation is established in the stone as soon as my knowledge depends upon it to measure the adequacy of my knowledge. These two are not logically prior or posterior but simultaneous. The rational relation of the measure to the measured is logically simultaneous to the real relation of the measured to the measure. What it means for God to terminate the relation from the possible creature to him is for God to have a rational relation to the possible creature. As they are logically simultaneous, there is no reason to distinguish their establishment into two instants. Since the rational relation from God to the stone as known is established in the second instant, the act of comparison that God makes according to a rational relation in the third instant is sufficient for knowing that relation.

If, as is the case in the *Reportatio*'s set of four instants, the second instant of the series establishes the stone in cognitive being but does not entail any relation or dependence on the stone's part, God's part, or both, then another instant of nature will be required to account for the establishment of a rational relation on God's part that can then be known in the fourth instant. The sets of instants in the *Reportatio* differ in number because they posit the relation to be established at different instants.

This seemingly minor shift in the number of instants reveals two critical developments in Scotus's thought: The first development, which we have already seen, is that divine cognitive being does not entail any relation or dependence from the thing known to God.[84] There are two ways to understand this claim: either divine cognitive being is some sort of independent, absolute being, or it is nothing. Scotus's move toward the nothingness explanation is the subject of the next section.[85] The second development holds that if there be a relation from the creature as known that God terminates, that relation automatically entails the corresponding rational relation on God's part. Scotus is emphasizing that even though not all relations are real for both terms, it cannot be the case that one thing is related to another without some sort of a relation existing in the other too. The sets of instants from the *Lectura*

---

84. See pp. 166–70.
85. See pp. 175–82.

and *Ordinatio* would have us believe that relations of the third mode involve a logical priority and posteriority. The possible creature as related to God would have a logical priority to God as related to the possible creature. But since the possible creature is the measured and God is the measure, Scotus would be committed to saying that the measure has a sort of logically posteriority to that which it measures. What depends is not logically prior to that on which it depends. Scotus does not tell us if this line of thinking has influenced the development in his thinking, but it seems probable that it did.

Before turning to the question of the existence of things in God, I should comment on the influence of Peter John Olivi and Petrus de Trabibus on Scotus's thought. Their Infinite Intellect Theory is faulty, but their criticisms of the Imitability Theory are spot on. Scotus adopts these arguments wholesale and completes some of them. Relations and knowledge of them cannot work the way the Imitability Theory requires. Scotus tacitly agrees with Olivi's claim that the Imitability Theory is contrary to reason.[86] Olivi's censure makes Scotus nervous. As a result, Scotus is anxious to emphasize that he does not deny that the character of divine ideas includes a rational relation. His emphatic language shows just how concerned he is that he will be lumped in with Olivi: "It is *certain* that there are distinct relations in God . . . . *everyone* concedes that such ideal *rationes* are in God . . . . it is clear that *I do not deny* there to be rational relations to creatures but I do say that they are not necessary for God's intellection of creatures."[87] Scotus's theory is innovative insofar as God knows creatures directly, but it is traditional insofar as divine ideas are characterized by known rational relations from God to creatures.

The Existence of Things in God

Henry of Ghent's theory of essential being looms large in Scotus's account of the existence of things in God.[88] He offers extended critiques of the traditional interpretation of essential being in the *Lectura* and *Ordinatio* and a brief critique in the *Reportatio*.[89] We will focus more on Scotus's own theory than his critiques. It is important to keep Henry's theory in mind because, I argue, it influences Scotus's move toward a theory of objective being as nothingness. I will first explain Scotus's theory of what it means to be a thing (*res*). Then, I will explain Scotus's theory of objective being (*esse obiectivum*) in general. Finally, I will look more closely at what sort of existence *esse obiectivum* is for Scotus.

---

86. Olivi, *Quaestio de ideis*, n. 9 (Piron, 3). See p. 124.

87. *Rep.* I-A, d. 36, qq. 1–2, nn. 27, 29, 64 (Noone, 404:11, 404:27–405:1, 422:6–9): "Certum enim est quod in Deo sunt relationes distinctae . . . omnes concedunt tales rationes ideales in Deo . . . Sic igitur patet quod non nego ibi relationes esse rationis ad creaturas sed dico quod non sunt necessariae ad intellectionem Dei circa creaturas." Emphasis mine. See Noone and Vater, "Sources of Scotus's Theory," 89.

88. See pp. 106–9.

89. *Lect.*, I, d. 36, q. un., nn. 13–22 (Vatican, 17.464:3–467:29); *Ord.*, I, d. 36, q. un., nn. 13–25 (Vatican, 6.276:5–281:4); *Rep.* I-A, d. 36, qq. 3–4, nn. 71–75 (Noone, 449:4–450:17).

Scotus on Res

Scotus's most comprehensive account of 'thing' (*res*) occurs in *Quodlibet*, q. 3 (Christmas 1306 or Easter 1307). He argues that *res* can be understood in three ways: most generally, generally, and most strictly. The most general sense matters for our purposes. In this sense, *res* extends to anything that is not 'nothing' (*nihil*). *Nihil* can be understood in two ways: First and most truly, what includes a contradiction that precludes both existence in the intellect and outside the intellect is *nihil*. It is not even something intelligible because it does not constitute a single intelligible thing. One can say "square circle" but there is no one intelligible object corresponding to those two words. Second, *nihil* can refer to what neither exists nor could exist as some being extramentally.[90]

Most generally, then, a *res* is whatever does not include a contradiction. Both rational beings (*entia rationis*), which only exist in the intellect, and real beings (*entia realia*), which exist extramentally, are *res* because they are not nothing in the first sense of *nihil*. In the second sense of *nihil* only what can or does have extramental existence is a *res*. *Res* contrasted to the second sense of *nihil* is more restricted than *res* contrasted to the first sense of *nihil*. Many thinkable things do not include a contradiction but do not exist nor could exist. Scotus uses the examples of logical intentions such as genus and species, and rational relations; "There is no contradiction included in the notion of what it is to be a species or what it is to be a genus.... Nevertheless, there is nothing in the extramental world whose essence is *to be a species* or *to be a genus*."[91] All extramental things fall into genera and species, but the second intentions *genus* and *species* do not themselves exist extramentally.[92]

This distinction between *res* as noncontradictory and *res* as possibly existing extramentally illuminates the distinction that Scotus makes between ratified beings (*entia rata*) in *Ordinatio* I, d. 36. In one sense, a ratified being is what has a firm and true being from itself. In another sense, a ratified being is distinguished from a fictional being (*figmentum*) since existence is not repugnant for it. Ratified beings in the first sense are such because they actually exist. God is a ratified being from himself. All other actually existing beings are ratified beings through their efficient cause. They are possible of themselves and they are ratified beings for as long as God wills them to exist. Beings are ratified in the second sense because extramental existence is not contrary to the thing as such.[93] Ratified beings in the second sense

---

90. *Quodlibet*, q. 3, n. 2 (Wadding-Vivès, 25.113–14), esp.: "Verissime enim illud est nihil quod includit contradictionem, et solum illud, quia illud excludit omne esse extra intellectum, et in intellectu; ... Alio modo dicitur nihil quod nec est, nec esse potest aliquod ens extra animam." See *Ord.*, I, d. 43, q. un., n. 15 (Vatican, 6.359).

91. Giorgio Pini, "Scotus and Avicenna on What It Is to Be a Thing," in *Scientia Graeco-Arabica: The Arabic, Hebrew, and Latin Reception of Avicenna's Metaphysics*, ed. Dag Nikolaus Hasse and Amos Bertolacci (Boston: De Gruyter, 2012), 376.

92. *Quodlibet*, q. 3, n. 2 (Wadding-Vivès, 25.114).

93. *Ord.*, I, d. 36, q. un., nn. 48–50 (Vatican, 6.290:5–291:9), esp.: "'ens ratum' aut appelatur illud quod habet ex se firmum et verum esse ... aut 'ens ratum' dicitur illud quod primo distinguitur a figmentis, cui scilicet non repugnant esse verum essentiae vel existentiae."

are creatable, but their actual existence cannot be known from the fact that they are ratified beings in this sense. Fictional beings such as chimera are not ratified beings in either sense because extramental existence is formally repugnant to them.[94] Scotus does not explain the impossibility of chimera existing extramentally, but rather views it "as a primitive fact."[95]

Comparing the distinctions between *res* and ratified beings, there are three distinct levels: First, *res* as noncontradictory is the broadest, including even fictional beings. Second and more narrowly, ratified beings as nonfictional are all *res* as possibly existing extramentally. Beings and things in this sense are possible of themselves, but only actually exist if God creates them. Scotus says these senses of *res* and *ens* are what Avicenna intends when he says that *ens* and *res* are impressed into the intellect by a primary impression.[96] The third and narrowest of the distinctions is ratified beings as true and firm.

These distinctions are indebted to the distinctions that Henry of Ghent draws between *res* in *Quodlibet* VII, qq. 1–2, but Scotus's account is unique.[97] Scotus drops all reference to essences and speaks merely of contradiction. Scotus determines what counts as a thing by "a merely formal and logical requirement. Quite simply, in order for something to be thinkable, it is sufficient for it not to include a contradiction. It is not necessary for it to be an essence or a combination of essences."[98] Scotus's account makes it easier to determine what is a thing. If it is thinkable, it is a thing, and no further investigation into whether it could exist extramentally is necessary. The logical criterion is sufficient; an ontological criterion only enters when we ask whether it is a *res* as possibly existing extramentally and a ratified being as nonfictional.[99]

When Scotus moves to consider *res* as possibly existing extramentally, he still does not speak of essences, which further distinguishes his account from Henry's. For Scotus, a *res* as possibly existing extramentally might be a real essence but not necessarily. It is a real essence if it is a ratified being as firm and true, but the mere possibility of extramental existence does not make a thing an essence. Nonexisting possibles are *res* as possibly existing extramentally, but they are not essences. For Scotus, "[s]omething is an essence if and only if it was made the object of God's act of creation."[100] This conclusion follows from Scotus's rejection of Henry's distinction between essential being and existential being. For Scotus, essential being and existential being are always found together, so if something does not exist extramentally (i.e., does not have existential being), then it cannot have the existence of an essence either.[101]

---

94. *Ord.*, I, d. 36, q. un., nn. 60–63 (Vatican, 6.296:1–297:11).
95. Pini, "What It Is to Be a Thing," 377.
96. *Quodlibet*, q. 3, n. 2 (Wadding-Vivès, 25.114b). See Avicenna, *Met.*, I, c. 5 (van Riet, I.31:2–3).
97. Note that Henry argues in terms of essence rather than in terms of possibility. See Henry, *Quodlibet* VII, qq. 1–2 (Leuven, 11.27:59–70). See p. 87.
98. Pini, "What It Is to Be a Thing," 378.
99. Pini, "What It Is to Be a Thing," 379.
100. Pini, "What It Is to Be a Thing," 380.
101. See *Ord.*, I, d. 36, q. un., n. 48 (Vatican, 6.290:5–8). For the traditional account of Henry's theory of essential being, see pp. 106–9.

The second level of Scotus's distinctions between *res* and ratified being, then, is populated by possible beings and he does not ask whether any of these ratified beings actually exist. The ones that actually exist do have essences, but that is not a consideration at this level. Since Scotus defines a divine idea as "an eternal notion in the divine mind in accordance with something formable according to its proper notion," it is clear that divine ideas fall at this second level.[102] They cannot be at the first level because not everything that is a *res* as noncontradictory is formable. They cannot be at the third level because not everything formable gets formed. Since things at this second level prescind from the question of essences, it follows that for Scotus divine ideas do not have essences. This denial has serious consequences for Scotus's account of the existence of things in God.

Scotus on Objective Being (Esse Obiectivum)

Immediately after offering his definition of a divine idea, Scotus emphasizes that "an idea is not some relation but the cognized object in the divine mind in which creatures exist objectively (*sunt creaturae obiective*)."[103] What Scotus says about the intelligible species in our intellects helps illuminate his account of existing objectively. At Scotus's time, many authors rejected intelligible species on the strength of arguments from Olivi and Henry of Ghent.[104] If an intelligible species is in the intellect, then it would inform the intellect as an accident informs its subject. Therefore, the intellect would receive a real reception (*passio*) from its object, not an intentional reception. Other accidents make their subjects have their intrinsic features. So, if an intelligible species is present in the intellect in the same way that any other accident is present in its subject, "the intelligible species, like whiteness, can then only make its subject have the features it engenders, and so *not* be 'intentionally directed' at something else—any more than the presence of whiteness in a white body somehow makes that white body to be 'about' whiteness."[105] The intelligible species could only make its subject know itself, not the intentional object to which it is supposed to point. Since the only reason to posit intelligible species is to explain the intentional presence of

---

102. *Rep.* I-A, d. 36, qq. 1–2, n. 57 (Noone, 419:17–19): "idea est ratio aeterna in mente divina secundum aliquid formabile secundum propriam rationem eius."

103. *Rep.* I-A, d. 36, qq. 1–2, n. 57 (Noone, 419:19–21): "idea non est relatio aliqua sed obiectum cognitum in mente divina in qua sunt creaturae obiective."

104. Olivi, *In II Sent.*, q. 58, ad 15 (Jansen, II.469); Henry, *Quodlibet* V, q. 14 (Badius, 175vF). On Olivi and Henry's rejections of intelligible species, see Robert Pasnau, *Theories of Cognition in the Later Middle Ages* (New York: Cambridge University Press, 1997), 236–47 and 306–10, respectively; Richard Cross, *Duns Scotus's Theory of Cognition* (New York: Oxford University Press, 2014), 84–90. As Pasnau points out, Olivi's rejection was more overarching than Henry's. For a brief discussion of Scotus's theory of intelligible species, see Adriaenssen, *Representation and Scepticism*, 135–37.

105. Peter King, "Duns Scotus on Mental Content," in *Duns Scot à Paris, 1302–2002: Actes Du Colloque de Paris, 2–4 Septembre 2002*, ed. Olivier Boulnois (Turnhout: Brepols, 2004), 72. Emphasis original.

objects of knowledge, the intelligible species could not do what it was posited to do.[106]

Scotus answers this difficulty by arguing that each intelligible species results in a twofold reception (*passio*): First, the intellect really receives the intelligible species as an accident and a real attribute. Thus, intelligible species "are real forms in the category of quality."[107] Second, there follows a cognizable or intentional reception through which the intellect receives the object in the species intentionally. Thus, the act of understanding is a motion for the soul because it is by the object as in the species. The first reception is in the intellect through the received species present in the intellect. The second reception is by the object as it shines forth again (*relucente*) in the species.[108]

Scotus accepts Olivi and Henry's objection and makes a distinction in the intelligible species that overcomes the problem and allows the intelligible species to make an object present in cognition. It is important to emphasize that the intelligible species makes the object present. Olivi and Henry argue that intelligible species just make themselves known, blocking the object from being known. Scotus's second reception makes the intelligible species self-effacing. It makes the knower think about the object that is cognitively present in the intellect, rather than making the knower think about himself or about the intelligible species. The object "shines forth again in the species."[109] As Peter King explains, "'once again' because it is the cognizable rather than the real presence of the object; and it 'shines forth' because the object transparently discloses itself in the act of thinking."[110] Objective being, then, is the way the object is cognitively present in the intellect and is contrasted to the subjective being that the intelligible species has according to its first reception. The content of the intelligible species has objective being because it makes the object present.

The two receptions of an intelligible species are caused in the knower in different ways: The first reception of the intelligible species is caused formally by the joint working of the phantasm and the agent intellect. The second recepcion is caused objectively, not formally.[111] Something is caused formally when it is caused as a form. In this case, the intelligible species becomes an accidental form in the intellect. Something is caused objectively when it is caused intentionally, that is, when the intelligible content of the thing is present without it being present formally. This distinction

---

106. *Rep.* I-A, d. 3, q. 4, n. 86 (Wolter-Bychkov, I.208). See *Ord.*, I, d. 3, p. 3, q. 1, n. 336 (Vatican, 3.336) and *Lect.*, I, d. 3, p. 3, q. 1, n. 254 (Vatican, 16.327). Scotus take this argument from Henry, *Quodlibet* V, q. 14 (Badius, 175vF).

107. Armand Maurer, "Ens Diminutum," 221. See Hoenen, *Marsilius of Inghen*, 130–31.

108. *Rep.* I-A, d. 3, q. 4, n. 119 (Wolter- Bychkov, I.218), esp.: "Prima ergo passio est in intellectu per speciem praesentem receptam in intellectu, secunda est ab obiecto ut in specie relucente."

109. *Rep.* I-A, d. 3, q. 4, n. 119 (Wolter-Bychkov, I.218): "in specie relucente."

110. King, "Scotus on Mental Content," 76–77.

111. *In VII Met.*, q. 18, n. 51 (OPh IV.352:19–353:4): "abstractio obiecti non est aliqua actio realis, sed causatur species intelligibiles a phantasmate et intellectu agente simul; qua causata in intellectu possibili formaliter, simul causatur obiectum abstractum ibi, non formaliter sed obiective."

makes sense of the fact that when I know *shark*, the intelligible content of *shark* is caused in me, but I do not cease to be a man and begin to be a shark. The first reception's being formally caused is a necessary condition for the second reception's being objectively (or intentionally) caused.[112] Since there is a twofold causality, there is a twofold being in the intellect: First, there is the formal or subjective being of the intelligible species as an accident in the category of quality existing in a subject. Second, there is the objective being of the object or mental content of the intelligible species. The question, then, is what sort of being is *esse obiectivum*?

The Existence of Esse Obiectivum

Scotus intends the term *esse obiectivum* to be contrasted with the subjective being of the intelligible species as form, but it is hard to know how this term relates to the myriad of similar terms. Things existing in the intellect are variously said to have diminished being, cognized or intellectual being, being in opinion, being in intellection, exemplified being, represented being, intentional being, and even spiritual being.[113] Scotus argues that these terms are synonymous by comparing the object of understanding to a statue of Hercules: "The universal object under the aspect of universal only has diminished being as cognized, as Hercules in a statue only has diminished being because he is represented in an image."[114] Diminished being, then, is representational; it is semiotic, pointing to something other than itself. For cognition, diminished being refers to the object being understood.

Scotus insists that the intentional object of cognition having diminished being cannot exist by itself because it is not caused in the intellect by itself. It exists in the intellect because of the work of the agent intellect. The agent intellect's work is not diminished being but something real. Its work terminates in a real form in the category of quantity that formally represents the universal as universal. This real form "is the form existing subjectively in the mind, which is not to be confused with the object existing objectively in the mind."[115] So, objective being is a sort of diminished being in the intellect.

Scotus gives two explanations of diminished being: The first explanation is found in the *Ordinatio*, where he says that diminished being is related to real being as what is *secundum quid* is related to what is *simpliciter*. The diminishment here does not affect the object itself, only the being that object enjoys as an object of

---

112. *In VII Met.*, q. 18, n. 51 (OPh IV.353:8–9): "illa numquam est intentionaliter nisi propter aliquam realem."; *Ord.*, I, d. 3, p. 3, q. 1, n. 386 (Vatican, 3.235:4–9). See Cross, *Duns Scotus's Theory of Cognition*, 30; Giorgio Pini, "Scotus on Objective Being," *Documenti e studi sulla tradizione filosofica medievale* 26 (2015): 353.

113. *Ord.*, I, d. 36, q. un., n. 34 (Vatican, 6.284:10–13). Scotus does not include the last two terms which come from Aquinas.

114. *Rep.* I-A, d. 3, q. 4, n. 105 (Wolter-Bychkov, I.213): "universale obiectum sub ratione universalis non habet nisi esse diminutum ut cognitum, quemadmodum Hercules in statua non habet esse nisi deminutum, quia repraesentatum in imagine."

115. King, "Scotus on Mental Content," 81.

cognition.[116] Diminished being is qualified being that can be reduced to the being of the intellection itself, which exists simply.[117] Since diminished being can be reduced to some absolute being, it is relative.[118] It necessarily implies a relation to the knower, regardless of whether the knower is a finite creature or the infinite God. Objective being, as diminished being, is reduced to the very act of divine knowing that produces it.[119]

On this account, objective being is nothing other than divine cognitive being, and it is similar to the more recent interpretation of Henry's theory of essential being that I endorsed in Chapter III.[120] The divine intellect establishes its objects of thought—possible creatures—in intelligible being. Some contemporary scholars have taken this account of objective being from the *Ordinatio* as an indication that Scotus thinks the objects of divine understanding constitute some sort of third realm ontologically distinct from existence in things and in finite intellects.[121]

As Garrett Smith points out, this interpretation cannot be correct. First, in *Ordinatio* I, d. 35, we find an insertion into the main text from Scotus's own hand which stresses that "God's act of understanding clearly does not have a simultaneous requirement or dependence to the stone nor vice versa. Proof: the object is nothing."[122] Scotus stresses that the object is nothing precisely to avoid the traditional reading of Henry.[123] He would not fight the interpretation so vigorously just to endorse it himself.[124] Scotus doubles down on this interpretation in the *Reportatio*. There, he says twice that the stone known by God is nothing in reality because it is not actually related to God.[125] So, when Scotus claims that the stone exists in God's mind objectively making it intellectually present to him, he still insists that objective existence is nothing in reality. It cannot be a third ontological realm because Scotus is not assigning any being to the objects of divine knowledge at all.

The claim that the objects of divine cognition are nothing in reality must not be taken too far. King and Cross have argued that Scotus's theory which emphasizes the nothingness of the objects of divine cognition amounts to an abandonment of

---

116. *Ord.*, I, d. 36, q. un., n. 34 (Vatican, 6.284:13–21)
117. *Ord.*, I, d. 36, q. un., n. 46 (Vatican, 6.289:4–14).
118. Maurer, "Ens Diminutum," 222.
119. *Ord.*, I, d. 36, q. un., n. 28 (Vatican, 6.281:18–282:12).
120. See pp. 109–11.
121. Calvin Normore, "Meaning and Objective Being," in *Essays on Descartes's Meditations*, ed. A. O. Rorty, 232–33 (Los Angeles: University of California Press, 1986); Dominik Perler, "What Am I Thinking About? John Duns Scotus and Peter Aureol on Intentional Objects," *Vivarium* 32, no. 1 (1994): 79–80.
122. *Ord.*, I, d. 35, q. un., n. 51 (Vatican, 6:267:7–9): "Intelligere Dei ad lapidem non habet coexigentiam (patet), nec dependentiam, nec e converso. Probatio: obiectum nihil est."
123. See pp. 106–9 for the traditional interpretation of Henry's essential being.
124. Garrett R. Smith, "*Esse Consecutive Cognitum*," 487n34.
125. *Rep.* I-A, d. 36, qq. 1–2, nn. 54 and 64 (Noone, 418:16–17 and 421:25–422:3): "quia lapis in esse cognito tantum nihil est secundum rem . . . . in secundo instanti quo Deus intelligit lapidem et constituitur in esse cognito non refertur lapis ad Deum nec dependet, quia sic adhuc nihil est in re."

diminished being.¹²⁶ Scotus does drop the entire discussion of diminished being, including the example of the Ethiopian who is white with respect to his teeth, in *Reportatio* I, d. 36, but the discussion appears in *Reportatio* II, d. 1, q. 2. This text, which Scotus certainly disputed after *Reportatio* I, d. 36, provides "a discussion of diminished being in terms of *esse simpliciter* and *secundum quid*, complete with the example of the Ethiopian, a discussion which is nearly *verbatim* with the account in the *Ordinatio*."¹²⁷ Moreover, in the same place, Scotus insists that the understood stone compared to being has true diminished being such that the being of the stone in cognition is the diminished being of the stone and *secundum quid*. Therefore, he concedes that the stone according to its truest being is understood eternally such that with respect to intellection it is taken according to *esse simpliciter*, but whole, as "understood stone," it is diminished being.¹²⁸ Objects of divine thought enjoy diminished being.

Moreover, objects of divine thought are nothing in reality, but they are not absolutely nothing. They are at least *res* as noncontradictory and many are also *res* as possibly existing extramentally.¹²⁹ To say that something has objective being is to say that it is intelligible, but that does not imply that the object could exist extramentally. Scotus frequently uses the example of a rock as the object of God's knowledge, but he could have easily used the example of *genus*. The second intention *genus* is not a *res* as possibly existing extramentally, but it is an object of divine cognition. Thus, we should conclude that the scope of objective being is wider than the scope of divine ideas for Scotus. Divine ideas must be ratified beings as nonfictional, but not necessarily ratified beings as firm and true.

This point solidifies two final, related aspects of Scotus's theory of the status of divine ideas: First, divine ideas are primarily cognitive principles for Scotus. A divine idea is more about *knowing* the possible creature as formable than it is about *making* the creature. This leads to the second point, which will be discussed more below. Divine ideas are not inherently to-be-made or not-to-be-made (*fiendum* or *non-fiendum*).¹³⁰ Scotus's theory of divine ideas examines God's knowledge of creatures at an instant logically prior to his choice to create some of those creatures. Thus, his theory of divine ideas does not include a distinction between reasons (*rationes*) and exemplars like Aquinas's.¹³¹

---

126. King, "Scotus on Mental Content," 65–88; Richard Cross, "Duns Scotus on the Semantic Content of Cognitive Acts and Species," *Quaestio* 10 (2010): 135–54; Cross, *Duns Scotus's Theory of Cognition*, 189–95. Pini seems to join their ranks but cautions that the change applies only to divine cognition ("Scotus on Objective Being," 337–67).

127. Smith, "*Esse Consecutive Cognitum*," 487n34. See *Rep.* II, d. 1, q. 2, nn. 12–13 (Wadding-Vivès, 22.527–28); *Ord.* I, d. 36, q. un., n. 45 (Vatican, 6.228).

128. *Rep.* II, d. 1, q. 2, n. 13 (Wadding-Vivès, 22.527b–28b), esp.: "concedo quod lapis secundum verissimum esse est intellectus aeternaliter, ita quod respectu intellectionis accipitur secundum esse simpliciter, sed totum ut lapis intellectus est esse diminutum." Quoted in Smith, "*Esse Consecutive Cognitum*," 487n34.

129. See *Quodlibet*, q. 3, n. 2 (Wadding-Vivès, 25.114) and pp. 176–78.

130. For a general overview of *fiendum* and *non-fiendum*, see pp. 91–92.

131. See pp. 46–51.

THE SCOPE OF DIVINE IDEAS

Scotus only addresses the scope of divine ideas in the *Reportatio*, where two aspects stand out: First, like all thinkers after the Condemnations of 1270, Scotus emphasizes the divine will as free and uncoerced by the divine intellect in general and with regard to divine ideas in particular. Second, Scotus's theory is a call to return to the plenitude of Bonaventure's theory.[132] There is a divine idea for every possible being and every possible aspect of those possible beings. Thus, he resists the growing trend to reduce the scope of divine ideas. Scotus asks two questions about the scope of divine ideas, which he treats together: The first of these questions, *Reportatio* I-A, d. 36, q. 3, asks whether God has distinct ideas of everything other than himself that may be distinctly cognized. The second of the questions, *Reportatio* I-A, d. 36, q. 4, considers whether God has an infinite number of ideas. Since Scotus does not follow the usual division of questions, I will again follow Scotus's division.

Ideas for Everything Distinctly Cognizable

The *sed contra* of *Reportatio* I-A, d. 36, q. 3—whether God has distinct ideas for all things other than himself that may be distinctly cognized—is noteworthy because it is based on imitability. Whatever God knows as other than himself, he knows as it imitates his essence. Therefore, whatever he knows distinctly, distinctly imitates his essence. But knowing all things other than himself to imitate his essence, God can know himself to be imitable by all things other than himself, and this is to have ideas of all things. Therefore, God has distinct ideas with respect to all things other than himself that he knows distinctly.[133]

This argument is a strong reinforcement of Scotus's declaration that he does not deny that divine ideas include relations, and even relations of imitability. When God knows a divine idea, he is knowing how this creature in particular can imitate him. The *Creatura Intellecta* Theory of divine ideas does not do away with imitability. It simply claims that imitability cannot be how God knows creatures. God's knowledge of the way a creature can imitate him is logically posterior to his knowledge of the creature itself.

Scotus begins his response to the question by explaining Aquinas and Henry of Ghent's theories and responding to them. Only after critiquing these predecessors does he offer his own answer to the question. Since his critiques reveal something about his own position, it will be useful to look at what he says about Aquinas and Henry first.

---

132. See pp. 36–40.
133. *Rep.* I-A, d. 36, qq. 3–4, n. 4 (Noone, 426:4–10), esp.: "quidquid Deus cognoscit ut aliud a se, cognoscit illud ut imitatur essentiam suam." Though this argument was likely given by Scotus's bachelor in the classroom, I think Scotus accepts the argument. Scotus redacted *Rep.* I-A, but he did not remove the argument or argue against it at the end of the question. See Stephen D. Dumont, "John Duns Scotus's *Reportatio Parisiensis Examinata*: A Mystery Solved," *Recherches de Théologie et Philosophie Médiévales* 85, no. 2 (2018): 377–438.

Scotus on Thomas Aquinas's Position

Scotus begins his account by explaining Aquinas's distinction between divine exemplars, which are principles of practical cognition according to which God wills to create at some time in history, and divine reasons, which are principles of speculative cognition according to which God never wills to create. This distinction, Scotus notes, causes Aquinas to exclude many things from the scope of divine exemplars. He eliminates nonexisting possible matter (Scotus seems to mean prime matter), genera, inseparable accidents, and individuals. Scotus thinks Aquinas only posits divine exemplars of the lowest species.[134]

Scotus replies to Aquinas on each of the five types of being excluded from divine exemplars. He rejects the exclusion of nonexisting possible beings because he thinks the distinction between divine exemplars and divine reasons is false, and he offers two arguments for this claim: First, divine exemplars and divine reasons are distinguished according as they are practical or speculative ideas, which in turn is based on whether the idea is to-be-made or not-to-be-made (*fiendum vel non-fiendum*). What uniformly relates to an idea does not distinguish a practical idea from a speculative one. Possibly *fiendum* and possibly *non-fiendum* uniformly and in the same manner relate to ideas before the act of the will. Therefore, *fiendum* and *non-fiendum* before any act of the will do not distinguish a practical idea from a speculative one, and since everyone agrees that ideas are in the intellect before any act of the will, it follows that possibly *fiendum* and possibly *non-fiendum* do not distinguish them. That ideas are equally *fiendum* and *non-fiendum* before any act of the will is clear from the fact that the divine will would be coerced into willing or not willing if an idea had *fiendum* or *non-fiendum* simply from an act of the divine intellect. If someone tries to preserve God's freedom by supposing that he could will contrary to the inherent *fiendum* or *non-fiendum* of the idea, he would be affirming that God acts contrary to right reason, which is impossible. Thus, ideas cannot be distinguished as speculative and practical, that is, as reasons and exemplars, from whether it is possible that something is going to come to be.[135]

I find this argument unconvincing because it misunderstands Aquinas's position. Scotus argues as if Aquinas distinguishes divine exemplars and reasons prior to any divine willing, but that is not how Aquinas understands it. An idea is "a form that something imitates from the intention of an agent who predetermines the end for himself."[136] The agent's intention comes from the will.[137] The character of an idea

---

134. *Rep.* I-A, d. 36, qq. 3–4, nn. 11–16 (Noone, 428:6–430:2). See pp. 89–98 and Hoenen, *Marsilius of Inghen*, 128 for Aquinas's account of the scope of divine ideas. Scotus gets Aquinas's position on individuals wrong. This error and its causes will be discussed at pp. 316–18.

135. *Rep.* I-A, d. 36, qq. 3–4, n. 18 (Noone, 430:7–25), esp.: "Quia si idea, ante actum voluntatis, respiceret diversimodi possible fiendum et non-fiendum, ergo intellectus ostens hoc voluntati ut unum possibile fiendum et aliud non-fiendum, aut voluntas non posset non velle illud fieri."

136. Aquinas, *De veritate*, q. 3, a. 1 (Leonine, 22/1.100:221–23): "idea sit forma quam aliquid imitatur ex intentione agentis qui praedeterminat sibi finem." See pp. 56–61.

137. See pp. 58–60.

is not complete simply when God knows which possible creatures could imitate him, but only after the divine will determines which of those possible creatures are *fiendum* and which are *non-fiendum* and the divine intellect knows what is willed. Admittedly, Aquinas could have been more explicit about this point. If he were, then I think Scotus would have known that a divine exemplar is not merely an intellectual object for Aquinas, but an intellectual object known to be willed by God for creation. If Scotus had seen this, I suspect he would have argued that his own theory of instants of nature is present in Aquinas's reasoning.

Scotus's second argument claims that Aquinas's distinction is not an essential distinction between ideas. Distinctions taken from objects and from ends on the part of the thing are essential, but distinctions from the part of the agent's will are not essential. If the latter were essential distinctions, then an artist would not have art unless he established his artistic habit to act as an end, which is impossible. The artist does not lose his habit of art simply because he does not act for the end of art in some particular case, but the distinction between *fiendum* and *non-fiendum* is not from the objects nor their ends on the part of the thing. Rather, it is only through the act of the divine will making this and not that. Therefore, possibly *fiendum* and possibly *non-fiendum* are not the primary differences of a speculative idea and a practical idea.[138] Since the distinction between *fiendum* and *non-fiendum* does not suffice to distinguish divine ideas, the distinction between divine exemplars and reasons does not hold either. Since the distinction between exemplars and reasons was Aquinas's reason for excluding nonexisting possibles from the scope of divine ideas, that exclusion is no longer justified.

Once again, Scotus offers an argument that is strong in itself but not when used against Aquinas. Aquinas's distinction between divine exemplars and divine reasons arises because God is not ignorant of what he has willed to do and not to do. It is worthless for Scotus to argue that *fiendum* or *non-fiendum* are not a primary distinction in ideas before the act of the divine will. Aquinas will readily grant that claim, but God still knows whether each idea has *fiendum* or *non-fiendum* because of the act of the divine will. Aquinas uses the terms 'practical' (*practica*) and 'speculative' (*speculativa*), as well as 'exemplar' (*exemplar*) and 'reason' (*ratio*) to articulate God's knowledge of the distinction. He uses the terms this way because he emphasizes the causal role of divine ideas. What Scotus needs to show is that Aquinas's emphasis on the causal role, which presupposes divine willing, is somehow irrational. Scotus's argument might be successful in showing that Aquinas is abusing the terms 'practical' and 'speculative,' but it is not sufficient to show that Aquinas's emphasis on the causal role of divine ideas is irrational.

Scotus notes that Aquinas rejects a proper idea of matter because it neither has being per se nor can it be cognized except on an analogy to form. Scotus rejects both of these reasons. Against the first reason—that matter does not have being

---

138. *Rep.* I-A, d. 36, qq. 3–4, n. 19 (Noone, 430:26–431:18), esp.: "Sed fiendum et non-fiendum non sunt aliquae differentiae essentiales, possibiles in obiectis vel in finibus, ideae practicae vel speculativae." This argument is clearly indebted to Henry of Ghent. See pp. 92–94.

per se—he argues that matter is a being (*ens*) from itself and according to itself. Therefore, it can come to be per se and as a result has a proper idea in God. It is beyond the scope of this study to adjudicate between Aquinas's and Scotus's theories of matter. It is enough here to say that for Scotus, if matter in the composite is nothing and the composite is composed from matter and form, then the composite will be composed from something and nothing and so is not composed at all. Thus, it must be able to exist per se, and thus Aquinas's reason for excluding it from the scope of divine ideas is removed.[139]

Against the second reason for excluding an idea of matter, Scotus grants that our intellects in this life only come to know matter from an analogy to form because we do not know the whole nature of being, even imperfectly. But Aquinas concludes too quickly to God. If an intellect perfectly knows all things, it knows them according to their proper *rationes* and natures as they are in themselves. Otherwise, the intellect would know discursively. God understands all things nondiscursively. Therefore, he knows matter according to its proper nature and the character of matter as it is in itself without any actual analogy to form, and not through the nature of form.[140]

Against Aquinas's third exclusion—genera—Scotus objects to the principle that if something cannot come to be per se, then it does not have an idea. Genera do not come to be per se, but that is not enough to deny divine ideas of them. If an artist produces both the whole and each part of the whole, he not only knows the whole per se, but he also knows distinctly whatever is in the whole as its per se parts. God, as an artist, not only produces the whole but even each part of the whole distinctly in the whole. Therefore, he distinctly knows each of the parts in the whole, not only according to the *ratio* of the whole, but through the proper *ratio* of each part. He will have a proper idea of the part through which idea he knows the part other than that of the whole and through which idea he knows the parts as in the whole through the character of the whole. Although the nature of a genus never comes to be except in a per se species of it, there is another idea proper to it from the idea of the species.[141] He applies the same reasoning to inseparable accidents, the fourth sort of being Aquinas excluded from the scope of divine exemplars.[142]

This argument is not entirely convincing on its own. Aquinas does not claim that God only knows the parts of the whole as parts. He readily admits that God knows each aspect of things distinctly and has a distinct divine *ratio* of each aspect,

---

139. *Rep.* I-A, d. 36, qq. 3–4, nn. 20–21 (Noone, 431:19–432:6). For Scotus's account of matter, see *Rep.* II, d. 12, qq. 1–2 (Wadding-Vivès, 23.1a–20a). See Hoenen, *Marsilius of Inghen*, 129–30; Robert Pasnau, *Metaphysical Themes: 1274–1671* (Oxford: Clarendon Press, 2011), 57–60; Thomas M. Ward, *John Duns Scotus on Parts, Wholes, and Hylomorphism* (Leiden: Brill, 2014), esp. 6–40.

140. *Rep.* I-A, d. 36, qq. 3–4, nn. 22–24 (Noone, 432:7–433:10).

141. *Rep.* I-A, d. 36, qq. 3–4, n. 25 (Noone, 433:11–434:6), esp.: "Quia artifex producens totum et quamlibet partem eius in toto, non solum cognoscit totum per se, sed etiam cognoscit distincte quidquid est in toto ut per se pars eius; aliter produceret aliquam per se partem in toto quam non distincte cognosceret."

142. *Rep.* I-A, d. 36, qq. 3–4, nn. 27–28 (Noone, 434:18–435:13).

which is why the scope of divine *rationes* vastly exceeds the scope of divine exemplars. What Aquinas claims is that when God makes a being, he does not require more than the exemplar idea of that being. He only needs the divine exemplar of Socrates to make Socrates, man, and animal because man and animal are, as it were, metaphysical parts of the individual Socrates. Since Scotus has switched the terms of the argument from divine making to divine knowing, his argument is a strawman. Scotus's argument could only be deemed accurate and successful if we restrict Aquinas's theory of divine ideas to divine exemplars. Even then, it remains an open question for Scotus how many divine ideas God uses when he creates some individual. Does he use the idea of Socrates only, or does he use the ideas of some or all aspects of Socrates as well?

Finally, Scotus turns to Aquinas's alleged exclusion of divine ideas of individuals, which he says is based on the fact that individuation is from matter and that the species, not the individual, is the intention of nature. Both, Scotus says, are false. Concerning individuation, Scotus argues that matter is a quidditative part of the species, so if an individual adds matter beyond the quidditative being of the species, it also adds form. Thus, as nature is individuated by matter, so too it is individuated by form.[143] This response is an abbreviated version of Scotus's theory of haecceity, which holds that the principle of individuation is an individual form that makes each individual to be a *this*.[144]

Scotus offers two critiques of the argument from the intention of nature of which the first is sufficient here: It is contradictory to say that individuals are not the intention of nature, but divine providence is primarily about individuals. Agents that do not know their end—like nature—only act for that end because they are directed to that end by a higher agent that knows the end. So, if nature produces an individual insofar as it is directed by God, and God's providence consists not only in species but principally in individuals, the intention of nature must be more principally for individuals, not just species.

Scotus simply gets Aquinas on ideas of individuals wrong. Aquinas undoubtedly holds that there are divine ideas of individuals from the very beginning of his career. As I argued in Chapter II, Aquinas could have been more explicit about affirming divine ideas of individuals in *ST* I, q. 15, a. 3, but he in no way denies them.[145] In that text, Aquinas used Plato's position as a foil to infer divine providence over individuals, but Scotus misses the inference. Noone has

---

143. *Rep.* I-A, d. 36, qq. 3–4, n. 29–30 (Noone, 435:14–436:1).

144. See *Ord.*, II, d. 3, p. 1, qq. 1–6 (Vatican, 7.391–494). For an overview of Scotus's theory, see, *inter alia*, Allan B. Wolter, "Scotus' Individuation Theory," in *The Philosophical Theology of John Duns Scotus*, ed. Marilyn McCord Adams, 68–97 (Ithica, NY: Cornell University Press, 1990); Allan B. Wolter, "John Duns Scotus," in *Individuation in Scholasticism: The Later Middle Ages and the Counter-Reformation 1150–1650*, ed. Jorge J. E. Gracia, 274–98 (New York: State University of New York Press, 1994); Timothy B. Noone, "Individuation in Scotus," *American Catholic Philosophical Quarterly* 69, no. 4 (1995): 527–42; Timothy B. Noone, "Universals and Individuation," in *The Cambridge Companion to Dun Scotus*, ed. Thomas Williams, 100–28 (New York: Cambridge University Press, 2003).

145. See pp. 78–81.

argued persuasively that Scotus misinterprets Aquinas's text because he is working with a faulty edition. Scotus educes the first four exclusions from a faithful reading of *ST* I, q. 15, a. 3, ad 1–3, but when he gets to ad 4, he suddenly ascribes the position of Plato to Aquinas, even though Aquinas clearly rejects it. So, it is likely that Scotus's text had no reference to Plato. Absent an explicit mention that the position is Plato's, it is reasonable that Scotus would think Aquinas was giving his own opinion.[146]

Scotus on Henry of Ghent's Position

Scotus next considers Henry of Ghent's position on the scope of divine ideas. As we saw in Chapter III, Henry limits the scope of divine ideas even more than Aquinas.[147] Henry eliminates divine ideas of second intentions, relations, artifacts, genera, differentiae, individuals, privations, and numbers.[148] There are divine ideas only of what is *secundum se* and *ad se ipsas* essentially. There are divine ideas of most specific species only, although Henry does allow for divine ideas of matter and form as the essential parts of things insofar as each of these are *per se* and makeable in themselves and insofar as they come to be in the composite.[149]

Scotus begins his criticism by noting his disagreement with Henry about the category of relations. On Scotus's reading of Henry, a respect does not denote a thing other than its foundation. As he sees it, Henry's rejection of ideas for the last seven categories depends on this view of relations. Since an idea corresponds to a thing, and since the last seven categories do not denote things other than the foundation, there is no proper idea of them in God.[150] Regarding respects of creatures compared to creatures, Scotus declares Henry's claim to be universally false.[151] If this criticism holds, then Henry's rejection of ideas in the last seven categories immediately comes to nothing.

---

146. Noone, "Scotus on Divine Ideas," 378–79. Chiara Paladini argues that Scotus and his followers deny that Aquinas holds ideas of individuals both because of his emphasis on the species as the intention of matter and because in *ST* I, q. 14, a. 11 (Leonine ed., 183a) Aquinas "explicitly states that purely speculative knowledge of matter along with that of the specific form (which corresponds to the divine ideas) is sufficient for a complete knowledge of individual compounds" ("Exemplar Causality as *Similitudo Aequivoca* in Peter Auriol," in *Divine Ideas in Franciscan Thought*, 207). For the reasons already given, I find this account less likely, at least for Scotus.

147. See pp. 114–19.

148. Henry, *Quodlibet* VII, qq. 1–2 (Leuven, 11.18:31–35).

149. Henry, *Quodlibet* VII, qq. 1–2 (Leuven, 11.20:97–21:15). See *Rep.* I-A, d. 36, qq. 3–4, nn. 33–37 (Noone, 436:22–438:19).

150. *Rep.* I-A, d. 36, qq. 3–4, n. 34 (Noone, 437:6–15), esp.: "Cum ergo idea correspondeat rei, sequitur quod nullum respectivum habeat suam propriam ideam in Deo."

151. *Rep.* I-A, d. 36, qq. 3–4, n. 38 (Noone, 438:21–24). Scotus argues against Henry's position at *Lect.*, II, d. 1, qq. 4–5, nn. 184–222 (Vatican, 18.61–70); *Ord.*, II, d. 1, qq. 4–5, nn. 200–230 (Vatican, 7.101–15); *In IV Met.*, q. 2, n. 73 (OPh III.337); *In V Met.*, qq. 5–6, n. 150 and qq. 12–14, n. 33 (OPh III.481–81 and 622); *In VII Met.*, q. 1, n. 13 and q. 13, n. 51 (OPh IV.94 and 235); *In IX Met.*, qq. 1–2, n. 26 (OPh IV.518). For discussions of Henry's theory and Scotus's critique, see Henninger, *Relations*, 40–58 and 68–97; Decorte, "'Modus' or 'Res'," 407–29.

The rest of Scotus's criticism is directed at Henry's rejection of ideas of individuals. Two arguments are sufficient to show how thoroughly Scotus devastates Henry's position: In the first argument, Scotus says that what can be distinctly known through no other *ratio* requires a proper *ratio cognoscendi*. An individual is such. Therefore, if individuals need to be known distinctly according to their proper *rationes*, this will be through their proper and distinct ideas. He proves the minor premise as follows: if an individual could be known distinctly through the *ratio* of another, this would be through the quidditative notion of the species. However, the quidditative notion of the species does not yield such distinct knowledge because what is only common through predication and does not virtually contain something other except in potency and confusedly is not the intelligible means of knowing distinctly the things contained under it. The species is such with respect to individuals, and so distinct knowledge of the species is not sufficient for distinct knowledge of individuals.[152]

This argument is devastating because it uses Henry's own epistemological principles against him. Henry thinks divine ideas are the only means by which God can know possible creatures.[153] But it turns out that his theory does not yield knowledge of individuals except in potency and confusedly. Even perfect knowledge of *man* only yields a confused knowledge of Peter. Thus, on Henry's theory, God does not have perfect knowledge.

In the second argument, Scotus argues that Henry's central claim—that a genus and an individual are *ad se* accidentally because it happens to the nature of the species that this individual subsists in it or that the genus is abstracted from it—comes to nothing. Nothing is more essential to something than that it is *per se* that thing in the first mode, which only belongs to the species because of the individual. Therefore, if the individual is *ad se* by the nature of the species, it will not be so accidentally, but essentially.[154]

This argument shows that Henry's reasoning about divine ideas is inconsistent with his metaphysical principles. The distinction between a genus and a species is not parallel to the case between a species and an individual as Henry claims. An individual "is not merely incidentally a member of the species any more than it is incidentally what it is."[155] It is incidental to *man* to be Socrates, but it is not incidental that Socrates is a man. Just as "both animal and rational belong essentially to the understanding of a third item, namely, man," so man and Socrates's unique individuation belong essentially to the understanding of Socrates.[156] The individual cannot be accidental in the way Henry's argument requires.

---

152. *Rep.* I-A, d. 36, qq. 3–4, n. 39 (Noone, 438:25–439:8), esp.: "Quia si per alterius rationem posset distincte cognosci, hoc esset per rationem quiditativam speciei; sed per illam non potest distincte cognosci. Quia quod solum est commune per praedicationem nec virtualiter contineat alia nisi in potentia et confuse, non est ratio distincte cognoscendi contenta sub eo."
153. See pp. 118–19.
154. *Rep.* I-A, d. 36, qq. 3–4, n. 41 (Noone, 439:20–27).
155. Noone, "Scotus on Divine Ideas," 382.
156. Noone, "Scotus on Divine Ideas," 382.

Scotus's Reply to the Question

Scotus relies on the authority of Bonaventure for his own position on the scope of divine ideas.[157] Regardless of whether we take the term 'idea' as a cognitive principle or a causal principle—every idea is both of these for Scotus—there is a distinct divine idea of every positive reality other than God, whether it be makeable in itself or in another, absolute or relational.[158] Scotus thinks that this conclusion holds regardless of how the status of divine ideas is interpreted. God must have ideas of each possible being and each of its possible aspects no matter whether ideas are the cognized objects or the *rationes cognoscendi*. If ideas are the cognized objects, then there will be an idea for everything and every aspect of everything precisely because they are known by God. God has a distinct idea of whatever object is distinctly knowable by him. If it is the mark of our intellect that it can know all things insofar as they are distinctly knowable, then even more is it a perfection in God.[159]

The same conclusion follows if we say divine ideas are *rationes cognoscendi*. The created intellect can compare the divine essence to every object and every aspect of every object as imitable by those objects. God can make the same comparisons. So, since our intellect can compare the divine essence to every positive reality, whether a whole, a part, absolute, or relative as imitable in diverse grades, the divine intellect can do so too with his one eternal act of knowledge. And if considering the divine essence under each of those comparisons constitutes an idea, then God will have ideas of everything and every one of its aspects.[160]

The fact that Scotus thinks the conclusion holds regardless of how the status of divine ideas is understood shows that he does not absolve his predecessors who reduced the scope of divine ideas simply because they understood the status of divine ideas differently. If their reduction of the scope of divine ideas followed from their claim that an idea is the relation of imitability from God to a possible creature, then in Scotus's eyes they might have committed just one philosophical sin, not two. But since God can compare his essence as imitable to every possible imitation, the scope of divine ideas should extend to every possible creature and aspect of that creature.

I think this conclusion further invalidates Henry's theory, but it scarcely touches Aquinas's. Like Scotus demands, Aquinas holds that God has a divine reason (*ratio*) for every possible creature and all its possible aspects. Aquinas only limits the scope of divine exemplars since there are only divine exemplars of what God wills to create, and God does not will to create every possible creature and all its possible aspects.

---

157. *Rep.* I-A, d. 36, qq. 3–4, n. 46 (Noone, 441:2–3): "cum alio doctore antiquo." Noone identifies Bonaventure as the "doctor antiquus," and the following discussion confirm this attribution. See Bonaventure, *In I Sent.*, d. 35, a. un., q. 1 and dub. 4 (Quaracchi, I.601 and 615) and pp. 36–40.

158. *Rep.* I-A, d. 36, qq. 3–4, n. 46 (Noone, 441:3–7), esp.: "sive sit factibile in se sive in alio, sive sit respectivum sive absolutum."

159. *Rep.* I-A, d. 36, qq. 3–4, nn. 47 (Noone, 441:8–19).

160. *Rep.* I-A, d. 36, qq. 3–4, nn. 48–49 (Noone, 441:20–442:8).

Scotus adds his thoughts about speculative and practical ideas as an epilogue to this question. Each idea is practical in its mode (*practica suo modo*). An idea is not absolutely practical such that its object will exist sometime according to it but such that its object is naturally suited to be produced if the divine will chooses it. The artist who produces something through cognition according to the whole has distinct knowledge of all that is in that thing, both its parts and its *per se* accidents. God is such an artist and so has distinct practical knowledge of all that he can produce in an operable thing and as a result has a distinct principle of practical cognition, which is an idea.[161]

Scotus does not address the issue here, but while he wants to extend the scope of divine ideas, he cannot conclude that God has an idea for every *res* that he knows. Some of the things that God knows are merely *res* as noncontradictory, for instance, chimerical fictions. These things are knowable because they do not imply a contradiction, but they could not be made. As Scotus notes, a *res* as possibly existing extramentally "only differs from fictional beings from the fact that it can exist in extramental reality and in effect."[162] Thus, God does not have an idea for every *thing* that he can cognize distinctly, but he does have an idea for everything and every aspect of every *producible* thing. The scope of divine ideas is thus limited to anything God can make.

The Infinity of Divine Ideas

Scotus's answer to the question whether God has an infinite number of ideas is easily gleaned from what was just said. Following Bonaventure, Scotus argues that God has an infinite number of divine ideas.[163] After offering a variety of arguments familiar from Bonaventure and Augustine, Scotus offers his own argument from divine infinity. An intellect that is comprehensive of a more perfect being is also comprehensive of a less perfect or equal being. The infinity of the divine essence is more perfect than the infinity of ideas, whether ideas are cognized objects or *rationes cognoscendi*. What is infinite of its very nature (*ex natura rei*) can perfectly comprehend the infinity of its essence, which is the cause of the other infinity— the infinity of divine ideas. Therefore, all the more can it comprehend every other infinity, whether it be in cognitive being or in a *ratio cognoscendi*. If an idea is the object cognized, the conclusion that God has an infinite number of ideas in his mind follows straightaway, since God comprehends an infinite number of objects.[164]

---

161. *Rep.* I-A, d. 36, qq. 3–4, nn. 51–52 (Noone, 15–26). It appears that this position is meant to distinguish Scotus from Aquinas, but, as I argued before, I think the two thinkers hold the same position with different emphases. See pp. 184–86.

162. *Rep.* I-A, d. 36, qq. 3–4, n. 74 (Noone, 450:2–7): "entitas quidditativa quae est ratitudo rei, et cuius est esse ratum, non differt a fictitiis nisi per hoc quod potest in re extra et in effectu existere."

163. *Rep.* I-A, d. 36, qq. 3–4, n. 64 (Noone, 446:9–10): "cum illo doctore antiquo." See Bonaventure, *In I Sent.*, d. 35, a. un., q. 5 (Quaracchi, I.612) and pp. 32–34.

164. *Rep.* I-A, d. 36, qq. 3–4, n. 68 (Noone, 447:2–11), esp.: "Sed infinitatem essentiae suae quae est causa alterius infinitatis potest comprehendere perfecte quae est infinitas ex natura rei."

The most contentious part of this argument is the claim that the divine essence is the most perfect infinity because his essence's infinity will be primary, unparticipated, and, as it were, the efficient cause of the other infinity in cognitive being or with respect to knowing. The other infinity is participated, as it were caused, and not first. Therefore, it is necessary to reduce the second infinity to the first, which is entirely one because every plurality must be reduced to what is one simply.[165]

RECAPITULATIONS AND CONCLUSIONS

Bl. John Duns Scotus's theory of divine ideas is both traditional and innovative. Like his predecessors, Scotus argues that God's only source of knowledge is his own essence. Divine ideas are secondary objects of the divine essence, and the character of an idea includes a known rational relation from God to the possible creature. Despite these points of agreement, Scotus's theory of divine ideas is at odds with the dominant theory of ideas at his time. Divine ideas are rational relations, but those relations are not how God comes to know possible creatures. Instead, direct knowledge of a possible creature makes it possible for God to have a rational relation to that creature. Scotus insists upon this reversal because the Imitability Theory requires an impossible theory of relations; a relation cannot be known before the terms of the relation.

A divine idea is "the eternal reason (*ratio aeterna*) in the divine mind in accordance with something formable according to its proper notion. Thus, it is clear that an idea is not some relation, but the cognized object in the divine mind in which creatures exist objectively."[166] What God knows exists in him objectively. The object known is nothing in reality, but as an object of thought it enjoys a sort of diminished being similar to the more recent interpretation of Henry of Ghent's essential being that I endorsed in Chapter III.[167]

Scotus's articulation of the scope of divine ideas is a defense of Bonaventure's theory. Scotus offers many of his own arguments in favor of the position, but most of his time is spent responding to the Thomistic and Henrician objections to the Bonaventurean position. Aquinas, he says, makes two errors: First, Aquinas's distinction between divine exemplars and divine reasons is tantamount to rejecting divine freedom. Since a divine exemplar has *fiendum*, then, Scotus argues, it must

---

165. *Rep.* I-A, d. 36, qq. 3–4, n. 69 (Noone, 447:12–19), esp.: "infinitas essentiae erit prima et imparticipata et quasi causa efficiens alterius infinitas in esse cognito vel respectibus cognoscendi; alia infinitas est participata et quasi causata et non prima, et ideo oportet eam reducere ad priorem quae omnino est una." For the principle that plurality must be reduced to what is one simply, see Aristotle, *Met.* II, c. 2, 994a1–b31 (AL 25.3.2.44:35–47:100); Ps.-Dionysius, *De div. nom.*, c. 13 (PG 3.978); Proclus, *Elementatio theologia*, c. 21 (Vansteenkiste, 273); Scotus, *Ord.*, I, d. 2, p. 2, qq. 1–4, n. 301 (Vatican, 2.305).

166. *Rep.* I-A, d. 36, qq. 1–2, n. 57 (Noone, 419:17–19): "idea est ratio aeterna in mente divina secundum aliquid formabile secundum propriam rationem eius. Et sic patet quod idea non est relatio aliqua sed obiectum cognitum in mente divina in qua sunt creaturae obiective."

167. See pp. 109–11.

either coerce the divine will to choose to create it or to choose to act against right reason. Second, Aquinas is wrong to limit the scope of ideas. On both points, I think Scotus overplays the difference between his theory and Aquinas's. Aquinas's distinction between divine exemplars and divine reasons is logically posterior, not prior, to God's act of will. Aquinas makes the distinction to emphasize that God knows what he has willed to make, and divine ideas are primarily causal principles. Aquinas's reduced scope of divine exemplars reflects the fact that God does not make everything he knows he could. Aquinas's theory of the scope of divine reasons is identical to Scotus's theory.

Scotus is more critical of Henry's theory of the scope of divine ideas in large part because Henry's theory is more restricted than Aquinas's. Henry's theory of the scope of divine ideas is so restricted as to be self-defeating.

I noted that for Scotus the scope of divine knowledge must be larger than the scope of divine ideas. Divine ideas must be producible, but there are many objects of divine knowledge that are not makeable, like chimeras. Chimeras are knowable because they do not entail a contradiction, but they cannot exist extramentally. Therefore, God does not have divine ideas of everything he can cognize distinctly. The fact that the scope of divine ideas is still more restricted than the scope of divine knowledge shows that for Scotus divine ideas must be both cognitive and causal principles. He emphasizes the cognitive role, but every divine idea still must be able to be a causal principle for God. If God had ideas of chimera, then not every divine idea would be a causal principle. Finally, Scotus's arguments for the scope of divine ideas naturally lead him to say that God has an infinite number of divine ideas. As he does in many places, Scotus takes the opportunity to offer a novel argument from divine infinity.

Chapter VIII.
Early Thomists and Scotists

A few words about the influence of Scotus's *Creatura Intellecta* Theory are in order before turning to the Nominalist Theories of Peter Auriol and William of Ockham. Scotus's theory exercises a considerable influence on both Thomists and Scotists. Thomists have no adequate response to Scotus. This phenomenon is exemplified in Thomas Anglicus's *Liber propugnatorius super primum sententiarum contra Johannem Scotum*. Having identified himself as the defender against Scotus, he says, "it seems to me that what he [Scotus] says about the eternal relations is true because it does not seem that they precede the intellection of the creatures. Similarly, even what he says—that ideas are the essences of creatures as understood by God— is highly probable."[1] Scotus's arguments are so thorough that Anglicus has to grant them. The same is true of the early Thomists John of Paris and Thomas of Sutton. Early Scotists begin to develop Scotus's arguments. I will examine how one early Scotist, Henry of Harclay, examines the relationship between Scotus's theory of direct knowledge of creatures and relations of imitability, which bears out the two possible interpretations of Scotus's theory that I examined in the previous chapter.[2]

JOHN OF PARIS (D. 1306)

John of Paris lectured on the *Sentences* in Paris from 1294–1295.[3] He does not respond directly to Olivi and Scotus, but his treatment of divine ideas shows that

---

1. Thomas Anglicus, *Liber Propugnatorius*, d. 35, q. un. (Venedig, 1523), 114vb.: "In ista quaestione videtur mihi quod id quod dicit de istis relationibus eternis est verum: quia non videtur quod praecedant intellectionem creaturarum. Similiter quod dicit etiam ideas esse essentias creaturarum ut intellectus a Deo: est valde probabile." Note that William de la Mare's earlier criticism of Aquinas's theory of divine ideas was limited to questions concerning the scope of divine ideas (*Correctorium Fratris Thomae*, aa. 4, 79–81, 97 in *Les Premières Polémiques Thomistes*, vol. 1, ed. P. Glorieux [Kain: Revue des Sciences Philosophiques et Théologiques, 1927], 25–26, 326–30, 389–90). For replies on behalf of Aquinas, see *Correctorii corruptorii 'Quare'*, aa. 4, 79–81, 97 in *Les Premières Polémiques Thomistes*, vol. 1, 27–28, 326–30, 389–90; John of Paris, *Correctorium corruptorii 'Circa'*, a. 4, in *Le correctorium corruptorii «Circa» de Jean Quidort de Paris*, ed., Jean-Pierre Muller, Studia Anselmiana 12/13, 32–37 (Rome: Herder, 1941); *Correctorium corruptorii 'Quaestione'*, c. 4 in *Le correctorium corruptorii 'Quaestione'*, ed. Jean-Pierre Muller, Studia Anselmiana 35, 24–28 (Rome: Herder, 1954). Since these replies can work within Aquinas's framework of the status of divine ideas, they can give adequate replies to William. Scotus's objections, on the other hand, challenge the very framework that Aquinas uses.
2. See pp. 170–71.
3. Duba and Schabel, "The Myth of the Two-Year Sentences Lecture," 156. In the introduction to the text, Jean-Pierre Muller argued for 1292–1294, but the argument from Duba and Schabel is overwhelming. See Jean-Pierre Muller, "Introduction," in Jean de Paris (Quidort) *Commentaire Sur Les Sentences: Reportation*, ed. Jean-Pierre Muller, vol. I (Rome: Herder, 1961), xxx.

he accepts their conclusions.[4] He never asks whether God's knowledge of the idea or the creature is prior, but he says that a divine idea arises from God's comparison of himself to a creature. He uses the language of diverse grades of imitability, but those grades of imitability are not how God knows creatures. They arise from direct knowledge of creatures.

He uses Aquinas's Argument from Divine-Self Knowledge. God knows things other than himself because he knows himself perfectly. Perfect knowledge of himself entails knowing each of his powers perfectly, which requires knowing everything to which the powers can extend themselves. Since divine power extends to every possible being, both insofar as they are beings and insofar as they are distinct from each other, God must know all possible beings.[5]

For John, an idea is the form of a thing existing in an agent that can produce it. Although he does not think that Plato taught a theory of independent subsisting forms, he agrees with criticisms of the theory.[6] There must be ideas subsisting in God as in an artist because only such a theory avoids the errors of creation by necessity and by chance. Without ideas God would produce naturally and necessarily. Creation is also not a matter of chance because what happens by chance happens rarely, which is not to be attributed to God. Thus, God must create intellectually. Every agent that acts through intellect has the reasons (*rationes*) of all the things that are produced by it in its intellect ahead of time. Therefore, God has these reasons in his intellect and produces according to them, looking to them as an exemplar of things coming to be. This description is what the term 'ideas' signifies, so God has ideas.[7]

This description of divine ideas can be specified: "An idea names the divine essence conceived by the divine intellect, not absolutely, but as it is imitable by a creature in such or such a grade of goodness or being, according to which God produces a creature in being."[8] This definition clarifies that the distinction between divine ideas is not from the divine essence absolutely. It is also not from the creature absolutely since the temporal is not a cause of the eternal. It is caused in God by the divine intellect from a comparison of the divine essence to creatures. From the divine intellect comparing the divine essence to a creature, the diverse respects (*respectus*) of the diverse grades arise, under which grades a creature is created or creatable by God.[9] Thus, in its principal signification, an idea signifies a respect to

---

4. See pp. 124–25 and 164–66 for Olivi and Scotus, respectively.

5. John of Paris, *Rep.* I, q. 115 (d. 35, q. 3) (Muller, I.350:31–45). See pp. 63–64 for a discussion of this argument in Aquinas.

6. John of Paris, *Rep.* I, q. 119 (d. 36, q. 3) (Muller, I.367:26–31 and 367:48–368:83).

7. John of Paris, *Rep.* I, q. 119 (d. 36, q. 3) (Muller, I.367:31–368:43), esp.: "Per istas autem rationes in intellectu divino existentes et insistentes, ad quas Deus tamquam ad rerum fiendarum exemplar inspiciens res producit, nihil aliud intelligimus quam ideas."

8. John of Paris, *Rep.* I, q. 120 (d. 36, q. 4) (Muller, I.370:13–16): "Idea enim nominat divinam essentiam a divino intellectu conceptam, non absolute, sed ut imitabilis est a creatura in tali vel in tali gradu bonitatis vel entitatis, secundum quem gradum Deus producit creaturam in esse."

9. John of Paris, *Rep.* I, q. 120 (d. 36, q. 4) (Muller, I.371:47–54), esp.: "Sed causatur in Deo distinctio idearum ab intellectu divino ex comparatione divinae essentiae ad creaturas, in quantum ex

a creature. It further follows that the formal aspect of an idea is the imitability directed to a creature.¹⁰

Despite using the language of the Imitability Theory, John of Paris subscribes to the *Creatura Intellecta* Theory. God has ideas because he compares his essence to *creatures*. He knows the diverse grades of imitability that creatures can bear to him because he knows the creatures themselves. Someone may object that in *Reportatio* I, q. 120, ad 3, John argues that although ideas are distinguished through a comparison to creatures, they are not caused by creatures, but by the divine intellect comparing the divine essence to creatures under diverse grades of imitability. He goes on to say that from the fact that God considers himself imitable in diverse ways, he produces diverse creatures.¹¹

This objection makes two errors: First, it mistakes creatures for creatures as understood. When John says that the distinction of divine ideas is not caused by creatures, he means that already created creatures do not cause the distinction. The actual distinction of creatures is a result, not a cause, of the distinction of divine ideas.¹² Note that he still says that the divine essence compares itself to *creatures*. God is comparing himself to something known, not something unknown.

Second, John grants that knowledge of diverse grades of imitability is prior to the creation of creatures. However, it does not follow from this claim that knowledge of diverse grades of imitability is prior to knowledge of possible creatures. The character of a divine idea entails knowledge of a respect to a possible creature, and those known respects are the exemplars by which God creates a creature. Nevertheless, God does not know the creature through those respects. The diverse grades are, as it were, the cause of God's knowledge that a creature is creatable by him, but God knows the creature directly first. This position is the *Creatura Intellecta* Theory.

Although John of Paris argues that there is an infinite number of divine ideas, he restricts the scope of divine ideas greatly.¹³ Properly speaking, an idea in God is a productive principle of things, not merely a cognitive principle like an intelligible species. Thus, God has distinct ideas of things that differ according to being (*esse*) and according to form. Individuals differ according to *esse*, but not according to form. Thus, there are no divine ideas of individuals.¹⁴ Further, there are no ideas of genera since genera do not have being except in a species. Again, the parts of the composite cannot exist essentially and according to themselves except in the composite, and there are not distinct ideas of them either. Prime matter cannot exist without form, and so does not have an idea distinct from the idea of the composite.

---

comparatione divini intellectus sic comparantis divinam essentiam ad creaturam insurgunt seu consurgunt diversi respectus diversorum graduum, sub quibus creatura est creata vel creabilis a Deo."

10. John of Paris, *Rep.* I, q. 120, ad 2 (d. 36, q. 4) (Muller, I.372:74–76).

11. John of Paris, *Rep.* I, q. 120, ad 3 (d. 36, q. 4) (Muller, I.372:80–91), esp.: "etsi ideae distinguantur per comparationem ad creaturas, non tamen ideae causantur a creaturis, sed a divino intellectu comparante divinam essentiam ad creaturas sub gradu diverso imitabilitatis."

12. See pp. 19 and 66–67 for this point in Bonaventure and Aquinas, respectively.

13. John of Paris, *Rep.* I, q. 121 (d. 36, q. 5) (Muller, I.372–78).

14. See Hoenen, *Marsilius of Inghen*, 125.

There are ideas of separable accidents, but no ideas of inseparable accidents. His reasoning is the same as Aquinas's: inseparable accidents do not have being distinct from the being of the subject, but separable accidents do have distinct being.[15]

John of Paris's account of the scope of divine ideas is indebted to Aquinas, and he frequently uses the same reasons as Aquinas.[16] John seems to admit ideas of non-existing possibles, but Aquinas does not admit exemplars of them. The most glaring departure concerns divine ideas of singulars. John does not admit them because they only satisfy one of the two criteria he sets for the existence of a distinct idea. Noone speculates that the fact that John of Paris is a Thomist and yet denies the existence of divine ideas of singulars might be a reason that Scotus thinks Aquinas himself denies divine ideas of singulars.[17]

THOMAS OF SUTTON (CA. 1250–1315)

Like John of Paris, Thomas of Sutton's theory of divine ideas cedes Scotus's arguments. He treats divine ideas primarily in two *Quodlibets:* II, q. 4 (after 1293), and IV, q. 5 (the early 1300s).[18] Although he has a large body of *Quaestiones Ordinariae*, that is, classroom disputations, he only mentions ideas when discussing Plato's theory.[19] Sutton's theory of divine ideas is curious because it could be read as a bridge between the *Creatura Intellecta* Theory and the Nominalist Theory. Sutton is not a nominalist thinker, neither in general nor regarding divine ideas, yet his account of divine ideas emphasizes divine simplicity in ways characteristic of the Nominalist Theory.[20] Moreover, his account of the imitability of the divine essence bears a certain resemblance to Peter Auriol's theory of an "equivocal likeness" (*similitudo aequivoca*).[21]

Sutton insists that the divine essence is God's only source of knowledge. His intellect is pure act. If God knew through species received, he would be in potency.[22] Moreover, since his intellect is pure act, it is identical to its knowledge, and God always understands all things in act.[23] It follows that the divine intellect has but one act of understanding, which is a direct act. By knowing his essence, God cognizes in himself all things perfectly in the same act. When he knows creatures, he does not turn from knowledge of himself, and when God knows himself to be imitable

---

15. John of Paris, *Rep.* I, q. 122 (d. 36, q. 5) (Muller, I.380:29–51). See pp. 83–84 for Aquinas's discussion of ideas of accidents.
16. See pp. 78–84.
17. Noone, "Scotus on Divine Ideas," 379.
18. For the chronology of Sutton's *Quodlibeta*, see Thomas of Sutton, *Quaestiones Ordinariae*, ed. Johannes Schneider, 46*–49* (München: Verlag der Bayerischen Akademie der Wissenschaften, 1977).
19. Sutton, *Quaestiones Ordinariae*, qq. 16; 22, arg. 24; 22, ad 24; 27, ad 24 (Schneider, 465, 599, 621, and 770).
20. See p. 207 for an overview of the Nominalist Theory.
21. See Chapter IX and Palatini, "*Similitudo Aequivoca*," 203–38.
22. Sutton, *Quaestiones ordinariae*, q. 2, a. 1 (Schneider, 50:404–51:411).
23. Sutton, *Quaestiones ordinariae*, q. 22 (Schneider, 605:407–9); Sutton, *Quaestiones ordinariae*, q. 17 (Schneider, 479:186–87).

by creatures, he is not turned back from knowledge of creatures to knowledge of himself. If he turned back and forth between himself and creatures, he would have more than one source of knowledge. Since there is no reflection when God knows both things in himself and outside of himself in a single act, God only has a single, direct act of knowing.[24]

Every author in this study admits that God does not have more than one act of knowing, but prior authors seem to allow that God can be said to have a secondary act of reflection according to our way of understanding. Even with the qualification "according to our way of thinking," Sutton will not allow this secondary act.[25] Sutton is more uncomfortable applying aspects of our knowledge to God than his predecessors. Man knows God by knowing a creature through a reflexive act, but God has an undistinguished direct act of knowing. Adherents of the Nominalist Theory will likewise emphasize the singularity of God's act of knowing. Ockham argues that just as our intellects can know a proposition (and so many terms) in a single, undistinguished act of knowing, so too God can know himself and all creatures in a single, undistinguished act of knowing.[26] Auriol compares the claim that God has a primary and secondary act of knowing to seeing something in a mirror and foolishly declaring that the thing has two presences: one in reality and one in the mirror.[27] I do not know of any explicit influence of Sutton on Auriol or Ockham, but Sutton's emphasis on the unity of God's act of knowing foreshadows the positions of Auriol and Ockham.

Turning to divine ideas, Sutton argues that "an idea is constituted from the divine essence and a respect of imitability."[28] This description makes it sound like divine ideas are constituted by two things that come together in a real composition. However, Sutton insists that this constitution consists of parts according to reason. He uses the example of a species, which is constituted from a genus and difference. In each constitution, one element is formally constitutive, and that is the element through which what is constituted is distinguished from others that are of its proximate genus. Thus, in the species *man*, the difference *rational* is formal, not the genus *animal* because man is distinguished by his rationality. In the case of divine ideas, the respect of imitability is formal because each idea is the divine essence.[29]

---

24. Sutton, *Quodlibet* II, q. 4 (Schmaus, 193:24–194:32).

25. Sutton, *Quodlibet* II, q. 4 (Schmaus, 194:37–195:54): "Sed posset aliquis credere quod, licet non posset dici quod intellectus Dei habeat actum reflexum secundum suum modum intelligendi, tamen potest dici quod habeat actum intelligendi reflexum secundum nostrum modum intelligendi..... Nullo modo potest concedi etiam cum ista additione: secundum nostrum modum intelligendi."

26. Ockham, *Ord.* I, d. 35, q. 4 (OTh IV.469:7–13). See pp. 234–35.

27. Auriol, *Scriptum*, d. 35, p. 2, a. 1 (E-Scriptum, 7:332–35). See pp. 214–15 and Alessandro D. Conti, "Divine Ideas and Exemplar Causality in Auriol," *Vivarium* 38, no. 1 (2000): 110–11; Palatini, "*Similitudo Aequivoca*," 214–15.

28. Sutton, *Quodlibet* IV, q. 5 (Schmaus, 533:28–29): "idea sit constituta ex essentia divina et respectu imitabilitatis."

29. Sutton, *Quodlibet* IV, q. 5 (Schmaus, 533:20–534:53).

Moreover, no creature is distinguished from another by imitating the divine essence, since they all do that.[30] Creatures are distinguished by imitating the divine essence according to different proper respects, that is, by the diverse proportions according to which they imitate the divine essence more or less perfectly. The divine essence as it is imitable according to that mode by which man can imitate it is the idea of man.[31] Thus, the character of an idea is formally constituted by a reason (*ratio*) of imitability, namely, a rational respect.[32]

A respect formally constitutes the character of an idea, but a respect is not an idea. An idea is a form according to which something is formed. A respect is not such a form, but the divine essence is. Thus, 'idea' names the divine essence directly and a respect indirectly (*in obliquo*).[33] Given what a divine idea is, Sutton concludes that the divine essence, which is one, is many ideas. It can be many ideas because it is one idea under one *ratio* and another idea under another *ratio*.[34] The divine essence is the one idea, and ideas are then multiplied according to the plurality of diverse respects.

The character of an idea includes a rational respect of imitability according to which a creature is creatable. Divine ideas are exemplars, and whatever exists has an idea in God.[35] But does God know creatures through these rational respects, or does he have rational respects because he knows creatures? Sutton examines Henry of Ghent's position that God needs ideas to know creatures, and he concludes that "this position seems to be contrary to reason."[36] He offers several arguments, the first of which is representative. The divine essence, as it is that by which God understands, is formally the proper *ratio* and likeness of all creatures and not only a common and exceeding likeness. His evidence is that God distinctly understands all creatures through his essence. Nevertheless, as the divine essence is that by which God formally understands a creature, it is not distinct according to diverse *rationes* by the divine intellect because it is not the object of the intellect in this way. Instead, it is the principle by which he understands. By the same reasoning, God already understands all creatures by understanding his essence as an object without any distinction of *rationes*.[37]

---

30. See pp. 124–25 and 164–66 for this point in Petrus de Trabibus and Scotus, respectively.

31. Sutton, *Quodlibet* IV, q. 5 (Schmaus, 533:20–534:53).

32. Sutton, *Quodlibet* IV, q. 5 (Schmaus, 534:60–61): "Et sic patet quod ista ratio imitabilitatis, quae ratio est respectiva, est formale in constitutione rationis ideae." Cf. Sutton, *Quaestiones ordinariae*, q. 10, ad 22 (Schneider, 313:456–61).

33. Sutton, *Quodlibet* IV, q. 5 (Schmaus, 535:100–536:106), esp.: "Et ita nomine ideae essentia intelligitur in recto. Sed respectus intelligitur quasi in obliquo." This distinction is used by Auriol and Ockham. See pp. 364–68 and 410–16. Ockham uses the distinction in a different way from Auriol.

34. Sutton, *Quodlibet* IV, q. 5 (Schmaus, 536:123–27), esp.: "essentia sub una ratione est una idea unius rei et ipsa sub alia ratione est alia idea alterius rei."

35. Sutton, *Quaestiones ordinariae*, q. 25, ad 24 (Schneider, 714:829–37), esp.: "quicquid producitur, habet formam exemplarem in Deo, quae respondet producto quantum ad terminum ad quem, scilicet ens, non autem quantum ad terminum a quo, scilicet non-ens."

36. Sutton, *Quodlibet* II, q. 4 (Schmaus, 196:103): "ista positio videtur esse contra rationem." See pp. 103–4.

37. Sutton, *Quodlibet* II, q. 4 (Schmaus, 196:103–197:112).

God has a rational respect to each creature according to which he knows himself to be imitable by that creature, but these respects are not how he knows creatures: "according to our reasoning, God's intellect knows creatures according to their absolute essences before he knows ideal respects."[38] He insists that this direct knowledge of creaturely essences does not make the distinction of ideas a result of reflexive knowledge. This insistence that there is no secondary consideration of the divine essence by the divine intellect separates Sutton's theory from Scotus's theory. However, Sutton's insistence that God's direct knowledge of creatures before the character of an idea is complete is sufficient to make him an adherent of the *Creatura Intellecta* Theory.

Sutton also follows Scotus in insisting that divine ideas only exist in God objectively, not formally or subjectively.[39] They have no positive reality in God because if they did, then they would induce a real composition in the divine mind.[40] Rational respects, which are formally constitutive of divine ideas, are only in God insofar as he knows his essence.[41] Sutton does not explicitly make this counterfactual, but if, *per impossibile*, God did not know his essence, there would be no divine ideas.

Since divine ideas have no positive reality in God according to actual existence, and since only God is from eternity, it follows necessarily that the respective reasons (*rationes respectivae*) were not distinct in something according to actual existence from eternity. However, divine ideas can be called "eternal" or "from eternity" because God's essence is eternal.[42]

Thomas of Sutton's theory of divine ideas is somewhat hodgepodge. He deploys Imitability Theory terminology, but he grants God's direct knowledge of creatures characteristic of the *Creatura Intellecta* Theory. He also denies that God has a secondary or quasi-secondary reflection upon the divine essence, like the Nominalist Theory. He endorses the divine essence as the one idea that every creature imitates and insists that divine ideas play a role in the production of creatures.

The early Thomists are keen to defend Aquinas from a variety of attacks, especially attacks from Scotus, but each succumbs to the force of Scotus's arguments on divine ideas.[43] Divine ideas are rational relations according to which God knows each creature as creatable, but these relations are not how God knows creatures' essences. The rational respects are (at least logically) posterior to God's knowledge

---

38. Sutton, *Quodlibet* II, q. 4, ad opp. (Schmaus, 200:194–96): "prius secundum rationem nostrum cognoscit intellectus Dei creaturas secundum suas essentias absolutas, quam cognoscat respectus ideales."

39. Sutton, *Quodlibet* II, q. 4 (Schmaus, 198:152–199:156). See pp. 178–82 for a discussion of *esse obiectivum* according to Scotus.

40. Sutton, *Quodlibet* IV, q. 5 (Schmaus, 535:67–70).

41. Sutton, *Quodlibet* IV, q. 5 (Schmaus, 536:131–32); Sutton, *Quaestiones ordinariae*, q. 10 (Scheider, 302:171–75).

42. Sutton, *Quodlibet* IV, q. 5 (Schmaus, 535:77–91 and 536:104–108).

43. Hoenen argues that Sutton is defending Aquinas's view against Henry (*Marsilius of Inghen*, 123–24). This claim follows from his prior claim that Aquinas admits that God has direct knowledge of creatures. See p. 71n122.

of the creature. Thomas Anglicus explicitly admits that Scotus is right. John of Paris does not address the issue much, but also admits that Scotus is right. Thomas of Sutton goes farthest of the three, seemingly arguing that Scotus did not go far enough. He articulates a theory of divine ideas that is on the border between the *Creatura Intellecta* Theory and the Nominalist Theory.

HENRY OF HARCLAY (CA. 1270–1317)

Henry of Harclay addresses the topic of divine ideas in his *Sentences Commentary* (ca. 1305–1308) and *Quaestiones ordinariae*, q. 15 (before 1313) and q. 2 (1313).[44] In the first two places, Harclay endorses the position that ideas are just the creatures themselves as known to be contained objectively in God's intellect. In the latter question, Harclay argues against this understanding of divine ideas in favor of the claim that a divine idea is the creature's essence with a respect of imitability. The respect of imitability is a *sine qua non*, not the object of God's act of knowing nor the *ratio cognoscendi*. Therefore, it is instructive to examine both views and especially Harclay's criticism of the first view.

Harclay arrives at his earlier theory of divine ideas through the question of whether they are rational relations. Like Scotus, he argues that knowledge of rational relations from God to creatures will not yield the cognition of the creatures.[45] In addition to the now-standard arguments that such a respect cannot cause understanding and that knowledge of a relation presupposes knowledge of the foundation, Harclay educes an original argument based on what it means to be a being of reason (*ens rationis*). There are two conditions for an *ens rationis*: First, an *ens rationis* is a being in the soul that only exists when the intellect considers it. It is in the soul objectively, not subjectively like a species. An *ens rationis*, understood rightly, is such that it never exists in reality but only in the intellect's consideration. Second, an *ens rationis* is made by the intellect and does not remain when the intellect ceases to consider it. It is only in the mind of the one considering or imagining it. Thus, it has diminished being, exists in a qualified sense, and is not in any of the ten categories of being. This claim is as true for God as it is for a creature because God's considering a relation of identity between extremes does not make it exist in reality anymore than a man's consideration does not make a relation

---

44. For the dating of Harclay's writings, see Franz Pelster, "Heinrich von Harclay, Kanzler von Oxford, Und Seine Quästionen," in *Miscellanea Fr. Ehrle*, vol. I (Rome, 1924), 323–29; Carlo Balić, "Adnotationes Ad Nonnullas Quaestiones circa Ordinationem I. Duns Scoti," in *Iohannis Duns Scoti Opera Omnia*, vol. IV, 1*–39* (Vatican City: Vatican, 1956); Carlo Balić, "Henricus de Harcley et Ioannes Duns Scotus," in *Mélanges Offerts à Étienne Gilson*, 93–121 (Paris, 1959); Armand Maurer, "Henry of Harclay's Questions on the Divine Ideas," *Mediaeval Studies* 23, no. 1 (1961): 165; Henry of Harclay, *Ordinary Questions*, vol. 1: Questions I–XIV, ed. Mark Gerald Henninger, trans. Raymond Edwards and Mark Gerald Henninger (New York: The British Academy, 2008), xix. For a discussion of Harclay's *Sentences* commentary, see William O. Duba, Russell L. Friedman, and Chris Schabel, "Henry of Harclay and Aufredo Gonteri Brito," in *Medieval Commentaries on the Sentences of Peter Lombard*, ed. Philipp W. Rosemann, 263–368 (Leiden: Brill, 2010).

45. See pp. 164–66.

of identity exist in reality. Therefore, the proper understanding of an *ens rationis* is a qualified and diminished being that in no way exists.[46]

Armed with the proper understanding of an *ens rationis*, Harclay argues that the comparison of the divine essence to imitating creatures cannot be the divine act of understanding comparing (*non est actus intelligendi comparans*). In that case, there would be but one idea just as there is one divine act of understanding. Therefore, it must be that the divine intellect considers the divine essence as imitable in diverse ways as if there were a diversity of grades in it according to the diversity of grades of creatures imitating it, even though there is no such diversity in the divine essence itself. An idea, then, is only in the intellect's consideration and an *ens rationis*, and it is only a diminished being not having existence in any way. No simple perfection in God nor anything that is in God by nature depends on a qualified being. Divine wisdom and knowledge are simple perfections in God, and they do not depend upon a rational relation. Understanding a stone or a man is a simple perfection, and so God understands them without a rational relation.[47]

Since ideas cannot be rational relations through which God understands creatures, Henry concludes that when his predecessors spoke of ideas, they understood by 'ideas' the very object known according to cognized being. Just as the statue of Hercules, which is something in reality, is a likeness of the man Hercules, in the same way, everyone admits that there is a likeness of the statue in the artist's mind to which he relates in making the artifact. Thus, the statue in his mind and in reality only differ as real being and cognized being. Cognized being is just the being that a true thing has when known by a mind. Cognized being is objective being, not subjective being like a species, and it is a complete likeness in the mind of the thing that will come to be. Before he makes a chest, the artist foreknows the same chest entirely according to all its conditions and so has a truthful likeness in his mind, not through a species existing subjectively in his mind. In the same way, God is related to knowing and making natural things through art and intelligence. Thus, the stone known by God from eternity, which is the same in reality with the stone already made, is an exemplar to the likeness of which God produces the stone. Therefore, ideas are not other than the object cognized from eternity. As cognized, things are said to be contained in the divine intelligence because they are contained objectively in it.[48]

---

46. Harclay, *Quaestiones ordinariae*, q. 15, nn. 13–16 (Henninger, II.688:75–690:104), esp.: "Ens rationis est ens in anima tantum, quod non est nisi dum intellectus considerat . . . . [A]lia condicio: quod est factum ab intellectu et non manet intellectu cessante considerare . . . . Unde relatio rationis, recte intellecta, est ens secundum quid et diminutum, in nullo existens." An earlier edition of this question was published as Question 1 in Maurer, "Harclay's Questions," 166–72.

47. Harclay, *Quaestiones ordinariae*, q. 15, nn. 17–19 (Henninger, II.690:105–692:126).

48. Harclay, *Quaestiones ordinariae*, q. 15, n. 23 (Henninger, II.694:157–80). The example of the statue is from Henry of Ghent. See p. 151. See also, Harclay, *In I Sent.*, d. 35, q. 2, and d. 36 (MS Casale Monferrato, Seminario Vescovila, fol., 73vb–76va), esp. from 74va: "Ideo dico ideae in mente divina non sunt aliquae relationes rationis quae necessario requirantur ad cognitionem ideatorum . . . Secundo dico quod ille ideae non sunt aliud nisi ipsamet obiecta cognita ab [ad *ms.*] intellectu divino inquantum cognita [cognitum *ms.*]."

A divine idea, then, is nothing but the creature's essence as known by God. The essence that exists (or could exist) in reality is the same essence that God knows. Harclay's insistence that the essence is in God's mind objectively and not subjectively shows that only the intelligible content of the essence is present. The essence itself has no actual existence, as would be the case if it were present subjectively.

Harclay rethinks this position when he disputes *Ordinary Questions*, q. 2. In particular, he is concerned that his former position isolates divine ideas from the divine essence. Augustine says, "the soul becomes beatified by the vision of them," but seeing a creaturely essence, even if that creaturely essence is in God's mind, is not beatifying.[49] Only the vision of the divine essence is beatifying.[50] Thus, he needs to revise his theory so that divine ideas are identical to the divine essence. He argues thus: if an idea is the *ratio* according to which everything that comes to be comes to be, it is necessary that the idea itself represent the makeable thing (*factibile*) according to every makeable aspect. Therefore, since a determinate grade of being pertains to the makeable thing according as it is makeable if God makes a limited thing according to an idea, which limitation cannot fall into the absolute character of an essence, then it is manifest that an idea will not be the essence only. However, it also cannot be a bare respect (*respectus*) both because respects cannot be principles for form alone and because a respect cannot be the principle of cognition or production. Therefore, an idea includes the essence with a respect.[51] After considering several options, Harclay specifies that the respect must have the character of imitability because such a respect is not contrary to divine simplicity and perfection.[52]

These respects are necessary for God to have distinct cognition of creatable beings but not as the object of the act or the *ratio cognoscendi*. They are required as a *sine qua non*. He outlines two acts—and he does call each an act—by which God knows his essence: In the first act, God knows his essence and the divine essence is the object of the act. There follows after (*postea*) the act by which he knows his essence is understood. This act is not the first act because it presupposes the first act. In this second act, God understands his essence as imitable such that the essence as imitable has the character of an object and a principle. Nevertheless, the essence so understood has the character of a foundation of an ideal respect, and the foundation is prior to the respect.[53]

---

49. Augustine, *De div. qq. 83*, q. 46, n. 2 (PL 40.31): "quarum visione fit beatissima."

50. Harclay, *Quaestiones ordinariae*, q. 2, n. 18 (Henninger, I.90:155–56): "beatus Augustinus dicit quod 'ipsarum visione anima fit beatissima', quod non esset nisi essent idem quod essentia." An earlier edition of this question was published as Question 2 in Maurer, "Harclay's Questions," 173–93.

51. Harclay, *Quaestiones ordinariae*, q. 2, n. 24 (Henninger, I.92:189–97), esp.: "Cum igitur determinatus gradus essendi pertineat ad factibile secundum quod factibile, si secundum Ydeam Deus faciat rem limitatam . . . manifestum est quod Ydea non poterit esse tantum essentia. Nec potest esse nudus respectus . . . . Ergo Ydea includit essentiam cum respectu." Notice that Harclay has borrowed the term *factibile* from Scotus's definition of an idea. See pp. 170–75 for Scotus's definition of divine ideas.

52. Harclay, *Quaestiones ordinariae*, q. 2, nn. 47, 80 (Henninger, I.102:353–56, 118:608–17).

53. Harclay, *Quaestiones ordinariae*, q. 2, n. 82–84 (Henninger, I.120:640–55), esp.: "ad distinctam cognitionem quam habet Deus ab aeterno de creabilibus requiruntur in eo distinctae rationes

Harclay is not sure whether the essence so understood either is the foundation of the respect as it has the character of an object or as it is the principle of the act of understanding. However, he is sure that the nature (*ratio*) of a foundation is prior to the *ratio* of a respect. Therefore, by considering his essence as imitable, God understands the creature, which has an idea, at the same time. Thus, an idea, according to this mode of understanding, is neither an object nor the *ratio cognoscendi* by which God knows a creature *per se*, but as a *sine qua non*. He explains this claim with an example of two white things. In two white things, when the second white thing comes into existence, a respect to the first white thing follows upon or is concomitant to the second white thing. Similarly, a respect to a creature is concomitant as a *sine qua non* to the divine essence understood as imitable.[54]

Harclay does not employ Scotus's theory of instants here, but something similar is at work.[55] As soon as God understands the creature, he understands the respect of imitability that he has to it. That respect of imitability is not the reason or means by which God knows the creature, but it comes along as a *sine qua non*. If the divine idea did not include the respect of imitability, then there would be something deficient about the creature as makeable. God would, perhaps, know the creature's essence *qua* essence, but Harclay indicates that God's knowledge of the creature's essence *qua* makeable (*factibile*) would suffer.

If God did not have intellect and will, he could produce creatures because he is productive before he understands himself to be productive.[56] Ideas are thus not necessary for divine production absolutely, but they are necessary for intellectual production in which they are a cause *sine qua non*.[57] Ideas are a sort of *per accidens* cause that the artist requires. Ideas are not the art itself but an instrument by which the artist produces, forms that direct the artist's operation. Divine ideas are exemplars, and exemplars are not the cause but instruments necessary for the cause.[58]

Harclay's two accounts of divine ideas parallel the two readings of Scotus that I identified in the previous chapter.[59] At first, Harclay seems so focused on the impossibility of God knowing through rational relations that he does not see any need to keep them. Thus, he focuses on Scotus's claim that "an idea is not some relation but the object known."[60] As Henry thinks over the issue, he realizes that Scotus also claims that the character of an idea is "according as something is

---

cognoscendi, quae vocantur Ydeae. Sed aliquid requiri ad distinctam cognitionem Dei quam habet de creabilibus neque sicud obiectum actus neque sicud ratio cognoscendi, sed sicud sine quo non."

54. Harclay, *Quaestiones ordinariae*, q. 2, n. 82–84 (Henninger, I.120:655–67), esp.: "semper ratio fundamenti prior est ratione respectus."

55. For Scotus's theory of instants of nature in divine ideas, see pp. 10–75.

56. Harclay, *Quaestiones ordinariae*, q. 2, n. 86 (Henninger, I.122:685–87).

57. Harclay, *Quaestiones ordinariae*, q. 2, n. 91 (Henninger, I.717–19).

58. Harclay, *Quaestiones ordinariae*, q. 2, n. 97, 99 (Henninger, I.128:769–77, 130:801–5).

59. See p. 171.

60. Scotus, *Rep. I-A*, d. 36, qq. 1–2, n. 57 (Noone, 419:19–20): "idea non est relatio aliqua sed obiectum cognitum."

formable."[61] To know it as formable is to have an exemplar of it, which includes a rational relation. Scotus denies that rational relations are necessary for God to understand creatures, but not that they are part of the character of divine ideas.[62] Harclay realizes that God has ideas when an ideal relation is caused by the divine intellect comparing its essence to the creature that he already knows directly.[63] Harclay's final position, then, coheres with what I think is the best reading of Scotus, and he shifts from his earlier position to his mature position for almost the same reasons that I gave for my reading of Scotus.

CONCLUSION

The Thomists were not equipped to handle Olivi and Scotus's objections to the Imitability Theory. Thus, they all formulated some version of the *Creatura Intellecta* Theory. Thomas of Sutton even pushes his theory farther than Scotus, emphasizing the unicity of God's act of knowing to the point that will be characteristic of the Nominalist Theory. God must have direct epistemological access to creatures because he cannot know them through a relation. Sutton even says that it seems contrary to reason to say that God can know possible creatures through a relation.[64] This claim is stunning when we consider that Peter John Olivi was censured for a similar claim just a decade earlier. The fact that Sutton feels justified in making such a claim in response to a public question reveals just how quickly authors felt the criticism's force.

Scotists make more progress in Scotus's thought than the Thomists. Henry of Harclay's thought on divine ideas is instructive because he changes his mind. Initially, he endorses a theory of divine ideas devoid of relations, which, as we saw in the previous chapter, is a tempting reading of Scotus. When Harclay returns to the subject, he instead endorses a version of the *Creatura Intellecta* Theory in which the character of a divine idea is not complete until God knows the rational relation that exists from him to the creature. Such relations are included in the theory as a *sine qua non*. This version of the *Creatura Intellecta* Theory seems more intellectually satisfactory and, as I argued in the previous chapter, is the best reading of Scotus.

In sum, early Thomists and one Scotist all work within the general Scotistic framework of divine ideas. The early Thomists accept that creatures cannot be known through a relation. The Scotist (Harclay) carries on Scotus's thought and examines certain ambiguities in his text. Importantly, at least one early Thomist (Sutton) and one early Scotist (Harclay) emphasize the unicity of the divine act of knowing in ways that become central for the last two thinkers in this study, Peter Auriol and William of Ockham.

---

61. Scotus, *Rep. I-A*, d. 36, qq. 1–2, n. 57 (Noone, 419:18): "secundum aliquid formabile."
62. See Scotus, *Rep. I-A*, d. 36, qq. 1–2, n. 64 (Noone, 422:6–9).
63. See Scotus, *Lect.* I, d. 35, q. un., n. 22 (Vatican, 17.452:28–453:3): " ita quod idea, ut ens quoddam est, sequitur intellectionem creaturae in tertio signo, et in alio instanti (scilicet in quarto), sequitur cognitio et intellectio istius ideae et illius relationis."
64. Sutton, *Quodlibet* II, q. 4 (Schmaus, 196:103).

Part V.
The Nominalist Theory of Divine Ideas

The fifth and final theory in this study is the Nominalist Theory. I call it the Nominalist Theory because the authors who subscribe to it—Peter Auriol and William of Ockham—are nominalists in the traditional sense of the word. They each argue that universals are just names. In contemporary parlance, we would call them "conceptualists" because they admit that universals exist, but universals are concepts constructed by the mind.[1]

Several aspects characterize the Nominalist Theory of divine ideas: First, its adherents reject the distinction between the primary terminating object and secondary terminating object. The distinction, they argue, is contrary to divine simplicity. The Godhead (*deitas*) or the divine essence is the only principle required to explain God's knowing and creating. The distinction between primary and secondary terminating objects is not a good theory, they say, but it still gets at a certain truth, namely, that God knows possible creatures by means of knowing himself. Second, the Nominalist Theory makes a semantic turn by saying that divine ideas are known connotatively when the divine essence is known. Bonaventure mentions connotations once in his discussion of divine ideas, but the Nominalist Theory takes the claim in ways Bonaventure would not recognize.[2] The third, and perhaps most important, aspect of the Nominalist Theory is that it results in a theory of divine ideas that is really a rejection of divine ideas. Divine ideas play no causal role and only play a nominal role in divine cognition.[3] The fourth characteristic is that Nominalist Theory subscribers always include a close and unfaithful analysis of Augustine's understanding of divine ideas. Denying divine ideas is tantamount to denying the divine Word, which is heretical.[4] Thus, they are anxious to be seen upholding an Augustinian account of divine ideas even as they undermine it.

---

1. Russell Friedman has rightly argued that Auriol retains a measuring or guaranteeing role to the extramental object in certain knowledge, but he still admits that Auriol's theory falls under the umbrella of conceptualist theories since the intellect is productive of the universal rather than receptive of it, as a realist theory would maintain. He calls Auriol's theory "moderate conceptualism." See Russell L. Friedman, "Peter Auriol on Intentions and Essential Predication," in *Medieval Analyses in Language and Cognition* (Copenhagen: The Royal Danish Academy of Sciences and Letters, 1999), 415–30.
2. Bonaventure, *In I Sent.*, d. 36, a. un., q. 3, ad 3 (Quaracchi, I.608b). See pp. 28–30.
3. Conti, "Divine Ideas in Auriol," 115; Palatini, "*Similitudo Aequivoca*," 203.
4. See Albert, *In I Sent.*, d. 35, a. 9 (Aschendorff, 190a); Bonaventure, *In I Sent.*, d. 6, a. un., q. 3 (Quaracchi, I.130a); Aquinas, *De veritate*, q. 3, a. 1 (Leonine, 22/1.98a). M. J. F. M. Hoenen, "*Propter Dicta Augustini*: Die Metaphysische Bedeutung Der Mittelalterlichen Ideenlehre," *Recherches de Théologie et Philosophie médiévales* 64, no. 2 (1997): 245–62.

Chapter IX.
Peter Auriol (ca. 1280–1322)

THE PLACE OF DIVINE IDEAS IN AURIOL'S THOUGHT

Peter Auriol's (Auriole, Aureol, Aureoli) life is largely unknown. It is speculated that he studied in Paris sometime between 1300 and 1310, making it possible that he heard some of Scotus's lectures. He was teaching at the Franciscan studium in Toulouse by the end of 1314. He must have been lecturing on Peter Lombard's *Sentences* in Toulouse because a complete draft of his massive *Scriptum super primum Sententiarum* (*Scriptum*) seems to be complete at that time. At the latest, the work was finished by late 1316 when he arrived in Paris to complete his degree. He lectured on the *Sentences* in Paris sometime between 1316–1318 and became *magister regens* in 1318. He was *magister regens* for no more than three years because he was made Archbishop of Aix-en-Provence in 1321. He died in January 1322.[1]

Much of the research on Auriol's theory of divine knowledge has focused on his account of divine foreknowledge and future contingents.[2] To my knowledge, Alessandro D. Conti and Chiara Paladini are the only two to have written articles on Auriol's theory of divine ideas, and both articles emphasize Auriol's account of divine exemplarity.[3] Both articles are excellent, but as a result of the emphasis on divine exemplarity, they focus more on what Auriol says in *Scriptum* d. 35 on divine knowledge in general and less on *Scriptum* d. 36 on divine ideas. On the one hand, their emphasis is proper since in d. 36 Auriol frequently refers to the arguments in d. 35. On the other hand, their emphasis ignores some of the ways Auriol applies his arguments to divine ideas. This chapter aims to supplement the good work begun by Conti and Paladini. It will focus primarily on Auriol's treatment of ideas in *Scriptum*, d. 36. Reference will be made to d. 35 to help elucidate what Auriol says in d. 36.

THE STATUS OF DIVINE IDEAS

Auriol investigates the status of an idea in *Scriptum*, d. 36, p. 2, a. 1. A complete account of the status of divine ideas requires a fourfold inquiry: We must know (1) what the term 'idea' means, (2) what an idea is in reality, (3) how many ideas there

---

1. *Dictionnaire de Théologie Catholique* (1935), s.v. "Pierre Auriol Ou Oriol." –Russell L. Friedman and Lauge O. Nielson, "Peter Auriol: An Introduction," *Vivarium* 38, no. 1 (2000): 1–2.
2. Calvin Normore, "Future Contingents," in *The Cambridge History of Later Medieval Philosophy*, ed. Norman Kretzmann, Anthony Kenny, and J. Pinborg, 369–70 (New York: Cambridge University Press, 1982); Calvin Normore, "Petrus Aureoli and His Contemporaries on Future Contingents and Excluded Middle," *Synthese* 96, no. 1 (1993): 83–92; Christopher Schabel, *Theology at Paris, 1316 - 1345: Peter Auriol and the Problem of Divine Foreknowledge and Future Contingents* (Aldershot: Ashgate, 2000).
3. Conti, "Divine Ideas in Auriol"; Paladini, "*Similitudo Aequivoca.*"

are, and (4) whether they exist and why they exist. This section will follow this fourfold division.

What Does 'Idea' Mean?

Auriol's explanation of the term 'idea' is a sustained interpretation of Augustine's definition of ideas.[4] The term is synonymous with a form or a species. 'Idea' can be reasonably understood as 'reason' (*ratio*), but this understanding is not ideal since *ratio* is more associated with the Greek term *logos*, not the Greek term *idea*. This distinction between (1) forms and species and (2) reasons could make it seem that ideas are called forms or species insofar as they are causal principles and that they are called reasons insofar as they are purely speculative and principles of cognition. Nevertheless, Auriol thinks that 'reason' and 'form' are synonymous because 'reason' is sometimes taken for that which is quidditative and formal in the thing.[5] Nevertheless, 'form,' 'species,' and 'reason' can have one of two meanings: They can mean the intrinsic form that is constitutive of a thing, or they can mean an extrinsic and exemplar form. Ideas, and consequently, forms, species, and reasons, are not intrinsic forms, so they are extrinsic and exemplars.[6]

Auriol further identifies seven characteristics that Augustine ascribes to divine ideas: First, they are principal forms because that to the imitation of which some other thing comes to be is more principal than that which comes to be. Second, they are stable, incommunicable, and eternal forms. They are not formed but are from themselves and always in the same mode. If they were formed after the fashion of other forms, then either there would be an infinite regress or the regress would arrive at other incommunicable, stable, and eternal forms. Third, everything that can or does arise or perish is formed according to these forms, which must be the case because everything subject to generation and corruption must be reduced to some invariable and immutable exemplar. Fourth, a holy and pure rational soul can intuit these forms. Fifth, the vision of these forms will be most blessed to the soul that "contuits" them. Sixth, the divine intelligence alone contains these forms because God intuits them when he makes something other than himself. It would be sacrilege to posit that he contemplates something outside himself. Seventh, these forms are not only ideas or likenesses, but they are true and having truth.[7]

He combines these seven characteristics into a (quasi-)definition of ideas.

> Ideas are certain principal, truly existing, stable, incommunicable, and eternal forms that are in no way formed, contained in the divine intelligence, according to which everything that perishes or arises is formed, to the contuition of

---

4. Augustine, *De div. qq. 83*, q. 46 (PL 40.29–30).
5. See Aristotle, *Met.* IV, c. 7, 1012a28 (AL 25.3.2.90:629–30), where Aristotle claims that a *ratio* is the name that is a thing's definition.
6. *Scriptum*, d. 36, p. 2, a. 1 (E-Scriptum, 3:127–41), esp.: "Ideae ergo non dicuntur formae aut species intrinsecae et constitutivae rei, sed potius extrinsicae et rationes exemplares."
7. *Scriptum*, d. 36, p. 2, a. 1 (E-Scriptum, 3:142–58).

which the rational soul can arrive, and, when it arrives, understands them in a most blessed vision.[8]

This (quasi-)definition would lead us to believe that Auriol will articulate a fairly traditional account of divine ideas. Like Aquinas, Henry of Ghent, and Scotus, Auriol emphasizes that ideas are extrinsic exemplars of possible creatures. His rejection of the distinction between forms and species as causal principles and *rationes* as speculative principles is even traditional in a sense. Aquinas endorses the view, but Henry and Scotus object to Aquinas's distinction. Auriol simply continues the tradition of Henry and Scotus.[9] However, Auriol completely rejects a causal role, and only offers divine ideas a marginal cognitive role.

The Reality of Ideas

Having determined the meaning of 'idea,' Auriol inquires what an idea is. He begins by arguing against Plato's Theory of Ideas, the Imitability Theory, and the *Creatura Intellecta* Theory, and then offers his own opinion. Rather than examine his treatment of Plato's theory, it is enough to note that Auriol's account is more penetrating and balanced than other Scholastics. Others seem content to reject Plato's theory on the authority of Aristotle. Auriol earnestly looks for a way to save the theory, although he ultimately concludes that Plato's account is incompatible with a Catholic account of divine knowledge.[10] He then argues that the Imitability Theory fails because it adheres to rational relations, and the *Creatura Intellecta* Theory fails because it posits a primary and secondary terminating object of the divine intellect. Each of these arguments deserves a close look.

Against the Imitability Theory

The Imitability Theory claims that divine ideas are the divine essence considered under diverse respects and are those respects. Auriol attacks this core claim with the conviction that *"even a purely logical* multiplication of the divine essence into different ideas, which all imitate the one essence of God in differing ways, necessarily entails a kind of *real* division of the divine essence and therefore posits a kind of real difference in God."[11] Two of Auriol's four arguments in *Scriptum* d. 36,

---

8. *Scriptum*, d. 36, p. 2, a. 1 (E-Scriptum, 3:159–64): "Sunt enim ideae formae quaedam principales, vere existentes, stabiles, incommutabiles, et aeternae, nullo modo formatae, in divina intelligentia contentae, secundum quas omne formatur quod interit vel oritur, ad quarum contuitum potest rationalis pervenire et, cum perveniret, intelligent eas beatissima visione." The word *contuitus* can mean either to look at directly or to view obliquely. Bonaventure uses the term in the second sense when discussing divine illumination, but I think Auriol intends the first sense here.
9. See pp. 46–52, 89–94, 170–75, and 191.
10. *Scriptum*, d. 36, p. 2, a. 1 (E-Scriptum, 3:165–5:226), esp.: "non intelligebat huiusmodi ideas esse in mente summi opificis realiter et per identitatem, sed tantummodo obiective, in se ipsis tamen subsistenter quasi aliquid realiter distinctum."
11. Paladini, "*Similitudo Aequivoca*," 213. Emphasis original.

p. 2, a. 1 stand out because they attack the cognitive and causal roles Aquinas ascribes to divine ideas.

The first argument concludes that God does not need rational respects to know creatures, which he had argued in *Scriptum*, d. 35, p. 3, a. 2. Where there are many distinct things, it is possible to take one of them without the other, but where there is only a single, indivisible, and simple thing, one cannot be taken without the other. Whoever takes anything takes the whole thing. If the perfections of things preexist in God, they preexist in the simplest and most indivisible being. Therefore, the divine intellect cannot take one perfection without another. God's simple essence, which no one can divide into many things that can be taken piecemeal, is not like the subtraction or addition of unity in numbers or the addition or subtraction of differences in a definition. Imitability Theorists cannot evade this difficulty by saying that the plurality is only a rational plurality (*secundum rationem*). Each *ratio* would be God's whole essence in reality since it cannot be merely part of it. God's whole essence is the likeness of all things, and as a result, each *ratio* would be a likeness of all things, including the other ideas. The perfections of every creature would be found under the same reason.[12]

Rational respects do not suffice to show how God knows creatures because they really divide God's simple essence. Thus, "Aquinas' conception of divine ideas hypostatizes them, so that God's being itself is nothing but the 'union' of divine ideas."[13] The divine essence cannot be divided piecemeal the way Aquinas's theory requires. Since God's essence is absolutely simple, a divine idea has to imitate the whole thing. A divine idea cannot take life but leave cognition the way Aquinas describes.[14]

This argument bears a certain similarity to Petrus de Trabibus's argument that imitability cannot be the characteristic of a divine idea since imitation of the divine essence is common to all divine ideas.[15] Auriol's argument strengthens Petrus's by insisting that each idea entails imitation of the whole divine essence.

Auriol's second argument is as follows: an idea and exemplar is that in God which every creature imitates. However, creatures do not imitate rational respects; they imitate the bare essence of the Godhead (*deitas*). Creatures do not imitate respects of imitability but the substratum of those respects. Therefore, those respects fall short of the formal character of an idea. Auriol argues that the example of color confirms the minor premise. Color is visible per se in the second mode, not because a respect of visibility is under the quiddity of color nor because sight attains color concerning visibility, but because sight attains the very color itself abstracted from such a respect.[16] Similarly, creatures imitate the divine essence

---

12. *Scriptum*, d. 35, p. 3, a. 2 (E-Scriptum, 11:566–79), esp.: "ubi tamen non est nisi unicum indivisibile et simplex non potest accipi unum sine alio, sed qui aliquid accipit totum capit."
13. Conti, "Divine Ideas in Auriol," 107.
14. Aquinas, *SCG* I, c. 54 (Leonine, 13.154–55). See p. 68.
15. See pp. 125–26.
16. Something is *per se* in the second mode when the subject falls in the definition of the predicate. In this case, 'color' falls in the definition of 'visible'. See *Post. An.* I, c. 4, 73a35–b4 (AL 4.12:22–13:7).

abstracted from every respect, although the apprehension of a respect of imitability could immediately arise.[17]

This second argument is directed against the causal role of divine ideas. Auriol seems convinced by Scotus's reasoning about God's knowledge of creatures and rational relations. As soon as we know that the creature imitates, we recognize a respect of imitability. Nevertheless, knowledge of the respect of imitability is logically posterior to knowledge of the creature. Auriol goes beyond Scotus in saying that the creature imitates the divine essence itself without any respect of imitability at all. Thus, Auriol criticizes Scotus's *Creatura Intellecta* Theory too.[18]

Lurking in the background of this argument seems to be an increased emphasis on Augustine's claim that the vision of divine ideas is the most blessed vision.[19] Although I claimed at the beginning of Part V that Nominalist Theories include an unfaithful interpretation of Augustine, Auriol seems to be more faithful to Augustine on this point. Since only the vision of the Godhead makes the soul most blessed, if the vision of the divine ideas makes the soul most blessed, the divine ideas must be the Godhead. By identifying divine ideas with rational relations, Imitability Theorists have created space between the Godhead and divine ideas. If such space exists, then it is the Imitability Theory that is unfaithful to Augustine because they would be holding—at least tacitly—that something other than the Godhead makes the soul blessed.

Despite Auriol's fidelity to Augustine on ideas as a most blessed vision, Auriol's second argument is dramatically unfaithful to Augustine because it denies that divine ideas play any causal role in creation. Creatures do not imitate divine ideas; they imitate the Godhead. If creatures imitated divine ideas, then God's divinity would not be the exemplar of all things.[20] God's essence would not be the exemplar cause of creatures essentially and formally, but only through a mode of subtraction. Since these ideas are not present in the Godhead's *ratio* except through an act of the intellect, God would be an exemplar neither from himself nor from his nature but through something that the divine intellect's consideration conferred upon him. In that case, divine ideas seem like accidents in a subject, and God's simplicity is lost. Note, too, that Auriol's criticism entails that divine ideas are not the Godhead, that is, they are not ultimately identical to the divine essence.

The critique of the Imitability Theory shows that Auriol's theory of divine ideas is more of a nod to the tradition of Augustine than a legitimate theory. He posits divine ideas, but they play no causal role. Since these roles (or at least one of them) are the only reason to posit divine ideas in the first place, Auriol is not really positing them at all.

For a good explanation of this chapter, see Aristotle, *Posterior Analytics*, trans. with a commentary by Jonathan Barnes, 2nd ed. (New York: Clarendon Press, 1993), 112–14.

17. *Scriptum*, d. 36, p. 2, a. 1 (E-Scriptum, 5:245–52), esp.: "creaturae non imitantur respectus rationis, immo ipsam nudam essentiam deitatis."

18. See p. 175.

19. Augustine, *De div. qq. 83*, q. 46, n. 2 (PL 40.30): "istas rationes, quarum visione sit beatissima."

20. *Scriptum*, d. 35, p. 3, a. 2 (E-Scriptum, 12:611–22 and 12:627–13:642). See Conti, "Divine Ideas in Auriol," 111–12.

Against the Creatura Intellecta *Theory*

Scotus's theory of divine ideas posits that the creatures themselves shine forth objectively in the divine mind.[21] This theory has the advantage of declaring that God's essence is directly representative of creatures.[22] Nevertheless, it too falls short and even commits the sin of sacrilege insofar as it declares that creatures are secondary terminating objects of God's act of understanding.[23] Creatures in no way terminate the divine intuition, neither as primary objects nor as secondary objects. Since creatures could only shine forth again if they were secondary terminating objects of God's intuition, Scotus's theory must be false.[24]

By positing a primary and secondary object of divine knowledge, Scotus considered the one, entirely simple divine essence as if it were two things. If creatures shined forth again in the divine essence as secondary objects, God would intuit something posited outside of himself. Creatures would not be spatially or locally (*situaliter*) outside God, but they would be entitatively (*entitative*) outside God because, in such existence, they are not the Creator himself.[25] Since the creature's being could not be identical with God's, if it exists at all, it has to exist outside of God. Auriol uses the example of a mirror to explain his point. When a mirror reflects some object, there are not suddenly two presences—the object and its image. There is but one presence: the object itself. In the same way, there is no additional presence of creatures in the divine essence than the essence itself.[26]

Auriol argues further that reliance on the mirror analogy tacitly abandons God's simplicity. God does not gaze upon (*intuetur*) a creature by another act of understanding (*intellectio*) than that by which he gazes upon his essence. Instead, to have seen his essence is to have seen every creature. Nevertheless, to have seen a mirror is not to have seen the thing in the mirror. They are diverse terms and diverse acts of having seen. Therefore, creatures are not seen by God through his essence as through a mirror.[27] Since seeing the mirror and seeing the thing in the mirror are two distinct acts, if God sees in a mirror, he has to have more than one, simple act of understanding. The two distinct cognitive principles (the essence and

---

21. *Scriptum*, d. 36, p. 2, a. 1 (E-Scriptum, 5:265–66).
22. *Scriptum*, d. 35, p. 3, a. 2 (E-Scriptum, 10:509–17), esp.: "iste modus dicendi licet in hoc verus sit quod habitudines istas tollit, deficit tamen in duobus." The two deficiencies are (1) how the simple essence could be a likeness of many dissimilar things, and (2) Scotus's endorsement of a primary and secondary terminating object of the divine intellect.
23. *Scriptum*, d. 35, p. 2, a. 1 (E-Scriptum, 7:353): "sacrilegium est quod creaturae reluceant in Deo tamquam obiecta secundaria."
24. *Scriptum*, d. 36, p. 2, a. 1 (E-Scriptum, 5:275–76:278).
25. *Scriptum*, d. 35, p. 2, a. 1 (E-Scriptum, 7:350–53), esp.: "Deus aliquid extra se positum intuetur. Extra . . . entitative, quia creaturae in tali esse positae non sunt ipse creator."
26. *Scriptum*, d. 35, p. 3, a. 2 (E-Scriptum, 10:515–24).
27. *Scriptum*, d. 35, p. 2, a. 1 (E-Scriptum, 7:332–35), esp.: "Sed vidisse speculum non est vidisse rem in speculum, immo sunt diversi termini et diversa vidisse." See Conti, "Divine Ideas in Auriol," 110–11; Paladini, "*Similitudo Aequivoca*," 214–15.

the ideas) would have to be known in two acts.[28] His understanding would be multiple and diverse.

Scotus's theory fails because it tacitly abandons God's simplicity. God is so simple that his essence alone is sufficient to exemplify all possible creatures. The divine intellect can know those likenesses directly when it terminates in its only object, the divine essence.

Auriol's Nominalist Theory

Some background in his general theory of knowledge and theory of divine knowledge is required to understand Auriol's theory of divine ideas. The central aspect of Auriol's account of knowledge is that the thing known appears to the knower: "the act of understanding (*intellectio*) is nothing other than that by which things appear to something."[29] Unlike his contemporaries, who emphasized the real presence of the object, Auriol points out that the mere appearance of the object is sufficient for cognition. There is cognition even if the thing is not present, and the appearance is the result of a hallucination.[30] The hallucinating or dreaming man has cognition even though the object of his cognition does not exist extramentally. Thus, Auriol rejects his predecessors' claims that cognition is a relation, passion, act, or quality.[31]

Instead of anything in these ontological categories, Auriol argues that "in every act of understanding (*intellectio*) the very thing cognized, not something else, emanates and proceeds in a certain objective being (*esse obiectivum*), according as it terminates the intellect's gaze (*intuitus*)."[32] As Russel L. Friedman explains, "for Auriol, concepts *are* extramental particulars, but having a different type of existence—a different *modus essendi*—than the real existence they have extramentally."[33] Auriol's theory of *esse obiectivum*, which he also calls intentional being (*esse*

---

28. *Scriptum*, d. 35, p. 2, a. 1 (E-Scriptum, 6:303–13).

29. *Scriptum*, d. 35, p. 1, a. 1 (E-Scriptum, 9:425): "Non enim est aliud intellectio quam id quo alicui res apparent." See Hamid Taieb, "What Is Cognition?: Peter Auriol's Account," *Recherches de Théologie et Philosophie Médiévales* 85, no. 1 (2018): 110, 117.

30. *Scriptum, proemium*, sect. 2, a. 3, nn. 81–87 (Buytaert, I.198:40–199:93). See Russell L. Friedman, "Act, Species, and Appearance: Peter Auriol on Intellectual Cognition and Consciousness," in *Intentionality, Cognition, and Mental Representation in Medieval Philosophy*, ed. Gyula Klima, 141–65 (New York: Fordham University Press, 2015); Lukáš Lička, "Perception and Objective Being: Peter Auriol on Perceptual Acts and Their Objects," *American Catholic Philosophical Quarterly* 90, no. 1 (2016): 49–76; Han Thomas Adriaessen, "Peter Auriol on the Intuitive Cognition of Nonexistents: Revisiting the Charge of Skepticism in Walter Chatton and Adam Wodeham," *Oxford Studies in Medieval Philosophy* 5 (2017): 151–80; Taieb, "What Is Cognition?: Peter Auriol's Account," 113–14; Adrianssen, *Representation and Scepticism*, 82–84.

31. *Scriptum*, d. 35, p. 1, a. 1 (E-Scriptum, 2:102–6:314 and 8:414–13:649). See Taieb, "What Is Cognition?: Peter Auriol's Account," 111–16.

32. *Scriptum*, d. 27, p. 2, a. 2, (E-Scriptum, 10:356–66): "in omni intellectione emanat et procidit, non aliquid aliud, sed ipsamet res cognita in quodam esse obiectivo, secundum quod habet terminare intuitum intellectus."

33. Friedman, "Act, Species, and Appearance," 143. Emphasis original.

intentionale) and apparent being (*esse apparens*), will be discussed below in the section on the Existence of Things in God.[34] What matters for now is that Auriol denies that the object of cognition is some numerically distinct thing from the thing itself.[35]

Auriol's predecessors all posited some ontological 'thing' between the knower and the thing known. However, "understanding (*intelligere*) does not formally include some determinate thing directly (*in recto*) but only connotes something as appearing to him who is said to understand."[36] *In recto*, there is no determinate object entailed by the term 'understanding.' The object is connoted or referred to indirectly (*in obliquo*). There are two things to note from this claim: First, cognition occurs anywhere appearing occurs. Auriol insists that a wall would have cognition of Caesar-depicted if the picture of Caesar on the wall were to appear to the wall.[37]

Second, and more important for understanding his theory of divine ideas, Auriol claims that understanding is connotative. The concept is "that by which things appear to something" and something as appearing is connoted in the concept.[38] A connotative concept expresses indirectly the thing connoted absolutely. Auriol uses the example of flesh. "Flesh, through the *ratio* by which it is flesh, is called *someone's* flesh."[39] A connotative concept inherently points to something else. An exemplar functions in the same way. It always points to the thing that it exemplifies. Since a connotative concept always points to something beyond itself, connotative concepts seem identical to relative concepts. However, Auriol denies that they are the same.

> A relative concept expresses the term through a relation (*habitudo*) added to the absolute *ratio*, as 'father' expresses 'son' through paternity added to Socrates. But the Philosopher indicates this distinction [between connotative and relative concepts] in the *Categories* when he says that the hand and foot and parts of the substance are relative in speech [*secundum dici*] not in being [*secundum esse*].[40]

---

34. See pp. 222–24.

35. *Scriptum*, d. 27, p. 2, a. 2 (E-Scriptum, 16:584–88): "res in esse formato posita non claudit in se aliquid absolutum nisi ipsam realitatem. Unde non ponit in numerum res et sua intentio quantum ad aliquid absolutum, claudit tamen aliquid respectivum, videlicet apparere." See Friedman, "Act, Species, and Appearance," 144.

36. *Scriptum*, d. 35, p. 1, a. 1 (E-Scriptum, 7:320–21): "intelligere formaliter non includit determinate aliquid in recto, sed solum connotat aliquid ut apparens illi quod dicitur intelligere."

37. *Scriptum*, d. 35, p. 1, a. 1 (E-Scriptum, 7:330–32): "Similiter etiam si per picturam in pariete existentem, Caesar pictus appareret parieti, paries diceretur cognoscere Caesarem pictum."

38. *Scriptum*, d. 35, p. 1, a. 1 (E-Scriptum, 9:424 and 7:321): "id quo alicui res apparent" and "aliquid ut apparens."

39. *Scriptum*, d. 8, p. 3, a. 6, n. 192 (Buytaert, II.1026:52; E-Scriptum, 33): "caro, per rationem qua caro est, dicitur alicuius caro." Emphasis mine.

40. *Scriptum*, d. 8, p. 3, a. 6, n. 192 (Buytaert, II.1026:54–1027:59; E-Scriptum, 33): "Conceptus autem relativus exprimit terminum per habitudinem additam rationi absolutae, sicut pater exprimit filium per paternitatem additam Sorti. Hanc autem distinctionem innuit Philosophus in *Praedicamentis*, cum dicit manum et pedem et partes substantiarum esse relativa secundum dici, et non secundum esse."

Connotative concepts are distinguished from relative concepts by the lack of a third thing—the relation; they immediately connect to what is connotated. The concept of a hand immediately connotes the person whose hand it is. Relative concepts only connect to that of which they are relative because of a relation or relatedness (*habitudo*). To Auriol's mind, the relation must be thought of as a disposition existing between two things. This is problematic, he thinks, because what could it mean for an accident to exist *between* two things? What would be the subject of that relation?[41] In contrast, connotative concepts "do not express the connotated thing because of a relatedness or relation, but from their proper condition."[42] The connotated thing is, as it were, built-in to the absolute *ratio*. It is built-in to the concept of 'hand' that it is *something's* hand. A relation is required to mediate between two absolute things, but in knowledge, there is only one thing, not two.[43] The only thing is the one, proper, absolute *ratio*, which immediately entails what is connoted.

Applying this general account to divine knowledge, Auriol argues that the Godhead (*deitas*) is the only thing that makes objects appear for the divine intellect. God has but one source of cognition, namely, himself. Moreover, the *deitas* is like the concept 'hand': "the Godhead, through its proper *ratio*, has that it connotes diverse things, like created justice that connotes one thing, and clemency that connotes another, and so on for the other created perfections."[44] Thus, "the act of understanding (*intelligere*) adds nothing directly (*in recto*), neither real nor rational, to the *ratio* of the Godhead (*deitas*), but a certain connotated thing, namely, the present-ness (*praesentialitas*) of the thing in apparent being (*esse apparens*)."[45] The Godhead always connotes all possible creatures. There is no need to appeal to any sort of secondary object because creatures are immediately, though indirectly, entailed in the concept of the Godhead. Auriol insists that the Godhead is itself absolute,

---

41. See *Scriptum*, d. 30, *expositio textus* (Vatican, 662aD–E): "Praeterea: illud, quod unum existens est imaginandum, intervallum inter duo non videtur esse in rerum natura, sed in solo intellectu: tum quia natura non facit talia intervalla: tum quia huiusmodi medium intervallum non videtur esse subiective in aliquo illorum, sed inter illa duo, ubi constat, quod non est aliqua res, quae subiecti non possit. Unde necesse est, quod tale intervallum sit solummodo in intellectu obiective, sed Commentator dicit tertio Physicorum, quod relatio est una dispositio existens inter duo, et apparet etiam sine ipso, quod paternitas concipitur, quasi per modum medii, connectentis patrem cum filio, et sic de aliis relationibus. Ergo non potest poni relatio, nisi in apprehensione sola." See Henninger, *Relations*, 153–154 and Brower, "Perspectives on Relations," 41–47.

42. *Scriptum*, d. 8, p. 3, a. 6, n. 192 (Buytaert, II.1097:63–64; E-Scriptum, 33): "ista non exprimunt connotatum propter habitudinem aut relationem, sed ex propria conditione."

43. See *Scriptum*, d. 35, p. 1, a. 3 (E-Scriptum, 25:11314–26:17): "non est verum quod addatur connotatio rationi absolutae, sed additur connotatum; unde non est connotatio aliquod intermedium inter duo absoluta, sed exprimit conceptum duorum absolutorum mutuo connexorum, non per habitudinem mediam, sed per rationem propriam alterius absolutam."

44. *Scriptum*, d. 8, p. 3, a. 6, n. 192 (Buytaert, II.197:59–62; E-Scriptum, 33): "deitas per propriam rationem sic habet quod connotet diversa, sicut iustitia creata quod connotet unum, et clementia quod connotet aliud; et sic de aliis perfectionibus creatis."

45. *Scriptum*, d. 35, p. 1, a. 3 (E-Scriptum, 24:1220–21): "intelligere ad rationem deitatis nihil addat in recto, nec reale nec rationis, sed certum connotatum, scilicet praesentialitatem rei in esse apparenti."

but the concept of the Godhead is always connotative.[46] God cannot know the Godhead without simultaneously having all possible creatures connotated, just as someone who knows a hand simultaneously knows that it is *someone's* hand.

Simply put, the Godhead contains all creatures. The divine essence's very intelligibility includes all creatures indirectly. Thus, Auriol argues that the Godhead is the eminent exemplar of all creatures.[47] By eminent, Auriol means that God exists more excellently than creatures exist in themselves. No creature is God or his ontological equal, yet they are contained in God's very intelligibility. When God creates creatures, he creates them after the pattern of the Godhead, but they exist in a lower way than God exists.

Much of Auriol's theory of divine ideas can already be gleaned from what has been said about divine knowledge. He first notes that the terms 'idea' (*idea*) and 'exemplar' (*exemplar*) are not absolute terms because an exemplar is called the exemplar *of* something, and an idea is called an idea *of* something. Reference to something other than itself does not belong to absolute terms. Nevertheless, the term is not formally relative either because to be an idea or an exemplar is just to be that which something else imitates. The thing that imitates does not imitate a relation; it imitates some absolute reason (*ratio*). As a result, an exemplar or idea cannot be a relation according to its formal *ratio*. Therefore, Auriol says, an idea is a connotative reason (*ratio connotativa*) in the same way that things in the genus of substance sometimes connotate another things according to their substantial *rationes*. He appeals to the examples of the hand and flesh again. A hand is called the hand of something, and flesh is called the flesh of something.[48]

Connotative reasons entail something directly and some connotated thing indirectly. As a connotative reason, a divine idea or exemplar directly and principally entails the simple nature of the Godhead, which ideates and exemplifies every creature and which all creatures imitate. Indirectly and connotatively, ideas entail the creatures. An idea does not differ from the divine essence except as the same *ratio* is taken with the connotated thing and without the connotated thing. Thus, recourse to respects of imitability, real *rationes*, or anything else of the like is unnecessary.[49]

This account of divine ideas replaces his predecessors' metaphysical systems with a grammatical and logical account. A connotation is not a relation, and so Auriol avoids positing anything like a respect of imitability. Paladini summarizes Auriol's position well:

> Such [respects] do not exist between connotative extremes, because their relationship *is not due to a common similarity*, as is the case with extremes related

---

46. See Taieb, "What Is Cognition?: Peter Auriol's Account," 118.
47. See, e.g., *Scriptum*, d. 36, p. 2, a. 1 (E-Scriptum, 8:402–4): "deitas est et sub propria ratione per quam est omnis entitas eminenter, quia similitudo eminens cuiuslibet entitatis."
48. *Scriptum*, d. 36, p. 2, a. 1 (E-Scriptum, 6:291–99), esp.: "Est igitur ratio connotativa."
49. *Scriptum*, d. 36, p. 2, a. 1 (E-Scriptum, 6:302–7), esp.: "idea et exemplar non sunt aliquid principaliter et in recto nisi ipsamet simplex ratio deitatis . . . in obliquo vero et connotative importat idea huiusmodi creaturas." See *Scriptum*, d. 35, p. 1, a. 3 (E-Scriptum, 26:1368–27:1375).

to one another. On the contrary, the connoting item (the divine *intelligere*) refers directly to something quite different (i.e., the divine essence) than that to which it refers indirectly (i.e., the creatures).[50]

Ideas are not relations because no relation is required to have two absolute things relate to one another here. Relations entail some third thing—the respect—that mediates between the two extremes. Peter and Paul are similar because of the white in each of them. Connotative concepts only include the absolute *ratio* with the term, without any middle connecting relatedness, since the absolute *ratio* itself connects because of its condition. The very intelligible content of the concept "wing" connects it to the winged-being.[51] Divine ideas are connotative reasons because they are implied from the divine essence, and they do not have any distinct existence of their own. Just as the "rudder" connotes what is ruddered, so "divine idea" always denotes directly (*in recto*) God's essence and connotes creatures.

Auriol finds further evidence that divine ideas are *rationes connotativae* and not relations because the creatures connoted by the divine ideas do not exist in reality, at least initially. Ideas point toward *possible* creatures, which means that divine ideas have to do with a productive potency. "A productive principle is not related to the product, except after the actual production.... And therefore, it must be said that the Godhead, with no added relatedness, posits things in formed esse (*esse formatum*)."[52] Since the creature does not exist from eternity, it is impossible for two absolute things to be related. There is just God and his knowledge of a possible creature from eternity, which means there is only one absolute thing. Since there is only one absolute thing, God's knowledge of the possible creature—the divine idea—must be a connotative reason, not a relation or a respect.

Auriol finishes his account of divine ideas by saying that "a divine idea does not differ from the divine essence except as the same *ratio* taken with the connotated thing and without the connotated thing."[53] This last claim is puzzling and seems problematic for Auriol. In particular, it seems to fall under the weight of his own objection against a primary and secondary terminating object of God's act of knowing. If the divine essence can be taken with or without what is connotated, then God's act of understanding would terminate primarily in the knowledge of his essence without any connotation. His act of understanding would terminate secondarily in the knowledge of his essence with the connotation of divine ideas.

---

50. Paladini, "*Similitudo Aequivoca*," 220–21. Emphasis original.
51. *Scriptum*, d. 35, q. 1, a. 3 (E-Scriptum, 25:1292–1301). He appeals to Augustine, *De Trinitate* VII, c. 1 (PL 42.935): "nec omnino ad se dicitur color, sed semper alicuius colorati est." See Paladini, "*Similitudo Aequivoca*," 221.
52. *Scriptum*, d. 8, p. 3, a. 6, n. 192 (Buytaert, II.1027:67–70; E-Scriptum, 33): "Principium autem productivum non refertur ad productum, nisi post actualem productionem.... Et ideo dicendum quod deitas, nulla habitudine addita, ponit res in esse formato." Auriol seems to use the term *esse formatum* synonymously with the terms *esse obiective*, *esse intentionale*, *esse apparens*, and *esse in anima*.
53. *Scriptum*, d. 36, p. 2, a. 1 (E-Scriptum, 6:305–6): "non differt idea a divina essentia nisi sicut eadem ratio sumpta cum connotato et sine connotato."

How is this connotative account exempt from his criticism of the mirror analogy? If God can consider his essence both (1) directly only and (2) directly and obliquely, how are these considerations distinct from considering the mirror itself and considering what is in the mirror?

The only defense I can see is that perhaps Auriol is talking about a human way of understanding. The man and his hand do not differ in reality, but we could consider his hand without considering that it belongs to him. Similarly, we could consider the Godhead without considering the creatures connotated by the Godhead. In that case, Auriol's point is that the Godhead and divine ideas are identical even if some finite being did not consider them together. God would always know the Godhead with the connotated creatures. Auriol does not clarify who is understanding the Godhead with and without the connotated creatures.

Even if Auriol does understand his claim in this way, he still encounters another difficulty that comes from Scotus.[54] If God had to understand the connotated divine ideas with the divine essence such that he could never just know the divine essence, God's beatitude would depend upon knowing possible creatures. Thus, God's beatitude would depend upon something other than himself, which is unfitting. Auriol might try to get around this problem by saying that divine ideas are God's very Godhead. Therefore, God's beatitude would only depend on himself and his exemplary power.

The Plurality of Divine Ideas

After determining that an idea is a connotative reason, Auriol turns to the unity and plurality of divine ideas. His predecessors had to say that there are many ideas in God because they held that an idea is formally and principally and directly (*in recto*) something. If ideas were certain formally distinct reasons in God from the nature of the thing, respects of imitability fabricated by the divine intellect knowing the divine essence, or the creatures themselves posited in the divine intellect objectively, there must be many of them. However, all those antecedents are false, so it does not necessarily follow that there must be a plurality of divine ideas. Auriol insists upon the unity of divine ideas. An idea formally and directly (*in recto*) only entails that what is ideated and exemplified imitate God. All things imitate God according to the Godhead, which is one thing that is supremely simple both in reality and in reason. Therefore, it follows that there is only a single, simple thing for all creatures. Strictly speaking, there is only one divine idea because the Godhead is the only thing entailed principally and directly (*in recto*). The Godhead is the lone connotative reason, but divine ideas are multiplied in the connotated things that are entailed indirectly (*in obliquo*).[55]

His predecessors' accounts flounder because of their appeal to indeterminate concepts that need further specification to produce distinct cognition. Indeterminate

---

54. See p. 162.
55. *Scriptum*, d. 36, p. 2, a. 1 (E-Scriptum, 6:309–19).

concepts cannot be distinguished by their proper reasons since they introduce nothing determinately. The idea of a rose expresses a concept other than the idea of a man, not because the principle that the rose imitates is entirely indifferent but because of the rose that is connotated. Therefore, God is full of such reasons insofar as all these concepts, which are many, can be applied to him. Indeed, they are abstracted from the one simple *ratio* of the Godhead and its attributes.[56] Thus, divine ideas are, strictly speaking, one because only one thing is imitated, the Godhead, yet they are many because many possible creatures are connoted.[57]

Auriol places far more weight on the unity of divine ideas than he does on the plurality of divine ideas. He emphasizes the unity of divine ideas because of his emphasis on the Godhead being the single exemplar for every creature. He admits the plurality of divine ideas so that his theory ensures God's perfect knowledge of all possible creatures, but the many divine ideas "ultimately play no role in creation. They exclusively serve God's knowledge of creatures."[58] Like Petrus de Trabibus, Auriol rejects the claim that divine ideas are formally *rationes cognoscendi*. Nevertheless, he admits that they do serve that role as an object denominating or connotating creatures. Divine ideas are necessary for God's knowledge of creatures, and if God knew his essence without what is connotated in it, he would not know creatures.[59] Nevertheless, creatures do not imitate divine ideas; they imitate the *deitas*.

Auriol's emphasis on the unity of divine ideas raises a question. If there are many ideas so that God will know all the creatures, how can God create many creatures if there is but one exemplar, the divine essence, and the plurality of divine ideas play no role in the act of creation? If divine ideas are not models for creation, how can Auriol explain the diversity of creatures that God has created? Auriol responds that the Godhead, as an exemplar cause, is an "equivocal likeness" (*similitudo aequivoca*).[60] This answer is an adaptation of the longstanding claim that God is an equivocal cause. Auriol's predecessors make a distinction between univocal causes and equivocal causes. Univocal causes share the nature of the effect that they produce. Reproduction is a standard example of univocal causality. Equivocal causes do not share the nature of what they effect. In the cosmology of the day, celestial bodies are frequently appealed to as equivocal causes, and God is the equivocal cause *par excellence*. They are the cause of the effect's form, and so can be called the cause of their being, not merely their coming-to-be.[61] Importantly, although equivocal causes do

---

56. *Scriptum*, d. 36, p. 2, a. 1 (E-Scriptum, 7:345–51).

57. See *Scriptum*, d. 36, p. 2, ad 3, 4, et 5 (E-Scriptum, 19:1030–35), esp.: "ideae formaliter non sunt plures rationes absolutae nec plures respectus, sed est una ratio connotans plura."

58. Paladini, "*Similitudo Aequivoca*," 236. See Conti, "Divine Ideas in Auriol," 115.

59. *Scriptum*, d. 36, p. 2, a. 1 (E-Scriptum, 8:418–29). See pp. 129–30.

60. *Scriptum*, d. 35, p. 3, a. 2 (E-Scriptum, 13:663–66): "non est impossibile, nec repugnatiam aut contradictionem includens, quod sit aliqua forma quae, per suam simplicem rationem formalem, similitudo sit inter se dissimilium quidditatum et naturarum, similitudo tamen aequivoca et alterius speciei seu generis ab eo cuius est similitudo."

61. For Aquinas on the nature of equivocal causality, see Aquinas, *SCG* I, c. 2 (Leonine, 13.89); *De veritate*, q. 10, a. 13, ad 3 (Leonine, 22/2.345:158–70); *ST* I, q. 4, a. 2 (Leonine, 4.51–52); *ST* I, q. 104,

not share in the nature of the effects they cause, the effect's nature is in the equivocal cause *in some way*. The effect must be in the cause in some way because every agent makes something like itself (*omne agens agit sibi simile*).[62] We saw Aquinas use this principle to argue that God has ideas in Chapter II.[63]

Auriol changes this vision of equivocal causality by rejecting the principle *omne agens agit sibi simile*. For earlier authors, a cause could be equivocal, but the likeness by which it was a cause still had to be univocal. The form in the mind of the artist, for example, had to be formally identical to the artwork he produces (barring some error in production). In accord with the Fourth Lateran Council, each author insisted that there is always a greater dissimilarity between God and creatures than similarity, but there is some similarity.[64] Auriol takes the claim even further, saying that the Godhead does not correspond to any creature in particular. If there were a corresponding likeness to one particular creature (or set of creatures), no other creatures could be made. As Paladini notes, "In order to represent all of them, it must represent no-one."[65] God is so unlike creatures that his essence can be a likeness of each despite not having any one-to-one correspondence to any creature. Auriol takes to the extreme Bonaventure's claim that God can exemplify possible creatures in every category of being because he transcends every category of being.[66]

Auriol's predecessors thought there must be a univocal likeness in God because they misunderstood God's transcendence. They thought that because both God and artists are exemplary causes that what is true of the created artist must be true of the divine artist, only in a higher (but univocal) way. This way of thinking, Auriol argues, is mistaken. The divine essence is an equivocal likeness.[67]

The Existence of Things in God

One of the marks of Auriol's theory of cognition is that the extramental thing and the concept of that thing appearing to the knower are numerically one.[68] The cognized object is not a distinct thing from the extramental thing. The concept and

---

a. 1 (Leonine, 5.464). See also Cornelio Fabro, *Participation et Causalité Selon s. Thomas d'Aquin* (Louvain: Publications Universitaires, 1961), 338–39; Wippel, *Metaphysical Thought*, 517–18; Meehan, *Efficient Causality*, 320.

62. See, for example, Aquinas, SCG II, c. 45 (Leonine ed., 13.372). See also, Wippel, *Metaphysical Themes II*, 152–72.

63. See p. 63.

64. Denzinger and Schönmetzer, *Enchiridion Symbolorum*, n. 806.

65. Paladini, "*Similitudo Aequivoca*," 233. See *Scriptum*, d. 35, p. 3, a. 2 (E-Scriptum, 12:617–20; 14:702–7; 15:744–47).

66. See p. 27.

67. This line of thinking is indebted to Averroes, who argues that we can only predicate 'knowledge' of God and man equivocally. See p. 5 and Paladini, "*Similitudo Aequivoca*," 230–32.

68. *Scriptum*, d. 27, p. 2, a. 2 (E-Scriptum, 16:584–88), esp.: "considerandum est quod res in esse formato posita non claudit in se aliquid absolutum nisi ipsam realitatem. Unde non ponit in numerum res et sua intentio quantum ad aliquid absolutum, claudit tamen aliquid respectivum, videlicet apparere." See Friedman, "Act, Species, and Appearance," 144.

the thing are the same thing, and they differ only according to their mode of existence (*modus essendi*). Extramental things have real existence, and concepts have *esse obiectivum*, which Auriol also calls *esse intentionale* and, most famously, *esse apparens*.[69] What sort of *esse* is *esse apparens*? What is its ontological status?

Auriol's answer to this question is deflationary, and it makes use of a variety of terms that are familiar from earlier chapters. Intentional being "is nothing other than *esse* in the soul."[70] Being in the soul is contrasted with extramental being. Extramental being is being absolutely (*simpliciter*), whereas being in the soul is qualified and diminished being (*secundum quid, deminuta*). When Auriol says diminished being, however, he does not mean to say that the objects of that being have any real, independent being. Being in the soul is, strictly speaking, nothingness (*nihilitas*) and nothing in itself (*nihil in se*).[71]

Many creatures are connotated when God knows the Godhead, but those creatures are not anything in and of themselves. Yet, the creatures cannot be absolutely nothing since God knows them. Only what does not exist in reality and is not even thought is absolutely nothing. God's knowledge raises the creatures connotated in the Godhead above pure or absolute nothingness, but it does not follow that they have any being of their own. If they had any being of their own, as the traditional interpretation of Henry of Ghent declares, then creatures would not be made from nothing (*de nihilo*).[72] Thus, Auriol insists that intentional being is nothing in itself.

The *esse intentionale* of divine ideas is nothing in itself because divine ideas are ontologically identical to the Godhead. If divine ideas had any sort of existence independent of the Godhead, then God would not be simple. Moreover, since the vision of the divine ideas is a most blessed vision and the only thing that gives a most blessed vision is the Godhead, the *esse* of divine ideas must be identical to the Godhead. The divine essence has the character of an idea, exemplar, and principal form but not insofar as it is a cognized object or *ratio cognoscendi*. It is an idea, exemplar, and principal form insofar as the Godhead under its proper *ratio* connotes every possible creature since it is an equivocal likeness of each being. Thus, *esse cognitum* (*esse intentionale, esse obiectivum, esse apparens*) does not give it the character of an idea. *Esse cognitum* belongs extrinsically to divine ideas, but it plays no role in the character of an idea. It certainly plays no role in the act of creation since creatures imitate the divine essence, not *esse cognitum*.[73]

Like his predecessors, Auriol holds that divine ideas are necessary since God necessarily knows them. By itself, this claim is unproblematic because it points to

---

69. *Scriptum*, d. 27, p. 2, a. 2, (E-Scriptum, 10:356–66): "in omni intellectione emanat et procedit, non aliquid aliud, sed ipsamet res cognita in quodam esse obiectivo, secundum quod habet terminare intuitum intellectus."
70. *Scriptum*, d. 27, p. 2, a. 2 (E-Scriptum, 12:445–46): "in esse intentionali, quod nihil aliud est quam esse in anima."
71. *Scriptum*, d. 27, p. 2, a. 2 (E-Scriptum, 17:603–11).
72. *Scriptum*, d. 36, p. 1 (E-Scriptum, 11:577–78). See pp. 106–9.
73. *Scriptum*, d. 36, p. 2, a. 1 (E-Scriptum, 8:401–10).

the perfection of God. Auriol's theory of divine ideas goes a step further, however. His emphasis on creatures being like the divine essence, not their idea, makes imitability characteristic of the divine essence. "God," Auriol says, "is a likeness of all things without any mediating relatedness or respect."[74] According to Conti, this shift makes creation necessary because the effect of imitability is creation. It follows that creation "becomes just as necessary as the divine essence itself—an evident heresy."[75] Auriol's novel explanation of future contingents and divine foreknowledge might allow him to escape this criticism, but, at minimum, Auriol's theory of divine ideas and divine exemplarity give cause for concern that creation becomes necessary.[76]

I think Auriol can escape Conti's criticism because Auriol rejects bivalence, the claim that a proposition is necessarily true or false. Propositions about the future are neither true nor false. If they were necessarily one or the other, then they would cease to be contingent. Instead, they would be immutable and necessary. Since future contingent propositions are neither true nor false, not even God knows them in a way that makes them true or false. Thus, future contingents remain contingent even though God knows them. Creation remains a contingent act. God's knowledge of the future does not make the contingent future proposition either true or false.[77]

THE SCOPE OF DIVINE IDEAS

Given that Auriol is a nominalist (conceptualist) and thinks that everything outside the mind is singular, we can easily guess that his theory of the scope of divine ideas includes singulars. Moreover, we can expect him to be critical of any theory that excludes divine ideas of singulars. Auriol does not disappoint. He begins *Scriptum*, d. 36, p. 2, q. 2—the question on the scope of divine ideas—by criticizing Aquinas

---

74. *Scriptum*, d. 35, p. 3, a. 2 (E-*Scriptum*, 13:648–49): "Deus est similitudo rerum omnium absque omni habitudine media seu respectu."

75. Conti, "Divine Ideas in Auriol," 115–16. Conti cites Lauge Olaf Nielson, "Dictates of Faith versus Dictates of Reason: Peter Auriole on Divine Power, Creation, and Human Rationality," *Documenti e studi sulla tradizione filosofica medievale* 7, no. 1 (1996): 213–41.

76. See, *inter alia*, Normore, "Future Contingents"; Normore, "Petrus Aureoli and His Contemporaries on Future Contingents and Excluded Middle"; Schabel, *Theology at Paris*; Mark N. A. Thakkar, "Peter Auriol and the Logic of Future Contingents" (Ph.D. diss., University of Oxford, 2010).

77. See *Scriptum*, d. 38, a. 3 (E-*Scriptum*, 14–21), esp.: "notitia divina quam de actualitatibus futurorum contingentium habet non dat ut propositio affirmativa praecise vel negativa praecise formata de futuro sit vera vel falsa, immo relinquit utramque neque veram neque falsam. Nulla enim notitia dat propositioni de futuro veritatem vel falsitatem nisi illa quae tendit in futurum ut distans per modum notitiae expectativae—et ratio huius est quia notitia quae dat determinationem alicui pro aliquo instanti, debet coexistere illi instanti; si ergo dat determinationem pro instantibus praecedentibus actualitatem, necessario debet illa notitia praecedere actualitatem et eam aspicere ut posteriorem et distantem, et per consequens est notitia expectativa; sed declaratum est supra quod notitia Dei non est expectativa futuri, nec tendit in ipsum tanquam in distans—unde non praecedit actualitatem futuri; ergo non dabit determinationem illi actualitati pro aliquo instanti praecedenti, et per consequens nec propositio formanda habebit a divina notitia quod sit vera vel falsa."

and Henry for denying divine ideas of singulars.[78] However, as we will see, he is unwilling to go as far as Bonaventure and Scotus on the scope of divine ideas and posit a complete plenitude of divine ideas.[79]

Auriol begins his account of the scope of divine ideas by reminding his readers not to fall back into a theory of rational relations. Things do not imitate divine ideas. Instead, all things have one common, simply indistinct idea, namely the *ratio* of the supremely simple Godhead. Therefore, the whole property and vast multitude of ideas must be taken in the things connotated, or even in general and confused concepts. Only the things connotated can distinguish these general and confused concepts because, as we saw above, the divine essence is an equivocal likeness of all possible creatures.[80] It can be applied indeterminately to anything that imitates it. Thus, the precision or imprecision does not hold on God's part, as his predecessors imagined, but only on the part of the thing connotated.[81] Since the divine essence is a likeness of creatures indeterminately, the determination by which God knows creatures cannot be immediate, but by a mediating demonstration, which comes on the part of the thing connotated. The divine intellect understands this or that signate stone to the extent that the divine essence represents not only *stone* certain and distinct in itself but knows it with demonstrability or a demonstration of that stone, which entails "this stone."[82]

With this caveat in place, Auriol determines the criterion by which to judge the scope of divine ideas. Everything that an angelic or human intellect can intuit distinctly and separately, the *ratio* of the Godhead connotes simply as distinct and separated. Thus, Auriol determines the scope of divine ideas by the criterion of separability. Certain things are inseparable from each thing understood. So, the Godhead connotes them as indistinct insofar as it is their exemplar and eminent likeness, not as separable or separated, but rather as impossible to separate.[83]

Auriol immediately sets to work applying this criterion. Neither form and matter nor relative and absolute accidents are independent things (*res praecisae*). Instead, these relate as act and actualizable. Thus, they do not have distinct ideas because they cannot be connotated as distinct. Second intentions are also not distinctly connotated since they are respects of reason, but Auriol is still willing to admit that they have co-ideas with the primary intentions, without which they are not understood. Primary intentions, like *man* and *animal*, are not distinct

---

78. Like Scotus, Auriol simply gets Aquinas's position wrong. It is unclear whether his error is due to a faulty version of the *ST*, following the errant position of certain Thomists like John of Paris, or if Auriol is just expressing the standard, but errant, interpretation of Aquinas. For his description of Aquinas's and Henry's positions, see *Scriptum*, d. 36, p. 2, a. 2 (E-Scriptum, 8:440-9:478). See pp. 287-88 for Scotus's misunderstanding of Aquinas and pp. 78-81 for Aquinas himself.
79. See pp. 36-40 and 190-91.
80. See pp. 221-22 above for equivocal similitude.
81. *Scriptum*, d. 36, p. 2, a. 2 (E-Scriptum, 9:491-504).
82. *Scriptum*, d. 35, p. 4, a. 3 (E-Scriptum, 23:1146-50).
83. *Scriptum*, d. 36, p. 2, a. 2 (E-Scriptum, 10:505-10), esp.: "omnia quae intellectus angelicus vel humanus potest intueri distincte et separatim connotat simpliciter ratio deitatis ut distincta et separata."

things for Auriol since neither genera nor species exist independently, but they have distinct ideas because they are distinctly conceivable. They are connoted as distinct, and they shine forth again in the divine intellect as distinct, as if something extramental were intuited. Since they are of another grade below the species, individuals of abstracted substances are represented and connoted as distinct. Similarly, signate individuals are represented by a distinct reason (*ratio*) and have distinct ideas.[84]

Auriol summarizes his theory of the scope of divine ideas, then, as restricted to individuals, species, and genera of the category of substance. There are no distinct ideas for anything other than these, although other things have co-ideas with those things from which they are inseparable. Accidents, form and matter, and second intentions are, as it were, co-understood with their substances, and so have co-ideas.[85] It is as if the accidents, for example, come along for free with their substance such that distinct knowledge of the substance is enough to know them distinctly.

With the scope of positive entities in place, Auriol turns to divine ideas of privations and negations. He is particularly concerned with the privation of evil. The Godhead is an eminent likeness of privations and negations such that the divine intuition terminated to the Godhead is said to have reached every negation and every privation equivalently in a certain eminent likeness.[86] This statement is true but vague. Moreover, this question is further complicated because negations and privations are not actually in things.[87]

As a result, Auriol distinguishes two ways of discussing evil: It is one thing to say that evils cannot be understood without some created good, and it is another thing to say that evils cannot be understood except through a created good as through a *ratio cognoscendi*. The first way of speaking is true because evils cannot be known without a twofold created good: the good that is being deprived, and the good substratum from which that good is deprived. Blindness is the deprivation of the good of sight from some seeing being. Neither of these goods is God since he is neither the subject of privation nor a deprivable good. The second way of speaking is false because no habit represents its privation, and so cannot be a formal principle of knowing that privation. Therefore, Auriol concludes, the divine intellect by knowing its essence knows all evils because the Godhead is a certain eminent likeness and exemplar, not through the notion of the good. He does not know evils insofar they are evil because, as such, they are privations and nothing. Neither does he know them insofar as they are in things because they cannot actually be in things according to real being. Thus, the Godhead is their likeness according as they are

---

84. *Scriptum*, d. 36, p. 2, a. 2 (E-Scriptum, 10:510–21).
85. *Scriptum*, d. 36, p. 2, a. 2 (E-Scriptum, 10:522–24): "individua, species, et genera de praedicamento substantiae habent distinctas ideas, cetera vero non, quamvis habeant aliqualiter co-ideas cum illis a quibus separari non possunt."
86. *Scriptum*, d. 36, p. 2, a. 2 (E-Scriptum, 10:535–37).
87. *Scriptum*, d. 36, p. 2, a. 2 (E-Scriptum, 11:579–81).

beings of reason having intentional being, but evils are not in God, nor do they live in him. They are in him only according to intentional being.[88]

Auriol does not explicitly consider the number of divine ideas. However, there must be an infinite number because an infinite number of possible individuals, species, and genera are connotated. This infinite is not quite as full as the infinite posited by Bonaventure and Scotus since the latter extended the scope of divine ideas to each thing and each of its aspects.[89]

Auriol is not entirely clear what he means by 'co-idea' (*co-idea*). The term only appears three times in *Scriptum*, dd. 35–36, and he never clarifies it. All that is clear about co-ideas is that they are of things that are not understood as distinct. But if those things are not understood as distinct, why say that there are ideas of them at all? Perhaps Auriol uses the term to emphasize that God knows each aspect of each thing even though he does not have a distinct idea of each aspect of each thing.

Auriol's theory of the scope of divine ideas also suffers the difficulty that Auriol does not adequately explain his separability criterion. Why does being able to exist separately determine the scope of divine ideas, especially since divine ideas play no role in the actual existence of things? Moreover, if separability is the criterion, why do first intentions (genera and species like *animal* and *man*) make the cut? First intentions do not exist extramentally for Auriol. How exactly can the species *man* be connotated as distinct if it cannot exist as distinct? They only exist in singulars. It would seem like Auriol's adherence to nominalism and the criterion of separability should reduce the scope of divine ideas to singulars only.

RECAPITULATION AND CONCLUSIONS

Peter Auriol's theory of divine ideas amounts to a rejection of divine ideas. Auriol places so great an emphasis on God's simplicity that divine ideas cannot really exist. It is the Godhead and the Godhead alone that functions as the exemplar of all creatures. Divine ideas play no role in the production of things. Auriol does seem to preserve the necessity of divine ideas for God's knowledge of creatures, but he is the first to articulate a theory of divine ideas in which divine ideas are not models of creatures.

He further breaks with his predecessors in denying that divine ideas are reasons or respects. He rejects all metaphysical speculation on divine ideas and replaces the metaphysical with a logical and grammatical account. Divine ideas are connotative reasons (*rationes connotativae*) of the divine essence. Since connotations always connote something, divine ideas are ideas of creatures. The divine essence, or in Auriol's technical language, the Godhead (*deitas*), connotes each creature since it is the *similitudo aequivoca* of each possible creature. This likeness is present in the divine essence

---

88. *Scriptum*, d. 36, p. 2, a. 2 (E-Scriptum, 13:662–86), esp.: "intellectus divinus cognoscendo suam essentiam cognoscit omnia mala non per rationem boni, sed quia deitas est quaedam similitudo eminens et exemplar."

89. See pp. 36–40 and 190–91.

logically before the act of the divine intellect. If he had articulated a metaphysically robust account of divine ideas, divine ideas would have been real relations in God and fallen under Scotus's criticism.[90] As it is, Auriol's grammatical and logical account, coupled with his innovative theory of divine foreknowledge and future contingents, avoids both Scotus's real relation criticism and divine necessitarianism. Moreover, the divine essence must have those connotations independent of the divine intellect's action because if they were not already there, then the divine intellect would not find them when it understood the divine essence.

The scope of divine ideas for Auriol extends to individuals, species, and genera in the category of substance. Form, matter, second intentions, and accidents do not have distinct ideas, although he says that they have co-ideas. The scope of divine ideas is infinite but not as plentifully infinite as we find in Bonaventure's and Scotus's theories. Bonaventure and Scotus posit an infinite number of individuals in an infinite number of species and genera in every category of being. Auriol's theory includes an infinite number of divine ideas, but they are not in an infinite number of species and genera in every category of being. In particular, his denial of divine ideas of accidents renders his account of the infinite number of divine ideas more restricted than Bonaventure's and Scotus's accounts. As in his account of the status of divine ideas, it is not clear that his account of the scope of divine ideas is entirely cogent, and he leaves a lot of questions unanswered.

---

90. See pp. 165–66.

Chapter X.
William of Ockham (ca. 1285–1347)

William of Ockham was born at about 1285 in the village of Ockham, just southwest of London. He joined the Franciscan order at the age of fourteen and was ordained a priest before June 19, 1318, when he received a license to hear confessions. Ockham began studying at about 1309 and commented on Peter Lombard's *Sentences* sometime between 1317–1319. He completed all the requirements to become a regent master. He even gave the first inaugural lecture (the *inceptio*) characteristic of becoming a regent master, but he never occupied the chair at Oxford. His writings are clearly distinguished into two periods. Ockham wrote primarily on logic, metaphysics, epistemology, and physics in the earlier period, developing his nominalist system. Ockham wrote almost exclusively on politics and the relationship between the Church and the state in the later period.

This dramatic shift can be attributed to two factors, the first of which was that John Lutteral, the Chancellor of Oxford, brought charges of heresy against Ockham. In 1324 Ockham was summoned to the papal court in Avignon to answer these charges. The committee investigating Ockham censured some of his teachings, but he was never formally condemned. The second factor was that the dispute over Franciscan poverty reignited while Ockham was in Avignon. The Franciscans insisted that neither the individual friars nor the order owned any property. Pope John XXII disagreed. On May 26, 1328, Ockham fled Avignon with the Minister General, Michael of Cesena, and the order's seal. The friars who fled were excommunicated and lived in Germany under the protection of the Emperor. There is no evidence that Ockham was reconciled to the Church at his death on April 10, 1347.[1]

---

1. For more on Ockham's life, see Léon Baudry, *Guillaum d'Occam: Sa Vie, Ses Oeuvres, Ses Ideés Sociales et Politiques*, vol. 1 (Paris, 1949); C. K. Brampton, "Traditions Relating to the Death of William of Ockham," *Archivum Franciscanum Historicum* 53 (1960): 442–49; Léon Baudry, "L'Ordre Franciscain Au Temps de Guillaume d'Occam," *Medieval Studies* 27 (1965): 184–211; James A. Weisheipl, "Ockham and Some Mertonians," *Mediaeval Studies* 30, no. 1 (1968): 164–74; Gedeon Gál, "William of Ockham Died 'Impenitent' in April 1347," *Franciscan Studies* 42, no. 1 (1982): 90–95; William J. Courtenay, *Schools & Scholars in Fourteenth-Century England* (Princeton, NJ: Princeton University Press, 1987); Francis E. Kelley, "Ockham: Avignon, Before and After," in *From Ockham to Wyclif*, ed. Anne Hudson and Michael Wilks (Oxford: Oxford University Press, 1987); Philotheus Boehner, "Editor's Introduction," in *Philosophical Writings*, rev. Stephen F. Brown (Indianapolis, IN: Hackett Publishing Co., 1990); Armand A. Maurer, *William of Ockham*, 1–3.

For Ockham's disagreements with Lutterell, especially on divine ideas, see Hoenen, *Marsilius of Inghen*, 139–40.

THE STATUS OF DIVINE IDEAS

Ockham endorsed the Nominalist Theory of divine ideas. As noted in the introduction to Part V, Nominalist Theories of divine ideas have several characteristic marks: They maintain a strict emphasis on divine simplicity, consider divine ideas as connotations rather than something more metaphysically real, emphasize their fidelity to Augustine's theory, and ultimately reject divine ideas. Each of these aspects is on full display in Ockham's theory of divine ideas since his theory is a direct outgrowth of his nominalism. Thus, to make sense of Ockham's theory of divine ideas, I will first make some remarks about Ockham's nominalism, his account of divine knowledge as a divine attribute, and his account of God's knowledge of things other than himself. After these preliminary remarks, we will be able to address the questions of what a divine idea is, the necessity of positing them, whether they are principles of speculative or practical knowledge, and how things exist in God.

Nominalism

Robert Guelluy claims that "Ockham's whole nominalism is contained in the way he treats the problem of distinction."[2] Ockham rejects anything less than a real distinction in extramental beings. "It is impossible," he writes, "that things differ formally in creatures unless they are really distinguished."[3] Thus, every singular thing is singular through itself, and every extramental thing is singular and numerically one.[4]

Anton Pegis has argued that this position is the consequence of accepting the Platonic assumption that being and unity are opposed.[5] The Platonic solution to the one and the many pits the intelligibility of being against unity. In the *Sophist*, Plato explains the multiplicity of Forms by arguing that the *logos* of Sameness is distinct both from the *logos* of Difference and from the *logos* of Being. Each of the Forms is the same as itself and different from all others. It is this sameness and difference that preserves the Form's intelligibility and its relation to other Forms.[6] Each Form has a qualified unity precisely because inherent in each Form is that it is the same as itself and different from all others. Difference and nonbeing are necessary to understand every Form, and they are intrinsic to the very character of the Form. Thus, "the whole of being must be considered not only as being but also as

---

2. Robert Guelluy, *Philosophe et Theologie Chez Guillaume d' Ockham* (Louvain: E. Nauwelaerts, 1947), 333.
3. *Ord.* I, d. 2, q. 6 (OTh II.173:12–13): "impossibile est in creaturis aliqua differre formaliter nisi distinguantur realiter."
4. *Ord.* I, d. 2, q. 6 (OTh II.196:3 and 13–14).
5. Anton C. Pegis, "The Dilemma of Being and Unity," in *Essays in Thomism*, ed. Robert E. Brennan (New York: Sheed and Ward, 1942), 153: "For it is only on the basis of a Platonic assumption that Ockham escapes from Platonism in the particular way that he does; which is the escape of a thinker who also remains a disciple."
6. Plato, *Sophist*, 243D–245E, 250BC, 257A, 258BC, 259A–E (Cooper, 264–67, 272, 280, 281–82, 282–83).

non-being, for non-being is the mysterious co-principle of its interior intelligibility."[7] Every being is interiorly constituted by being and nonbeing.

Given that every being is intelligible only insofar as it is a complex of sameness and difference, no being can have unity, strictly speaking. Every being will lack unity insofar as it is intelligible. Only what is beyond being and beyond intelligibility could be completely unified. Thus, it is no surprise that Plato posits the Form of the Good as beyond being and that Plotinus does the same with the One.[8] So, Pegis notes, "the intelligible character of being makes radically impossible the identification of being and unity. By nature, a being can be whole, but it cannot be one."[9] Being is, at least to a certain extent, opposed to unity.

Christian thinkers will be especially troubled by this opposition because they want to ascribe supreme unity, supreme intelligence, and intelligibility to God. Most authors in this study reject this dilemma—God is both the highest being and supremely one. Ockham accepts the opposition of being and unity and consistently identifies what is indistinguishable with the individual. There can be no universals outside of the mind precisely because then singular beings would not be one.

Even if we assume that some universal, *a*, exists extramentally, close analysis reveals that this universal is singular, not universal. Does *a* contain many things essentially, or is it precisely one thing? If *a* contains many things, then those things included essentially must be either numerically finite or infinite. They cannot be infinite because the existence of an actual infinite is impossible. If they are numerically finite, then each of them is one in number. Thus, the resulting whole will be one in number. Of course, if *a* is precisely one thing, it is singular because something that does not include many distinct things is numerically one thing. Thus, despite assuming otherwise, the universal *a* will be singular.[10] The whole notion of a universal or common reality comes to nothing.

Ockham argues further that every extramental being will still be singular even if we ignore this argument and grant that *a* is added to Socrates. Are *a* and Socrates, he asks, many things or not? If not, *a* is a singular thing because Socrates is a singular thing. If they are many things but not infinitely many, then they will be numerically finite. In fact, on this supposition, *a* and Socrates must be exactly two things, each of which is numerically one. Therefore, this universal *a* is numerically one and so singular.[11]

The world is composed entirely of singulars because there are no universal essences, and nothing in the world is common to more than one thing. There are only individual essences, some of which are maximally similar to other individual

---

7. Pegis, "Being and Unity," 157.
8. See Plato, *Republic* VI–VII (Cooper, 1107–55); Plotinus, *Enneads* VI, 9, 1–2 (Armstrong, VII.302–11).
9. Pegis, "Being and Unity," 157.
10. *In Porph.*, proem., §2 (OPh II.11:35–48).
11. *In Porph.*, proem., §2 (OPh II.11:49–12:56), esp.: "Sed quando sunt tantum duae res, utraque illarum est una secundum numerum; ergo ista rest universalis est una secundum numerum et per consequens est singularis."

essences. Socrates's essence is an essential part of him that is not distinct from him or shared by anyone else.[12] Thus, a singular "is one in the sense of being indistinct and indistinguishable from the standpoint of the intellect."[13] We cannot inspect a singular and find rational or formal distinctions. Ockham's theory "maintains unity by driving out intelligibility."[14] If singulars had universal essences, then they would not be one.

Divine Attributes

Our inability to find rational or formal distinctions in singulars is especially true of God. Strictly speaking, God does not have any attributes.

> I say that there are not any attributable perfections [in God], but there is only one perfection indistinct in reality and in reason, which properly and by virtue of speech ought not to be said to be in God or in the divine essence, but is in every way the divine essence itself.[15]

If they were distinguished in reality, then there would be as many gods as divine attributes, which is abhorrent. Divine attributes are not even distinguishable by reason because everything that is distinguished is distinguished by something.[16] However, there is nothing already distinguished on God's part by which we could distinguish by reason.

Ockham only grants that God has many attributes if we use terms improperly. Divine attributes are distinguished rationally because they are nothing but certain mental, vocal, or written predicables that are naturally suited to signify and supposit for God. These predicables can be investigated by natural reason and applied to God.[17] The divine attributes are just concepts or signs that can be predicated of God truly.[18] These attributes fall into three categories: The first sort implies the divine essence absolutely and affirmatively, like intellect and will. The second sort implies the divine essence connotatively by connoting something other than it, like creating. The third sort implies the divine essence negatively, like incorruptibility. Ockham stresses that these divine attributes are not the divine essence because they are just concepts or names. The divine essence is not many concepts or names.[19] We distinguish them rationally, but they are not rationally distinct in

---

12. See *Ord.* I, d. 2, q. 5 (OTh II.158:20–159:2).
13. Pegis, "Being and Unity," 167.
14. Pegis, "Being and Unity," 168.
15. *Ord.* I, d. 2, q. 2 (OTh II.61:18–21): "dico quod non sunt plures perfectiones attributales, sed tantum est ibi una perfectio indistincta re et ratione, quae proprie et de virtute sermonis non debet dici esse in Deo vel in divina essentia, sed est omnibus modis ipsa divina essentia."
16. *Quodlibet* III, q. 2 (OTh IX.210:45): "proprie loquendo si aliquid distinguitur, ab aliquo distinguitur." For Ockham's denial of rational distinction, see *Ord.*, d. 2, q. 3 (OTh II.75:4–77:6).
17. *Quodlibet* III, q. 2 (OTh IX.211:58–62).
18. *Ord.* I, d. 2, q. 2 (OTh II.61:22–23).
19. *Ord.* I, d. 2, q. 2 (OTh II.62:5–17).

God. All these concepts or names are various ways that we understand God's supremely simple essence.[20]

Ockham holds, then, that we can predicate 'intellect' of God. If God has intellect, then it is natural to affirm that he knows, since it would be unfitting for God's intellect to be in potency. Nevertheless, it proves hard to show how God has knowledge. The first problem to emerge concerns the term 'knowledge' (*scientia*). As two objectors point out, knowledge is the effect of a demonstration, passing from the knowledge of premises to true and necessary conclusions. Moreover, knowledge is a certain habit inclining the knower to exercise an act of knowledge. But God does not come to know by demonstrating conclusions, nor does he have any habitual disposition to know conclusions.[21] As Maurer points out, given what Ockham says about divine attributes, "we should not say that he *has* knowledge or that knowledge is *in* him, but that he *is* his knowledge, for it is identical with his essence."[22] So, how can God's knowledge be explained?

Ockham considers Aquinas's theory that immateriality is the reason that something is cognitive. Knowers are distinguished from non-knowers because the former can have the form of another thing as a species in it, whereas the latter only have their own forms. The natures of non-knowers are thus more limited than the natures of knowers. Since limitation is only through matter, a thing's immateriality makes it a knower. Since God is supremely immaterial, he is supremely a knower.[23] Aquinas's conclusion is true, but his reasoning is insufficient for several reasons, Ockham says: First, if the reception of other forms is characteristic of knowledge, then so is potency-to-receive. Since no one wants to posit potency in God, "[i]t seems that Aquinas's argument that God is a knower is based on an epistemological premise that Aquinas did not want, in the end, to apply to God!"[24] This objection is a strawman. Aquinas never states that the knower must receive other forms, only that it is characterized by having them. A being that has other forms without receiving them would qualify as a knower for Aquinas, and God is just such a knower.

Ockham's second objection hits closer to home, even though it still depends on reception. By Aquinas's own admission, the medium between the thing known and the knower receives the species of the thing known.[25] Thus, the medium should be a knower, but it is not. If Aquinas were to respond that the medium does not receive the species immaterially but materially, then his argument loses all its force. Whatever is received is received through the mode of the receiver, so a species is received immaterially because the receiver is immaterial. Therefore, such a reception should be concluded more from the immateriality of the thing than vice versa.[26]

---

20. See Maurer, *William of Ockham*, 184–204; Marilyn McCord Adams, *William Ockham* (Notre Dame, IN: University of Notre Dame Press, 1987), II.903–60.
21. *Ord.* I, d. 35, q. 1, arg. 1–2 (OTh IV.424:10–15).
22. Maurer, *William of Ockham*, 205. Emphasis original.
23. *Ord.* I, d. 35, q. 1 (OTh IV.425:4–11); See Aquinas, *ST* I, q. 14, a. 1 (Leonine, 4.166).
24. Adams, *William Ockham*, II.1018.
25. Aquinas, *De veritate*, q. 18, a. 1, ad 1 (Leonine, 22/2.532:227–533:302).
26. *Ord.* I, d. 35, q. 1 (OTh IV.426:4–12).

Even if we consider the immateriality only, Aquinas's argument would still fail. Immateriality is not the reason that something is cognitive. Many accidents are immaterial, and, as Averroes argues, the form of heaven is immaterial, but neither of these are cognitive. Ockham does not think the form of heaven is immaterial, but he finds no formal contradiction in the claim, which would have to be found if immateriality were the reason for knowledge.[27]

Ockham's answer to the question begins by recalling that the word 'knowledge' (*scientia*) can be used generally for all knowing and not merely in the technical sense of knowing caused through demonstration. God's knowledge is not caused in any way. He then offers an *a priori* demonstration that God has knowledge, although it is a demonstration in the broadest sense. Strictly speaking, a demonstration ascertains the reason why the conclusion is true. In this case, the argument cannot assign a reason or cause why God is a knower since his knowledge has no cause. All Ockham has is an argument from one proposition to another by a one-way formal inference: "God is the supreme being; therefore, he is understanding, knowing, and cognizing." This proposition is not convertible. It does not follow from the fact that a being is understanding, knowing, and cognizing that it is God. Thus, God knows.[28]

Ockham turns from the fact of God's knowledge to how God knows. Like every other author in this study, Ockham insists that divine essence is the primary object of God's intellect. If it were not, then that other primary object would be prior, and so there would be something prior to the divine essence, which is false.[29] Like Auriol, Ockham insists that the divine essence admits only a single consideration; there is no secondary consideration or object.[30] Ockham takes particular issue with Scotus's explanation of this secondary consideration, which involves instants of nature. Instants of nature rely on the principle that whatever real order really distinct things would have, they have a similar order according to reason where they are only distinct according to reason.[31] The problem with this approach, Ockham

---

27. *Ord.* I, d. 35, q. 1 (OTh IV.426:17–21 and 427:4–10). See Averroes, *De substantia orbis*, c. 3 (Iunctina, IX.5va).

28. *Ord.* I, d. 35, q. 1 (OTh IV.428:3–19), esp.: "Deus est summe ens, igitur est intelligens, sciens et cognoscens." Adams argues that Ockham's argument fails: "Ockham seems mistaken in regarding 'God is the highest being' as a necessary proposition, however. For even if we assume that God exists necessarily, it will not follow that He is necessarily the highest being any more than it will follow that He is necessarily the Lord of creation. For the existence of everything other than God is contingent; and God will be the highest being only if something else exists to which His excellence can be compared" (*William Ockham*, II.1021). This objection does not convince me. It does not seem to be the case that more than one being is required for a being to be supreme. A comparative term requires at least two instances, but a superlative only seems to require one, especially if any other possible instances would not change the superlative status. A family with one child can meaningfully speak of their firstborn child even though there are no other children since any other children would not be first. Similarly, God is the supreme being both if he is the only being and because any other beings that could come into existence would be lesser beings.

29. *Ord.* I, d. 35, q. 3, ad opp. (OTh IV.445:5–7).

30. See pp. 214–15.

31. Scotus, *Rep.* prol., q. 1, a. 4, n. 117 (Wolter-Bychov, I.44); Scotus, *Quodlibet*, q. 6, n. 20 (Wadding-Vivès, 24.157). See pp. 170–71.

argues, is that wherever something is prior in perfection, there corresponds something posterior in perfection. But nothing in God is posterior in perfection. Therefore, nothing is prior in perfection there either. Ockham's proof for the minor premise is that everything posterior in perfection is more imperfect, but nothing in God is imperfect in any way, as there is no imperfection in God.[32]

Ockham's banishing of everything posterior in perfection from God includes both his act of understanding and the objects he understands. God's act of understanding is entirely indistinct from his essence in reality (*ex natura rei*). Nothing about it is prior or posterior. Just as man understands an entire proposition—and thus many terms—in a single, indistinct act of knowing, all the more God understands everything that he knows in one indistinct act.[33]

Ockham also argues that there are two ways for things to be ordered according to prior and posterior: First, things are called "ordered" (*ordinata*) because something extrinsic to the ordered things corresponds to them such that one corresponds to one, and the other corresponds to the other. Things ordered according to time and place are ordered in this way. This way of speaking is the proper way of speaking of things ordered according to time and place because the prior is in something prior in which the posterior is not. Second, things are ordered in which no extrinsic order corresponds at all. God is prior to a creature in this way, even though no time or place is imaginable. Parts and whole, and universally everything ordered according to nature and according to causality, dignity, and community are ordered in this second way. This way of speaking of things being ordered is not the proper way because the prior is not in something prior in which the posterior is not.[34]

It is clear that Scotus's theory of instants, at least when applied to God, entails the second way of understanding things ordered according to prior and posterior. However, "[u]nless there is a measure really distinct from what is measured, then there is no such correspondence for the prepositional phrase 'in something prior' to signify."[35] There is nothing extrinsic that measures the divine essence. Scotus would object that an extrinsic measure's actual existence is irrelevant because his claim is not that God knows in a temporally or locally prior way. Scotus is talking about a natural priority and posteriority. However, as Adams points out, "it is far from clear why the fact that God is naturally prior to creatures and prior to them in perfection should have the consequence that God's understanding of Himself is naturally prior to His understanding of creatures."[36] If God does not have a quasi-secondary object of understanding but instead has a single, indistinct act of understanding, what is there to render one object of knowledge prior and another posterior?

---

32. *Ord.* I, d. 35, q. 3, (OTh IV.448:9–18).
33. *Ord.* I, d. 35, q. 4 (OTh IV.469:7–13), esp.: "in nobis unicus actus indistinctus est quo intelligimus totum complexum, et per consequens plures terminus. Igitur multo fortius Deus intelligit omnia quaecumque intelligit unico actu indistincto."
34. *Ord.* I, d. 9, q. 3 (OTh III.302:4–24).
35. Adams, *William Ockham*, II.1048.
36. Adams, *William Ockham*, II.1049.

God's Knowledge of Things Other Than Himself

Ockham's insistence upon the unicity of the divine act of understanding and our inability to make distinctions within it has important ramifications for his account of God's knowledge of things other than himself. Ockham takes Averroes's objections to God's knowledge of creatures seriously and responds to each individually.[37] Each of the arguments is manifestly false and contrary to the authority of Sacred Scripture, but Averroes's arguments from God's nobility are the strongest. If it could be proved that God does not understand things other than himself, it would only be because of his supreme nobility.[38] His nobility might prevent knowing other things in two ways: his knowing less noble things might make him less noble, or his knowledge of other things might make him dependent upon them, which would be ignoble.

Experience incorrectly teaches that knowledge of something vile makes the knower vile. The thought of vile things can frequently impede man's ability to know more noble things, and knowledge of vile things can even incline him to do vile acts. If such impediments or inclinations result, then it is indeed ignoble to have that knowledge at that time, but these effects need not result.[39] God is not impeded from knowing himself or another noble object, nor does knowledge of something vile tempt God to commit some vile act. Thus, knowledge of things other than himself is not contrary to God's nobility.[40]

Experience further incorrectly teaches that the knower necessarily depends upon what he knows. Man's knowledge depends upon an object because it is caused by that object.[41] This experience should not be generalized too quickly because it cannot even be proved that the object causes all his acts of knowing, never mind every act of knowing whatsoever. Thus, it is not characteristic of an act of understanding that it be caused by the object or depend upon it.[42] Since God's knowledge is not caused at all, his knowledge entails no dependence.

After showing that it cannot be proved that God does not know things other than himself, Ockham argues that it cannot be proved that God *does* know things other than himself. If God's knowledge of other things could be proved, the best argument would be Aquinas's Argument from Divine Self-Knowledge. God knows the full extent of his power. A thing's power is not perfectly known unless that to which the power extends is known too. Divine power extends to all things. Therefore, God knows all things.[43]

---

37. Averroes, *In XII Met.*, com. 51 (Iunctina, VIII.157va–158rb) and pp. 3–6.
38. *Ord.* I, d. 35, q. 2 (OTh IV.434:19–436:8 and 440:18–20).
39. See Adams, *William Ockham*, II.1022.
40. *Ord.* I, d. 35, q. 2 (OTh IV.443:5–10). See Augustine, *De civ. Dei*, XIV, c. 23, n. 3 (PL 41.451), where Augustine chastises those who are tempted to lust by his discussion of the chaste intercourse that would have occurred before the Fall. Those tempted to vile acts should blame their unchastity, not the chaste words Augustine uses about a chaste subject.
41. *Ord.* I, d. 35, q. 2 (OTh IV.443:1–2).
42. *Ord.* I, d. 35, q. 2 (OTh IV.441:3–11).
43. *Ord.* I, d. 35, q. 2 (OTh IV.436:10–15), quoting Aquinas, *ST* I, q. 14, a. 5 (Leonine, 4.172). See pp. 63–64.

Ockham likes this argument but thinks that it can only be probable for two reasons: First, it cannot be proved sufficiently that perfect knowledge of a power entails perfect knowledge of everything to which that power extends. Simple knowledge of one thing does not suffice for simple knowledge of another thing. Thus, someone could know a power perfectly but not know everything to which that power extends. His proof of the minor is taken from the senses, which perfectly know their objects. As a result, the senses perfectly know their power since their objects and the objects' power do not differ. Nevertheless, no sense power knows something else to which the sense extends itself.[44] Ockham can separate knowledge of the power of a cause from the knowledge of its actual or possible effects because causes are distinct from their effects.[45]

Second, Aquinas's argument is only probable because it cannot be sufficiently proved that God is the cause of all things or even that God is an efficient cause. From the notion of causality, it can be shown that a cause knows its immediate effect, but we cannot show that God is the immediate cause of all creatures. Ockham thinks that Avicenna's account of creation in which God creates the first intelligence immediately and the rest of creation is caused by a chain of intermediate, creaturely causes is the best that reason can do.[46]

Although the arguments are not demonstrative, Ockham thinks we have good reason to think that God is the immediate cause of some effect. It is probable that something exists such that, *per impossibile*, if God were destroyed, that thing would be destroyed too, whether mediately or immediately. Every case where the destruction of one thing follows the destruction of something else has the character of a cause, so it is probable that God is the immediate cause of something.[47] Moreover, if God could not effectively cause something in the universe, his existence would be posited in vain. Therefore, he is probably the efficient cause of some effect.[48] Furthermore, it is not probable that the first efficient cause does not know what it produces because then it would produce and not know what it produced. Thus, God is probably an efficient cause and knows what he produces, that is, God probably knows some effect.[49]

The preliminary investigations into Ockham's account of nominalism, divine attributes, and God's knowledge of things other than himself make it clear that Ockham's theory of divine ideas will differ significantly from most of his predecessors. Ockham's emphasis on divine simplicity ensures that the plurality of divine ideas cannot be identical to the divine essence. Divine ideas cannot be 'in' God subjectively because then God would not be one. The best Ockham can do is say that

---

44. *Ord.* I, d. 35, q. 2 (OTh IV.437:17–437:6).
45. See Adams, *William Ockham*, II.1028.
46. *Ord.* I, d. 35, q. 2 (OTh IV.441:7–18); *Quodlibet* II, q. 1 (OTh IX.107:11–108:20). See Avicenna, *Met.* IX, c. 4 (van Riet, II.476–88).
47. Adams, *William Ockham*, II.1031.
48. *Quodlibet* II, q. 1 (OTh IX.109:43–45).
49. *Ord.* I, d. 35, q. 2 (OTh IV.441:19–442:5). For Ockham's account of God's causality, see Maurer, *William of Ockham*, 295–311.

they are in God's knowledge as objects known. We should also note how little reason can accomplish in the realm of divine knowledge. If the arguments that God knows things other than himself are only probable, any argument that God has divine ideas will be probable as well.

What Is an Idea?

Ockham takes up the question of divine ideas in *Ordinatio* I, d. 35, q. 5. He criticizes Henry of Ghent's theory before turning to his account. It is not uncommon for Ockham to criticize Henry, but it is curious that he chose to take up Henry's account rather than Scotus's account. There are several likely factors that contribute to this choice. First, Henry's thought was still dominant in England. Scotus converts early Thomists to his position, but Henry's position must still be influential. Second, critiquing Henry's position allows Ockham to emphasize the unity and simplicity of the divine essence. Third, we saw Scotus repeatedly emphasize that he does not deny that rational relations are part of the character of a divine idea even if those relations are not how God knows possible creatures.[50] Thus, when Ockham directs his criticism against those who conclude that "an idea really is the divine essence and differs from it in reason," he is tacitly attacking at least part of Scotus's theory.[51]

Contra Henry of Ghent

Henry and others conclude that divine ideas are both really identical to the divine essence and rationally distinct from it to account for God's knowledge of creatures as they are identical with him and other than him. On Henry's account, God knows a creature as other than him insofar as his essence is its reason (*ratio*) and exemplar form. For the divine essence to be the *ratio* and exemplar form is nothing other than the imitability by which others imitate it. The formal character of a divine idea is nothing other than a respect of imitability from the intellect's consideration upon the divine essence.[52]

In response, Ockham denies divine ideas could be the divine essence. This conclusion is alarming because if divine ideas are not the divine essence, then it is unclear what they are. The only other option would seem to be creatures, which would seem to make creatures eternal and necessary. Nevertheless, divine ideas cannot be the divine essence because "[e]very attempt to explain them in these terms runs into insuperable difficulties."[53] It is simply not the case that something "can be both really the same as something else and distinct in reason from it."[54]

---

50. See p. 175.
51. *Ord.* I, d. 35, q. 5 (OTh IV.480:2–3): "idea est realiter divina essential et tantum differ ratione ab ea."
52. *Ord.* I, d. 35, q. 5 (OTh IV.480:5–19). See Henry, *Quodlibet* IX, q. 2 (Leuven XIII.29:79–81) and pp. 88–91.
53. Maurer, *William of Ockham*, 214.
54. Adams, *William Ockham*, II.1038.

Ockham offers the following argument: A divine idea refers to (1) the divine essence precisely, (2) the respect precisely, or (3) the aggregate of essence and respect.[55] If a divine idea were (1) the divine essence, then there could only be one idea, which Henry and company deny. If a divine idea were (2) the respect only, then it must be either (2a) a real respect or (2b) a rational respect. If (2a) a real respect, then a divine idea would have to be a relation of the Divine Persons. Everyone denies this, and they further deny that God has any real relation to a creature. If (2b) a divine idea were a rational respect, then a being of reason would really be the same as a real being, which is impossible because everything that is really the same as a real being is truly a real being and so not a being of reason.[56] Besides, if a divine idea were only a respect of reason, it is not the divine essence. Finally, (3) the aggregate of divine essence and respect option fails because an aggregate or composite is not really any of the parts, as the composite is neither really the matter nor the form.[57] By process of elimination, a divine idea cannot be the divine essence.

After offering this argument, Ockham takes aim at Henry's four reasons for the necessity of divine ideas. Henry argued that divine ideas are necessary based on (1) divine self-knowledge, (2) formal and exemplar causality, (3) efficient causality, and (4) final causality.[58] Ockham admits that Henry's reasons seem true, but they cannot be true if we consider that Henry takes ideas as respects of imitability, not the creatures themselves. As such, he argues against all four. Maurer points out that Ockham's principle of economy—his so-called razor—"is clearly operative in his rejection of relations of imitability as an explanation of the divine knowledge of creatures. They are indeed superfluous. A created artist does not need them in order to produce his works of art; why should the divine artist need them?"[59] Worse yet, positing relations of imitability as necessary for God's knowledge of creatures degrades the divine intellect. If God requires relations of imitability, then the divine essence would not be the only moving principle of God's intellect. Relations of imitability would be required as something else and so degrade the divine intellect.[60]

Even if such relations are not unnecessary or degrading, they cannot perform the role for which Imitability Theorists posit them. Ockham takes up Scotus's argument against the Imitability Theory, saying that these respects either presuppose

---

55. Ockham admits that, in principle, an idea could entail the essence and something absolute, or precisely something absolute beyond the essence. Since no one argues for these positions, he omits them.

56. This point is contentious as Henry thinks that a rational respect is, in fact, identical to a real being. Unsurprisingly, Ockham assumes his "own understanding of real distinction and identity" (Jenny Pelletier, "William Ockham on Divine Ideas, Universals, and God's Power," in *Universals in the Fourteenth-Century*, ed. Fabrizio Amerini and Laurent Cesalli [Pisa: Edizioni della Normale, 2017], 196).

57. *Ord.* I, d. 35, q. 5 (OTh IV.481:2–482:6), esp.: "aut idea dicit praecise divinam essentiam, aut praecise respectum, aut aggregatum ex essentia et respectu." This argument explains why, "Unlike Thomas and others, Ockham never spoke of an idea as a *ratio*, but always simply of *idea* or *exemplar*." (Hoenen, *Marsilius of Inghen*, 137. Emphasis original.)

58. For Henry's arguments, see pp. 95–98.

59. Maurer, *William of Ockham*, 215.

60. *Ord.* I, d. 35, q. 5 (OTh IV.483:8–485:9).

knowledge of the creatures or follow upon knowledge of the creatures. They cannot presuppose the knowledge because rational respects necessarily follow some divine act of knowing. The respect would follow the act of divine knowledge by which God knows his essence absolutely, not by comparing it to each other thing, which Imitability Theorists deny. They cannot follow the knowledge of creatures because then they would play no role in God's knowledge of creatures, which is the central claim of the Imitability Theory.[61] The Imitability Theory of divine ideas thus fails to show what a divine idea is or even why God should need divine ideas.

Ockham's Theory of Divine Ideas

Ockham begins his account of divine ideas by determining the meaning of the word 'idea.'

> ['Idea'] is a connotative term (*nomen*), or a relative term according to another way of speaking. For every idea necessarily is the idea of something ideal or the ideated. And therefore, it does not precisely signify some one thing, but signifies one thing and connotates something else or that same thing that it signifies.[62]

Like all connotative terms, then, an idea has only a nominal quiddity (*quid nominis*) and only admits a descriptive or nominal definition.[63] Thus, he defines an idea as "something known by an effective intellectual principle, looking to which the active principle can produce something in real being."[64]

Augustine and Seneca confirm this definition, Ockham says. Augustine's description of a divine idea emphasizes three things, which are all found in Ockham's nominal definition: Divine ideas are known by the Creator, are in his mind, and are that to which he looks when he creates.[65] Seneca's authority adds

---

61. *Ord.* I, d. 35, q. 5 (OTh IV.484:4–15), esp.: "aut iste respectus rationis praesupponit intellectionem creaturae aut consequitur intellectionem. Non primum quia, secundum istum, respectus rationis necessario consequitur aliquem actum intelligendi.... Nec potest dici secundum. Tum quia tunc nihil facerent ad hoc quod Deus distincte intelligeret alia a se."; See *Ord.* I, q. 35, a. 4 (OTh IV.465:14–20). For similar arguments in Scotus, see *Rep.* I-A, d. 36, qq. 1–2, n. 35–38 (Noone, 408–9). See pp. 164–66 for an analysis of Scotus's argument.

62. *Ord.* I, d. 35, q. 5 (OTh IV.485:19–486:1): "[idea] est nomen connotativum, vel relativum secundum alium modum loquendi. Nam omnis idea necessario est alicuius idealis vel ideati idea. Et ideo non praecise significat aliquid unum, sed significat unum et connotat aliquid aliud vel illud idem quod significat." For Ockham's general account of connotative terms, see *Summa logicae* I, c. 10 (OPh I.36:38–38:94), esp.: "Nomen autem connotativum est illud quod significat aliquid primario et aliquid secundario. Et tale nomen proprie habet definitionem exprimentem quid nomen, et frequenter oportet ponere unum illius definitionis in recto et aliud in obliquo."

63. *Summa logicae* I, c. 28 (OPh I.90:1–3): "Descriptiva autem definitio est mixta ex substantialibus et accidentalibus. Verbi gratia 'homo est animal rationale, erecte ambulativum, latas habens ungues."

64. *Ord.* I, d. 35, q. 5 (OTh IV.486:2–4): "idea est aliquid cognitum a principio effectivo intellectuali ad quod ipsum activum aspiciens potest aliquid in esse reali producere."

65. Augustine, *De div qq. 83*, q. 46 (PL 40.30).

further weight to the veracity of this definition. After positing Aristotle's four causes, Seneca adds a fifth cause taken from Plato, namely, the exemplar cause, which he calls an idea. An idea "is that looking to which the artist produces that which he deigned to carry out."[66] Ockham rejects Seneca's claim that there is a fifth species of cause, but Seneca is right to say that an idea is a known exemplar and that a knower can produce something in real being by looking at it.[67]

Ockham continues saying that only the creatures themselves fit this description of ideas, not the divine essence nor some rational respect. He reiterates that a rational respect cannot be a creature's exemplar just as a being of reason (*ens rationis*) cannot be the exemplar of a real being (*ens reale*). He argues against the divine essence as a divine idea because there are many ideas, a fact everyone admits. But the divine essence is one and not capable of being made many in any way.[68] The only option left is creatures, and it turns out that creatures fit the parts of his description of an idea quite well. A creature is known by an intellectual agent, and God looks to it such that he produces rationally. For however much God knows his essence, if he did not know what is producible by him, he would produce ignorantly and not rationally, not through an idea. Therefore, God truly looks to the producible creature itself, and by looking at it, can produce it.[69]

In a stroke of irony, Ockham affirms this conclusion by appealing to the ubiquitous analogy to the finite artist.

> Ideas ought to be posited proportionally in the created and uncreated artist. If the created artist knew that work of art that he produces precisely, he would truly act through an exemplar. As a result, he would act through an idea, just as if he knew one thing of which he ought to produce a similar thing. Therefore, with respect to the created artist, the idea and exemplar would truly be the producible thing itself,—since authors understand the same thing by 'ideas' and 'exemplars.' Therefore, since God foreknows the very producible creature, it will truly be an idea.[70]

---

66. Seneca, *Ad Lucilium Epistulae Morales*, epist. 65, n. 7 (Gummere, I.448): "ad quod aspiciens artifex illud quod destinavit efficit."

67. *Ord.* I, d. 35, q. 5 (OTh IV.486:4–487:3).

68. *Ord.* I, q. 35, q. 5 (OTh IV.487:4–488:14), esp.: "secundum omnes, plures sunt ideae. . . . Sed essentia divina est unica, nullo modo plurificabilis; igitur ipsa non est idea. . . . Nec respectus rationis: tum quia nullus talis est Dei ad creaturam qui possit importari per nomen ideae; tum quia ille non potest esse exemplar creaturae, sicut nec ens rationis potest esse exemplar entis realis."

69. *Ord.* I, q. 35, q. 5 (OTh IV.488:15–22). See Gordon Leff, *William of Ockham: The Metamorphosis of Scholastic Discourse* (Totowa, NJ: Rowman and Littlefield, 1975), 439–40; Adams, *William Ockham*, II.1054; Maurer, *William of Ockham*, 217.

70. *Ord.* I, q. 35, q. 5 (OTh IV.489:9–16): "ideae, proportionaliter sunt ponendae in artifice creato et increato. Sed si artifex creatus praecise cognosceret illud articifiatum quod produceret, ita vere ageret per exemplar, et per consequens per ideam, sicut si cognosceret unum cuius simile debet producer. Igitur respectus artificis creatae ipsummet producibile vere esset idea et exemplar,—quia idem intelligent auctores per ideas et exemplaria. Igitur cum Deus ipsammet creaturam producibilem praecognoscat, ipsamet vere erit idea."

Ockham's use of the analogy to the created artist is interesting. We saw in the last chapter that Auriol criticizes the analogy in his critique of the Imitability Theory. For Auriol, the uncreated artist is completely unlike created artists because he does not have to use a univocal likeness.[71] We might have expected that Ockham would also be critical of the analogy since he also adheres to the Nominalist Theory. However, Ockham accepts the analogy of the created artist wholesale. The analogy works, but his predecessors misunderstood how it works. Earlier thinkers got the created artist wrong, and so they were misled about the uncreated artist. The created artist knows the very work of art that he will produce, not some likeness of it. Ockham can accept the analogy because he applies his epistemology to it.

At the heart of Ockham's argument is the claim that an idea is anything known to which the knower looks in producing with the result that he produces something like it and produces it in real being. Given this description, an external exemplar (say, a house) is just as much an idea as an exemplar that the knower thinks up himself. The distinction between the two is that in the case of the external exemplar, the already existing house is the idea, and in the thought-up exemplar, it is the producible house that is the idea. The case of the thought-up exemplar is particularly striking because Ockham says that if the house itself in particular were foreknown by the artist and by his power, he could produce the same house, the house itself would be its own exemplar and idea, to which the artist, looking, could produce it in real *esse*.[72]

Ockham applies this general description of an idea to divine ideas:

> An idea signifies (*importat*) the creature itself both directly (*in recto*) and indirectly (*in obliquo*). It also signifies (*importat*) indirectly (*in obliquo*) divine cognition itself or the divine cognizer. Therefore, 'idea' is predicable of the creature itself as it is. However, it is not predicable of the knowing agent or his cognition because neither cognition nor knowing is an idea just as it is not an exemplar.[73]

The secondary literature is divided on how to interpret this passage. Fr. Harry Klocker says that a divine idea's "function is to signify the creature directly and indirectly its producibility by God."[74] Maurer, however, says that a divine idea "signifies both directly (*in recto*) and indirectly (*in obliquo*) the creature itself, conceived by God as something creatable, though indirectly it also signifies the same creature

---

71. See pp. 221–22.

72. *Ord.* I, d. 35, q. 5 (OTh IV.490:5–14), esp.: "si ipsamet domus in particulari esset ab artifice praecognita et virtute illius posset domum illam eandem producer, ipsa domus esset exemplar et idea sui ipsius, ad quam artifex aspiciens posset ipsammet producer in esse reali."

73. *Ord.* I, q. 35, q. 5 (OTh IV.490:15–20): "idea importat ipsammet creaturam in recto et etiam ipsammet in obliquo, et praeter hoc importat ipsam divinam cognitionem vel cognoscens in obliquo. Et ideo de ipsamet creatura et praedicabilis ut ipsa sit idea, sed non est praedicabilis de agente cognoscente vel cognitione, quia nec cognitio nec cognoscens est idea sicut non est exemplar."

74. Harry R. Klocker, "Ockham and the Divine Ideas," *The Modern Schoolman* 47, no. 4 (1980): 358.

produced in reality and the divine knowledge or knower."[75] There are two points at stake in this disagreement: First, does a divine idea signify the creature as producible directly? Second, does a divine idea signify the actual production of the creature indirectly?

Neither Klocker nor Maurer explains why he interprets Ockham's text as he does, so the only recourse to resolve the issue is Ockham's text itself. A possible interpretive key is Ockham's claim that "authors understand the same thing by 'ideas' and 'exemplars.'"[76] At first, this quotation seems unhelpful because Ockham only seems to be reporting that others think the terms 'idea' and 'exemplar' have the same signification. Nevertheless, I think this quotation can show that Maurer's interpretation is closer to Ockham's intended meaning, although the evidence is not especially strong. At the end of the block quotation above, Ockham insists that "neither cognition nor a cognizer is an idea *just as it is not an exemplar.*"[77] The significations of 'idea' and 'exemplar' are connected for Ockham just as they are for other authors. This connection in signification means that producibility is central to an idea, not merely something added on or signified obliquely. A divine idea cannot directly signify the creature itself as created for the obvious reason that it is not (yet) created. Nor can it directly signify the creature independent of its producibility. Producibility is part of the intelligibility of a creature. If God could not create it, it could not be a creature. Ockham admits as much in the conclusion of his argument that the creature itself is the idea: "Therefore, since God foreknows the producible creature itself, it itself will truly be an idea."[78] As Maurer says, a divine idea directly signifies the producible creature itself directly and indirectly, and it also signifies God's knowledge and God himself as a knower indirectly. It even indirectly signifies the creature itself as created, if God wills to create it. This last indirect signification is added since Ockham insists that the very thing produced is its exemplar.[79]

Ockham's claim that a divine idea signifies the creature itself directly and indirectly, and also signifies the divine act of knowing indirectly departs sharply from Auriol's claim that a divine idea signifies the Godhead (*deitas*) directly and the creature itself indirectly.[80] The two men are united in deflating the metaphysically robust accounts of divine ideas held by their predecessors to a logical account of connotative terms, but their understandings of the connotation are opposed. The differences seem to stem from emphasizing different aspects of Augustine's account of divine

---

75. Maurer, *William of Ockham*, 218.
76. *Ord.* I, d. 35, q. 5 (OTh IV.489:13–14): "idem intelligunt auctores per ideas et exemplaria."
77. *Ord.* I, d. 35, q. 5 (OTh IV.490:19–20): "nec cognitio nec cognoscens est idea sicut non est exemplar." Emphasis mine.
78. *Ord.* I, d. 35, q. 5 (OTh IV.489:15–16): "Igitur cum Deus ipsammet creaturam producibilem praecognoscat, ipsamet vere erit idea."
79. *Ord.* I, d. 35, q. 5 (OTh IV.490:10–14): "si ipsamet domus in particulari esset ab artifice praecognita et virtute illius posset domum illam eandem producere, ipsa domus esset exemplar et idea sui ipsius, ad quam artifex aspiciens posset ipsammet producere in esse reali."
80. See pp. 217–19.

ideas. Auriol emphasized Augustine's claim that the vision of the divine ideas is a most blessed vision. Since man is only beatified by seeing the Godhead, divine ideas must signify the *deitas* directly.[81] Ockham seems to focus on Augustine's claim that divine ideas are in the divine mind.[82] A divine idea can signify the creature directly because God knows the creature directly. Ockham thinks his emphasis is justified because of the way he understands distinctions. It is impossible for the same thing to be really the same and yet differ in reason.[83] Thus, he can emphasize that divine ideas are in the divine mind without losing the vision of divine ideas as a most blessed vision. Since the divine understanding and what is understood by it are ultimately identical to the divine essence, vision of divine ideas is a most blessed vision.[84]

Ockham's emphasis that a divine idea signifies the creature directly and indirectly and signifies divine cognition or God as knower indirectly also seems to follow from his nominal definition of an idea. "An idea," he says, "is something known by an effective intellectual principle, looking to which the active principle can produce something in real being." When God produces a creature, he does so by looking at the creature itself. Thus, the creature as producible is signified directly by a divine idea. On Ockham's definition of an idea, Auriol's claim that divine ideas signify the *deitas* directly amounts to be a sort of divine navel-gazing. For Ockham, it is unclear how God looking directly at the *deitas* could be called an idea, especially since he thinks neither knowledge nor a knower is an idea or exemplar.[85] Worse yet, since the *deitas* is not producible in real being in the first place, it would be inappropriate to say that a divine idea signifies the divine essence directly. Finally, since an idea is an idea *of* something, it seems to make more sense to say that divine cognition would be signified obliquely by a divine idea. It is a creature *of* God's knowledge.

This analysis clarifies why Ockham would say that a divine idea signifies the producible creature directly and God's knowledge or knowing indirectly, but it still leaves obscure why a divine idea would also signify the very creature indirectly. As quoted above, Maurer says that "indirectly it also signifies the same creature produced in reality."[86] This interpretation is reasonable since the creature as producible naturally leads us to think of the creature as actually produced. Once the builder builds the chair, we can reasonably say that his idea of the chair is not just an idea of the producible chair but also an idea of the chair he has produced. Since ideas are ordered to production, an idea signifies actual production indirectly.

---

81. See p. 213.
82. Augustine, *De div. qq. 83*, q. 46, n. 2 (PL 40.30).
83. *Ord.* I, d. 2, q. 3 (OTh II.75–98). Ockham uses this conclusion as part of his argument against the Imitability Theory's claim that the divine essence is many insofar as it is comparable to diverse creatures. See *Ord.* I, d. 35, q. 5 (OTh IV.487:11–18).
84. It is debatable whether Ockham is entitled to this conclusion, given how strongly he emphasizes that divine ideas are not the divine essence or in God subjectively. Ockham himself sees this objection and raises it against himself. For his discussion of this objection, see pp. 248–53.
85. *Ord.* I, d. 35, q. 5 (OTh IV.490:18–20).
86. Maurer, *William of Ockham*, 218.

This distinction between ways that divine ideas signify creatures raises a question about divine ideas of non-existing possible. Although it has not yet been determined whether Ockham thinks God has ideas of non-existing possibles, if he does have these ideas, do these ideas signify the creatures themselves indirectly? There are several options at this point: First, perhaps the indirect signification of the creature itself as produced is not necessary for the character (*ratio*) of an idea. Since by supposition these creatures are not produced, the *ratio* of a divine idea of a non-existing possible would not include the indirect signification of the produced creature. It would only signify the creature itself as producible directly and signify the divine knowledge or knowing indirectly. Second, perhaps the produced creature's indirect signification is necessary for the *ratio* of a divine idea. In that case, either there could not be divine ideas of non-existing possibles or the actual production of a non-existing possible would still be signified indirectly by the divine idea even though the creature is not produced. Ockham does not consider this difficulty, so I will leave this matter as an open question in Ockham's thought.

The Necessity of Positing Divine Ideas

Ockham's description of divine ideas as the creatures themselves to which God looks when he produces them has important ramifications for the necessity of positing divine ideas. Most importantly, Ockham has denied any cognitive role for divine ideas. Divine ideas are not *rationes cognoscendi*, that is, they do not make or cause God to know. God's knowledge is uncaused; "God knows simply because he is God."[87] Divine ideas are not cognitive principles or means for God, and so we should not posit them to account for God's knowledge.

One could object that Ockham does allow for God to know "through ideas" (*per ideas*) if the '*per*' refers to "the circumstance of the terminating object, as we say that we will see God through (*per*) his essence because the very divine essence itself will be seen."[88] Perhaps Ockham is making use of a distinction parallel to Aquinas's distinction between the principle object and the terminating object of the intellect.[89] Creatures do not reduce God from potency to act with respect to knowing creatures—as principle objects—but they are what he knows: the terminating objects.

This objection is sufficient to show that God does not have creatures as sources or principles of knowledge. His only source of knowledge is himself. However,

---

87. Leff, *William of Ockham*, 440. See *Ord.* I, d. 35, q. 1 (OTh IV.428:3–19). Ockham applies this claim to divine ideas explicitly at *Ord.* I, d. 35, q. 5 (OTh IV.494:11–13): "ideae nec movent intellectum divinum, nec sunt intellectus ipse, nec obiectum medium inter Deum et alia a se cognita." See also Hoenen, *Marsilius of Inghen*, 135.

88. *Ord.* I, d. 35, q. 5 (OTh IV.494:7–9): "Vel [ly per] potest dicere circumstantiam obiecti terminantis, sicut dicimus quod videbimus Deum per essentiam suam quia ipsamet divina essential in se erit visa." See lines 13–14 just below: "Sed quarto modo potest concedi quod ideae sunt ispamet cognita a Deo, alia ab eo."

89. See p. 67. This distinction also appears in Henry and Scotus. See pp. 88–89 and 160–61, respectively.

Ockham's theory of divine ideas is so drastically different from his predecessors' that his theory has no place for divine ideas' cognitive role as his predecessors posited it. For his predecessors, God knows the creature as producible *through* the divine idea because the divine idea is not the creature itself. As Doolan notes, commenting on Aquinas's theory, "The divine Idea that God has of me is *not* me."[90] This statement is even true for Scotus despite his claim that God knows the creature directly because, while God knows the creature directly in the second instant, he only knows the creature as producible and has an idea of it in the fourth instant. Even though Scotus alters the Imitability Theory's vision of divine ideas' cognitive role, he still preserves the cognitive role of divine ideas since God only knows the creature as producible when God knows the rational respect between him and the possible creature. Ockham's theory of divine ideas does not permit divine ideas to be cognitive *means by which* he knows creatures as creatable at all. The divine idea is not the means of knowing the creature as creatable or created. It is just the creature as creatable (directly) and the creature as actually created (indirectly). For Ockham, the divine idea God has of me *is* me, not how he knows me. Thus, divine ideas can serve a cognitive role in Ockham's theory, but that cognitive role bears almost no resemblance to the cognitive role posited by his predecessors.

Similarly, divine ideas are not to be posited as certain likenesses representing creatures to the divine intellect. Such likenesses cannot be the divine essence since they are many, and the divine essence is entirely incapable of being many. They do not even need to be beings of reason because no such thing is required for production or knowledge.[91]

It is necessary to posit divine ideas, then, precisely as exemplars looking to which the divine intellect produces creatures. The authority of Augustine is evidence that some causal role is to be preserved for divine ideas.[92] Divine ideas safeguard God's reasonable operation. There are only two requirements for an agent to operate reasonably: (1) a productive or operative power, and (2) an exemplar to which he looks in operating. Ideas are not the productive or creative power of producing, so they must be the exemplars, and as exemplars, they must be posited.[93]

I am not sure how Ockham can be entitled to this claim. Gordon Leff says that "to call ideas exemplars is simply to say that God knows what he produces."[94] This interpretation seems accurate, but its plausibility stems from an ambiguity in the phrase "what he produces." As Ockham understands it, the phrase requires a drastic shift in our understanding of the term 'exemplar.' An exemplar must be logically prior to the act of production since it informs what the artist is producing. If divine ideas are the creatures themselves and exemplars, in what sense is the creature itself

---

90. Doolan, "The Really Real," 1086. Emphasis original.
91. *Ord.* I, d. 35, q. 5 (OTh IV.492:7–12).
92. Augustine, *De div. qq. 83*, q. 46 (PL 40.30).
93. *Ord.* I, d. 35, q. 5 (OTh IV.492:13–493:2), esp.: "Ideo dico quod ideae sunt ponendae praecise ut sint exemplaria quaedam ad quae intellectus divinus aspiciens producat creaturas."
94. Leff, *William of Ockham*, 440.

prior to the act of producing it? The creature cannot be logically prior as a real being because it would exist before it existed, an obvious absurdity. Neither can the creature be the divine essence for the reasons Ockham has given. Since there are no other real beings, divine ideas could only be exemplars as non-real beings. But what is a non-real exemplar? This confusion leads Ward to argue that for Ockham, "God cannot know creatures in advance of creation by knowing himself."[95] Because of his insistence on divine simplicity and his being wholly other than creatures, Ockham has made it clear that there is no place in the divine essence for divine ideas. He has argued that they are in God's mind, but it is hard to know what to make of this claim, especially given that creatures are nothing at all prior to creation.[96] If divine ideas are creatures, and if before their actual creation, creatures are nothing at all, what exactly does it mean to say that God has divine ideas? This question will be addressed more fully below in the section on the existence of things in God. For now, all that is clear is that we cannot stipulate the ontological status of divine ideas.

Principles of Practical Cognition

Ockham asks whether God's ideas are practical or speculative because he is expected to ask the question, but he does not find much merit in doing so. Strictly speaking, the question seems null because speculative and practical seem to be differences of acts of cognition, not of their objects. Divine ideas are objects of cognition, not acts of cognition, so they are neither practical nor speculative. However, the sense of the question is whether God's knowledge of things that can be made is practical or speculative, and this question is worth asking.[97]

Those who argue that God's knowledge cannot be practical mistakenly think that the practical concerns what is to be done. However, on this account, logic, rhetoric, grammar, and the mechanical arts would not be practical, which is false. These arts are practical but not dictative.[98] God's knowledge of things he could make is practical in the same way. For Ockham, practical knowledge "is concerned with what is in the will's power."[99] Divine volition, which everyone admits is really God himself, would not be praxis only if the act is not in God's power. It is in God's power to produce a creature contingently and make all other things about creatures. In a certain sense, this production can be called praxis because it is contingently from the divine will. Thus, the corresponding knowledge can truly be called practical. Divine ideas are not properly practical or speculative, but if it is meant that the knowledge of the things to be done through the ideas is practical, then divine ideas can be called practical.[100]

---

95. Ward, *Divine Ideas*, 52.
96. *Ord.* I, d. 36, q. 1 (OTh IV.547:11–19).
97. *Ord.* I, d. 35, q. 6 (OTh IV.508:2–509:4).
98. *Ord.* I, d. 35, q. 6 (OTh IV.509:19–510:1). See *Ord.*, prol., q. 11 (OTh I.316).
99. Leff, *William of Ockham*, 441.
100. *Ord.* I, d. 35, q. 6 (OTh IV.512:15–513:9).

The Existence of Things in God

Ockham identifies seven consequences that follow from his claim that divine ideas are the very things known by God, namely, the creatures themselves. Consequences two through seven concern the scope of divine ideas, and they will be treated below.[101] The first consequence, however, concerns the existence of divine ideas in God.

> First, it follows that ideas are not in God subjectively and really (*subiective et realiter*). They are only in him objectively (*obiective*) as certain things known by him (*cognita ab ipso*), because the ideas are the very things producible by God.[102]

Two aspects of this claim need to be examined: (1) the claim that ideas are not in God subjectively and really; (2) the claim that ideas are in God objectively. This distinction between subjective and objective is paramount for Ockham because, as Pelletier points out, it is "devised precisely to preserve divine simplicity."[103] He will eventually deny it because he comes to see it as opposed to divine simplicity. Thus, the distinction helps explain why Ockham initially thinks it safeguards divine simplicity and why he later thinks it is contrary to divine simplicity.

Ockham explains in the quotation above that both claims result from saying that ideas are the very things God can produce, but he does not explain the inference. To say something is in something subjectively is to say that that thing really is in the other thing. Brown is subjectively in Fido because Fido's hair is brown.[104] Thus, to say that divine ideas are in God subjectively is to say that God really is those ideas in the same (or at least a proportional) way as brown is subjectively in Fido. Two consequences that Ockham cannot accept immediately arise: First, divine ideas are many, so if the creatures themselves existed subjectively in God, then God would be many things subjectively. He would no longer be simple; he would be complex.[105] Second, if the creatures themselves existed subjectively in God, then creatures would be God, which is pantheism (or at least panentheism). Ockham does not speak to this second consequence specifically, but he would reject it.

Since they cannot exist in God subjectively, divine ideas must exist in God's mind objectively. Ockham argues in *Ordinatio*, d. 2, q. 8 that, among other objects, *figmenta*, logical objects, conceptual relations, and artificial things in the artist's mind exist objectively in the soul.[106] He further qualifies that "artificial things in

---

101. See pp. 253–54.
102. *Ord.* I, d. 35, q. 5 (OTh IV.493:5–7), esp.: "Primo sequitur quod ideae non sunt in Deo subiective et realiter, sed tantum sunt in ipso obiective tamquam quaedam cognita ab ipso, quia ipsae ideae sunt ipsaemet res a Deo producibiles."
103. Pelletier, "Ockham on Divine Ideas," 207.
104. This distinction is parallel to Bonaventure and Aquinas's distinction between natural agents and intellectual agents. See pp. 19–21 and 52–54, respectively. In Aquinas's case, it is especially close to his distinction between *esse naturale* and *esse spirituale*.
105. See *Ord.* I, d. 35, q. 5, (OTh IV.488:4–6): "aut ideae sunt in mente divina subiective aut obiective. Non subiective, quia tunc essent ibi plura subiective, quod est manifeste falsum."
106. *Ord.* I, d. 2, q. 8 (OTh II.273:15–274:6).

the mind of the artist do not seem to have subjective being, and neither do creatures in the divine mind before creation."[107] But what does it mean to exist objectively in God's mind? Ockham hints toward an answer when he says that ideas are in God objectively "as certain things known by him."[108] This qualification indicates that divine ideas will exist with a sort of cognitive being, but this answer just pushes the problem further down the road, for what is cognitive being?

Ockham works out his answer to this question—and the question on objective being more generally—through an objection. Ockham's claim that divine ideas are the creatures themselves raises difficulties about the existence of things in God. Whatever is eternal is really in God because otherwise, something other than God would be eternal. According to Augustine, divine ideas are eternal, and therefore, really in God.[109]

Ockham responds to this objection in *Ordinatio* I, d. 35, q. 5, and offers his account of the existence of things in God in the following distinction (d. 36). This objection has a particular force because of the authority of Augustine, but Ockham argues that the objection is not, in fact, faithful to Augustine's teaching. Specifically, it does not take into account Augustine's distinction between the divine essence and the divine intellect. Augustine only posits divine ideas in the divine intellect, not in the essence. Thus, ideas are not really and subjectively in God, but only objectively, just like all creatures were in God from eternity because God knew them from eternity. Ideas are only in God as known and not as really existing.[110]

Merely positing a distinction between the divine essence and the divine intellect does not solve the problem. Ockham still has to explain what it means to say that creatures were in God from eternity because God knew them from eternity. Ockham argues that the term 'eternal' (*aeternum*) has two senses: In one sense, 'eternal' is taken properly for what truly, properly, and really is actually existing eternally. In another sense, "eternal" is taken improperly and extendedly for that which is eternally and immutably known or cognized. Ideas are not eternal in the first sense because only God actually exists eternally. Ideas are eternal in the second sense.[111]

Ockham insists three times that this interpretation is the best reading of Augustine, but this account departs from Augustine, who is clear that God's ideas

---

107. *Ord.* I, d. 2, q. 8 (OTh II.274:1–2): "artificialia in mente artificis non videntur habere esse subiectivum, sicut nec creaturae in mente divina ante creationem." See Pelletier, "Ockham on Divine Ideas," 207–8.
108. *Ord.* I, d. 35, q. 5 (OTh IV.493:6–7): "sunt in ipso [sc. in Deo] tamquam quaedam cognita ab ipso."
109. *Ord.* I, d. 35, q. 5 (OTh IV.494:16–495:9). See Augustine, *De div. qq. 83*, q. 46, n. 2 (PL 40.30).
110. *Ord.* I, d. 35, q. 5 (OTh IV.497:15–21), esp.: "ideae non sunt in Deo realiter et subiective sed tamquam obiective, sicut omnes creaturae ab aeterno fuerunt in Deo quia ab aeterno fuerunt cognitae a Deo. . . . et non sicut ibidem realiter existentia."
111. *Ord.* I, d. 35, q. 5 (OTh IV.498:1–10; 500:2–4; 501:1–2). See Adams, *William Ockham*, II.1056–57.

are just as eternal as he is.¹¹² Earlier theorists who posit divine ideas as identical to the divine essence are more faithful to Augustine. Even if Ockham were more faithful to Augustine, it is not clear how his response is explanatory. The response reiterates that ideas, that is, creatures, do not truly, properly, really, and actually exist from eternity, but what exactly does it mean to be eternal by being eternally understood? Since what it means to *be* eternally understood is what Ockham needs to explain, merely repeating that they are eternally understood seven times in two paragraphs does not explain anything.¹¹³

Even if his explanation did explain what it means to be eternally understood, it is unclear how his system can sustain what he has said. In the first place, the distinction between the divine essence and the divine intellect required is contrary to Ockham's unflagging insistence that the divine essence admits of no distinctions whatsoever. If, as he says, "there are not many attributive perfections, but there is only one perfection indistinct in reality and in reason, which properly and in virtue of speech ought not to be said to be in God or in the divine essence, but is in every way the divine essence itself," how could God's knowledge (or at least the objects of that knowledge) not be eternal like his essence?¹¹⁴ What justifies the distinction? Insistence on divine simplicity drives Ockham to banish divine ideas from the divine essence but doing so seems to commit him to offending divine simplicity all the same.

Divine ideas exist in God objectively, but it is not clear what this objective existence is. Ockham insists in *Ordinatio* I, d. 36 that creatures are nothing in themselves from eternity.¹¹⁵ When Ockham says nothing, he means nothing. Creatures do not have some sort of cognized being or diminished being in God before their creation. Before their creation, they are pure nothing.¹¹⁶

Ockham consistently offers this response throughout his career, but it suffers a certain ambiguity. Creatures themselves are pure nothing prior to their creation, but what of their status as known by God? Ockham's answer to this question depends upon which theory of cognition he endorses. At the time of the *Ordinatio*, Ockham held the *ficta* theory of cognition. On this theory, the entire being of an

---

112. Augustine, *De div. qq. 83*, q. 46, n. 2 (PL 40.30): "non solum sunt ideae, ses ipsae verae sunt, quia aeternae sunt, et eiusmodi atque immutabiles manent." Notice that Augustine posits without qualification that divine ideas are eternal. See Ward, *Divine Ideas*, 52: "[Ockham] was paying mere lip service to St. Augustine and the divine ideas tradition when he wrote that a divine idea of a creature just is the creature itself."

113. *Ord.* I, d. 35, q. 5 (OTh IV.495:5–496:8).

114. *Ord.* I, d. 2, q. 2 (OTh II.61:18–21): "non sunt plures perfectiones attributales, sed tantum est ibi una perfectio indistincta re et ratione, quae proprie et de virtute sermonis non debet dicit esse in Deo vel in divina essentia, sed est omnibus modis ipsa divina essentia."

115. *Ord.* I, d. 36, q. un., ad oppositum (OTh IV.524): "Illud quod nihil est in se, a nullo distinguitur realiter; sed perfectio hominis ab aeterno nihil fuit in se reale; igitur a nullo distinguebatur realiter."

116. *Rep.* IV, q. 9 (OTh VII.178:11): "omnia creabilia sint purum nihil." See Maurer, *William of Ockham*, 220; Ward, *Divine Ideas*, 52: "Prior to creation, creatures are nothing at all: not creatures, not proto-creatures, and not even twinkles in God's eye—just nothing at all."

object of thought (*fictum*) is its being known.[117] God's act of thinking is identical to his essence and so has real existence, but what God thinks has objective existence even though nothing exists in reality because of this objective existence.[118] Adams explains this position well: "since objective existence is a mind-dependent existence, the ideas depend for their necessary objective existence on the divine act of thought."[119] Ideas have mental existence, but mental existence does not make creatures more than pure nothing.

By the time he disputed *Quodlibet* IV, Ockham had abandoned the *ficta* theory of cognition in favor of the *intellectio* theory of cognition because God's understanding of things other than himself includes fictitious beings.[120] As a result, there would be as many fictitious beings as diverse intelligible things from eternity. Furthermore, the existence of these beings would be so necessary that not even God could destroy them.[121] On the *ficta* theory, divine ideas are entirely dependent upon God's thinking them. Nevertheless, "even if their objective existence is dependent upon God's thought, it is independent of His will—which Ockham had come to regard as too close to Platonism for comfort!"[122] Even though he insists that the objective being of divine ideas is pure nothing, it is hard not to read "objective being" and think they had some sort of being. The *intellectio* theory holds that nothing more than the act of understanding is required. A divine idea is just God's act of understanding some creature, and that creature is a pure nothing prior to its being created.

Ockham distinguishes several senses of the term 'nothing' and several senses of '*esse*' that help explicate what he means when he says a creature is a pure nothing. In one way, 'nothing' is taken syncategorematically, and so is one, universal, negative sign, including the term it can distribute ('being'). In this sense, we say, "nothing runs" and "nothing is understanding." In another way, 'nothing' can be taken categorematically for something said to be a nothing. This sense can be further distinguished because 'nothing' can be taken and called (1) that which does not really exist nor had some real *esse* or (2) that which not only has no real *esse* but having real *esse* is repugnant to it. In the former sense, angels and men were nothing from eternity, and in the second sense, chimeras are nothing. Divine ideas are nothing

---

117. *Ord.* I, d. 2, q. 8 (OTh II.273:20–21): "igitur tantum habent esse obiectivum, ita quod eorum esse est eorum cognosci."

118. *Ord.* I, d. 35, q. 5 (OTh IV.500). See Adams, *William Ockham*, II.1057.

119. Adams, *William Ockham*, II.1058.

120. For an explanation of the *ficta* and *intellectio* theories of cognition, see Pasnau, *Theories of Cognition*, 277–89; Timothy B. Noone, "William of Ockham," in *A Companion to Philosophy in the Middle Ages*, ed. Jorge J. E. Gracia and Timothy B. Noone, 704–6 (Malden, MA: Blackwell Publishing Co., 2003).

121. *Quodlibet* IV, q. 35 (OTh IX.473:92–96). See Adams, *William Ockham*, II.1058; Maurer, *William of Ockham*, 221.

122. Adams, *William Ockham*, II.1058. As Pelletier points out, this position makes it seem as if there is "a special non-real mode of diminished existence that mental objects enjoy." ("Ockham on Divine Ideas," 208.)

in the first categorematic sense of nothing. They do not have any real *esse*, but real *esse* is not repugnant to them.[123]

Ockham also distinguishes three senses of *esse*: First, *esse* can be taken for actual existence (*esse-existere*). Second, *esse* can be taken for the *esse* that is convertible with a being to which actual existence (*esse in rerum natura*) is not repugnant. Third, *esse* can be taken for the copula joining subject and predicate.[124] The second sense of *esse* overlaps with the first categorematic sense of nothing.[125] Therefore, since the first categorematic sense of nothing includes non-existing possible beings, Ockham seems committed to the existence of non-existing possible beings and their being divine ideas of them. Divine ideas are thus the creatures God *could* make and not merely what God actually makes. The scope of possible beings limits the scope of divine ideas. There are no ideas of chimeras.

There is no consensus in the secondary literature about whether Ockham posits ideas of non-existing possible creatures.[126] In addition to the reason stated in the last paragraph, A. S. McGrade has argued that Ockham could be seen as

---

123. *Ord.*, I, d. 36, q. un. (OTh IV.547:6–23), esp.: "Alio modo [nihil] accipitur categorematice pro aliquo quod dicitur esse unum nihil. Et hoc potest accipi dupliciter. Quia uno modo 'nihil' accipitur et dicitur illud quod non est realiter nec habet aliquod esse reale.... Aliter accipitur 'nihil' pro illo quod non tantum non habet esse reale, sed etiam sibi repugnat esse reale."

124. *Ord.* I, d. 36, q. un. (OTh IV.538:3–7): "'esse' potest multipliciter accipi: vel pro esse-exsistere, vel pro esse quod convertitur cum ente cui non repugnat esse in rerum natura,—sed sic non est multum usitatum—, vel in propositione accipitur secundum quod est copula uniens praedicatum cum subiecto."

125. See Pelletier, "Ockham on Divine Ideas," 209.

126. The following authors think Ockham is ontologically committed to ideas of non-existing possibles: Marilyn McCord Adams, "Ockham on Identity and Distinction," *Franciscan Studies* 36, no. 1 (1976): 5–74; Elizabeth Karger, "Would Ockham have shaved Wyman's Beard?" *Franciscan Studies* 40, no. 1 (1980): 244–64; A. S. McGrade, "Plenty of Nothing: Ockham's Commitment to Real Possibles," *Franciscan Studies* 45, no. 1 (1985): 145–56; Adams, *William Ockham*, I.400–16; Elizabeth Karger, "Référence et non-existence dans la sémantique de Guillaume d'Ockham" in *Lectionum Varietates, Hommage á Paul Vignaux (1904–1987)*, ed. J. Jolivet, Z. Kaluza, and A. de Libera, 163–76 (Paris: Vrin, 1991); Claude Panaccio, *Les mots, les concepts et les choses* (Paris: Vrin, 1991), 28–29; Cyrille Michon, *Nominalisme: La théorie de la signification d'Occam* (Paris: Vrin, 1994), 299–332; Jenny E. Pelletier, *William Ockham on Metaphysics: The Science of Being and God* (Leiden: Brill, 2013), 126n109, and Pelletier, "Ockham on Divine Ideas," 208–9.

The following authors think that Ockham is not ontologically committed to ideas of non-existing possibles: Alfred J. Freddoso, "Ockham's Theory of Truth Conditions," in *Ockham's Theory of Propositions: Part II of the Summa logicae* (Notre Dame, IN: University of Notre Dame, 1980), 39; Pierre Alféri, *Guillaume d'Ockham: Le Singulier* (Paris: Éditions de Minuit, 1989), 30; Calvin G. Normore, "Some Aspects of Ockham's Logic," in *The Cambridge Companion to Ockham*, ed. Paul Vincent Spade, 34–35 (New York: Cambridge University Press, 1999).

To say that Ockham is ontologically committed to divine ideas of non-existing possibles is to say that he should hold the position because of other positions that he holds. Given his other ontological commitments, most notably his commitment to "entities for which the terms of true propositions personally supposit," Ockham should also endorse divine ideas of non-existing possibles (Pelletier, *Ockham on Metaphysics*, 126n109). The conception of ontological commitment has its origin in twentieth-century analytic philosophy. Even though not everyone holds all the positions to which he is ontologically committed, it is also unclear whether the concept can even be applied to Ockham. See Normore, "Some Aspects of Ockham's Logic," 35.

positing divine ideas of non-existing possibles. If so, "Ockham's real possibles might be thought of as 'beyond being'" like Plato's Idea of the Good.[127] This interpretation seems plausible given the (at least tacit) influence of Plato expounded above.

Those who argue that Ockham would reject the claim that non-existing possibles are beings in some sense point to texts where Ockham argues that the distinction between a being in act (*ens in actu*) and a being in potency (*ens in potentia*) does not entail that a being in potency exists in reality.[128] Moreover, Ockham rejected the *ficta* theory of cognition because it necessitated "another little world of objective entities."[129] If the idea of these entities was strange to Ockham, "he should have found unreduced, unactualized possible even stranger. . . . For assuming that possible are necessarily possible, it would follow that possible have this 'occult' status eternally and necessarily and independently of both the divine will and the divine intellect."[130] The only way to remove their occult status is to eliminate them.

Ultimately, I do not think this question can be answered for Ockham because either answer requires saying something contrary to divine omnipotence. If God necessarily has ideas of non-existing possibles, he would not be able to destroy them, that is, their possibility. If he cannot destroy their possibility, then he does not seem to be omnipotent. If there are no ideas of non-existing possibles, God must create the world in only one way. Moreover, since he would not have ideas of non-existing possibles, he would have to create if he had any ideas at all. If he must create and create in only one way, he is not omnipotent.

Ockham seems to hint toward ideas of non-existing possibles. He argues that God has distinct ideas of everything that he could make. It follows that God has an infinite number of ideas because he can create an infinite number of distinct things.[131] However, an actual infinite cannot exist, and so God has ideas of non-existing possibles. This argument does nothing to alleviate the concern about their 'occult' status though. The question of divine ideas of non-existing possibles seems an open question in Ockham's thought.

THE SCOPE OF DIVINE IDEAS

Ockham offers a concise treatment of the scope of divine ideas. The conciseness of the account is due, in part, to the fact that his system is metaphysically minimal. Just as things themselves are distinct from each other, so there are distinct ideas of all makeable things. The scope of divine ideas is limited to what God can make, namely, what can have real existence. Since God could make matter, form, and

---

127. McGrade, "Plenty of Nothing," 156.
128. *Summa logicae* I, c. 38 (OPh I.108:54–66); *In III Phys.*, c. 2, n. 1 (OPh IV.415:23–416:45); Quodlibet II, q. 9 (OTh IX.153:72–79). See Pelletier, *William Ockham on Metaphysics*, 126n109.
129. *Quodlibet* III, q. 4 (OTh IX.218:98–219:99): "est unus parvus mundus alius entium obiectivorum."
130. Adams, *William Ockham*, 1060–61; Marilyn McCord Adams, "Ockham's Nominalism and Unreal Entities," *The Philosophical Review* 86, no. 2 (1977): 174.
131. *Ord.* I, d. 35, q. 5 (OTh IV (493:7–9 and 19–21).

universally all integral and essential parts of things exist separately, Ockham argues that God has distinct ideas of them.[132]

Ockham further specifies that divine ideas are primarily of singulars. Singulars alone are producible extramentally, so there are ideas of them alone. This claim clarifies Ockham's claim about matter, form, and parts. When he says that God has an idea of matter, he does not mean the species *matter*, but of some singular matter. God has ideas of matter, form, and parts of things because he could create them separately, but these are not primary singulars. Divine ideas are primarily of individual substances, like this dog, rather than this dog's matter or this dog's form.[133]

Since only singulars exist extramentally, God does not have divine ideas of genus, difference, and other universals except insofar as they are certain things existing subjectively in the soul and only common to external things by predication. God has an idea for each of our thoughts, but each of those thoughts is singular. They are only universal by being predicable of many. Thus, God only has ideas of universals in an extended sense.[134] The scope of divine ideas ends there. There are no ideas of negations, privations, evil, guilt, or anything else like these. They do not exist in reality, and so there are no ideas of them.[135] Finally, God has an infinite number of divine ideas because he could produce an infinite number of things, otherwise God's omnipotence would be curtailed.[136]

RECAPITULATION AND CONCLUSIONS

William of Ockham's theory of divine ideas is closely linked to Peter Auriol's theory and certain trends in Scotus's theory. Like Auriol, Ockham rejects any possibility of a primary and secondary object of the divine essence. A twofold object and consideration of the divine essence would be contrary to divine simplicity. None of the rational or formal distinctions his predecessors used to justify a secondary consideration will do because Ockham does not admit distinctions less than a real distinction. Just as we know many terms in a single act when knowing a proposition, so God knows both himself in a single, undistinguished act when knowing his essence.

Like Auriol's, Ockham's theory completes the trend toward identifying divine ideas with the creatures themselves. Scotus argued for direct knowledge of creatures, but he did not argue that divine ideas are identical to creatures. Ockham grants the arguments that led Scotus to posit direct cognition, and he furthers them in two ways: First, he argues that the creature as known cannot be one with the divine essence. If it were, then either the divine essence would be complex, or there would be only one idea. No one is willing to grant either option, so divine ideas are not one with the divine essence. Second, Ockham argues that no relations at all are required for divine ideas. The created artist does not need any rational respects

---

132. *Ord.* I, d. 35, q. 5 (OTh IV.493:7–11).
133. *Ord.* I, d. 35, q. 5 (OTh IV.493:12–14).
134. For an extended discussion of this issue, see Pelletier, "Ockham on Divine Ideas," 201–7.
135. *Ord.* I, d. 35, q. 5 (OTh IV.493:14–19).
136. *Ord.* I, d. 35, q. 5 (OTh IV.493:19–21).

to know or produce his artifacts, so why would God need them?[137] From these arguments, Ockham concludes that divine ideas are the creatures as known that are exemplars, but they are not in the divine essence. It is unclear how Ockham can claim that divine ideas are exemplars if there are no relations involved. An exemplar measures what is exemplified, but Ockham does not explain how something could be a measure without any relation in the measure or the measured. Moreover, it is not clear how the creature could be the measure of itself.

Ockham also continues Scotus's argument that divine ideas are nothing in themselves. Since divine ideas are not in the divine essence, if they are anything in themselves, then Ockham will either have introduced complexity into the divine essence or claimed that something other than God is eternal. At least at one point in his career, Ockham admits that divine ideas are in the divine intellect objectively, but that just means that the divine intellect knows them.

Ockham's theory of divine ideas is a sophisticated way of explaining them away. His descriptive definition of divine ideas as "something cognized from an effective intellectual principle looking to which that active principle can produce something in real being," is deceptively close to his predecessors' definitions.[138] Ockham's account strips divine ideas of both the cognitive and causal roles that they played for his predecessors.

> God does not need anything else because he requires nothing to act. Therefore, God does not need ideas in order to act, nor are the ideas, properly speaking, required for God to act. Only cognition of the ideas, which is God himself in every way, is required. From the fact that God is God, God cognizes all.[139]

Divine ideas do not make God know, and they are not God. In the absence of an explanation for how an exemplar and what it exemplifies can have no relation, it is at best unclear how divine ideas can play a causal role for Ockham. God does not really have ideas because the divine essence is not the exemplar of creatures. Their ideas are meant to be their exemplars, but, as we have seen, it is unclear how this is the case.

Like the status Ockham accords to divine ideas, his theory of divine ideas is a theory of pure nothingness. Divine ideas are superfluous to his account of divine knowledge and creation. Divine ideas are nothing and utterly unrelated to God. Gilson criticized Aquinas for articulating divine ideas without needing them, but

---

137. *Ord.* I, d. 35, q. 5 (OTh IV.483:16-20 and 484:16-21). See *Ord.* I, d. 34, q. 4 (OTh IV.169: 7-13).
138. *Ord.* I, d. 35, q. 5 (OTh IV.486:2-4): "idea est aliquid cognitum a principio effective intellectuali ad quod ipsum activum aspiciens potest aliquid in esse reali producere."
139. *Ord.* I, d. 35, q. 5 (OTh IV.506:18-23): "Deus nullo alio indigent quia nihil requirit ad hoc quod agat. Et ideo Deus non indigent ideis ad hoc quod agat, nec ipsae ideae requiruntur proprie loquendo ad hoc quod Deus agat, sed tantum requiritur cognitio ipsarum idearum quae est ipse Deus omni modo. Et ex hoc ipso quod Deus est Deus, Deus cognoscit omnia."

this critique is better directed at Ockham.[140] Ockham only includes an account of divine ideas as a nod to the venerable tradition of Augustine and perhaps to avoid the claim that he tacitly denies the Second Person of the Trinity.[141] For Ockham, God knows just because he is God. Divine ideas are a needless complication for his system. His so-called razor should have cut out a discussion of divine ideas entirely.

---

140. Gilson, *Introduction*, 173–74.
141. See Augustine, *De div. qq. 83*, q. 46, n. 2 (PL 40.30).

Conclusion

There is a noticeable development in theories of divine ideas from St. Bonaventure through William of Ockham. Most of the development is driven by increased investigation of relations. The Imitability Theory was dominant for many years and argued that divine ideas are relations by which God knows possible creatures. Authors begin to find weaknesses in the Imitability Theory because it requires an impossible theory of relations. As a result, the Infinite Intellect Theory and *Obiecta Cognita* Theory are developed. These two theories are short-lived because Bl. John Duns Scotus takes their objections to their logical conclusions and develops the *Creatura Intellecta* Theory. This theory is well received by every author who accepts relations as necessary for exemplarity. Nominalist authors, who reject the need for relations in both knowledge and exemplarity, articulate theories of divine ideas that are tantamount to rejections of divine ideas. Thus, the two theories left standing historically at 1325 A.D. are the *Creatura Intellecta* Theory and the Nominalist Theory. Authors choose between them based on prior commitments to realism or nominalism.

There are many points of disagreement in the various theories of divine ideas, even among adherents to the same theory. However, there are also several points on which each of the authors agree. The remainder of this chapter will offer a systematic account of the points of agreement and disagreement among the theories and will conclude with some tentative considerations about which theory is best.

POINTS OF AGREEMENT

There are six points on which every author in this study agrees: First, the divine essence is the only principle and source of divine knowledge. Second, there are many ideas, the plurality of which is not contrary to divine simplicity. Third, divine ideas explain God's production of the world, that is, divine ideas are exemplars of creation. Fourth, divine ideas establish the intelligibility of the world. Fifth, God necessarily has divine ideas. Sixth, the scope of divine ideas extends only as far as it is necessary for God to know and produce every creature distinctly.

The first point is the strongest point of agreement among the authors. They unanimously and emphatically reject the theory of divine knowing and production found in Plato's *Timaeus*, and many authors reject Plato by name. God is pure act and lacks all potency. Receiving knowledge from another entails potency, even if there is no temporal progression from not knowing to knowing. Thus, God's only source of knowledge is God himself. His knowledge is uncaused, and he does not begin to know anything *de novo*.

There are many divine ideas. Augustine's claim that "it is absurd to judge that man and horse are made by the same reason" is the common point of inspiration.[1] To this authority, authors further argue that if God had but one idea, then at best, his knowledge of possible creatures would be confused and in potency, and his production of them would be mediate. Authors insist that this plurality is neither the plurality of the Divine Persons nor contrary to divine simplicity. The need to preserve divine simplicity was a powerful motivator for Nominalist Theorists. The sort of rational relations proposed by all their predecessors could only violate divine simplicity.

Divine ideas are exemplars. Creatures come to be after the pattern of their divine ideas. If God did not have divine ideas as exemplars, he would not create each creature with knowledge and love. Chance or necessity would be the cause of the world, not divine love. The world would be, at best, a happy accident, not something eternally known and loved into existence by God's knowing and willing. Not only would God be producing the world out of ignorance or necessity, but he could not be provident. Divine reward or punishment would be arbitrary and not based on the creature's good or bad actions. Peter Auriol's agreement on this point is tenuous at best. He argues that the divine essence, not divine ideas, is an equivocal exemplar of creatures. Since Ockham says that divine ideas are exemplars, we can at least say that at least one adherent to each of the five theories of divine ideas identified in this study holds that divine ideas are exemplars.

The first three claims together yield the fourth claim. Divine ideas establish the intelligibility of the world. The plurality of actually existing creatures results from God knowing himself capable of producing a plurality of creatures. God determines the essences of things ahead of time. Each essence is what it is because God knows it. The world is intelligible precisely because God knows each aspect of it.

The fifth point of agreement is that God necessarily has divine ideas and necessarily has each of his ideas. God's knowledge is perfect, and so includes each possible creature that he could create. Bonaventure sums up this position well: "although the actual production of a creature be voluntary, yet the potency of producing and the knowledge is necessary."[2] God does not have ideas because he wills to have them; he has ideas because he knows himself.

The final point of agreement is that the scope of divine ideas should not be multiplied superfluously. The scope of divine ideas should extend precisely as far as it is necessary for God to know and produce each creature distinctly. Authors vary significantly about how to apply this principle, but they each hold the principle. Bonaventure and Scotus argue for an infinite scope of divine ideas extending to every possible creature and every aspect of each creature. Henry of Ghent argues that the scope is finite, extending to the most specific species of possible creatures. Nevertheless, each author holds the position that he does because of what is

---

1. Augustine, *De div. qq. 83*, q. 46 (PL 40.30): "Nec eadem ratione homo, qua equus: hoc enim absurdum est existimare."
2. Bonaventure, *In I Sent.*, d. 27, a. un., q. 2, ad 2 (Quaracchi, I.486a): "quamvis actualis productio creaturae sit voluntaria, tamen potentia producendi et scientia est necessaria."

required on his system for God to know and produce all creatures. No author argues for this principle explictly, but they all hold it.[3]

POINTS OF DISAGREEMENT
The Status of Divine Ideas

Divine Ideas as the Term of Divine Understanding

There are two connected primary concerns for the authors of the study: First, whether divine ideas arise from a secondary consideration or object of the divine intellect upon the divine essence, and second, whether divine ideas are relations or the creatures themselves. Authors who argue that divine ideas are a secondary object of the divine intellect almost invariably argue that divine ideas are relations. Authors who reject a secondary consideration argue that ideas are the creatures themselves. Scotus and Richard of Mediavilla are somewhat unique about this. They think divine ideas arise as the secondary terminating object of the divine intellect, and they argue that the character of a divine idea includes a relation. Nevertheless, they argue that the relation is not how God knows the creature.

All authors through Scotus hold that divine ideas are the secondary terminating object of the divine intellect. Auriol and Ockham hold that there cannot be a secondary consideration of the divine intellect upon the divine essence. Thus, divine ideas are connotations of the divine essence. The earlier authors argue that when God knows his essence, he primarily knows himself. Since the divine essence is the principle informing the divine intellect, the divine essence is what God knows primarily, and he knows it primarily as his essence. Secondarily, God knows things other than himself. For Imitability Theorists, God knows things other than himself by knowing the divine essence as imitable in diverse ways. A divine idea is the divine essence considered as imitable in a particular way. Thus, the divine intellect 'expresses,' 'discovers,' and 'thinks out' the ways of imitating the divine essence.[4] Possible creatures do not imitate the divine essence by agreeing with a third thing (as two white things agree in the third thing *whiteness*). The imitation is of one to another, and the likeness is itself like.[5]

Since divine ideas are likenesses by which the divine essence is imitable, these authors argue that divine ideas are rational respects. Divine ideas cannot be the creatures themselves since they are identical to the divine essence. To say that a

---

3. In Aquinas, *In I Met.*, lect. 15, nn. 234–35 (Marietti, 81) and Aquinas, *De sub. sep.*, c. 11 (Leonine, 40.61–62), St. Thomas argues that a multiplicity of exemplars for an individual is unfitting because the multiplicity would prevent the creature from being one. However, he does not connect this point to divine ideas explicitly.

4. See, for example, Bonaventure, *In I Sent.*, d. 35, a. un., q. 1 (Quaracchi, I.601b); Aquinas, *De veritate*, q. 3, a. 2 (Leonine, 22/1.104:165–67).

5. Bonaventure, *De scientia Christi*, q. 2 (Quaracchi, V.8b–9a); Aquinas, *De veritate*, q. 3, a. 1 (Leonine, 22/1.99:183–96); Richard of Mediavilla, *In I Sent.*, d. 36, a. 3, q. 2 (Brexiae, I.110vb); James of Viterbo, *Quodlibet* I, q. 5 (Ypma ed., 65:107–8).

divine idea is the creature is tantamount to pantheism or panentheism. A divine idea is God's knowledge of the possible real relation a creature could have to him.[6] His knowledge of the real relation is a rational respect for him. If divine ideas were real relations for God, they would be additional Persons of the Trinity, or they would make God dependent upon his knowledge of creatures.

Scotus agrees with his predecessors that divine ideas are a secondary object of the divine essence and that the divine intellect is the measure of possible creatures, but he disagrees over imitability. Imitability is insufficient to distinguish divine ideas "because imitation is not the specific difference of this or that being."[7] God might know that he is perfectly imitable yet not know the absolute specific difference of those imitations. This theory can succeed only if he knows the imitation's foundation, the creature itself. Furthermore, since the Imitability Theory posits imitability as how creatures are known, Scotus has emptied the theory of all explanatory power.

Scotus further objects to the idea that God could know a relation before knowing both terms of the relation. Since a creature is the term of the relation, it must be known before the relation between it and God could be known. To drive this point home, Scotus says that "an idea is not some relation but the known object in the divine mind."[8] This statement does not mean to deny that the character of divine ideas includes rational respects, however. A divine idea's character (*ratio*) includes the known rational respect from God to the possible creature, but such respects are not how God knows possible creatures. The respects follow upon knowledge of the possible creatures.[9]

Scotus's position on the direct knowledge of creatures is similar to Auriol's and Ockham's positions, although their positions differ more than they agree. Auriol and Ockham argue that no secondary object of the divine intellect upon the divine essence is possible. Such a theory, they say, tacitly admits that God has two acts of knowing, not just one. Moreover, it treats the one divine essence as if it were two things. Auriol's example of the mirror is helpful. When an image reflects in the mirror, the thing in the image and the presence of the thing in the mirror are not two presences, but a single presence. Similarly, creatures do not have a second presence in the divine essence beyond the essence itself. God also does not require relations to mediate his essence and possible creatures because there are no extremes to be mediated.[10] Ockham adds that just as we can understand many distinct terms in a single act of knowing a proposition, so too God can know himself and all possible creatures in the single act of knowing his essence.[11]

---

6. Aquinas, *In I Sent.*, d. 36, q. 2, a. 2, ad 3 (Mandonnet, I.843); Henry, *Quodlibet* IX, q. 1, ad 1 (Leuven, 13.7:1–7).

7. Scotus, *Rep. I-A*, d. 36, qq. 1–2, n. 22 (Noone, 403:3): "Quia imitatio non est differentia specifica huius vel illius entis." See Olivi, *Quaestio de ideis*, n. 13 (Piron, 3–4).

8. Scotus, *Rep. I-A*, d. 36, qq. 1–2, n. 57 (Noone, 419:19–20): "idea non est relatio aliqua sed obiectum cognitum in mente divina."

9. Scotus, *Rep. I-A*, d. 36, qq. 1–2, n. 64 (Noone, 421–22).

10. Auriol, *Scriptum*, d. 35, p. 3, a. 2 (E-Scriptum, 10:515–24).

11. Ockham, *Ord.* I, d. 34, q. 4 (OTh IV.469:7–13).

Auriol and Ockham replace the metaphysical conception of a divine idea as a relation with the grammatical conception of a divine idea as a connotative term. For Auriol, an idea denotes the divine essence or Godhead directly and the creature indirectly and obliquely. For Ockham, an idea signifies the creature as predicable directly and divine knowledge or knowing indirectly.[12] If God has a single, indistinct act of knowing the divine essence, he does not need relations to connect his knowledge of the divine essence to his knowledge of creatures. A significant source of their predecessors' error is thinking that the divine ideas are the divine essence. Despite their best efforts to avoid these conclusions, if divine ideas are the divine essence, then either the multiplicity of divine ideas will be denied, or divine simplicity will be denied.[13]

There is a strong correlation between arguing for the existence of divine ideas through a secondary object of the divine intellect and arguing that divine ideas are rational respects or relations of God to creatures. Every author in this study who denies that the divine intellect has anything like a secondary object denies that divine ideas are or entail relations. It seems possible to hold that divine ideas arise by a quasi-secondary reflection and deny that they are rational relations, but no author takes this position. Scotus comes the closest to this position since he argues that God does not know possible creatures through divine ideas, which are relations, and he insists that the character of a divine idea is only complete when God knows the rational relation from him to the possible creature. God only knows a creature as formable when he understands the rational relation.[14]

Principles of Speculative or Practical Cognition

Almost all the authors in the study argue that divine ideas are cognitive principles. But if they are cognitive principles, are they principles of speculative or practical cognition? Even Ockham, who denies the cognitive role, asks this question. An author's answer to this question must ensure that God produces creatures intelligently. An author who posits divine ideas that play no role in creation posits divine ideas in vain. Nevertheless, divine ideas must not coerce the divine will into creating (as opposed to not creating) or creating any particular creature or set of creatures. Auriol and Ockham posit theories that run afoul of the first error. On Auriol's theory, divine ideas play no role in creation. On Ockham's theory, divine ideas do not play a cognitive role. Ockham does claim that they are exemplars that God uses in his act of creating, but since they have no relation whatsoever to that which is exemplified, it is not clear how he is entitled to this claim.

The debate over whether divine ideas are principles of speculative or practical cognition was hotly contested, but the debate's terms belie a substantial agreement

---

12. Auriol, *Scriptum*, d. 36, p. 2, a. 1 (E-Scriptum, 6:291–307); Ockham, *Ord.* I, d. 35, q. 5 (OTh IV.486:2–4).

13. Ockham, *Ord.* I, d. 35, q. 5 (OTh IV.481:2–482:6). See Adams, *William Ockham*, II.1038–39; Maurer, *William of Ockham*, 214–15.

14. Scotus, *Rep. I-A*, d. 35, qq. 1–2, n. 57 (Noone, 419:16–19).

by all authors that divine ideas are partially speculative and partially practical. This agreement stands even though Aquinas argues that divine ideas are, strictly speaking, principles of practical cognition, and Henry argues that divine ideas are only principles of speculative cognition.

Aristotle argues that speculative knowledge and practical knowledge are distinguished in three ways: from the object, from the mode of cognizing, and from the end.[15] Knowledge is speculative if it seeks truth, cannot produce its object, or cognizes its object scientifically. It is practical if it seeks an act or operation, can produce its object, and cognizes its object consultatively. Given this description, God's knowledge of himself is speculative because he could in no way make himself. Since God knows things other than himself as creatable by him, his knowledge cannot be purely speculative. If his knowledge of possible creatures were purely speculative, God would know them merely as possible and not as produced by him.

The issue becomes complicated by the worries of *fiendum* (having-to-come-to-be). One of the propositions condemned in 1270 concerned intellectualism, namely, that the intellect can determine absolutely what the will must choose. Intellectualism denies the freedom of the will. When applied to God, intellectualism makes the creation of this particular world necessary. God's intellect is a purely natural power, and so he necessarily has the divine ideas that he has. If those ideas included *fiendum* or *non-fiendum*, then the divine will would be coerced into making the *fiendum* ideas and not making the *non-fiendum* ideas. God would not be free to create differently or not to create at all.

Henry seeks to avoid this conclusion by arguing that God is indifferently related to everything that he knows. His intellect does not determine whether anything that he knows will be created. His intellect prescinds from *fiendum* and *non-fiendum*.[16] There is a twofold end of knowledge: the end of the knowledge itself and the knower's end. Only the end of the knowledge itself is properly speculative or practical. The end of the knower does not make knowledge speculative or practical. If someone does not put his ethical knowledge into action, he does not make ethics a speculative science. Since divine ideas do not include *fiendum* or *non-fiendum*, the knowledge is not practical. Thus, divine ideas are principles of speculative cognition. God's knowledge is only practical accidentally.[17]

This argument is decisive, given Henry's definition of a divine idea as including only God's knowledge and not his intention. Nevertheless, Henry's admission that God's knowledge is accidentally practical is telling. Since God knows his will's free action, he knows according to which divine ideas he will create. Put differently,

---

15. Aristotle, *EN*, VI, c. 2 1138b35–1139a16 (AL 26.1.3.253:5–23); Aristotle, *De anima*, III, c. 10, 433a14–15 (Leonine, 45/1.244). See Henry, *Summa*, a. 36, q. 4 (Leuven, 28:106:21–107:36).
16. Henry, *Summa*, a. 36, q. 4 (Leuven, 28.110:01–18). See Averroes, *In III De anima*, com. 46 (Crawford, 514:15).
17. Henry, *Summa*, a. 36, q. 4, ad 2 (Leuven, 28.115:34–117:59 and 118:93–120:40). Henry quotes Aquinas, *ST* I, q. 14, a. 16 (Leonine, 4.196b–197a). See Scotus, *Rep. I-A*, d. 36, qq. 3–4, n. 51 (Noone, 442:15–18).

God knows which divine ideas are *fiendum* as a result of the divine will and which are *non-fiendum*. Divine ideas do not have *fiendum* or *non-fiendum* from the divine intellect alone, but they do as a result of the divine will. Since Aquinas argues that a divine idea's character includes God's intention, he can profitably distinguish ideas into exemplars and reasons (*rationes*) without violating divine freedom. The character of a divine idea is logically posterior to the divine will's act. Henry's account does not admit such a division because the character of divine ideas is logically prior to the action of the divine will. Divine ideas are thus partially principles of practical cognition and partially of speculative cognition.

The Unity and Plurality of Divine Ideas

Most of the diversity among theories of divine ideas stems from a reflection on divine ideas' unity and plurality. Authors disagree strongly about how to safeguard God's simplicity and his exhaustive knowledge of all possible creatures. They unanimously declare the divine essence as the only source of divine knowledge, but if God had but one idea, he would not have distinct knowledge of every possible creature. There are five accounts of this plurality, which I have called the Imitability Theory, *Obiecta Cognita* Theory, Infinite Intellect Theory, *Creatura Intellecta* Theory, and Nominalist Theory.

The Imitability Theory is the earliest of the theories, held by Bonaventure, Aquinas, and Henry. On this theory, divine ideas are rational respects of imitability. God knows his essence as it is imitable by creatures. The divine essence is one, but the possible expressions or imitations of it are many. Even in God, the possible imitations are many, and it is the distinction of divine ideas that makes possible the distinction of creatures. God is the divine artist who thinks up the possible imitations of the divine essence. Significantly, God knows creatures by means of knowing his essence as imitable (or, in Bonaventure's terminology, expressive). He knows the relation that a creature would bear to him if created. He does not know the creature or its essence directly. The fact that God does not have direct epistemological access to creatures does not concern these authors because creatures are imitations of the divine essence. Thus, it is fitting that God would know creatures by knowing the divine essence's imitability.

The Infinite Intellect Theory, endorsed by Peter John Olivi and Petrus de Trabibus identifies divine ideas with the very act of divine knowing. Olivi is the first to attack the Imitability Theory. Olivi argues that the Imitability Theory is contrary to faith and reason. A central claim of the Imitability Theory is that God knows a relation prior to knowing both terms; God knows the creature through knowing the relation. But relations cannot be known in this way. They are only known once the terms of the relation are known. God must have direct epistemological access to creatures before he can know any possible relation between him and creatures.[18] Relations of imitability cannot perform the role for which they were posited.

---

18. Olivi, *Quaestio de ideis*, nn. 9–18 (Piron, 3–5); Olivi, *In II Sent.*, q. 55 (Jansen, II.346); Olivi, *Quodlibet* III, q. 2 (Defraia, 174).

In addition to a sustained critique of the Imitability Theory, the Infinite Intellect Theory argues that God's intellect, his object understood, and his act of understanding, are identical. As a result, divine ideas are God's very act of understanding because he is his understanding of any particular thing. Insofar as he understands a creature, he has an idea and exemplar of it. Unlike the created artist who exists by a natural form and knows by an intellectual form, God has but one form by which he exists and knows. His nature and knowledge are only distinct according to reason. In reality, his form is his knowledge.

The *Obiectum Cognitum* Theory is found in James of Viterbo. An idea, he says, is called an exemplar because the concept of the thing is the thing itself, in a certain sense.[19] Every idea entails an actual respect to a creature and is the quiddity of the *ideatum*. James distinguishes between causal quiddities and essential quiddities. Divine ideas are the former because they are quiddities that God knows he could cause, not already existing quiddities that he comes to know.[20]

On the *Obiectum Cognitum* Theory, God knows his essence in two ways: as it is an essence, and as potency and cause. God knows possible creatures as identical to him when he knows his essence as essence, and he knows them as distinct from him when he knows his essence as potency and cause. Before any creature is created, it is in God's knowledge as identical to him and distinguished from him. As the object cognized, the essences of possible creatures must be something because what does not exist in any way is not even understood. Thus, a creature is something as an *obiectum cognitum* even before it actually exists. When God knows possible creatures, his essence is simultaneously the object cognized and the creature's *ratio cognoscendi*. Since God knows his essence as a means of knowing as cause, there must be a further object because a cause is always *of* something. Nothing is the *ratio cognoscendi* of itself as cause, so when God knows his essence as cause, the *obiectum cognitum* must be something other than his essence, that is, he must know a creature. Creatures, then, are the divine ideas and the cognized objects.[21]

The *Obiectum Cognitum* Theory of divine ideas departs from the Imitability Theory by denying that divine ideas are relations through which God knows creatures. Creatures are known directly and not through a relation. This theory does not directly attack the Imitability Theory. However, it marks the first move toward a direct cognition of creatures, which becomes a hallmark of the *Creatura Intellecta* and Nominalist Theories of divine ideas.

The *Creatura Intellecta* Theory of divine ideas is held tacitly by Richard of Mediavilla and explicitly by John Duns Scotus. They develop the *Creatura Intellecta* Theory in light of Olivi's criticisms of the Imitability Theory. They insist that God has direct knowledge of possible creatures, but they hold that the character of a divine idea is only complete once God compares himself to the possible creature and knows the rational relation, which is that comparison. God has many ideas

---

19. James, *Quodlibet* III, q. 15 (Ypma, 195:17–196:52); *Quodlibet* I, q. 5 (Ypma, 65:107–8).
20. James, *Quodlibet* III, q. 15 (Ypma, 197:72–198:102).
21. James, *Quodlibet* I, q. 5 (Ypma, 64–65).

because he knows many creatures. Just as our intellects can compare every creature and every aspect of every creature to God, so God can make those comparisons. The *Creatura Intellecta* Theory of divine ideas is thus in continuity with its predecessors by upholding the necessity of rational relations, but novel in declaring that those relations arise because of the knowledge of creatures, not as a means of knowing creatures.[22]

The Nominalist Theory of divine ideas, held by Peter Auriol and William of Ockham, argues that divine ideas are connotative notions and the creatures themselves. God knows his essence directly, and he knows creatures as connotations from the essence. Ockham argues that God has many ideas simply because he can know many things when he knows his essence in the same way we can know many terms when we know a proposition.[23] Auriol goes further. God must have distinct cognition because he is perfect. But distinct cognition of one thing only yields distinct cognition of that thing, nothing else. Ideas are distinguished because of the thing connoted. Since God is full of such connotations, he must have many ideas.[24]

The Existence of Things in God

Authors take three distinct positions on the existence of things in God: The first and earliest position emphasizes that divine ideas have God's very *esse divinum* and that the possible creatures have *esse cognitum*. The second position holds that divine ideas have *esse essentiae*, and this existence is really distinguished from the divine essence. The final position is that divine ideas have *esse obiectivum* but are nothing in themselves.

The first position flows from the conviction that divine ideas are likenesses with a causal potency in their cause. In reality, divine ideas are one and identical to the divine essence, and so they share God's existence, that is, they are eternal and divine.[25] Divine ideas have uncreated being in the same way that a material house has immaterial existence in the builder's mind.[26] In a certain sense, their eternal existence is a truer existence than the finite existence creatures enjoy in their proper natures. They even share in divine life, regardless of whether they live in their proper genera.[27]

The second position was universally attributed to Henry of Ghent, although I do not think he held it. Developing a distinction in Avicenna, it is claimed that essences have three modes of being and three modes of consideration. They can be considered in singulars, in the intellect, or absolutely. The absolute consideration

---

22. Scotus, *Rep. I-A*, d. 36, qq. 1-2, nn. 26-28 (Noone, 404:8-26).
23. Ockham, *Ord.* I, d. 35, q. 5 (OTh IV.487:4-488:7).
24. Auriol, *Scriptum*, d. 36, p. 2, a. 1 (E-Scriptum, 7:331-52).
25. Bonaventure, *In I Sent.*, d. 36, a. 1, q. 1 (Quaracchi, I.620b-621a).
26. Aquinas, *ST* I, q. 18, a. 4, ad 2 (Leonine, 4.230a); Bonaventure, *In I Sent.*, d. 36, a. 2, q. 1 (Quaracchi, I.623b).
27. Bonaventure, *In I Sent.*, d. 36, a. 2, q. 2, fm. 2 (Quaracchi, I.625a); Aquinas, *De veritate*, q. 4, a. 5 (Leonine, 22/1.134:66-77).

is prior because it considers the essence only and does not consider the accidental attributes that accrue to the essence from existence in singulars or the intellect. An essence absolutely considered has its own type of being: essential being (*esse essentiae*). This sort of being comes from God, the formal exemplar of the essence.[28] Since it has essential being, an essence is naturally suited to exist—it is a *res a ratitudine*.[29] The relationship between essential being and God is rational on God's part, "but conversely, that of the creature to him is a real relation."[30] Since everything that exists is either God or a creature, divine ideas are relegated to creaturely status since they are really related to God. Thus, they must have some sort of creaturely existence independent of God. Just as we bestow cognitive being on essence in our intellects that is diminished from their true being, so God bestows essential being on possible creatures that is diminished from his own being.[31]

This position is dangerous in two ways: First, God is a formal exemplar of essences naturally and not voluntarily. Thus, if divine ideas have creaturely being, then creation is necessary and independent of the divine will. Second, the position tacitly denies *creatio ex nihilo*.[32] When God produces creatures in existential being, namely, in their proper natures, he produces them according to divine ideas' likeness. Since divine ideas already exist, God will be creating out of actually existing essences, not out of nothing.

The third account of divine ideas as having *esse obiectivum* arises in response to the second account. To emphasize that divine ideas and possible creatures do not have any sort of independent, real existence, authors begin to insist that creatures are nothing in themselves. Scotus's account insists that divine ideas still have *esse obiectivum* because they make the object known.[33] Divine ideas are present intentionally; they make the object known. Nevertheless, Scotus does not think this intentional presence entails any being or existence at all. When God understands a stone, the stone is not related to him at all; the stone is nothing in reality.[34] For Scotus, *esse obiectivum* is cognitive being and signifies that the object is noncontradictory and so intelligible.

Ockham's mature thought on the issue denies that divine ideas have *esse obiectivum* because the theory results in "another little world of objective entities."[35] The

---

28. Henry, *Quodlibet* IX, q. 2 (Leuven, 13.30:30–31:32).

29. Henry, *Quodlibet* VII, qq. 1–2 (Leuven, 11.27:71–28:87); Henry, *Quodlibet* V, q. 2 (Badius, 154rD).

30. Henry, *Quodlibet* V, q. 4 (Badius, 158vO): "e converso [relatio] creaturae ad ipsum sit secundum rem." Note that while he uses the word 'creature', he is talking about a divine idea.

31. Paulus, *Henri de Gand*, 89; Gómez Caffarena, *Ser Participado*, 32; Maurer, "Ens Diminutum," 220.

32. See Giles of Rome, *De esse et essentia*, q. 2 (Venice, 17va); Godfrey of Fontaines, *Quodlibet* II, q. 2 (PB I.53–68); Godfrey of Fontaines, *Quodlibet* VII, q. 3 (PB II.285–87); James of Viterbo, *Quodlibet* I, q. 5 (Ypma, 63). See also Hocedez, "La Distinction Réelle," 360; Wippel, *Godfrey of Fontaines*, 130–45.

33. See King, "Scotus on Mental Content," 76–77.

34. Scotus, *Rep. I-A*, d. 36, qq. 1–2, nn. 54 and 64 (Noone, 418:16–17 and 421:25–422:3).

35. Ockham, *Quodlibet* III, q. 4 (OTh IX.218:98–219:99): "unus parvus mundus alius entium obiectivorum."

theory is too close to Platonism for Ockham. Thus, he holds that divine ideas have no existence in themselves; they are present as known but are nothing in themselves.[36] Since divine ideas are nothing, they can only be present in God as known. They are in the divine intellect, but not the divine essence. If they were in the divine essence, God could not legitimately be called simple.

The Scope of Divine Ideas

All authors agree that the scope of divine ideas must extend as far as is necessary for God to have distinct cognition of each creature and produce them distinctly. The authors give many answers to this question. Their theories of the character of an idea, individuation, participation, and knowledge significantly impact their answers.

Singulars, Species, and Genera

There are three positions on whether God has ideas of singulars, species, and genera. The first position, held by Bonaventure, Scotus, and Auriol, argues that God has all three. The second position, held by Henry, argues that God has ideas of the lowest species only, and no ideas of singulars or genera. The last position, held by Aquinas and Ockham, argues that properly speaking, God only has ideas of singulars.

Bonaventure and Scotus arrive at their position by different but compatible arguments. Bonaventure argues that divine truth is supremely expressive and that there are as many divine ideas as expressible truths. Both universals and singulars are such expressions, and so there are ideas of all singulars, species, and genera.[37] Scotus argues from comparison rather than expression. God can do anything we can do. We can compare every individual and every part of every individual, including its species and genus, to God's essence. Thus, God can make those comparisons too. Divine ideas result from such comparisons. Thus, God has ideas of singular, species, and genera.[38] Auriol reaches a similar conclusion by saying that primary intentions like man and animal are connoted as distinct things as if they could exist extramentally.[39]

Henry of Ghent argues that God only needs ideas of natural things that are *secundum se* and *ad se ipsas* essentially. Only the lowest species of essences are such. Genus and difference differ from species as incomplete to complete. Thus, distinct cognition of the species is sufficient for perfect knowledge of genera and differences. Since individuation occurs by a double negation for Henry, individuals do not add anything formally distinct from the species. God can know them through the idea of the species.[40]

---

36. Ockham, *Ord.* I, d. 36, q. un, ad opp. (OTh IV.524); Ockham, *In IV Sent.*, q. 9 (OTh VII.178:11).
37. Bonaventure, *In I Sent.*, d. 35, a. un., q. 4 (Quaracchi, I.610a).
38. Scotus, *Rep. I-A*, d. 36, qq. 3–4, n. 49 (Noone, 441–42).
39. Auriol, *Scriptum*, d. 36, p. 2, a. 2 (E-Scriptum, 10:505–24).
40. Henry, *Quodlibet* VII, qq. 1–2 (Leuven, 11.8:8–9); Henry, *Quodlibet* IX, q. 2 (Leuven, 13.33:91–92). See Godfrey of Fontaines, *Quodlibet* II, q. 2 (PB I.53–68).

Aquinas and Ockham argue that the scope of divine ideas is limited to what can have real existence. They agree that everything that exists extramentally is singular, and so there are only ideas of singulars. For Aquinas, this argument holds for ideas *qua* exemplars only. *Qua rationes*, God has divine ideas for everything that can be distinguished intellectually, and so has ideas of genera and species.[41] Ockham admits that God can be said to have ideas of genera and species since he has an idea for every concept of our minds, and we have concepts of genera and species. Even so, Ockham argues that those concepts are singular. Thus, God only has ideas of universals in an extended and inappropriate sense.[42]

Accidents

The authors that ask about divine ideas of accidents conclude that there are divine ideas of all, some, or no accidents. Scotus and Ockham argue that there are divine ideas of all accidents. Scotus argues that accidents are ways that creatures can be compared to the divine essence. Accidents are distinctly cognizable, and it is a mark of perfection to know everything that is distinctly cognizable.[43] Ockham argues that God has an idea of everything that he could create separately. God can make every possible accident exist separately.[44] Bonaventure does not explicitly address this issue, but his arguments in favor of divine ideas for singulars, species, and genera could equally apply to all accidents.

Aquinas and Henry argue that God only has ideas of some accidents. Aquinas claims that God has only divine exemplars of separable accidents because proper accidents are never separated from their subject but are produced in being by the same act that produces their subject. Thus, the idea of the subject includes the inseparable accidents. Distinct acts produce separable accidents, and so they have distinct exemplars.[45] His reasoning about the scope of divine *rationes* of singulars, species, and genera would lead him to admit a distinct divine *ratio* for every possible accident, but he does not make this point explicitly.[46] Henry further restricts divine ideas of accidents. First, he reduces the traditional nine categories of accidents to just quantity and quality. Then, Henry argues that God only has ideas of the lowest species of accidents in those two categories. He restricts divine ideas to the lowest species for the same reasons above.[47]

Auriol is the lone adherent to the position that there are no ideas of accidents. Accidents, he says, are inseparable from their substances and so connotated with their subjects. But there are only ideas of what is distinctly connotated.[48]

---

41. Aquinas, *De veritate*, q. 3, a. 8, ad 2 (Leonine, 22/1.116:74–84).
42. Ockham, *Ord.* I, d. 35, q. 5 (OTh IV.493:12–19).
43. Scotus, *Rep. I-A*, d. 36, qq. 3–4, nn. 47–49 (Noone, 441:8–442:8).
44. Ockham, *Ord.* I, d. 35, q. 5 (OTh IV.493:7–11).
45. Aquinas, *ST* I, q. 15, a. 4, ad 4 (Leonine, 4.204).
46. See Doolan, *Aquinas on Divine Ideas*, 137.
47. Henry, *Quodlibet* VII, qq. 1–2 (Leuven, 11.6:74–8:2).
48. Auriol, *In I Sent.*, d. 36, p. 2, a. 2 (E-Scriptum, 10:505–24).

Evil

Authors almost unanimously argue that God does not have a divine idea of evil properly, but he does have an idea of evil through his ideas of good things.[49] Auriol explains it best when he points out that evil is a twofold privation: It is the privation of some good with regard to some good subject. God does not have an idea of evil directly, but he does have an idea of evil in the sense that he knows how creatures fall short of the ideal.

Ockham alone denies that God has an idea of evil in any way. God only has ideas of distinct things because he can make them separately, but evil, guilt, and other negations and privations are not distinct things. Since they are not distinct things, God could not produce them separately and does not have ideas of them.[50]

Prime Matter

After the question of a divine idea of evil, most authors ask whether God has an idea of prime matter. For the most part, the authors answer with a definitive affirmation or denial. Bonaventure, Henry, Scotus, and Ockham affirm a divine idea of prime matter. Bonaventure and Scotus argue that even imperfect things have a certain degree of perfection. There are no divine ideas of imperfect things *qua* imperfect, but there are insofar as they are perfect. Even minimal assimilation between a creature and God is enough for God to be its exemplar, and so God has an idea of prime matter.[51] Henry says that God has a distinct idea of form and matter insofar as they are integral parts of the composite. God cannot make prime matter without form, but it is other than form and merits its own idea.[52] Unlike Henry, Ockham thinks that God could create prime matter without form. Since Ockham holds that God has an idea for anything he could create separately, God has an idea of prime matter.

Auriol firmly denies that God has a divine idea of prime matter. Like Ockham, he thinks that God has a distinct idea of anything that can be created separately. Nevertheless, he denies that God could create matter without form. Form and matter are related as act and capable-of-actualization. It is impossible for what is merely capable-of-actualization to be actualized without act, that is, prime matter cannot exist without form.

Aquinas insists that God does not have a distinct divine exemplar of prime matter independent of the exemplar of the composite, as there are only divine exemplars of what is producible in being. Prime matter cannot exist without form, and so is not strictly producible in being. Therefore, there is no divine exemplar of matter. Aquinas also insists that there is no distinct divine *ratio* of prime matter. God has divine *rationes* of anything that is distinctly cognizable. Prime matter is

---

49. Bonaventure, *In I Sent.*, d. 36, a. 3, q. 1 (Quaracchi, I.627b); Aquinas, *De veritate*, q. 3, a. 4, ad 7 (Leonine, 22/1.111:124–30); Auriol, *In I Sent.*, d. 36, p. 2, q. 2, a. 2 (E-Scriptum, 13:661–86).
50. Ockham, *Ord.* I, d. 35, q. 5 (OTh IV.763:12–19).
51. Bonaventure, *In I Sent.*, d. 36, a. 3, q. 2 (Quaracchi, I.629b).
52. Henry, *Quodlibet* VII, qq. 1–2 (Leuven, 11.20:97–21:3).

not, of itself, cognizable. Therefore, God does not have a divine idea of prime matter in the sense of an exemplar or a *ratio*.[53]

The Number of Divine Ideas

Given that a divine idea is, for most authors, a principle of divine knowledge of possible creatures, we might assume that at least most authors would argue that God has an infinite number of divine ideas. The preceding summary of the theories clarifies that not every author will endorse an infinity of divine ideas.

Bonaventure and Scotus argue that God has, as it were, divine ideas of an infinite number of infinities. God has ideas of every possible individual and every possible aspect of those possible individuals. There is an infinite number of divine ideas since there is an infinite number of possible individual substances and accidents and possible species of substances and accidents.[54] God has divine ideas of an infinite number of species and genera in every category of being. Each of those species and genera has an infinite number of possible individuals within it. Auriol and Ockham agree that God has an infinite number of divine ideas, but their infinities are less plentiful. There is an infinite number of divine ideas of individuals, but not an infinite number of species and genera. Divine ideas are the creatures as known. God could create an infinite number of creatures, and so has an infinite number of ideas.[55] They do not emphasize, or in some cases admit, ideas of the aspects of possible creatures.

Henry and Richard defend that God could not, even in principle, have an infinite number of divine ideas. Henry's argument is representative. Divine ideas are rational respects of imitability known by the divine intellect. Each imitation of God occupies a distinct and unrepeatable grade of imitation and has a certain degree of perfection. If God had an infinite number of ideas, then there would be an infinite number of degrees of perfection among possible creatures. One of those infinite degrees of perfection would have to be infinite perfection. Since no creature can imitate God perfectly, he could not have an infinite number of divine ideas.[56]

Aquinas's theory posits an infinite number of divine *rationes* and a finite number of divine exemplars. God only has exemplars of what he actually wills to produce in time in the sense of divine exemplars. Since it cannot be proven philosophically that the world is not eternal, it is philosophically possible for him to have an infinite number of divine exemplars. Theologically, it is certain that the world began to be and will exist for only a finite amount of time. Since only a finite number of creatures can exist in a finite amount of time, God has a finite number of exemplars. Divine *rationes* are not restricted by what God produces, so God must have an infinite number of *rationes* because he knows an infinite number of possible creatures.[57]

---

53. Aquinas, *ST* I, q. 15, a. 3, ad 3 (Leonine, 4.204).
54. See also Scotus's argument from infinity, *Rep.* I-A, d. 36, qq. 3–4, n. 68 (Noone, 447:2–11).
55. Ockham, *Ord.* I, d. 35, q. 5 (OTh IV.493:19–21).
56. Henry, *Quodlibet* V, q. 3, ad 1 (Badius, 156vT).
57. Aquinas, *ST* I, q. 15, a. 3 (Leonine, 4.204).

CONCLUSION

A SUGGESTION FOR THE BEST THEORY

This study shows that an author's theory of divine ideas is, in part, an outgrowth of his logical, metaphysical, and epistemological commitments. Since divine ideas are, in a sense, a secondary line of metaphysical inquiry, the best theory of divine ideas depends upon the best metaphysical theory. This dependence is the primary reason it is beyond this study's scope to make definitive arguments about the best theory of divine ideas. Nevertheless, some preliminary judgments are in order by way of conclusion.

In the absence of a definitive judgment about the best metaphysical theory, I think the best theories of divine ideas are Scotus's and Bonaventure's. It would be impossible to hold both theories, but the metaphysical systems that undergird each make it impossible for one of the theories of divine ideas to rule out the other definitively. Scotus's theory offers a devastating critique of the Thomistic and Henrician versions of the Imitability Theory, the *Obiecta Cognita* Theory, and the Infinite Intellect Theory. The arguments he offers for the claims that divine ideas cannot be how God knows possible creatures, would be real relations, and could not yield distinct cognition of creatures are decisive. Without some manner of direct epistemological access to creatures, God could not know them distinctly. Moreover, Scotus's application of instants of nature gives an adequate account of God's knowledge of himself and possible creatures. Finally, it is a strength of Scotus's theory that it includes rational respects in the *ratio* of a divine idea, which ensures that Scotus offers a robustly metaphysical—and not merely logical or grammatical—account of divine ideas.

These comments, coupled with Chapter VII's arguments, show the strength of Scotus's position. My endorsement of Bonaventure's position will require more defense since it appears to fall under the weight of Olivi's and Scotus's arguments against the Imitability Theory. Bonaventure's theory escapes the critique because of his emphasis on exemplarity. The metaphysician must study exemplarity and even has it as his unique task to study exemplarity because being-exemplified is the most fundamental aspect of a creature. At its innermost core, a creature is an imitation of God. Put another way, for Bonaventure, the central characteristic of a creature is its being related to God as an imitation. Since creatures are imitative relations fundamentally, Bonaventure's theory of divine ideas can claim enough direct access to creatures to make his theory workable. In the *Itinerarium*, Bonaventure foreshadows Scotus's arguments about relations: "No one knows," he says, "that something is more assimilated to another unless he knows that other. For I do not know that this [man] is like Peter unless I know or cognize Peter."[58] Unless the terms of the relation are known, the relation remains unknown. Now it is possible to read this text as saying that the measure must be known to know how things are related

---

58. Bonaventure, *Itinerarium*, c. 3, n. 4 (Quaracchi, V.304b–305a): "Nullus autem scit, aliquid alii magis assimilari, nisi illud cognoscat; non enim scio, hunc esse similem Petro, nisi sciam vel cognoscam Petrum."

to it, but the text cannot be read as saying that knowledge of the measured can be had simply from the knowledge of the measure and a relation.

If Bonaventure accepts this point, how can his theory of divine ideas, which argues that they are *rationes cognoscendi*, avoid contradiction? The answer is found in Bonaventure's account of the nature of creatures and his emphasis on divine ideas as expressions of truth. Creatures, because they are created *ex nihilo* and composed of form and matter, have unstable existence.[59] What stability they do have comes from their matter. The form gives the act of existence to a substance, and matter gives it the stability to existing *per se*.[60] However, understanding a creature's form and matter is not enough to comprehend it. Creatures are parts of a whole, and so they are only comprehended if understood in relation to the whole. For Bonaventure, understanding a creature in relation to the whole entails an ascent of being because every creature is, at its core, a vestige of God: "All things or substances are signs, intentionally expressed by a sign-giver."[61] Substances are fundamentally signs of their transcendent source.[62] No creature is fully understood unless it is understood as a sign of God, which explains why exemplarism is at the core of Bonaventure's metaphysics. At its deepest level, a creature is a likeness of God.

This account of creatures as signs already shows how Bonaventure's theory escapes Scotus's criticism. The character of a sign is to be related to what it signifies. A sign is a certain relation. If creatures are signs, then the most fundamental aspect of what it means to be a creature is to signify God. Creatures are certain relations. To know the creature is to know the relation. Knowledge of the creature can come through a relation because the creature is the relation at its core. This claim follows because God cannot know the creature before he establishes its signification.

This response becomes even more evident when we consider Bonaventure's claim about divine ideas as expressions of truth. God's way of knowing is the opposite of ours. When we know, the thing known is the truth, and our *ratio cognoscendi* is a likeness. We know this way because we receive our knowledge *ab extra*. The likeness of the thing makes us know the thing. But with God, the *ratio cognoscendi* is truth itself, and "what is known is a likeness of the truth, namely, the creature itself."[63] God knows the creatures themselves because they *are* likenesses of the truth. Creatures are not numerically identical to their divine ideas since that claim amounts to pantheism. Yet, a creature's essence is a likeness for Bonaventure in a way that it is not a likeness for other Imitability Theorists, who take a stronger, more Avicennian account of essences. Comprehension of an essence could be

---

59. Bonaventure, *In I Sent.*, d. 8, p. 1, a. 1, q. 1, arg. 5 (Quaracchi, I.150b); Bonaventure, *In I Sent.*, d. 37, p. 1, a. 1, q. 1 (Quaracchi, I.639a); Bonaventure, *Dominica III adventus*, Sermo 14 (Quaracchi, IX.73a). See Bissen, *L'exemplarisme Divin*, 170; Cullen, "Semiotic Metaphysics," 271.

60. Bonaventure, *In II Sent.*, d. 3, p. 1, q. 2 (Quaracchi, II.97b).

61. Cullen, *Bonaventure*, 77. See Bonaventure, *Itinerarium*, c. 2, n. 11 (Quaracchi, V.302b); Cullen, "Semiotic Metaphysics," 228.

62. Cullen, "Semiotic Metaphysics," 323.

63. Bonaventure, *In I Sent.*, d. 35, a. un., q. 1 (Quaracchi, I.601b): "cognitum est similitudo veritatis, scilicet ipsa creatura."

possible without recourse to divine ideas, according to them. This way of thinking is especially true of Aquinas, who denies divine illumination.

Bonaventure's system gains further credibility when we consider the weight he places on likenesses in knowing. All knowledge requires the use of likenesses. Even if an intermediate likeness is not required to mediate between the knower and the thing known, the knower's essence would still be a *ratio cognoscendi* and so possess the character of a likeness.[64] God's essence is the likeness of every possible creature, and each creature is, in turn, a likeness of the divine essence. So, when God knows a likeness, he has direct epistemological access to the creature. From Bonaventure's point of view, it makes no sense to say, as Scotus does, that God knows the creature in an instant logically prior to knowing the rational relation because there is no creaturely essence to know prior to the rational relation. At its core, the creature is that relation, and so by knowing that relation, God knows the creature.

Bonaventure's Imitability Theory escapes Scotus's critique unscathed because it posits that creatures are fundamentally signs. It preserves the sort of direct epistemological access to creatures that Olivi's and Scotus's arguments show a good theory of divine ideas needs. Without this sort of account of essences, the Imitability Theory is not explanatory.

The truth about the best theory of divine ideas depends on the truth about the best theory of essence. If creatures are inherently signs of the divine essence, then God will know the creature by knowing the relation by which it is a sign of him. If creatures are not inherently signs but have more robust, independent essences, relations can only arise after direct acquaintance with the creature itself. In both cases, however, Scotus's critiques of the Imitability Theory hold sway. God cannot know a creature through a relation unless that relation is, in some way, the creature itself.

---

64. Bonaventure, *De scientia Christi*, q. 2, ad 11 (Quaracchi, V.10b), esp.: "Nihilominus tamen ipsa essentia, in quantum est ratio cognoscendi, tenet rationem similitudinis; et hoc modo ponimus similitudinem circa divina cognitionem, quae non est aliud quam ipsa essentia cognoscentis."

Bibliography

PRIMARY SOURCES

Albert the Great. *Sancti Doctoris Ecclesiae Alberti Magni Ordinis Fratrum Praedicatorum Episcopi Opera Omnia*. Aschendorff: Monasterii Westaflorum, 1951.

Alexander of Hales. *Glossa in Quatuor Libros Sententiarum Petri Lomardi*. 4 vols. Bibliotheca Franciscana Scholastica Medii Aevi 12–15. Quaracchi: Collegium S. Bonaventura, 1591.

———. *Summa Theologica*. 6 vols. Quaracchi: Collegium S. Bonavenura, 1924.

Anselm of Canterbury. *S. Anselm Cantuariensis Archiepiscopi Opera Omnia*. Edited by F. S. Schmitt. 6 vols. Edinburgh: Thomas Nelson and Sons, 1946.

Aristotle. *Aristoteles Latinus*. Leiden: Brill, 1939–.

Augustine. *Opera Omnia*. Edited by J. P. Migne. Patralogia Cursus Completus. Series Latina 32–47. Paris, 1844–.

Averroes. *Aristotelis Opera Cum Averrois Commentariis*. Venice: Iunctina, 1574.

———. *Commentarium Magnum in Aristotelis De Anima Libros*. Edited by F. Stuart Crawford. Cambridge, MA: The Medieval Academy of America, 1953.

———. *The Book of the Decisive Treatise Determining the Connection between the Law and Wisdom & Epistle Dedicatory*. Translated by Charles E. Butterworth. Provo, UT: Bringham Young University Press, 2001.

Avicenna. *Avicenna Latinus: Liber de Philosophia Prima, Sive Scientia Divina*. Edited by Simone van Riet. 3 vols. Leiden: Brill, 1977–1983.

Bessa, Bernardi a, ed. *Analecta Franciscorum*. Vol. 3, *Chronica XXIV generalium Ordinis minorum*. Rome, 1897.

Bonaventure. *Doctoris Seraphici S. Bonaventurae . . . Opera Omnia*. 10 vols. Quaracchi: Collegium S. Bonaventura, 1882.

Denifle, Henricus, ed. *Chartularium Universitatis Parisiensis*. 5 vols. Paris, 1899.

Denzinger, Henricus, and Adolfus Schönmetzer, eds. *Enchiridion Symbolorum Definitionum et Declarationum de Rebus Fidei et Morum*. 32nd ed. Rome: Herder, 1963.

Ghazali, Abu Hamid al-. *Algazel's Metaphysics: A Medieval Translation*. Edited by Joseph Muckle. Toronto: St. Michael's College, 1933.

Giles of Rome. *De Esse et Essentia. De Mensura Angelorum. De Cognitione Angelorum*. Venice, 1503.

Glorieux, P., ed. "Correctorium Corruptorii 'Quare.'" In *Les Premières Polémiques Thomistes*, 1:1–432. Kain: Revue des Sciences Philosophiques et Théologiques, 1927.

Godfrey of Fontaines. *Les Philosophes Belges*. Edited by M. De Wulf and A. Pelzer. 5 vols. Louvain: Institut Supérior de philosophie, 1904.

Hamesse, Jacqueline, ed. *Les Auctoritates Aristotelis: Un Florilège Médiéval Étude Historique et Édition Critique*. Louvain: Publications Universitaires, 1974.

Henry of Ghent. *Quodlibeta*. Paris, 1518.

———. *Summa Quaestionum Ordinarium*. 2 vols. Paris, 1520.

———. *Henrici de Gandavo Opera Omnia*. Leuven: Leuven University Press, 1969–.

Henry of Harclay. "In I Sententiarum." MS Casale Monferrato. Seminario Vescovile, B.2, fols. 1r–84r.

———. *Ordinary Questions*. Edited by Mark Gerald Henninger. Translated by Raymond Edwards and Mark Gerald Henninger. 2 vols. Auctores Britannici Medii Aevi 17–18. New York: The British Academy, 2008.

James of Viterbo. *Disputationes de Quolibet*. Edited by Eelcko Ypma. 4 vols. Wûrzburg, 1968–1975.

———. *Quaestiones de Divinis Praedicamentis I–X*. Edited by Eelcko Ypma. Rome, 1983.

———. *Quaestiones de Divinis Praedicamentis XI–XVII*. Edited by Eelcko Ypma. Rome, 1986.

John Duns Scotus. *Joannis Duns Scoti Doctoris Subtilis Ordinis Minorum Opera Omnia*. Editio nova. Paris: Wadding-Vivès, 1891.

———. *Ioannis Duns Scoti Doctoris Subtilis et Mariani Opera Omnia*. Civitas Vaticana: Typis Polyglottis Vaticanis, 1950.

———. "Scotus on Divine Ideas: *Rep. Paris. I-A*, d. 36." Edited by Timothy B. Noone. *Medioevo* 24, no. 1 (1998): 395–453.

———. *B. Ioannis Duns Scoti Opera Philosophica*. St. Bonaventure, NY: Franciscan Institute, 1999.

———. *The Examined Report of the Paris Lecture: Reportatio I-A*. Edited by Allan B. Wolter and Oleg V. Bychkov. 2 vols. St. Bonaventure, NY: The Franciscan Institute, 2004.

John of Paris. *Le Correctorium Corruptorii «Circa» de Jean Quidort de Paris*. Edited by Jean-Pierre Muller. Studia Anselmiana 12/13. Rome: Herder, 1941.

———. *Commentaire Sur Les Sentences*. Edited by J. P. Muller. Rome: Herder, 1961–1964.

Muller, Jean-Pierre, ed. *Le Correctorium Corruptorii 'Quaestione'*. Studia Anselmiana 35. Rome: Herder, 1954.

Pattin, Adriaan. "Le *Liber de Causis*: Édition Établie à l'aide de 90 Manuscrits Avec Introduction et Notes." *Tijdschrift Voor Filosofie* 28, no. 1 (1966): 90–203.

Peter Auriol. *Petri Aurioli Commentariorum in Primum Librum Sententiarum*. E-Scriptum. Accessed January 1, 2017. http://www.peterauriol.net/editions/electronic-scriptum/contents.

Peter John Olivi. *Quaestiones in Secundum Librum Sententiarum*. Edited by B. Jansen. 3 vols. Quaracchi: Collegium S. Bonavenura, 1922.

———. "Tria Scripta Sui Ipsius Apologetica Annorum 1283 et 1285." Edited by Damasus Laberge. *Archivum Franciscanum Historicum* 28, no. 1 (1935): 115–55, 374–407.

———. *Quodlibeta Quinque*. Edited by S. Defraia. Grottaferrata: Collegium S. Bonaventura, 2002.

———. "Quaestio de Divino Velle et Scire (Summa I, 6)." Edited by Sylvain Piron. *Oliviana* 6, no. 1 (2020). http://journals.openedition.org/oliviana/977.

———. "Quaestio de Ideis (Summa I, 6 Bis)." Edited by Sylvain Piron. *Oliviana* 6, no. 1 (2020). http://journals.openedition.org/oliviana/1023.

Peter Lombard. *Sententiae in IV Libris Distinctae.* Edited by Ignatius Brady. Grottaferrata: Editiones Collegii S. Bonaventurae ad Claras Aquas, 1971.

Plato. *Plato: Complete Works.* Edited by John M. Cooper. Indianapolis, IN: Hackett Publishing Co., 1997.

Plotinus. *Enneads.* Translated by A. H. Armstrong. Cambridge, MA: Harvard University Press, 1988.

Proclus. "Procli Elementatio Theologica Translata a Guilelmo de Moerbeke (Textus Ineditus)." Edited by C. Vansteenkiste. *Tijdschrift Voor Filosofie* 13, no. 2–3 (1952): 263–302, 491–531.

Pseudo-Dionysius. *Opera Omnia.* Edited by J. P. Migne. Patralogia Cursus Completus. Series Graeca 3. Paris, 1857.

Richard of Mediavilla. *Sacratissimi Theologi Richardi de Mediavilla Ordinis Seraphici Minorum Conventualium.* Brixiae, 1591.

Robert Grosseteste. *Die philosophischen Werke des Robert Grosseteste, Bischofs von Lincoln.* Edited by Ludwig Baur. Münster: Aschendorfsche Verlagsbuchhandlung, 1912.

———. *Hexaemeron.* Edited by Richard C. Dales and Servus Gieben. Auctores Britannici Medii Aevi 6. New York: Oxford University Press, 1983.

Roger Marston. *Fr. Rogeri Marston, OFM, Quodlibeta Quatuor.* Edited by Gerald J. Etzkorn and Ignatius Brady. Quaracchi: Collegium S. Bonavenura, 1968.

Seneca, Lucius Annaeus. *Ad Lucillum Epistulae Morales.* Translated by Richard M. Gummere. 3 vols. New York: G. P. Putnam's Sons, 1935.

Thomas Anglicus. *Liber Propugnatorius Super Primum Sententiarum Contra Johannem Scotum.* Venedig, 1523.

Thomas Aquinas. *Sancti Thomae de Aquino Opera Omnia.* Rome: Comissio Leonina, 1882.

———. *Scriptum Super Libros Sententiarum.* 4 vols. Edited by R. P. Mandonnet. Paris: Lethielleux, 1929.

———. *Scriptum Super Sententiis.* Edited by M. F. Moos. Vols. 3–4. Paris: Lethielleux, 1933.

———. *In Librum Beati Dionysii De Divinis Nominibus Expositio.* Edited by C. Pera. Turin: Marietti, 1950.

———. *Super Evangelium S. Ioannis Lectura.* Edited by R. Cai. 5th ed. Rome: Marietti, 1952.

———. "Quaestiones Disputatae de Potentia." In *Quaestiones Disputatae*, edited by P. M. Pession, 8th ed., 2:7–276. Rome: Marietti, 1965.

———. *In Duodecim Libros Metaphysicam Aristotelis Expositio.* Edited by R. M. Spiazzi. Rome: Marietti, 1971.

Thomas of Sutton. *Quodlibeta.* Edited by Michael Schmaus. München: Verlag der Bayerischen Akademie der Wissenschaften, 1969.

———. *Quaestiones Ordinariae*. Edited by Johannes Schneider. München: Verlag der Bayerischen Akademie der Wissenschaften, 1977.

William de la Mare. "Correctorium Fratris Thomae." In *Les Premières Polémiques Thomistes*, edited by P. Glorieux, 1:1–432. Kain: Revue des Sciences Philosophiques et Théologiques, 1927.

William of Alnwick. "Determinationes." Palatini lat. 1805. Civitas Vaticana, n.d.

William of Ockham. *Guillelmi de Ockham Opera Philosophica et Theologica*. 17 vols. St. Bonaventure, NY: Franciscan Institute, 1974–1988.

SECONDARY SOURCES

Adams, Marilyn McCord. "Ockham on Identity and Distinction." *Franciscan Studies* 36, no. 1 (1976): 5–74.

———. "Ockham's Nominalism and Unreal Entities." *The Philosophical Review* 86, no. 2 (1977): 144–76.

———. *William Ockham*. 2 vols. Notre Dame, IN: University of Notre Dame Press, 1987.

Adamson, Peter. "On Knowledge of Particulars." *Proceedings of the Aristotelian Society* 105, no. 1 (2005): 257–78.

Adriaenssen, Han Thomas. "Peter Auriol on the Intuitive Cognition of Nonexistents: Revisiting the Charge of Skepticism in Walter Chatton and Adam Wodeham." *Oxford Studies in Medieval Philosophy* 5, no. 1 (2017): 151–80.

———. *Representation and Scepticism from Aquinas to Descartes*. New York: Oxford University Press, 2018.

Aertsen, Jan A. *Medieval Philosophy as Transcendental Thought: From Philip the Chancellor (ca. 1225) to Francisco Súarez*. Studien Und Texte Zur Geistesgeschichte Des Mittelalters, Band 107. Leiden: Brill, 2012.

Alféri, Pierre. *Guillaume d'Ockham: le singulier*. Paris: Éditions de Minuit, 1989.

Aristotle. *Posterior Analytics*. Translated by Jonathan Barnes. 2nd ed. New York: Clarendon Press, 1993.

Balić, Carlo. "Adnotationes Ad Nonnullas Quaestiones circa Ordinationem I. Duns Scoti." In *Iohannis Duns Scoti Opera Omnia*, IV:1*–39*. Vatican City: Vatican, 1956.

———. "Henricus de Harcley et Ioannes Duns Scotus." In *Mélanges Offerts à Étienne Gilson*, 93–121. Paris, 1959.

Baudry, Léon. *Guillaum d'Occam: Sa Vie, Ses Oeuvres, Ses Ideés Sociales et Politiques*. Vol. 1. Paris, 1949.

———. "L'Ordre Franciscain au Temps de Guillaume d'Occam." *Medieval Studies* 27, no. 1 (1965): 184–211.

Beckmann, Jan P. "Entdecken oder Setzen? Die Besonderheit der Relationstheorie des Duns Scotus und ihre Bedeutung für die Metaphysik." In *John Duns Scotus: Metaphysics and Ethics*, edited by Ludger Honnefelder, Rega Wood, and Mechthild Dreyer, 367–84. Leiden: Brill, 1996.

Bissen, R. P. J.-M. "Des Idées Exemplaires En Dieu d'après Saint Bonaventure." Ph.D. diss., The University of Freibourg, 1927.

———. *L'exemplarisme Divin Selon Saint Bonaventure*. Paris: Vrin, 1929.

Black, Deborah. "Avicenna on Individuation, Self-Awareness, and God's Knowledge of Particulars." In *The Judeo-Christian-Islamic Heritage: Philosophical and Theological Perspectives*, edited by Richard C. Taylor and Irfan A. Omar, 255–81. Milwaukee: Marquette University Press, 2012.

Bobillier, Stève. "Divine Ideas and Beatific Vision by Peter John Olivi." In Falà and Zavattero, 51–73.

Boehner, Philotheus. "Editor's Introduction." In *Philosophical Writings*, Revised by Stephen F. Brown. Indianapolis, IN: Hackett Publishing Co., 1990.

Boland, Vivian. *Ideas in God According to Saint Thomas Aquinas: Sources and Synthesis*. New York: Brill, 1996.

Bonaseo, Olivier. "The Question of an Eternal World in the Teaching of St. Bonaventure." *Franciscan Studies* 34, no. 1 (1974): 7–33.

Boulnois, Olivier. "Jean Duns Scot." In *Sur La Science Divine*, edited by J.-C. Bardout and O. Boulnois, 245–52. Paris: Presses Universalitaires de France, 2002.

Boureau, Alain. "Le Concept de Relation Chez Pierre de Jean Olivi." In *Pierre de Jean Olivi (1248–1298)*, edited by Alain Boureau and Sylvain Piron, 41–55. Paris: Vrin, 1999.

Brady, Ignatius. "Prooemium." In *Fr. Rogeri Marston O.F.M., Quodlibeta Quatuor*, edited by Gerald J. Etzkorn and Ignatius Brady. Quaracchi: Ex typographia collegii S. Bonaventurae, 1968.

Brampton, C. K. "Traditions Relating to the Death of William of Ockham." *Archivum Franciscanum Historicum* 53, no. 1 (1960): 442–49.

Branick, Vincent P. "The Unity of the Divine Ideas." *The New Scholasticism* 42, no. 2 (1968): 171–201.

Brower, Jeffrey E. "Aquinas on the Problem of Universals." *Philosophy and Phenomenological Research* 92, no. 3 (2016): 715–35.

———. "Aristotelian vs Contemporary Perspectives on Relations." In *The Metaphysics of Relations*, edited by Anna Marmodoro and David Yates, 38–54. New York: Oxford University Press, 2016.

———. "Medieval Theories of Relations." In *The Stanford Encyclopedia of Philosophy*, edited by Edward N. Zalta, Winter 2018. Metaphysics Research Lab, Stanford University, 2018. https://plato.stanford.edu/archives/win2018/entries/relations-medieval/.

Brown, Stephen F. "Henry of Ghent (b. ca. 1217; d. 1293)." In *Individuation in Scholasticism: The Later Middle Ages and the Counter Reformation 1150–1650*, edited by Jorge J. E. Gracia, 195–219. Albany, NY: State University of New York Press, 1994.

Coccia, Antonius. "De Aeternitate Mundi apud S. Bonaventuram et Recentiores." In *S. Bonaventura 1274–1974*, 279–306. Rome: Collegio S. Bonavenura, 1974.

Conti, Alessandro D. "Divine Ideas and Exemplar Causality in Auriol." *Vivarium* 38, no. 1 (2000): 99–116.

———. "Late Medieval Exemplarism: A Philosophical Assessment." In Falà and Zavattero, 461–87.

Cooper, John W. *Panentheism, the Other God of the Philosophers: From Plato to the Present*. Grand Rapids, MI: Baker Academic, 2006.

Côté, Antoine. "Review of Gregory T. Doolan, Aquinas on Divine Ideas as Exemplar Causes." *Journal of the History of Philosophy* 47, no. 4 (2009): 624–25.

———. "James of Viterbo on Divine Ideas and the Divine Cognition of Creatures." In Côté and Pickavé, 70–97.

Côté, Antoine, and Martin Pickavé, eds. *A Companion to James of Viterbo*. Leiden: Brill, 2018.

Courtenay, William J. *Schools & Scholars in Fourteenth-Century England*. Princeton, NJ: Princeton University Press, 1987.

———. "Scotus at Paris." In *Via Scoti: Methodologia Ad Mentem Joannis Duns Scoti*, edited by Leonardo Sileo, 1:149–63. Atti Del 244 Duns Scotus Bibliography Congresso Scotistico Internazionale Roma 9–11 Marzo 1993. Rome: Edizioni Antonianum, 1995.

Cross, Richard. "Duns Scotus on the Semantic Content of Cognitive Acts and Species." *Quaestio* 10, no. 1 (2010): 135–54.

———. "Henry of Ghent on the Reality of Non-Existing Possibles—Revisited." *Archiv Für Geschichte Der Philosophie* 92, no. 2 (2010): 115–32.

———. *Duns Scotus's Theory of Cognition*. New York: Oxford University Press, 2014.

Cruz Hernandez, Miguel. *Abu-L-Walid Ibn Rusd (Averroes): Vida, Obra, Pensamiento, Influencia*. Cordoba: Monte de Piedad y Caja de Ahorros de Cordoba, 1986.

Cullen, Christopher M. "The Semiotic Metaphysics of Saint Bonaventure." Ph.D. diss., The Catholic University of America, 2000.

———. *Bonaventure*. Great Medieval Thinkers. New York: Oxford University Press, 2006.

De Carvahlo, Mário S. "On the Unwritten Section of Henry of Ghent's Summa." In *Henry of Ghent and the Transformation of Scholastic Thought: Studies in Memory of Jos Decorte*, edited by Guy Guldentops and Carlos Steel, 327–70. Leuven: Leuven University Press, 2003.

De Konick, Thomas. "Aristotle on God as Thought Thinking Itself." *Review of Metaphysics* 47, no. 3 (1994): 471–515.

Decorte, Jos. "'Modus' or 'Res': Scotus's Criticism of Henry of Ghent's Conception of the Reality of a Real Relation." In *Via Scoti: Methodologica ad Mentem Joannis Duns Scoti*, edited by Leonardo Sileo, 1:407–29. Atti Del 244 Duns Scotus Bibliography Congresso Scotistico Internazionale Roma 9–11 Marzo 1993. Rome: Edizioni Antonianum, 1995.

———. "Relatio as Modus Essendi: The Origins of Henry of Ghent's Definition of Relation." *International Journal of Philosophical Studies* 10, no. 3 (2002): 309–36.

———. "Relation and Substance in Henry of Ghent's Metaphysics." In *Henry of Ghent and the Transformation of Scholastic Metaphysics: Studies in Memory of Jos Decorte*, edited by Guy Guldentops and Carlos Steel, 3–14. Leuven: Leuven University Press, 2003.

Dewan, Lawrence. "St. Thomas, James Ross, and Exemplarism: A Reply." *American Catholic Philosophical Association* 65, no. 2 (1991): 221–34.

Dezza, Ernesto. "Giovanni Duns Scoto e gli *Instantia Naturae*." In Falà and Zavattero, 135–59.

Doolan, Gregory T. *Aquinas on the Divine Ideas as Exemplar Causes*. Washington, DC: The Catholic University of America Press, 2008.

———. Aquinas on the Divine Ideas and the Really Real." *Nova et Vetera* 13, no. 4 (2015): 1059–91.

Duba, William O. "Henry of Harclay and Aufredo Gonteri Brito." In *Mediaeval Commentaries on the Sentences of Peter Lombard: Current Research*, edited by Philipp W. Rosemann, Russell L. Friedman, and Chris Schabel, 2:263–368. Leiden: Brill, 2002.

Duba, William, and Chris Schabel. "Remigio, Auriol, Scotus, and the Myth of the Two-Year Sentences Lecture at Paris." *Recherches de Théologie et Philosophie Médiévales* 84, no. 1 (2017): 143–79.

Dumont, Stephen D. "The *Propositio Famosa Scoti*: Duns Scotus and Ockham on the Possibility of a Science of Theology." *Dialogue* 31, no. 3 (1992): 415–29.

———. "Henry of Ghent and Duns Scotus." In *Medieval Philosophy*, edited by J. Marenbon, 41–57. Routledge History of Philosophy 3. New York: Routledge, 2003.

———. "Duns Scotus's Parisian Question on the Formal Distinction." *Vivarium* 43, no. 1 (2005): 7–62.

———. "James of Viterbo on the Will." In Côte and Pickavé, 249–305.

———. "John Duns Scotus's *Reportatio Parisiensis Examinata*: A Mystery Solved." *Recherches de Théologie et Philosophie Médiévales* 85, no. 2 (2018): 377–438.

Elders, Leo. *Aristotle's Theology: A Commentary on Book Λ of the Metaphysics*. Assen, The Netherlands: Koninklijk Van Gorcum & Co., 1972.

Endres, J. B. "Appropriation." In *New Catholic Encyclopedia*, 1:606–7. Washington, DC: The Catholic University of America Press, 2003.

Fabro, Cornelio. *Participation et Causalité Selon S. Thomas d'Aquin*. Louvain: Publications Universitaires, 1961.

Falà, Jacopo Francesco. "Divine Ideas in the *Collationes Oxonienses*." In Falà and Zavattero, 101–33.

Falà, Jacopo Francesco, and Irene Zavattero, eds. *Divine Ideas in Franciscan Thought: XIIIth–XIVth Century*. Flumen Sapientiae 8. Rome: Aracne editrice, 2018.

Farthing, John Lee. "The Problem of Divine Exemplarity in St. Thomas." *The Thomist* 49, no. 2 (1985): 183–222.

Feser, Edward. *Scholastic Metaphysics: A Contemporary Introduction*. Editiones Scholasticae 39. Heusenstamm: Editiones Scholasticae, 2014.

Freddoso, Alfred J. "Ockham's Theory of Truth Conditions." In *Ockham's Theory of Propositions: Part II of the Summa Logicae*, 1–76. Notre Dame, IN: University of Notre Dame Press, 1980.

Friedman, Russell L. "Peter Auriol on Intentions and Essential Predication." In *Medieval Analyses in Language and Cognition*, 415–31. Copenhagen: The Royal Danish Academy of Sciences and Letters, 1999.

———. *Intellectual Traditions at the Medieval University: The Use of Philosophical Psychology in Trinitarian Theology among the Franciscans and Dominicans, 1250–1350*. Studien Und Texte Zur Geistesgeschichte Des Mittelalters, Bd. 108. Leiden: Brill, 2013.

———. "Act, Species, and Appearance: Peter Auriol on Intellectual Cognition and Consciousness." In *Intentionality, Cognition, and Mental Representation in Medieval Philosophy*, edited by Gyula Klima, 141–65. New York: Fordham University Press, 2015.

Friedman, Russell L., and Lauge O. Nielson. "Peter Auriol: An Introduction." *Vivarium* 38, no. 1 (2000): 1–4.

Gál, Gedeon. "William of Ockham Died 'Impenitent' in April 1347." *Franciscan Studies* 42 (1982): 90–95.

Galluzzo, Gabriele. "Aquinas on Common Natures and Universals." *Recherches de Théologie et Philosophie Médiévales* 71, no. 1 (2004): 71–131.

Gauthier, R. A., and J. Y. Jolif. *L'Ethique à Nicomaque*. Vol. 2. Louvain: Publications Universitaires de Louvain, 1970.

Geach, Peter T. *God and the Soul*. London: Routledge and Kegan Paul, 1969.

Geiger, Louis B. "Les Idées Divines Dans l'oeuvres de S. Thomas." In *St. Thomas Aquinas, 1274–1974, Commemorative Studies*, edited by Armand Maurer, 1:175–209. Toronto: Pontifical Institute of Mediaeval Studies Press, 1974.

Gilson, Étienne. *Jean Duns Scot: Introduction a Ses Positions Fondamentales*. Paris: Vrin, 1952.

———. *La Philosophie de Saint Bonaventure*. Troisième édition. Paris: Vrin, 1953.

———. *History of Christian Philosophy in the Middle Ages*. London: Sheed and Ward, 1955.

———. *Introduction à La Philosophie Chrétienne*. Paris: Vrin, 1960.

———. *Le Thomisme*. 6th ed. Paris: Vrin, 1965.

———. "Quasi Definitio Substantiae." In *St. Thomas Aquinas, 1274–1974, Commemorative Studies*, edited by Armand Maurer, 1:111–29. Toronto: Pontifical Institute of Mediaeval Studies Press, 1974.

Gómez Caffarena, José. "Cronología de La «Suma» de Enrique de Gante por relacion a Sus «Quodlibetos»." *Gregorianum* 38, no. 1 (1957): 116–33.

———. *Ser Participado y Ser Subsistente en La Metafisica de Enrique de Gante*. Rome, 1958.

Gossiaux, Mark D. "James of Viterbo and the Late Thirteenth-Century Debate Concerning the Reality of Possibles." *Recherches de Théologie et Philosophie Médiévales* 74, no. 2 (2007): 483–522.

Gracia, Jorge J. E. "Cutting the Gordian Knot of Ontology: Thomas's Solution to the Problem of Universals." In *Thomas Aquinas and His Legacy*, edited by David M. Gallagher, 16–36. Washington, DC: The Catholic University of America Press, 1994.

Grajewski, Maurice J. *The Formal Distinction of Duns Scotus*. Washington, DC: The Catholic University of America Press, 1944.

Greenstock, David L. "Exemplar Causality and the Supernatural Order." *The Thomist* 16, no. 1 (1953): 1–31.

Guelluy, Robert. *Philosophe et Theologie chez Guillaume d' Ockham*. Louvain: E. Nauwelaerts, 1947.

Hayes, Zachary. *The Hidden Center: Spirituality and Speculative Christology in St. Bonvaenture*. New York: Paulist Press, 1981.

———. "Bonaventure: Mystery of the Triune God." In *The History of Franciscan Theology*, edited by Kenan B. Osborne, 39–125. St. Bonaventure, NY: Franciscan Institute, 1994.

Henle, R. J. *Saint Thomas and Platonism*. The Hague: Martinus Nijhoff, 1956.

Henninger, Mark Gerald. *Relations: Medieval Theories 1250–1325*. New York: Oxford University Press, 1989.

Hocedez, E. *Richard de Middleton: Sa Vies, Ses Oeuvres, Sa Doctrine*. Louvain: Spicilegium Sacrum Louvanienses, 1925.

———. "Gilles de Rome et Henri de Gand Sur La Distinction Réelle (1276–1287)." *Gregorianum* 8, no. 3 (1927): 358–84.

Hödl, L. "'Opus Naturae Est Opus Intelligentiae.' Ein Neuplatonisches Axiom im aristotelischen Verständnis des Albertus Magnus." In *Averroismus im Mittealter und in der Renaissance*, edited by F. Niewöhner and L. Sturlese, 132–48. Zürich: Spur Verlag, 1994.

Hoenen, M. J. F. M. *Marsilius of Inghen: Divine Knowledge in Late Medieval Thought*. Vol. 50 of Studies in the History of Christian Thought. Leiden: Brill, 1993.

———. "*Propter Dicta Augustini*: Die Metaphysische Bedeutung der mittelalterlichen Ideenlehre." *Recherches de Théologie et Philosophie Médiévales* 64, no. 2 (1997): 245–62.

———. "Nominalismus als universitäre Spekulationskontrolle." *Recherches de Théologie et Philosophie Médiévales* 73, no. 2 (2006): 349–74.

Hoffmann, Tobias. "Ideen Der Individuen und Intentio Naturae: Duns Scotus im Dialog mit Thomas von Aquin und Heinrich von Gent." *Freiburger Zeitschrift für Philosophie und Theologie* 46, no. 1/2 (1999): 138–52.

———. *Creatura Intellecta: Die Ideen und Possibilien bei Duns Scotus mit Ausblick auf Franz von Mayronis, Poncius und Mastrius*. Münster: Aschendorff, 2002.

———. *Free Will and the Rebel Angels in Medieval Philosophy*. New York: Cambridge University Press, 2021.

Honnefelder, Ludger. Ens Inquantum Ens: *Der Begriff des Seienden als solchen als Gegenstand der Metaphysik nach der Lehre des Johannes Duns Scotus*. Beiträge zur Geschichte der Philosophie und Theologie des Mittelalters—Neue Folge 16. Münster: Aschendorff, 1989.

Hünermann, Peter, Helmut Hoping, Robert L. Fastiggi, Anne Englund Nash, Heinrich Denzinger, and Catholic Church, eds. *Compendium of Creeds, Definitions, and Declarations on Matters of Faith and Morals*. 43rd ed. San Francisco: Ignatius Press, 2012.

Jansen, Lawrence F. "The Divine Ideas in the Writings of St. Augustine." *Modern Schoolman* 22, no. 3 (1945): 117–31.

Janssens, Jules. "Henry of Ghent and Avicenna." In *A Companion to Henry of Ghent*, edited by Gordon A. Wilson, 63–83. Leiden: Brill, 2011.

Jordan, Mark D. "The Intelligibility of the World and the Divine Ideas in Aquinas." *The Review of Metaphysics* 38, no. 1 (1984): 17–32.

Jordan, Michael Joseph. "Duns Scotus on the Formal Distinction." Ph.D. diss., Rutgers University, 1984.

Karger, Elizabeth. "Would Ockham Have Shaved Wyman's Beard?" *Franciscan Studies* 40, no. 1 (1980): 244–64.

———. "Référence et Non-Existence Dans La Sémantique de Guillaume d'Ockham." In *Lectionum Varietates, Hommage á Paul Vignaux (1904–1987)*, edited by J. Jolivet, Z. Kaluza, and A. de Libera. Paris: Vrin, 1991.

Kelley, Francis E. "Ockham: Avignon, Before and After." In *From Ockham to Wyclif*, edited by Anne Hudson and Michael Wilks. New York: Oxford University Press, 1987.

King, Peter. "Bonaventure (b. ca. 1217; d. 1274)." In *Individuation in Scholasticism: The Later Middle Ages and the Counter-Reformation 1150–1650*, edited by Jorge J. E. Gracia, 141–72. Albany, NY: State University of New York Press, 1994.

———. "Scotus on Metaphysics." In *The Cambridge Companion to Duns Scotus*, edited by Thomas Williams, 15–68. New York: Cambridge University Press, 2003.

———. "Duns Scotus on Mental Content." In *Duns Scot à Paris, 1302–2002: Actes Du Colloque de Paris, 2–4 Septembre 2002*, edited by Olivier Boulnois. Turnhout: Brepols, 2004.

Klocker, Harry R. "Ockham and the Divine Ideas." *The Modern Schoolman* 47, no. 4 (1980): 351–60.

Klubertanz, George P. "*Esse* and *Existere* in St. Bonaventure." *Mediaeval Studies* 8, no. 1 (1946): 169–88.

Kondoleon, Theodore J. "Exemplar Causality in the Philosophy of St. Thomas Aquinas." Ph.D. diss., The Catholic University of America, 1967.

———. "Divine Exemplarism in Augustine." *Augustinian Studies* 1 (1970): 181–95.

König-Pralong, Catherine. *Avènement de l'aristotélisme en terre chrétienne: l'essence et la matière: entre Thomas d'Aquin et Guillaume d'Ockham*. Études de philosophie médiévale 87. Paris: Vrin, 2005.

———. *Être, essence et contingence*. Sagesses médiévales. Paris: Belles lettres, 2006.

Kovach, Francis J. "Divine Art in Saint Thomas Aquinas." In *Arts Libéraux et Philosophie Au Môyen Age: Actes Du Quatrième Congrès International de Philosophie Médiévale*, 663–71. Montreal: Institut d'études médiévales, 1969.

———. "The Question of the Eternity of the World in St. Bonaventure and St. Thomas: A Critical Analysis." *Southwestern Journal of Philosophy* 5, no. 2 (1974): 141–72.

Lahey, Stephen E. *John Wyclif*. New York: Oxford University Press, 2009.

Leff, Gordon. *William of Ockham: The Metamorphosis of Scholastic Discourse*. Totowa, NJ: Rowman and Littlefield, 1975.

Lička, Lukáš. "Perception and Objective Being: Peter Auriol on Perceptual Acts and Their Objects." *American Catholic Philosophical Quarterly* 90, no. 1 (2016): 49–76.

Macken, Raymond. "Les Diverses Applications de La Distinction Intentionnelle Chez Henri de Gand." In *Sprache Und Erkenntnis Im Mittelalter*, edited by W. Kluxen, 769–76. Berlin: De Gruyter, 1981.

Marmura, Michael E. *Probing in Islamic Philosophy: Studies in the Philosophies of Ibn Sīnā, al-Ghazālī, and Other Major Muslim Thinkers*. Binghamton: Global Academic Pub., 2005.

Marrone, Stephen P. *Truth and Scientific Knowledge in the Thought of Henry of Ghent*. Cambridge, MA: Medieval Academy of America, 1985.

———. "Henry of Ghent in Mid-Career as Interpreter of Aristotle and Thomas Aquinas." In *Henry of Ghent: Proceedings of the International Colloquium on the Occasion of the 700th Anniversary of His Death (1293)*, edited by W. Vanhamel, 193–209. Leuven: Leuven University Press, 1996.

———. *The Light of Thy Countenance: Science and Knowledge of God in the Thirteenth Century*. 2 vols. Leiden: Brill, 2001.

Maurer, Armand. "Ens Diminutum: A Note on Its Origin and Meaning." *Medieval Studies* 12, no. 1 (1950): 216–22.

———. "Henry of Harclay's Questions on the Divine Ideas." *Mediaeval Studies* 23, no. 1 (1961): 163–93.

———. "James Ross on the Divine Ideas: A Reply." *American Catholic Philosophical Quarterly* 65, no. 2 (1991): 213–20.

———. *The Philosophy of William of Ockham: In the Light of Its Principles*. Toronto: Pontifical Institute of Mediaeval Studies, 1999.

McGinnis, Jon. *Avicenna*. New York: Oxford University Press, 2010.

McGrade, A. S. "Plenty of Nothing: Ockham's Commitment to Real Possibles." *Franciscan Studies* 45 (1985): 145–56.

Meehan, Francis X. *Efficient Causality in Aristotle and St. Thomas*. Washington, DC: The Catholic University of America Press, 1940.

Meinert, John. "*In Duobus Modis*: Is Exemplar Causality Instrumental According to Aquinas?" *New Blackfriars* 95, no. 1055 (2014): 57–70.

Michon, Cyrille. *Nominalisme: La Théorie de La Signification d'Occam*. Paris: Vrin, 1994.

Muller, Jean-Pierre. "Introduction." In *Commentaire Sur Les Sentences: Reportation*, by Jean de Paris (Quidort) O.P., edited by Jean-Pierre Muller, Vol. I. Rome: Herder, 1961.

Nielson, Lauge Olaf. "Dictates of Faith versus Dictates of Reason: Peter Auriole on Divine Power, Creation, and Human Rationality." *Documenti e Studi Sulla Tradizione Filosofica Medievale* 7, no. 1 (1996): 213–41.

Noone, Timothy B. "Individuation in Scotus." *American Catholic Philosophical Quarterly* 69, no. 4 (1995): 527–42.

———. "Aquinas on Divine Ideas: Scotus's Evaluation." *Franciscan Studies* 56, no. 1 (1998): 307–24.

———. "Scotus on Divine Ideas: *Reportatio Paris*. I-A, d. 36." *Medioevo* 24, no. 1 (1998): 359–453.

———. "Universals and Individuation." In *The Cambridge Companion to Dun Scotus*, edited by Thomas Williams, 100–28. New York: Cambridge University Press, 2003.

———. "William of Ockham." In *A Companion to Philosophy in the Middle Ages*, edited by Jorge J. E. Gracia and Timothy B. Noone, 696–712. Malden, MA: Blackwell Publishing Co., 2003.

———. "Ascoli, Wylton, and Alnwick on Scotus's Formal Distinction: Taxonomy, Refinement, and Interaction." In *Philosophical Debates at Paris in the Early Fourteenth Century*, edited by Stephen F. Brown, Thomas Dewender, and Theo Kobusch, 127–49. Leiden: Brill, 2009.

Noone, Timothy B., and Carl A. Vater. "The Sources of Scotus's Theory of Divine Ideas." In Falà and Zavattero, 85–111.

Norman, Richard. "Aristotle's Philosopher-God." *Phronesis* 14, no. 1 (1969): 63–74.

Normore, Calvin. "Future Contingents." In *The Cambridge History of Later Medieval Philosophy*, edited by Norman Kretzmann, Anthony Kenny, and J. Pinborg, 358–81. New York: Cambridge University Press, 1982.

———. "Meaning and Objective Being." In *Essays on Descartes's Meditations*, edited by A. O. Rorty, 223–41. Los Angeles: University of California Press, 1986.

———. "Petrus Aureoli and His Contemporaries on Future Contingents and Excluded Middle." *Synthese* 96, no. 1 (1993): 83–92.

———. "Some Aspects of Ockham's Logic." In *The Cambridge Companion to Ockham*, edited by Paul Vincent Spade, 31–52. New York: Cambridge University Press, 1999.

———. "Ockham on Being." In *Categories of Being: Essays on Metaphysics and Logic*, edited by Leila Haaparanta and A. M. Mora-Márquez, 389–402. Leiden: Brill, 2012.

Normore, Calvin G. "Duns Scotus's Modal Theory." In *The Cambridge Companion to Duns Scotus*, edited by Thomas Williams, 129–160. New York: Cambridge University Press, 2003.

Oberman, H. A. *The Harvest of Medieval Theology: Gabriel Biel and Late Medieval Nominalism*. Cambridge, MA: Harvard University Press, 1963.

Osborne, Kenan B. "The Trinity in Bonaventure." In *The Cambridge Companion to the Trinity*, edited by Peter C. Phan, 1st ed., 108–27. New York: Cambridge University Press, 2011.

Owens, Joseph. *The Doctrine of Being in the Aristotelian Metaphysics: A Study in the Greek Background of Mediaeval Thought*. 3. ed., rev. Toronto: Pontifical Institute of Mediaeval Studies, 1978.

———. "The Relation of God to World in the Metaphysics." In *Études Sur La Métaphysique d'Aristote: Actes Du VIe Symposium Aristotelicum*, edited by Pierre Aubenque, 207–28. Paris: Vrin, 1979.

Paladini, Chiara. "Exemplar Causality as *Similitudo Aequivoca* in Peter Auriol." In Falà and Zavattero, 203–38.

Panaccio, Claude. *Les Mots, Les Concepts et Les Choses*. Paris: Vrin, 1991.

Pasnau, Robert. *Theories of Cognition in the Later Middle Ages*. New York: Cambridge University Press, 1997.

———. *Metaphysical Themes: 1274–1671*. Oxford: Clarendon Press, 2011.

Paulus, Jean. *Henri de Gand: Essai sur les tendances de sa métaphysique*. Paris: Vrin, 1938.

Pegis, Anton C. "The Dilemma of Being and Unity." In *Essays in Thomism*, edited by Robert E. Brennan, 149–83. New York: Sheed and Ward, 1942.

Pelletier, Jenny E. *William Ockham on Metaphysics: The Science of Being and God*. Studien Und Texte Zur Geistesgeschichte Des Mittelalters, Bd. 109. Leiden: Brill, 2013.

———. "William Ockham on Divine Ideas, Universals, and God's Power." In *Universals in the Fourteenth-Century*, edited by Fabrizio Amerini and Laurent Cesalli, 187–223. Pisa: Edizioni della Normale, 2017.

Pelster, Franz. "Heinrich von Harclay, Kanzler von Oxford, Und Seine Quästionen." In *Miscellanea Fr. Ehrle*, I:323–29. Rome, 1924.

Perler, Dominik. "What Am I Thinking About? John Duns Scotus and Peter Aureol on Intentional Objects." *Vivarium* 32, no. 1 (1994): 72–89.

———. "What Are Intentional Objects? A Controversy among Early Scotists." In *Ancient and Medieval Theories of Intentionality*, 203–26. Leiden: Brill, 2001.

Pickavé, Martin. "Henry of Ghent on Metaphysics." In *A Companion to Henry of Ghent*, edited by Gordon A. Wilson, 153–79. Leiden: Brill, 2011.

Pini, Giorgio. "Scotus and Avicenna on What It Is to Be a Thing." In *Scientia Graeco-Arabica: The Arabic, Hebrew, and Latin Reception of Avicenna's Metaphysics*, edited by Dag Nikolaus Hasse and Amos Bertolacci, 365–87. Boston: De Gruyter, 2012.

———. "Scotus on Objective Being." *Documenti e Studi Sulla Tradizione Filosofica Medievale* 26, no. 1 (2015): 337–67.

Piron, Sylvain. "La Liberté Divine et La Destruction Des Idées Chez Olivi." In *Pirre de Jean Olivi (1248–1298)*, edited by Alain Boureau and Sylvain Piron, 71–89. Paris: Vrin, 1999.

———. "Pierre de Jean Olivi." In *Sur La Science Divine*, edited by J.-C. Bardout and O. Boulnois, 204–25. Paris: Presses Universalitaires de France, 2002.

Plevano, Roberto. "Divine Ideas and Infinity." In *Henry of Ghent and the Transformation of Scholastic Thought: Essays in Memory of Jos Decorte*, edited by Guy Guldentops and Carlos Steel, 177–97. Leuven: Leuven University Press, 2003.

Porro, Pasquale. "Universaux et Esse Essentiae: Avicenna, Henri de Gand et Le «troisième Reichs»." In *Le Réalisme Des Universaux*, 10–50. Caen: Presses Universitaires de Caen, 2002.

———. "Doing Theology (and Philosophy) in the First Person: Henry of Ghent's Quodlibeta." In *Theological Quodlibeta in the Middle Ages: The Thirteenth Century*, edited by Christopher Schabel, 171–231. Brill's Companions to the Christian Tradition 1. Leiden: Brill, 2006.

Quinn, John Francis. "The Chronology of St. Bonaventure (1217–1257)." *Franciscan Studies* 32, no. 1 (1972): 168–86.

———. *The Historical Constitution of St. Bonaventure's Philosophy*. Toronto: Pontifical Institute of Mediaeval Studies, 1973.

Rosier-Catach, Irène. "*Res Significata* et *Modus Significandi*: Les Enjeux Linguistiques et Théologiques d'une Distinction Médiévale." In *Sprachtheorien in Spätantike und Mittelalter*, edited by S. Ebbensen, 135–68. Tübingen: Gunter Narr Verlag, 1995.

———. "Grammar." In *The Cambridge History of Medieval Philosophy*, edited by Robert Pasnau and Christina Van Dyke, 106–216. New York: Cambridge University Press, 2010.

Ross, James. "Aquinas's Exemplarism; Aquinas's Voluntarism." *American Catholic Philosophical Quarterly* 64, no. 2 (1990): 171–98.

———. "Response to Maurer and Dewan." *American Catholic Philosophical Quarterly* 65, no. 2 (1991): 235–43.

Saak, Eric L. "The Life and Works of James of Viterbo." In Côte and Pickavé, 11–32.

Saccenti, Riccardo. "*Sic Bonum Cognoscitur et Similiter Lux*: Divine Ideas in the First Franciscan Masters (Alexander of Hales and John of La Rochelle)." In Falà and Zavattero, 1–24.

Schabel, Christopher. *Theology at Paris, 1316–1345: Peter Auriol and the Problem of Divine Foreknowledge and Future Contingents*. Aldershot: Ashgate, 2000.

Sertillanges, A. D. *S. Thomas d'Aquin, Somme Théologique, Dieu: Tome II (Ia 12–17)*. Paris: Éditions de la Revue de Jeunes, 1933.

Smith, Garrett R. "The Origin of Intelligibility According to Duns Scotus, William of Alnwick, and Petrus Thomae." *Recherches de Théologie et Philosophie Médiévales* 81, no. 1 (2014): 37–74.

———. "*Esse Consecutive Cognitum*: A Fourteenth-Century Theory of Divine Ideas." In *Contemplation and Philosophy: Scholastic and Mystical Modes of Medieval Philosophical Thought*, edited by Roberto Hofmeister Pich and Andreas Speer, 477–527. Leiden: Brill, 2018.

———. "The Analogy of Being in the Scotist Tradition." *American Catholic Philosophical Quarterly* 93, no. 4 (2019): 633–73.

Spade, Paul Vincent. "Degrees of Being, Degrees of Goodness: Aquinas on Levels of Reality." In *Aquinas's Moral Theory: Essays in Honor of Norman Kretzmann*, edited by Scott MacDonald and Eleonore Stump, 254–75. New York: Cornell University Press, 1999.

Spruit, Leen. *Species Intelligibilis: From Perception to Knowledge*. 2 vols. Vols. 48–49 of Brill's Studies in Intellectual History. Leiden: Brill, 1994.

Taieb, Hamid. "What Is Cognition?: Peter Auriol's Account." *Recherches de Théologie et Philosophie Médiévales* 85, no. 1 (2018): 109–34.

Teetaert, A. "Pierre Auriol ou Oriol." In *Dictionnaire de Théologie Catholique*. Vol. XII/2. Paris: Letouzey et Ané, 1935.

Teske, Roland J. *Essays on the Philosophy of Henry of Ghent*. Milwaukee: Marquette University Press, 2012.

Thakkar, Mark N. A. "Peter Auriol and the Logic of Future Contingents." Ph.D. diss., University of Oxford, 2010.

Torrell, Jean-Pierre. *Initiation à saint Thomas d'Aquin*. Vol. 1 of Nouvelle édition profondément remaniée. Paris: Les Éditions du Cerf, 2015.

Vater, Carl A. "An Inconsistency in Aquinas's *De Veritate* Account of Divine Ideas." *Nova et Vetera* 18, no. 2 (2020): 639–52.

Vos, Antoine. *The Philosophy of John Duns Scotus*. Edinburgh: Edinburgh University Press, 2006.

Wanke, Otto. "Die Kritik Wilhelms von Alnwick an der Ideenlehre des Johannes Duns Skotus." Universität Bonn, 1965.

Ward, Thomas M. *John Duns Scotus on Parts, Wholes, and Hylomorphism*. Investigating Medieval Philosophy 7. Leiden: Brill, 2014.

———. *Divine Ideas*. New York. Cambridge Elements in Religion and Monotheism. Cambridge: Cambridge University Press, 2020.

Weisheipl, James A. "Ockham and Some Mertonians." *Mediaeval Studies* 30, no. 1 (1968): 164–74.

———. "The Axiom 'Opus Naturae est Opus Intelligentiae' and Its Origins." In *Albertus Magnus, Doctor Universalis: 1280/1980*, edited by Gerbert Meyer and Albert Zimmerman. Mainz: Matthias-Grünewald-Verlag, 1980.

Wilson, Gordon A. "Henry of Ghent's Written Legacy." In *A Companion to Henry of Ghent*, edited by Gordon A. Wilson, 23:3–23. Leiden: Brill, 2011.

Wippel, John F. "The Dating of James of Viterbo's Quodlibet I and Godfrey of Fontaine's Quodlibet VIII." *Augustiniana* 24, no. 1 (1974): 348–86.

———. *The Metaphysical Thought of Godfrey of Fontaines: A Study in Late Thirteenth-Century Philosophy*. Washington, DC: The Catholic University of America Press, 1981.

———. *Metaphysical Themes in Thomas Aquinas*. Washington, DC: The Catholic University of America Press, 1984.

———. *Thomas Aquinas on the Divine Ideas*. Toronto: Pontifical Institute of Mediaeval Studies, 1993.

———. *The Metaphysical Thought of Thomas Aquinas: From Finite Being to Uncreated Being*. Washington, DC: The Catholic University of America Press, 2000.

———. *Metaphysical Themes in Thomas Aquinas II*. Washington, DC: The Catholic University of America Press, 2007.

Wolter, Allan B. *The Transcendentals and Their Function in the Metaphysics of Duns Scotus*. St. Bonaventure, NY: Franciscan Institute, 1946.

———. "Scotus' Individuation Theory." In *The Philosophical Theology of John Duns Scotus*, edited by Marilyn McCord Adams, 68–97. Ithaca, NY: Cornell University Press, 1990.

———. *The Philosophical Theology of John Duns Scotus*. Edited by Marilyn McCord Adams. Ithaca: Cornell University Press, 1990.

———. "Scotus on the Divine Origin of Possibility." *American Catholic Philosophical Quarterly* 67, no. 1 (1993): 95–107.

———. "John Duns Scotus." In *Individuation in Scholasticism: The Later Middle Ages and the Counter-Reformation 1150–1650*, edited by Jorge J. E. Gracia, 271–98. New York: State University of New York Press, 1994.

———. "Scotus at Oxford." In *Via Scoti: Methodologia Ad Mentem Joannis Duns Scoti. Atti Del 244 Duns Scotus Bibliography Congresso Scotistico Internazionale Roma 9–11 Marzo 1993*, edited by Leonardo Sileo, 1:183–92. Rome: Edizioni Antonianum, 1995.

Ypma, E. "Recherches Sur La Carrière Scolaire et La Bibliothèque de Jacques de Viberbe †1308." *Augustiniana* 24, no. 1 (1974): 247–92.

Index

agent: by nature vs. by intellect, 19, 20, 22, 23, 51, 60, 63, 129, 138, 187, 248, univocal vs. equivocal, 69, 221
Albert the Great, 63, 207n4
Alexander of Hales, 13n1, 16n20
Algazel, 66n95, 97n41
Aristotle, 2–3, 6, 14, 15n17, 20, 32, 38–39, 46, 54–55, 73, 91, 101, 117n28, 160n17, 166–68, 192n165, 210n5, 211, 213n16, 241, 262
art, 19–21, 37, 57, 60–61, 167, 169, 185–86, 222, 239, 241–42, 243n79, 247
Augustine, 1–2, 7, 14n12, 29, 32–33, 40, 41n113, 43, 44, 45n11, 47, 53n42, 95n34, 117, 131, 162n27, 191, 204, 207, 210, 213, 219n51, 230, 236n40, 240, 243–44, 246, 249–50, 256, 257, 258n1
Averroes, 2–6, 32, 34, 38–39, 40, 88n6, 99, 101, 113n115, 158, 222n67, 234, 236, 262n16,
Avicenna, 2–3, 5–6, 29, 58n68, 66, 73n138, 97, 106, 158, 164n42, 177, 237, 265

being (*esse/ens*): act of being (*actus essendi*), 43, 56n56, 69–70, 78; diminished, 108, 110, 113, 180–82, 192, 202–3, 223, 250, 251n122, 266; *esse cognitum*, 108, 110, 144, 171, 180–81, 184, 203, 223, 265; *esse essentiae* vs. *esse existentiae*, 93n29, 96, 105–13, 176n93, 177, 265–66; *esse obiectivum* (*esse intentionale, esse apparens*), 175, 178–82, 215–17, 219n52, 222–23, 227, 248–53, 266; natural being vs. intelligible being, 22, 51–52, 63, 73, 171n77; 173; 181; and nothing, 169–70, 172, 174, 175–77, 181–82, 223, 250–53, 255, 265–67; real vs. of reason, 176–78, 202–3, 241; ways of being in God. *See* divine ideas
Bonaventure, 7, 9, 13–42, 43, 46, 58n69, 65, 69, 70, 90, 92, 96n40, 97, 104–5, 114n117, 117, 120, 121n2, 124n6, 126–27, 129, 131n36, 132–33, 135, 138n6, 143, 147, 153–55, 157, 161, 164n42, 168n60–61, 183, 190, 191, 192, 197n12, 207, 211n8, 222, 225, 227, 228, 248n104, 257–58, 259n4–5, 263, 265n25–27, 267–73

Condemnations of 1270, 91–92, 183, 262–63
connotation, 28–30, 41–42, 128–29, 151–53, 207, 216–21, 223, 225–28, 230, 232, 240, 243, 259, 261, 265, 267, 268
contuition, 210–11
creation: *ex nihilo*, 108, 111–13, 120, 145, 266, 272
Creatura Intellecta Theory of divine ideas, 71n122, 121, 147, 264–65
critique of (Auriol), 214–15

distinction: assimilation by essence and by likeness, 15; end of generation and end of the generated, 60; *esse/res* and *ratio* of relation. *See* relation; *esse essentiae* and *esse existentiae*. *See* being; *esse* and supposit, 114–15; essential quiddity vs. causal quiddity, 139; 143; exemplars and reasons (*rationes*), 22, 46–52, 57n61, 58–59, 78, 85, 182, 184–85, 263, 268–70; intentional, 107n81; knowledge causing a thing and knowledge caused by a thing. *See* divine knowledge, knowledge; moments in divine knowledge. *See* Instants; natural exemplars and thought-up exemplars. *See* exemplars; natural agent vs. intelligent agent. *See* agent; possible, 77–78; principle of knowledge and term of knowledge. *See* knowledge; real distinction, 26, 37, 129, 168–69, 230–32, 239, 254; real distinction and eminent distinction, 168–69; real relation and rational relation. *See* relation; in reality (*ex natura rei*), 103, 104n69, 167, 235; *res a reor* vs. *res a ratitudine*, 87, 108n85, 266; *res* as noncontradictory vs. *res* as possibly existing, 176–78; speculative cognition and practical cognition. *See* divine ideas; univocal agent/cause and equivocal agent. *See* agent
divine essence: beyond every genus, 26–27, 126, 129, 222; contains all creaturely essences eminently, 69–70, 93n29, 94, 96, 98, 112, 161, 168–69, 218, 225–26, 141, 153, 218, 226; as imitable, 154n22, 151–55, 161, 196, 212, 224; imitability in

diverse ways, 67–68, 99–100, 104, 109, 119–20, 204–5; known to be imitable, 11, 17, 57–59, 67, 70, 89–91, 96–97, 104, 111, 120, 141, 154n22, 162–63, 120–21, 124, 141, 155, 161–62, 183, 196–97, 199–201, 204, 259, 263; principle of divine knowledge, 67, 88, 139, 150, 160, 198–99, 210–11, 234, 245, 257, 259, 263; simplicity of. *See* divine simplicity; unlimited, 96–97

divine freedom: to create, 22, 52, 59, 76, 78, 91–92, 94, 143, 183–84, 224, 262–63

divine ideas: of accidents, 83–84, 116–17, 198, 226, 268; Aquinas's distinction into *rationes* and exemplars, 22, 46–52, 57n61, 58–59, 78, 85, 132, 182, 184–85, 263, 268–70; analogous to ideas of human artist, 20, 129, 185–86, 196, 203, 205, 222, 239, 241–42, 243n73, 246–47, 248–49, 254–55, 263–64. *See also* art; arguments that God has ideas, 23–25, 61–65, 95–98, 196; causal role, 8, 11, 22, 50–56, 137–40, 155–56, 197, 210–11, 213, 221, 243, 255, 258–59; cognitive role, 8, 11, 16–25, 40, 46–50, 137–41, 155–56, 210–11, 245–46, 255, 257, 261–63; are connotations, 216–21, 261, 265. *See also* connotation; the creature itself, 139–41, 170, 190, 202, 202–3, 240–45, 254–55, 259–61, 265; definition of, 45, 56–61, 89–91, 119, 161n24, 170–71, 192, 196–97, 199, 210–11, 240, 244, 255; determine the end of creatures, 21, 60–61, 258; distinct from the creatures ideated, 56, 76, 138–39, 144–45, 150, 246, 196; eternity of, 2, 34, 104, 201, 210–11, 219, 249–50; of evil, 38–39, 81–82, 131, 226–27, 253–54, 269; exclude relations, 172; are exemplars, 17–23, 46–56, 94, 128, 138–41, 210–11, 218, 241, 246, 257–58; existence enjoyed in God, 34–36, 74–76, 89, 105–13, 143–45, 151, 201, 222–24, 248–53, 265–67; *fiendum* and *non-fiendum*, 91–92, 183–84, 127–28, 192, 262, 183–85, 247, 262–63; of forms, 117–18, 226, 253–54; of genera, 36–38, 78–81, 114–16, 186–87, 197, 225–26, 253–54, 267–68; heretical to deny, 7–, 14, 43, 207, 256; identical to God himself, 20, 91, 128–30, 139–40, 199–200, 249; knowing through ideas vs. knowing in ideas, 152–53, 155; as likenesses, 15, 22, 41, 150, 154, 199, 204; of matter, 39–40, 82–83, 117–18, 131, 185–86, 197, 226, 253–54, 269–70; nature/character of, 15–22, 45–61, 88–91, 126–30, 137–40, 149–56, 164–75, 195–97, 199–201, 202–6, 211–20, 238–45; necessity of, 19, 65, 92, 145, 223–24, 239, 245–47, 257–58; of non-existing possibles, 34–36, 76–78, 84, 144–45, 245, 252–53; not secondary objects of divine knowledge, 198–99, 214–15, 217–18, 234–35; number of, 32–34, 73–74, 78, 81, 104–5, 131, 149, 191–92, 197, 227, 270; of numbers, 32–33, 117, 253, 254; are *obiecta cognita*, 140–41, 145, 245n88; plurality of, 11–12, 28–32, 41, 65–70, 98–100, 130–31, 140, 141–43, 151–52, 199–200, 203, 220–22, 257–58; principles of practical or speculative cognition, 17, 46–50, 91–94, 149, 184–85, 191, 247, 261–63; *rationes cognoscendi*, 15–16, 22, 27, 37, 40, 93–94, 99, 111, 118–19, 150, 152, 190–91; are relations, 24, 68, 71–74, 89–91, 147, 151, 157, 164–65, 196–97, 199–200, 204–5, 259–61, 263–64; secondary objects of divine knowledge, 8, 11, 88–89, 94, 109, 120, 139, 147, 151, 154, 157, 161, 164, 204, 259–61; of singulars, 36–38, 78–81, 114–16, 130–31, 187–88, 189, 197, 224–26, 253–54, 267–68; of species, 36–38, 78–81, 114–16, 131, 197, 225–26, 253–54, 267–68; of things produced by secondary causes, 131; unity/oneness of, 11–12, 25–27, 41, 109, 140, 141–43, 220–22

divine knowledge: analogies to human knowing, 5, 20, 32, 37, 129, 169, 178–80; of creatures directly, 147, 155, 167, 200, 202–3; establishes possible creatures as essences, 95–96, 138–40; of evil or base things, 4–5, 38–39, 81–82, 113, 236. *See also* divine ideas; *ficta* theory vs. *intellection* theory, 250–53; of the infinite, 5–6, 32–34; *See also* divine ideas; knows creatures as in his essence or in his power, 139–40; omniscient, 113, 118, 198; perfectly in act, 4, 198, 233–34; purely natural power, 19, 92, 108, 127, 151; source of, 4, 27, 64, 67, 88–89, 128, 150, 160, 215–15, 198–99, 217, 263

divine providence, 1, 80, 187, 258

divine simplicity, 5, 11–12, 25–26, 30–31, 36, 44, 62, 65, 73–74, 76, 98, 121, 130, 132, 139, 141, 198–99, 204, 206–7, 212–13, 214–15, 227, 230, 237, 238, 247, 248, 250, 254, 257–58, 261, 263,

divine truth: as expressive 17, 20, 22, 24–25, 27–30, 35–36, 40–41, 70, 126–27, 155, 267, 272

INDEX

divine will: and creation, 107–8, 125, 127–28; establishes an idea as an exemplar, 58, 127–28, 130, 263; *fiendum* and *non-fiendum*, 92, 94; 184–85, 192–93, 262. *See also* divine ideas; free, 57n61, 59, 68–69, 94, 120, 149, 152, 184–85, 247, 251, 258, 261; generates the Divine Word concomitantly, 19; necessary to complete the definition of an idea, 58; not necessary to complete the definition of an idea, 76, 92, 105

essence: Avicenna's theory of, 106, 272–73; essential quiddity vs. causal quiddity, 138–39, 145
exemplar: causality, 39, 54–56, 57, 59n70, 63, 95–97, 111, 145, 213, 221, 239, 241; external vs. thought-up, 67–68, 138, 242; as final causes, 54–56; as formal causes, 54–56, 89, 95–97, 110, 112, 138–41; ideas are. *See* divine ideas; natural vs. intellectual, 52–53, 138, 142, 242

Henry of Ghent, 7, 9, 28n62, 37n100, 76n147, 87–120, 124, 138, 139n15, 145, 149, 151, 159, 166n49, 168n61, 175, 177, 178, 183, 185n138, 188–89, 192, 200, 203n48, 211, 223, 238–40, 258, 265, 267
Henry of Harclay, 8–9, 170n73, 195, 202–6

idea: translation of the term from Greek to Latin, 2, 210
Infinite Intellect Theory, 8, 121–33, 135, 146, 175, 257, 263–64, 271; critique of (Scotus), 165–66
Imitability: formal aspect of an idea, 196–97, 199; of God. *See* divine essence, divine ideas; not a specific difference of any creature, 125–26, 162–64, 260
Imitability Theory of divine Ideas, 7–9, 11–120, 121, 128, 132–33, 135, 137, 140–41, 145–46, 147, 149, 153–56, 157, 160, 161, 175, 192, 197, 201, 206, 242, 244n83, 246, 257, 260, 263–64, 271, 273; critique of (Auriol), 211–13; critique of (Ockham), 238–40; critique of (Olivi and Petrus), 123–26, 263; critique of (Scotus), 162–66, 184–89, 264; has a faulty theory of relation, 126, 132, 162–66, 200–201, 257
imitation, 11, 16, 20–21, 23–25, 41, 53–54, 57–61, 63, 68, 81–82, 89–91, 125–26, 137–38, 153, 162–64, 190, 204, 210, 212, 259–60, 263, 270, 271

intention: intentional being. *See* being; irrelevant to ideas, 92–93, 262–63; in knowledge, 178–80, 266; of nature, 78, 80–81, 187; necessary aspect of ideas, 18, 21, 45, 48, 50, 52, 56, 58–60, 66, 80, 184–85; second intentions, 114–15, 176, 182, 188, 225–26, 227, 267; in things, 272
instants, 57n61, 58–59, 65, 127–28, 147, 168, 171–75, 182, 185, 205, 206n63, 224n77, 234–35, 246, 271, 273

John Duns Scotus, 7–9, 34n8, 38n107, 42, 59n70, 64, 71n122, 71n124, 101, 106, 119n135, 123n5, 125–26, 137, 144, 146, 147, 149, 154n22, 155, 157–93, 195, 196n4, 198, 200n30, 201–2, 204n51, 205–6, 209, 211, 213–15, 220, 225, 227–28, 234–35, 238–40, 245n89, 246, 254–55, 257–62, 264, 265n22, 266–73
John of La Rochelle, 13n1
John of Paris, 8, 195–98, 202, 225n78

Knowledge: end of, 92–93; measure and measured (causing the thing and being caused by the thing), 16–17, 21, 59–60, 73, 97–98, 161, 166–67, 271–72; as principle vs. as term, 29, 65–67, 88–89, 150, 160–61, 259–61. *See also* divine knowledge

Lateran: Fourth Council of, 21n42, 222
Liber de causis, 35, 63n86, 66n98
Likeness, 16–17, 19, 41, 90, 97, 129, 259, 272–73; equivocal likeness, 198, 221–22, 225; imitative vs. exemplative, 14, 16–18, 22, 41; univocal vs. of imitation, 129, 222, 242

nominalist theory of divine ideas, 9, 135, 198–99, 201–2, 206, 207–56, 257, 263, 265

Obiectum Cognitum Theory of divine ideas: overview, 8, 135, 264

pantheism/panentheism 15, 23, 63, 248, 260, 272
participation, 7, 16, 53, 68, 70, 75, 82, 90, 95–98, 100, 124–26, 162, 192, 267
perfection: grades of, 53–54, 90, 105, 107, 114–15, 161; preexistence in a cause, 69, 96, 98–99, 141
Peter Auriol, 9, 195, 198–99, 200n33, 206, 207, 209–28, 234, 242–44, 254, 258, 259–61, 265, 267–70

Peter John Olivi, 7–8, 42, 121–33, 137, 146, 147, 149–50, 152–54, 157, 161, 163–64, 166, 175, 178–79, 195, 196n4, 206, 260n7, 263–64, 271, 273

Petrus de Trabibus, 8, 121–33, 147, 161–62, 164, 175, 200, 212, 221, 224, 263

Plato/Platonism, 2, 4, 14, 20, 52, 54, 57, 75, 78, 80, 91, 151, 187–88, 196, 198, 211, 230–31, 241, 251, 253, 257, 267

potency: active vs. passive, 77–78, 144

Pseudo-Dionysius, 1–2, 32, 34, 131n37 and n39, 161, 192n165

Quiddity: *See* being, essence

relations: Aristotle's three modes of, 73, 166–70, 174–75; ideas are. *See* divine ideas; God not really related to creatures, 29–30, 31, 70–73, 102–4, 239; of imitability, 8, 89–90, 93, 128, 141, 163, 190, 212, 218, 220, 239, 263, 270; knowledge of, 104, 107, 121, 124–25, 147, 151–53, 162–63, 165–66, 192, 201, 203–4, 206, 213, 260, 264–65; not necessary for God's knowledge of creatures, 167–68, 196–97; rational relations (*relationes rationis*), 9, 11, 30–34, 70–74, 103–4, 149, 151–52, 155–56, 157, 164–75, 264–65; *relatio* vs. *respectus*, 37n100, 102; relative concepts vs. connotative concepts, 216–19; relative terms, 218; *res/esse* and *ratio* of, 71–73, 100–102

Richard of Mediavilla, 8, 123, 125–26, 146, 147, 149–56, 159, 259, 264, 270

Sacred Scripture, 1–2, 19n30, 236

Seneca, 54, 240–41

signification: *modus significandi* vs. *res significata*, 142

Stephen Tempier, 91

Themistius, 5–6

Thomas Aquinas, 3n17, 7–9, 21n43, 22, 43–85, 87–88, 91n23, 95–97, 99, 100–101, 104–5, 115, 116, 120, 124, 126, 127, 131–32, 137–38, 140, 143, 145n42, 150n7 and n9, 151n12–13, 155, 158–59, 161–63, 168n60–61, 180n113, 182, 183–88, 190, 191n161, 192–93, 195n1, 196, 197n12, 198, 201, 207n4, 211–12, 221n61, 222, 224, 225n78, 233–34, 236–37, 245–46, 248n104, 255, 259n3–5, 260n6, 262–63, 265n26–27, 267–70

Thomas Sutton, 8, 195, 198–202, 206

transcendentals, 52–54, 158

William of Ockham, 3, 7, 9, 54n47, 64n89, 172, 195, 199, 206, 207, 229–56, 257–61, 265–70

www.ingramcontent.com/pod-product-compliance
Lightning Source LLC
Chambersburg PA
CBHW071955290426
44109CB00018B/2032